Varieties

of

Monetary Experience

ECONOMICS RESEARCH STUDIES

of the

ECONOMICS RESEARCH CENTER

of the

UNIVERSITY OF CHICAGO

This volume is a publication of the
Workshop in Money and Banking

Varieties
of
Monetary Experience

Edited and with an Introduction by
DAVID MEISELMAN

With Essays by
JOHN V. DEAVER
ADOLFO CESAR DIZ
MICHAEL W. KERAN
GEORGE MACESICH
MORRIS PERLMAN
COLIN D. CAMPBELL

THE UNIVERSITY OF CHICAGO PRESS
CHICAGO & LONDON

International Standard Book Number: 0–226–51930–9
Library of Congress Catalog Card Number: 70–116027

THE UNIVERSITY OF CHICAGO PRESS, CHICAGO 60637
THE UNIVERSITY OF CHICAGO PRESS, LTD., LONDON

Printed in the United States of America

Contents

Introduction

DAVID MEISELMAN

Introduction

MORE than a decade ago four research studies which had been conducted at the Workshop in Money and Banking of the University of Chicago were published in a book bearing the then unlikely—and evocative—title, *Studies in the Quantity Theory of Money*.[1] The book appeared at a time when it was widely believed that the quantity theory approach, which emphasizes the importance of monetary phenomena in explaining the price level and short-period changes in business conditions, had been refuted by the events surrounding the Great Depression of the 1930s and had been superseded by the new and superior income-expenditure theory of Keynes, which assigned only a minor role to the stock of money. The book contained empirical studies of monetary phenomena by Phillip Cagan, John Klein, Eugene Lerner, and Richard Selden plus an introductory essay by Milton Friedman, its editor, which set forth a theoretical framework for the analysis of some of the consequences of monetary change. The studies played an important role in the subsequent dramatic revival of widespread support for the book's central thesis "that money does matter—that any interpretation o short-term movements in economic activity is likely to be seriously at fault if it neglects monetary change and repercussions. . . ."[2]

Partly because of the high level of its scholarship, partly because its results pointed to the importance of the stock of money, partly because it did not attempt to substitute one untested and rigid orthodoxy for another, the book gave strong impetus to much of the large and impressive body of research in the field of monetary economics which has been an important element in the worldwide revival of interest in monetary phenomena and in the step-by-step evolution of the modern quantity theory of money. As has so often occurred, techniques

1. Milton Friedman, ed., *Studies in the Quantity Theory of Money* (Chicago: University of Chicago Press, 1956).

2. Friedman, "The Quantity Theory of Money—a Restatement," in *Studies in Quantity Theory*, p. 3.

developed to solve one class of problems turned out to be applicable to a much wider range of problems. A notable example is the set of techniques developed in Phillip Cagan's classic study, "The Monetary Dynamics of Hyperinflation."

The six studies in the present volume (like the two volumes by individual authors published earlier under the auspices of the Workshop, A. James Meigs's *Free Reserves and the Money Supply*[3] and George Morrison's *Liquidity Preferences of Commercial Banks*[4]) continue the tradition of *Studies in the Quantity Theory of Money* both in subject matter and in general research strategy. All are empirical analyses of the role of monetary behavior in shaping economic events. All seek the greatest explanatory power for the fewest variables and relationships by systematic search for stable, invariant, and simple relationships consistently applicable over a broad range of different circumstances. Some of the studies improve basic statistics of monetary phenomena and other data. All systematically test and retest, extend and refine a growing set of related hypotheses about the effects of monetary change, and all experiment with widening the tested range of implications.

Because fruitful research is an evolutionary process requiring cumulative learning and testing, these studies have systematically built on the foundations of previous work, much of it initially reported in *Studies in the Quantity Theory of Money*. Pursuit of this research strategy provided the principal motivation for initiating and then assembling in one volume these studies of monetary phenomena in such apparently dissimilar conditions as those found in a cross section of forty-seven countries during the post–World War II period (Morris Perlman, "International Differences in Liquid Asset Portfolios"); in Canada over the century from 1867 to 1965 (George Macesich, "Supply and Demand for Money in Canada"); in Chile, over an only slightly shorter period from 1879 to 1955 (John Deaver, "The Chilean Inflation and the Demand for Money"); in South Korea from 1953 to 1961, where the deceleration of inflation provides an almost mirror-image to the acceleration of inflation in Brazil from 1948 to 1965 (Colin Campbell, "The Velocity of Money and the Rate of Inflation: Recent Experience in South Korea and Brazil"); in Argentina during the period spanning the establishment of a Central Bank in the depression year of 1935 and the tumultuous decade of the 1950s when prices increased about tenfold (Adolfo Cesar Diz, "Money and Prices in Argentina, 1935–62"); and in Japan during the post–World War II economic "miracle" of Japanese

3. Chicago: University of Chicago Press, 1962.
4. Chicago: University of Chicago Press, 1966.

recovery and rapid growth (Michael Keran, "Monetary Policy and the Business Cycle in Postwar Japan").

The vast array of varieties of monetary experience in the midst of such wide diversity of circumstances (rather than the work of William James) first suggested the title of this volume.

The same quest for understanding the determinants of the price level and of short-period economic fluctuations can and has been pursued by research traditions that differ from the one underlying these studies either in the variables deemed important or in the strategy used to test hypotheses. Monetary variables may not be given as important a role. Or, even if money is given an important role, some research workers prefer to follow the strategy of constructing and testing complex and sophisticated models employing many variables, rather than systematically tracing the behavior of a small number of variables. This alternative strategy rests on the basic hypothesis that the connections between monetary and other disturbances and resulting economic change are complex and indirect, that there exists no way of organizing the evidence that will reveal a fairly simple and direct connection.[5] The two strategies can complement one another and only time can tell which will prove the more fruitful. However, one clear cost of the alternative research strategy is that more complex models like the Brookings and Federal Reserve Board quarterly econometric models, each containing two hundred or more equations, must necessarily be restricted to a small range of experience by both lack of data and the resources required to construct and test the models.

Either strategy accepts, rejects, or modifies hypotheses as new evidence or better ways or organizing and viewing the evidence are developed. However, because large-scale models are both complex and have a smaller range of observations for a wider range of variables, step-by-step experiments and modifications, comparisons and reconciliations of findings, and the like are bound to be cumbersome and in many cases inconclusive. In this respect in particular, the research strategy embodied in the Workshop volumes can effectively implement the large-model strategy.

The present group of studies provides many excellent examples of the cumulative process of science. Some studies include development of basic data for the stock of money, aggregate income, and the like. Some

5. In this context it would seem that the difference between the two research strategies is not accurately captured by the difference between single equation and simultaneous equation estimates but rather by the level of abstraction and the complexity of the interrelations imposed on the structure of the model.

studies emphasize replication, using new evidence to retest hypotheses which have been successfully tested on other bodies of data. Some studies modify empirical techniques useful in one context and experiment to determine whether they might be useful in another. Some studies emphasize additional implications and add new complexity, some develop and test new hypotheses, and some broaden the range of phenomena under examination. All essentially conclude that from Argentina to Canada, from Brazil to South Korea, and from Chile to Japan, "money does matter—that any interpretation of short-term movements in economic activity is likely to be seriously at fault if it neglects monetary changes and repercussions."

There is another important and more personal tie among these studies. All of the authors have been directly associated in one way or another with the Workshop in Money and Banking of the University of Chicago and all but one have been Workshop members. The studies by Deaver, Diz, and Perlman were originally doctoral dissertations done while they were members. Macesich, an early member and alumnus, presented preliminary drafts of several sections of his study at Workshop meetings. Campbell spent a semester's leave there while working on his study. Keran was never formally associated with the Workshop, but was brought into contact with the work of its members by Milton Friedman who happened to meet him during a visit to Japan. Keran was then a member of the Treasury Department staff at the United States Embassy in Tokyo and was in the early stages of a study of postwar economic fluctuations in Japan as the subject of his doctoral dissertation for the University of Minnesota.

Finally, for his generous help, all of the authors owe a special debt to Milton Friedman, who founded the Workshop in Money and Banking at the nadir of the quantity theory and whose scholarship and zealous devotion to positive economies sparked the revival of concern for monetary phenomena and the development of the modern quantity theory.

I

The Chilean Inflation and the Demand for Money

JOHN V. DEAVER

The Chilean Inflation and the Demand for Money

1. INTRODUCTION

CHILE has had inflation since at least 1879. During the next eighty years prices increased at an average rate of 8 per cent a year. The rise has not been smooth, of course; there have been periods of relative price stability, and even periods of price decline. But the overall picture is one of inflation, decade after decade, at progressively higher rates. The following sections examine this inflation mainly in terms of four variables: the price level, the rate of change in the price level, the stock of money, and income. In the final section, Chile's inflation as a tax on cash balances is shown to have been substantial, but collected only in part by the government.

Inflation imposes a cost on anyone holding cash balances, equivalent in any period to the average rate of inflation, times the amount of cash he holds.[1] So presumably, in a country like Chile, changes in the rate of inflation will influence the amount of real cash balances individuals and firms will desire to hold. One of the purposes of this study is to find out to what extent the actual rate of inflation—or the rate of inflation that individuals may regard as likely to occur—affects the holdings of money.

The demand for money. More generally, the purpose of this study is to analyze the demand for real money balances in Chile. There have been few quantitative studies of this nature. One of the most successful efforts was made by Phillip Cagan in a study of seven hyperinflations.[2]

1. This effect of inflation was fairly well recognized by the neoclassical writers. Alfred Marshall, in *Money Credit and Commerce*, makes several allusions to it (see pages 6, 18, 47 in the 1st ed. [London, 1923]). J. M. Keynes, in his *Tract on Monetary Reform* (London, 1922), devotes all of chapter II to a discussion of the tax on money produced by inflation. In recent years the concept has been developed much more thoroughly by Phillip Cagan, in "The Monetary Dynamics of Hyperinflation," in *Studies in the Quantity Theory of Money*, ed. Milton Friedman (Chicago, 1956); and by Martin Bailey in "The Welfare Cost of Inflationary Finance," *Journal of Political Economy*, vol. 64 (1956).

2. Cagan, "Monetary Dynamics."

He found that changes in the anticipated cost of holding money, as measured by a weighted average of past price changes, could explain over 90 per cent of the variation in the real stock of money. Since he was dealing with relatively short periods—the longest inflation over which he attempted to define a demand curve was twenty-six months—he did not try to account for changes in income. And by calculating a regression of the real stock of money on the expected rate of inflation he assumed implicitly (*a*) that income did not change appreciably over the period, or (*b*) that he was measuring income velocity and that the income elasticity of demand for money was equal to one. He defined hyperinflation as an inflation beginning with a rate of price increase of 50 per cent a month or more. By this standard, inflation in the United States and most other countries has been negligible.

In contrast to the short-run nature of Cagan's study, and to the relative unimportance of the income variable, is the historical study of demand for money in the United States by Milton Friedman and Anna Schwartz.[3] This study shows that a high long-run income elasticity of demand for money in the United States can be reconciled with the low short-run income elasticity if one substitutes for measured current income an index of permanent income designed to measure the income that individuals and firms regard as normal in any given time. The small part of the short-run changes in real money balances that is not explained in this way appears only slightly correlated with the rate of inflation or interest rates; and both these variables have very slight effect relative to income.[4] In the American case changes in the cost of holding money are extremely small compared with such changes in countries undergoing hyperinflation, while changes in income are substantial. In hyperinflations the reverse is true.

These two different hypotheses about the demand for money can be successfully tested without contradiction, since money holders may respond to large changes in the cost of holding money and to substantial changes in expected income as well. It just happens that the tests were made in each case when only one of the variables changed enough to be important. However, these results leave a blank space in the testing of a general money-demand hypothesis. What would be the result if the cost of holding money were high and variable relative to

3. *A Monetary History of the United States, 1867–1960* (Princeton, 1963).

4. Richard Selden also found that inflation in the United States could explain very little of the change that occurred in velocity between 1919 and 1951. See "Monetary Velocity in the United States," in *Studies in Quantity Theory*, ed. Friedman.

that occurring in the United States, yet low by comparison with the hyperinflations? And what if, at the same time, income were changing substantially, so that according to the experience in the United States, it should have an effect on money holdings also?

Chile as an intermediate case. If the hypotheses have general applicability, it should be possible to answer these questions with the data for a country like Chile. During the twenty-four years after 1932 the rate of inflation averaged almost 20 per cent a year, with a maximum annual rate of about 85 per cent in 1955. This is still very small compared with the hyperinflations, but is very large compared with inflation in the United States. Moreover, the period is long enough to encompass substantial changes in income per capita. This study, then, is intended to fill part of the gap between the hypothesis in which income is the major determinant of real money stocks, and that in which the cost of holding money is the major determinant.

The analysis of money demand in Chile is undertaken in several steps. The first, contained in section 2, is to observe the movements of prices and money over the seventy-six years between 1878 and 1955, and to make tentative inferences about changes in income velocity for the first fifty years of that period. The second step, undertaken in the first part of section 3, is to examine the annual data for the years between 1932 and 1955 to determine the effect of the rate of inflation on the income velocity. The third step, in the last half of section 3, is to use quarterly data to test a more precisely stated demand hypothesis, that the demand for real cash balances is a function of the expected rate of inflation and income. These tests show that a stable demand schedule can be defined for Chile that explains most of the variations that took place in the real money stock between 1878 and 1955.

As progressively more complete and accurate data are used, more precise results are obtained. But these results, in turn, raise questions. For instance, income elasticities estimated with quarterly data are uniformly less than one. Moreover, when the twenty-four-year period is broken into shorter periods covering inflationary cycles, income elasticities are lower than for the period as a whole. Friedman's work with permanent income in the United States suggests that the difficulty may stem from using measured income rather than permanent income. Therefore a weighted series of past income was substituted for the measured income series. The result tends to confirm Friedman's hypothesis, for generally higher income elasticities were obtained in the short periods.

A second question comes from including time deposits as part of the total money stock. What results would be obtained if they are removed? It turns out that the same basic relationships hold. However, time deposits are more sensitive to changes in the cost of holding money, because as the marginal cost of holding money rises, the marginal cost of holding a given quantity of time deposits rises even faster. So there is substitution of demand deposits and cash for time deposits, making the cost elasticity of time deposits appear much greater than the cost elasticity of other kinds of money. This problem is taken up in section 4.

2. Money and Prices 1879–1955

> An ill-considered increase in the volume of an inconvertible currency is likely to lower the value of each unit more than in proportion to the increase: for it will lower the credit of the currency; and incline everyone to hold a rather smaller share of his resources in that form than he otherwise would. [Alfred Marshall, in *Money, Credit, and Commerce*]

The following pages deal with seventy-six years of Chile's inflation, from 1879 to 1955. In the next section, the hypothesis expressed by Marshall in the caption will be tested against the data for the period 1932 to 1955. While some statements can be made in this section that bear on the hypothesis for the period 1879 to 1928, they must remain vague because there are so few data to work with.

The first of the following sections will give a bird's-eye view of the inflation from 1879 to 1955, and the second section will examine the period before 1932 for evidence of velocity changes.

A. THE LONG INFLATION

Chile has suffered from "an ill-considered increase in the volume of an inconvertible currency" for a long time. But it was not always so. From the early days of the colonization until 1879 Chile was on a bimetallic standard, and historians credit the Chileans with an abhorrence for paper money that began to diminish only after 1850. While this attitude retarded the growth of banks—since they were not generally allowed to issue notes as negotiable receipts for deposits—it also gave their country a moderately stable monetary system.[5]

A few commercial houses had small banking facilities to complement their regular business. Before 1860 a small volume of notes had been issued by some of these houses. But paper money was not in general

5. Guillermo Subercaseaux, *Monetary and Banking Policy in Chile* (Oxford, 1922), pp. 34–43; Agustin Ross, *Los Bancos de Chile* (pamphlet) (Santiago, 1886), p. 42.

circulation until after 1860, when the first general banking law was passed. Even then issues were small at first since there was no developed banking system to take immediate advantage of the new law.

The banking law contained few restrictions on note issues. Only denominations of twenty pesos and over could be used, and note liabilities of any bank could not exceed a fixed proportion of its capital. But there were no reserve requirements, no restrictions on the kinds of loans that could be made, no prohibition against lending to officers or directors of the banks. This law remained without major modification until 1898 when the note issue privilege was taken from the banks and given exclusively to the treasury.[6]

The inflation started in 1879. Private banks had been encouraged to increase their note issue in order to lend to the government. The rise in prices this produced led to a severe drain of gold and silver; and in order to prevent the failure of the banks, specie payments were suspended.

This was the beginning. It was generally thought that specie payments would be resumed after the financial crisis was over, and agitation to do so persisted for many years. Two times, once in 1887 and once in 1925, a metallic standard was readopted. But both reforms were unsuccessful, and the voices raised in their support came to have less influence. Inflation became an accepted aspect of economic life.

Chart 1 shows the growth in money and prices after 1879. The measure for prices before 1913—no published series covers that period—is the peso-sterling exchange rate multiplied by the British wholesale price index.[7] This is linked to a cost-of-living index that is carried forward to 1955. Companion to the price series is an index of the quantity of money. This is measured by the amount of paper money in the hands of the public from 1879 through 1928. Thereafter it is linked to an index of the total money stock, including time and demand deposits.

The use of exchange rates before 1913 and the absence of deposits from the stock of money before 1928 are serious shortcomings in this comparison. Nevertheless, some important characteristics of the Chilean inflation can be seen from it.

First, it is evident that the rise in prices, which started with relatively small momentum in the 1880s, gained speed over the years, despite the

6. Frank Fetter, *Monetary Inflation in Chile* (Princeton, 1931), pp. 8, 111.

7. This index is based on the purchasing power parity hypothesis; it is, of course, only an approximation. Many factors may produce significant divergences between a price index of foreign exchange and one representative of all goods sold in an economy. However, considering its modest burden of indicating broad price behavior, the index is adequate.

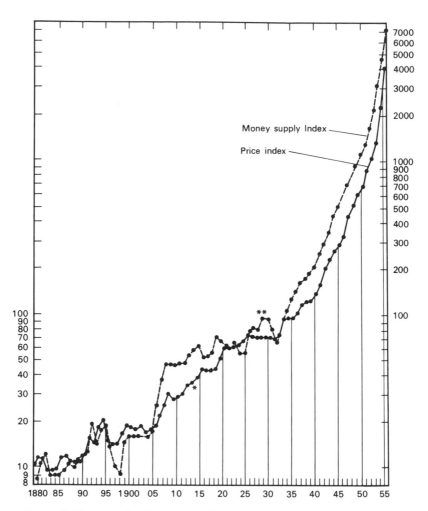

CHART 1. Money and prices in Chile, 1879–1955

SOURCES: Total fiduciary issue, 1879–1912, *Anuario Estadistico*, vol. 6, 1925; notes and coins in circulation, 1912–28, *Sinopsis Geografico-Estadistica*, 1933; total money stock, 1928–55, Appendix B; exchange rate on British penny, *Anuario Estadistico*, vol. 6, 1925; wholesale prices in England, Warren & Pearson, *Prices* (Sauerbeck), p. 75; cost-of-living index, 1937–27, *Sinopsis Geografico-Estadistica*, 1933; cost-of-living, 1928–55, *Estadistica Chilena*.

* Before 1913: index of the peso exchange rate on the British penny multiplied by British wholesale price index; after 1913: cost-of-living index for Santiago.

** Before 1929: index of notes in circulation; after 1929: total money stock including demand and time deposits.

existence of periods of relative price stability. The seventy-six-year span seems to break naturally into three sub-periods: 1879 to 1904, 1904 to 1931, and 1931 to 1955. The average annual rate of inflation was about 2 per cent in the first period, 7 per cent in the second, and 20 per cent in the third.

Second, the shapes of the trends during the three phases differ: the first, though rising, is virtually flat at the early and the late years, most of the rise occurring in the middle; the second rises more rapidly, and more steadily, but tends to flatten out in the final years; the third rises much more rapidly than the others and at an ever increasing rate.

The upward sweep of the final phase is most impressive. Two main factors appear to set the third period apart. Most important was the public attitude. During each of the first two phases a monetary reform involving the adoption of a metallic standard was carried out, and many individuals—businessmen, editors, and legislators—opposed inflation.[8] Although the reforms were short-lived,[9] they did result in halting the rise in prices for a time. During most of the final period, however, the mood of Congress, the business community, and most of the press favored monetary expansion. And after 1937 there was little inclination in the government or in the central bank to hold out against this mood. Only in 1956, after a year when the cost-of-living index went up 85 per cent, were significant reform measures again taken.[10]

A second factor that set the final phase apart was an altered monetary mechanism. In 1925 a central bank was set up and the gold standard adopted. While the gold standard soon perished in the Great Depression, the central bank continued to function.

Before the central bank was set up all note issue had been a liability of the treasury, and additions to the money supply generally had depended upon government deficits financed by such issues. But the new bank took over all note liabilities, and had the authority to lend to commercial banks and to the public as well as to the treasury. Thus inflation could proceed independently of government deficits.

Between 1930 and 1933 the bank was called upon to purchase large blocks of government paper, and during 1931 and 1932 the stock of

8. Agustin Ross, *Chile, 1851–1910* (Valparaiso, 1910 [?]), chap. 10.

9. Ross, *Chile*, pp. 58–62; Fetter, *Inflation*, pp. 190–91.

10. In the late 1940s and until 1955 there was a mild but growing agitation for monetary reform. In 1955 Klein and Saks Incorporated, a private U.S. consulting firm, was commissioned by the Chilean government to study the Chilean economy and suggest measures of reform. Many of their anti-inflationary proposals were officially accepted, and began to be adopted in 1956. Through 1958 little political strength appeared behind the reforms.

money grew by about 120 per cent on this account. As a result both the wholesale price index and the cost-of-living index moved up rapidly.

However, from the early months of 1933 until 1938 the ruling political forces seemed to be leading to eventual monetary stability. The president and the minister of finance held the traditional views on monetary and fiscal policy. The president of the central bank, Guillermo Subercaseaux, tried to prevent the bank from using its inflationary potential. Although he was not entirely successful, it is noteworthy that the loans of the central bank to other banks, to the public, and to the government, from the end of 1933 to the end of 1938, increased an average of slightly more than 5 per cent per year.[11] In the years that followed his resignation, these loans increased at about 20 per cent per year.

A new political regime committed to aggressive, centralist policies; new central bank management; a severe earthquake which excited public demands for more government intervention—all these combined to give the growth in money and prices after 1938 an upward momentum that has come to be commonly regarded as economically damaging only in recent years.

The *third* characteristic of the comparison of money and prices over the seventy-six-year period is the striking correspondence between the two series—over the period as a whole and over individual cycles. Large upward or downward movements do not appear to take place in either series independent of a similar movement in the other. This could indicate that income velocity did not undergo large swings, assuming income moved up steadily. However, incompleteness of the data for the first two periods precludes firm conclusions. This problem will be taken up in the following section.

B. MONETARY RELATIONSHIPS BETWEEN 1879 AND 1931

Before passing to the period between 1931 and 1955—which will be the subject of the later sections of this study—let us look at the period from 1879 to 1931, which can shed some light on two questions that are relevant to events in the later period. Specifically, how important were the commercial banks in the monetary system during this time, and what inferences may be drawn about long-term changes in velocity and the demand for money?

Commercial banking developed rapidly during the twenty years after the first general banking law was enacted in 1860. In that year there

11. For Subercaseaux's own defense of the relatively conservative policies he was instrumental in shaping, and his growing doubts as to whether they would be pursued, see his *Seis Años de Política Monetaria, 1933–1938* (Santiago, 1938).

were no fully operating banks. By 1878 eleven banks of issue with numerous branches were operating in the major cities of the country; and the currency and deposit liabilities of these banks accounted for over 80 per cent of the total money stock.[12]

Commercial banks continued to expand their activities after 1878. Although there are huge gaps in the available statistics, it is possible to make rough comparisons over widely spaced points in time. Consolidated bank records are available for the years 1878, 1914, and 1928. While the figures are not entirely comparable, they indicate the growth in the money supply and the changes that took place in its composition (see table 1).

TABLE 1

MONEY STOCK AND ITS COMPOSITION IN CHILE
(In Millions of Pesos)

	1878	1914	1928
Total money stock................	54	578	1,687
Total commercial bank liabilities ...	47	460	1,425
Deposits.....................	38[a]	460	1,425
Currency (notes)..............	8	0	0
Currency in hands of public.......	8	118	262
Gold and silver in circulation......	7[b]	—[c]	—[d]
Bank liabilities as percentage of money stock	87	79	85
Deposits as percentage of money stock......................	71	79	85

SOURCES: 1879, Ramon E. Santelices, *Los Bancos Chilenos* (Santiago, 1893), p. 214; 1914, 1928, *Boletin Mensual del Banco Central de Chile*, December 1929.

a. Actual deposits were 37.17 million pesos. An additional 1.26 million pesos of other liabilities to the public were also included.

b. Gold and silver circulation was estimated at two times the average gold holdings of the banks for the years 1876, 1877, and 1878. No official estimate of specie in circulation at that time is available.

c. There was undoubtedly some gold and silver in private hoards, and perhaps some in circulation at this time, but I have assumed that the quantities involved were negligible.

d. Specie in circulation in 1928 is included in the currency category.

On the basis of these figures, between 1878 and 1914 the total money stock rose about 970 per cent, or an average of 6.5 per cent, a year.

12. Ramon E. Santelices, in *Los Bancos Chilenos* (Santiago, 1893), gives a consolidated balance sheet of the Chilean banks for the years 1876, 1877, and 1878. In 1876, currency liabilities stood at 9 million pesos; deposits—which may include inter-bank balances—were 39.1 million pesos. No estimate of gold and silver in circulation is available. Bank holdings at the time were 3.6 million pesos, and I have guessed that the public held $2\frac{1}{2}$ times this amount outside the banks, giving a figure of 9.1 million pesos in specie circulation. This implies a total money stock of 57.2 million pesos, of which 84% consisted of commercial bank liabilities.

Between 1914 and 1928 the money stock increased by another 190 per cent, or almost 8 per cent a year. The total increase for the fifty years was about 3,020 per cent, or an average of about 7 per cent a year.

Specific evidence that the banks were of growing importance during the fifty-year period was the increase in deposits relative to the total money stock. Deposits accounted for about 71 per cent of the total in 1878. In 1914 they were almost 80 per cent, and in 1928 they were 85 per cent of the total. However, total bank monetary liabilities as a percentage of the total money supply dropped over the period. In the 1890s the note-issuing privilege was withdrawn from the banks, leaving all paper currency a liability of the treasury.

The banks were clearly an important part of the monetary system in 1878, just before the long inflationary period began. The fact that they continued to grow in importance—though slightly—as the inflation became more intense must be mainly due to the growing usefulness of banks, and to increasing familiarity with and acceptance of banking services by those holding money and making monetary transactions. If it had not been for such additional services—and the growing demand for them—it is likely that the interest paid on deposits would have risen during the period rather than fallen. As it was, interest on deposits was quite high, but after the 1880s, rates generally declined. The highest rates, of course, were paid on time deposits—up to 8 per cent on one-year deposits. Sight deposits paid as much as 4 per cent during the 1880s, but fell gradually to 1 per cent toward the end of the century, and remained at that level until the middle of the 1920s.[13]

Income velocity. Chart 1 suggests that velocity had considerable short-run stability because prices and note issue moved roughly in the same pattern. But this tells little about the trend in velocity. Not only is the money index only a partial one, but we have no direct measure of the growth in income.

However, table 2 has been constructed on the basis of stated assumptions about income growth. From the consolidated bank balance sheets recorded in table 1, the 1928 monetary accounts, and the price information given in chart 1, changes in velocity are computed under different assumptions about income growth.

The fifty years after 1878 was a period of general economic expansion. It encompasses the building of most of the major railways, great growth in the nitrate industry, construction of basic public works,

13. Subercaseaux, *Monetary and Banking Policy*, p. 189.

TABLE 2

Income Velocity in Chile

	1878	1914	1928
Total money stock index...	100	1,070	3,120
Price index................	100	398	675
Income index			
Assuming 2% growth....	100	206	273
Assuming 3% growth....	100	284	444
Assuming 4% growth....	100	410	710
Income velocity index			
Assuming 2% growth....	100	75	63
Assuming 3% growth....	100	102	97
Assuming 4% growth....	100	149	155

development of the public school system, progress in agriculture,[14] and expansion of foreign trade.[15] Therefore it does not seem unreasonable to assume that during this period per capita income was rising, perhaps by as much as 2 per cent a year on the average. An overall growth rate between 2.5 and 3.5 per cent a year is probably not far wrong (population was rising at about 1.35 per cent a year).

As computed in table 2, a 3 per cent growth rate would imply that income velocity underwent only small secular change over the fifty years. This result does not seem to fit the experience of other growing economies during this period. In countries such as the United Kingdom and the United States, velocity tended to decline; rising incomes were associated with an even more rapidly rising stock of money. For example, Professor Friedman estimated the income elasticity for money in the United States, adjusted for cyclical changes, at about 1.8 for the years between 1878 and 1954.[16] If there was a comparably high income elasticity in Chile, it follows that (a) the price and money data used in table 2 are wrong, (b) income growth was lower than 3 per cent, or (c) one or more other variables were pressing down on cash balances—especially in 1914.

Alternatively, the income elasticity of demand for money in Chile may have been much lower than in the United States. My guess is that

14. Agustin Ross, in *Chile, 1851–1910*, suggests that between 1871 and 1906 agricultural production may have risen 330%, or about 4% a year.

15. Chile's exports rose almost 510%, or 3.5% a year, between 1879 and 1925. Exports for this period are recorded in Fetter's *Inflation*, and are calculated in pounds sterling. To bring these figures closer to a physical basis I deflated them by Sauerbeck's index of wholesale prices in the United Kingdom.

16. Milton Friedman, "The Demand For Money: Some Theoretical and Empirical Results," *Journal of Political Economy* (August, 1959).

income elasticity was only slightly above unity, and that over most of the period a rising inflation cost of holding money prevented cash balances from rising even moderately faster than income.

In talking about changes in velocity it is desirable to distinguish between the period ending in 1914 and that ending in 1928. Under the assumptions used in table 2, income velocity fell more, or rose less, in the second period than in the first. Part of the explanation may be that 1914 was a year of inflation following other years of inflation, and that 1928 was a year of price stability following other years of price stability.

In 1879 there was no inflation; in 1914 prices had been rising at a rate of 8 to 10 per cent a year for several years. Therefore, the cost of holding money must have appeared higher in 1914 than it had in 1879. This could have induced money holders to keep down their cash balances, making income velocity higher than it otherwise would have been. Indeed, it could have more than offset a fall in velocity that would be expected to occur on the assumption that the income elasticity of the demand for money in Chile was greater than one.

Conditions in 1928 were quite different. Although prices rose much faster on the average between 1914 and 1928 than between 1879 and 1914, they had risen hardly at all during the three years just before 1928. So it seems doubtful that any inflation was generally anticipated at that time. The fact that inflation then was much lower than in 1914 implies that the incentive to economize on cash was weaker. Therefore, one would expect velocity to fall between 1914 and 1928, other conditions remaining the same. Further growth in income—assuming an income elasticity greater than one—would also press down velocity. With a 3 per cent annual rise in income, as computed in table 2, velocity fell by about 5 per cent.

Conclusions based on the monetary data available for the period before 1928 must be especially tentative. But the analysis in this section suggests the following:

1. Banks were quite well developed at the beginning of the inflation in 1879, but became more active in later years, as indicated by the growth in deposits relative to the total money stock.

2. The fairly close relationship between prices and money suggests that velocity did not undergo wide swings from year to year.

3. Additional data on the total money stock, along with reasonable assumptions about economic growth, indicate that there was no substantial rise or fall in income velocity. However, it seems likely that

velocity rose more, or fell less, between 1878 and 1914 than between 1914 and 1928.

4. On the basis of experience in the United States one might expect velocity to have declined substantially in Chile during this time. There may well have been a rise in demand for money relative to income, but Chile's inflation could have largely offset this by imposing a rising cost on holdings of money.

3. THE DEMAND FOR MONEY, 1932–1955

> The demand for a metal for the purposes of hoarding is increased by a continued rise in its value and diminished by a continued fall, because those people who hoard believe that what has been rising in value for some time is likely to go on rising and vice versa. [Alfred Marshall, in *Official Papers*]

In the last section it was observed that during the fifty years of Chile's inflation before 1928, income velocity did not appear to have risen or fallen appreciably; the real stock of money tended to keep pace with the rise in real income. It was tentatively concluded that this was a result of offsetting forces. On the one hand, a rise in real money balances relative to real income that might have been expected to occur on the basis of United States experience may have been partly offset by efforts to economize cash due to a moderately rising inflation cost of holding it.

Yet, it was also pointed out that during this period there were times of price decline and of relative price stability—and there was a persistent, though uneven, undercurrent of disaffection with the inflationary policies of the government. This may have kept alive the expectation that inflation might be stopped, thus causing the expected cost of holding money to fall short of the actual cost and weakening the urge to economize cash.

These conditions keeping down velocity were altered in the period after 1932.[17] Not only was inflation more severe, but there was less public opposition to an inflationary government program. The following figures tell the story: from the beginning of 1932 to the end of 1955 the total money supply in Chile rose 12,000 per cent, and the cost-of-living index rose 12,850 per cent. In the space of twenty-three years prices

17. The three-year gap between 1928 and 1932 was a period of severe economic disturbance. There was a sharp drop in Chilean exports and in foreign investments to Chile. Gold left the country as a result of the balance of payments deficit, and also helped draw down the money stock. Wholesale prices fell about 27% during the period and there was widespread unemployment. Thus 1928 was the end of a period; 1932 was the beginning of another.

rose almost twenty times as much as they had in the previous fifty-three years.

At the same time income velocity increased, reaching 70 per cent above the 1932 level at the end of 1955. Moreover, there were substantial fluctuations in velocity during this time. These changes did not wash out the visible relationship between money and prices, but they were large enough to invite the inquiry made in this chapter to explain them. The attempt is possible because there are adequate price, money, and income data for this period.

This section is divided into three parts: a review of the basic money-demand model; two tests of simple money-demand hypotheses based on annual data; and two tests of a more precise hypothesis based on quarterly data, one in which measured income and the other in which expected income is an independent variable.

A. THEORY OF MONEY DEMAND

The theoretical approach used in the following analysis is in the tradition of the quantity theory of money. The central theme of this tradition is that there is a logical and empirically observable relationship between the stock of money and the level of prices and income. The modern version of this theory can be reached in two stages. At the first stage the theory states that, *given certain factors*, there is a linear relationship between income, prices, and money, such that the real stock of money, M/P, is equal to a constant fraction, k, of real income, y. This is the familiar Cambridge equation of exchange,

$$M = kPy. \tag{1}$$

The equivalent equation, $MV = Py$, is obtained by designating V as the inverse of k.[18]

As with most successful conjectures, this relationship was often observed in the real world before it gained the status of a theory. So it is not surprising that nearly all the broad movements in prices that have taken place in the countries throughout the world can be explained by it. In section 2 this relationship was shown to hold for Chile, in a gross way, over the past seventy-six years.

---

18. The equation has been frequently used merely to define total income expenditures, Py, in a given period in terms of the stock of money and the average number of times it is used in that period, V, without specifying what happens to V. Given the stock of money and real income, the two variables P and V cannot be determined by this one equation. In this form it is merely nomenclature.

But it is both undesirable and unnecessary to leave the theory at this stage. The fact that k (or V) is fairly stable only suggests that the original approach is worth carrying further. Prices often rise faster or slower than the stock of money, and usually this can only be partly explained by changes in income as it is usually measured. It is the effort to take account of changes in k in a systematic and simple way that characterizes the modern quantity-theory approach.

One way of reaching the second stage is to regard changes in velocity as a result of changes in the amount of money people desire to hold. The empirical question then is, what variables determine the amount of money people want to hold, and what quantitative effect do changes in these variables have on changes in demand for money. Stated in this way the problem is to find a demand function of the general form,

$$M/P = f(x_1, x_2, \ldots, x_n, y), \tag{2}$$

in which income is one of the independent variables.

Once the form of this function, and the values of its parameters, is known, k (or V) can be easily determined, and the relationship between money and prices can be found for any set of values of the independent variables.

The demand functions tested in the following sections are based on this formulation, with the independent variables restricted to income, y, and the cost of holding money, C, thus:

$$M/P = h(y). \tag{2'}$$

Other variables are not included, mainly because the data for Chile are not available.[19] However, this may not be an important loss. Price

19. Milton Friedman, in "The Quantity Theory of Money—A Restatement," has suggested a list of variables that should be included in a complete demand equation. They are (i) the nominal return on bonds, (ii) the nominal return on equities, (iii) the expected rate of change in a price index (reflecting changes in the yield of durable goods relative to money), (iv) the ratio of human to nonhuman wealth (reflecting, in the long run, the relative yield on human capital), (v) expected income, defined so as to be an index of total wealth, and (vi) tastes and preferences. Equation (2') only includes (iii) and (v), and those in rather imperfect form.

The principal excluded variables are (i) and (ii), covering real yields on alternative investments. Equity yields in Chile are not published. All that is available is a weighted geometric mean of prices of traded stocks. Arnold Harberger, in an unpublished manuscript (1957), estimated a total interest charge on stock market loans for the years 1948 through 1953. However, these rates theoretically contain the expected rate of inflation as well as the expected real return on capital. In addition the series may contain many other elements due to the narrowness of the market.

and income data are frequently sufficient to determine statistical demand schedules for other commodities within tolerable limits; and there is an advantage in keeping the number of independent variables at a minimum consistent with the precision desired in the results.

The cost of holding money. The problems associated with using income as an independent variable are fairly straightforward and will be discussed in operational terms as the tests of the demand hypotheses are taken up. However, the cost variable is more complex, both from the theoretical and from the operational point of view.

The main problem is that the cost of holding any asset cannot be observed in the market, except in retrospect; at the time of purchase it can only be estimated. The actual cost of holding any asset for a given period is the discounted real yield on the best alternative investment that might have been made. But neither the real *ex post* yield on the investment made, nor that on other alternatives, can be known in advance. This raises two subsidiary questions: what are the alternative yields that must be estimated, and how can their expected value—which is by definition a subjective magnitude—be observed empirically?

In practice, there are numerous assets carrying different kinds and degrees of risk, nominal yields, and nonpecuniary yields (such as the liquidity rendered by riskless short-term loan instruments). Individuals and firms will choose among these assets according to their attitude toward risk, their knowledge of the various alternatives, and their opinion as to relative future yields. For an economy as a whole there is some weighted average of these alternative yields that can be regarded as the expected real return on all capital investments currently being made. This is one component of the cost of holding money for the economy as a whole. For convenience it can be assumed that in the

---

Yields on bonds can be computed, but they are meaningless for the purposes of this study. There is a minute amount of government paper in private hands, and a slightly larger amount of mortgage bonds held by the public. All these issues have computed yields in the neighborhood of the bank rate of interest. This rate is negative in real terms for a good deal of the period, and very low for all of it. The income from these assets is small, amounting to about 1.5% of direct property income from all sources in 1954 (*Cuentas Nacionales de Chile, 1940–54*, CORFO [Santiago, 1957]).

No attempt is made to estimate (iv), the yield on human capital. Even the approximation suggested by Friedman ("Quantity Theory"), taking the ratio of human to nonhuman income, would be possible for only part of the period studied.

absence of inflation particular market rates of interest measure this particular cost.[20]

A second part of the cost of holding money is the rate at which the value of money is expected to decline due to rising prices, or to rise due to falling prices.

The sum of these two expected costs—real alternative yields and the rate of price change—is the total expected cost of holding money. Thus if an individual money holder anticipates that prices will rise by 5 per cent a year, and that the net yield on an alternative asset that appears most attractive to him is 7 per cent, then the total expected cost of holding money instead of other assets is approximately 12 per cent of his holdings.

It is not possible to find any reliable measure of the real return on capital in Chile. So it is necessary to measure the cost of holding money by its inflation cost, *as if changes in the real return on capital were not significant.* The actual rate of inflation, measured by the cost-of-living index, during the period between 1932 and 1955 ranged from a minus 5 per cent to a plus 85 per cent a year. It seems quite improbable that the real return on capital had even one-tenth this range. Thus, on deductive grounds, the absence of this fraction of the cost of holding money in my calculations does not appear very damaging.

In a given period the actual cost of holding money may be quite different from the cost that is generally anticipated at the time decisions are made about how much money to hold in the period. Therefore, the second problem raised by the cost variable is that of measuring *expected* cost.

In this case the variable is the expected rate of inflation. In the following tests, the method for obtaining the expected rate of inflation can be stated simply as follows:[21] the year's (quarter's) measured rate of inflation is initially given a weight of B, the measured rate of inflation of the year (quarter) before that is given a weight of $B(1 - B)$, that of the year (quarter) before that a weight of $B(1 - B)^2$, and so on. Thus,

20. The question of which observed rate, or rates, are relevant, and how they should be entered into a demand equation, need not be discussed here, since this is not one of the variables for which useful data on Chile are available. However, it should be emphasised that no market rate of interest, nor any other concrete rate, needs to be in the mind of anyone or any group choosing between different assets. All that would be required for the theory to be useful is that people in the market act as if they choose on the basis of some determinable rate of return.

21. For a review of the literature on this technique for inferring anticipated costs and prices from current data, see Marc Nerlove's *Distributed Lags and Demand Analysis*, Agricultural Handbook No. 141 (Washington, 1958).

if the weight given to last year's rate of inflation is $\frac{1}{2}$, that given to the rate of inflation of the year before last would be $\frac{1}{4}$, and that given to the rate of inflation of three years ago would be $\frac{1}{8}$, and so on. This weighting principle would dictate that the expected rate of inflation at any time would receive some influence from the rate of inflation in *every* past period, but the influence of the rate of inflation of periods very far back would be negligible. In practice, the weights were computed as indicated above until a given percentage of the total weight would be accounted for when six past periods entered into the average. To make the weights for these six years add up to one, the initial figures ($\frac{1}{2}$, $\frac{1}{4}$, $\frac{1}{8}$, $\frac{1}{32}$, and $\frac{1}{64}$) would be multiplied by $\frac{64}{63}$.[22] B is less than unity and greater than 0. It is inversely proportional to the number of observations in past periods required to use up a given percentage of the weights.

By this procedure a time series is derived for the cost of holding money. In order to discover what weighting system is most appropriate—how far into the past it is relevant to consider actual changes in the rate of inflation—several such time series are derived, using different values of B. Each is fitted by least squares to the other variables in the demand equation, and the one which yields the highest correlation is regarded as most nearly reflecting aggregate expectations of how rapidly prices will rise.

22. In more general terms the method is as follows: Call the expected rate of inflation in period t, C_t. If P_{t-1} and w_1 are the actual rate of price change and its weight in period $t - 1$, and if $w_0 > w_1 > \cdots > w_n$, then we have:

$$C_t = \frac{\sum\limits_{i=0}^{n} P_{t-i} w_i}{\sum\limits_{i=0}^{n} w_i}. \tag{3}$$

For an alternative method of describing the derivation of weights in this type of model see Cagan, "Monetary Dynamics," pp. 37–41; and Nerlove, "Estimates of the Elasticities of Supply of Selected Agricultural Commodities," *Journal of Farm Economics* 38 (1956): 496–509.

This approach is to assume that individuals modify their expectations about future prices on the basis of the error they made in anticipating prices in the previous period. Expectations in the previous period are determined, in turn, by the error in anticipating the price in that period from the period before, and so on back. Thus current expectations are based on previous price changes indefinitely into the past. This approach is more restrictive than the one used above, since the function relating weights in various periods is predetermined by it. However, it is mathematically neater, and there is considerable advantage in limiting the number of relevant weighting patterns. Two of the tests in the following section employ estimating equations that are basically the same as those used by Cagan and Nerlove.

This is the basic technique used in the following sections to determine the expected rate of inflation. The method of selecting the weighting patterns will be taken up as the tests themselves are discussed.

B. THE HYPOTHESES

This and the following section contain the results of tests of money-demand hypotheses of the general form, $M/P = f(C,y)$, as in equation (2'). In the first test velocity is the dependent variable, assumed to depend on the cost of holding money; in the second test the real stock of money is the dependent variable, assumed to depend on the cost of holding money and on real income. The following equations are estimated statistically:

Hypothesis #1: $\log V = a_0 + a_1 C.$ $\qquad\qquad$ (4)

Hypothesis #2: $\log M/P = b_0 + b_1 C + b_2 \log y.$ $\qquad$ (5)

The first of these formulations, as indicated before, is more restrictive than the second. However, the two are identical if the income elasticity of the demand for money is constant and equal to one.[23]

Two tests of the first hypothesis are made with annual data. The first is a least squares regression of velocity on the first differences of the logarithms of the wholesale price of the cost-of-living index; the second is a regression of a transformed equation that yields estimates of the parameters in (5), where C is the "expected" annual first difference of the wholesale price index.[24]

The tests of the second hypothesis are made with quarterly data. They are least squares regressions of the real stock of money on the "expected" first difference of a cost-of-living index and on real income. The technique for finding the expected cost variable is adapted from that used by Phillip Cagan in his study of hyperinflations.

Test of hypothesis #1a. In the first of these tests, the *actual* rate of change of a price index is regarded as the cost of holding money. It cannot be thought of as the "expected cost" unless it is assumed that individuals know the rate at which prices will rise during a current year. However, it is reasonable to assume that the rate of increase in prices in a given year is partly anticipated, so that the higher the rate of inflation, the higher the rate of inflation that is generally anticipated.

23. Log $V = -\log M/Py$, by definition. If, in equation (5), $b_2 = 1$, then equation (5) is equal to (minus) equation (4).

24. This test follows procedures set out by Marc Nerlove in "Estimates of Elasticities."

The rise in the wholesale and cost-of-living price indices from 1929 to 1955 is far from smooth. After a decline from 1928 to 1931, there was a sharp rise to the end of 1932, followed by a leveling off (with an actual fall in the wholesale index). Then came another rise in 1937, another leveling off, followed by a rise at an increasing rate to about 1943. From then on the rate of rise tended to become larger, but there were still two periods in which the rate of increase declined: 1948–49 and 1953.

To the extent that these rates of change were anticipated by money holders, they represent the expected cost of holding money. Hypothesis #1 implies that these changes will be accompanied by roughly corresponding changes in velocity. Chart 2 compares velocity with the

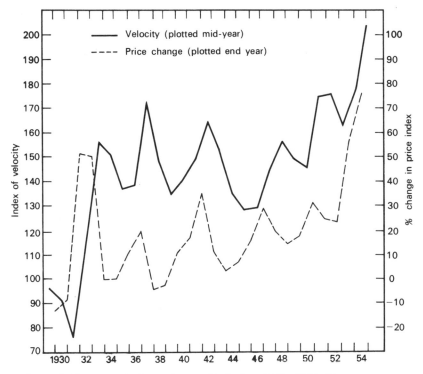

CHART 2. Income velocity and rate of inflation, Chile, 1929–55
SOURCES: Wholesale price index, *Estadistica Chilena*; money stock and output indices, *Estadistica Chilena* and *Boletin Mensual del Banco Central*.
NOTE: The price-change variable is based on the average monthly wholesale price index of each calendar year; it is a difference of annual monthly averages and is therefore plotted at the end of the year. Velocity is equal to the annual index of industrial and agricultural production multiplied by the wholesale price index (both yearly averages) and divided by the stock of money (centered end-year data). It is computed as a mid-year index.

annual first difference in the wholesale price index: the simple co-efficient of determination between the two series is .301.

Between 1932 and 1955 there were five cycles in the annual first differences of prices and in velocity. These can be seen in chart 2. Of the eleven turning points over the cycles eight show a one-and-a-half-year lag in velocity and three cycles show a half-year lag, which suggests that quarterly or monthly data would reveal an average lag in velocity of something over a year.

This lag indicates that velocity may be a function of the expected rate of inflation, as defined in the previous section. For if velocity is a function of a weighted average of past price changes, then velocity should lag behind actual price changes.

Hypothesis #1b. In order to test this supposition the annual data were fitted by least squares to a model with an implicit weighting pattern for past price changes like this:

$$C_t^* = B \sum_{i=1}^{\infty} C_{t-i}(1 - B)^{i-1} \tag{6}$$

where B is the parameter governing the size of the price-change weights in past periods.

In this model the sum of the weights is equal to one, which makes it possible to estimate the values of B in a relatively simple way. Recall that the demand equation to be estimated is

$$\log V = a_0 + a_1 C^* + u. \tag{7}$$

Inserting (6) into (7) and taking the difference between (7) at time t and (7) at time $t - 1$, the following equation is derived:

$$\log V_t - (1 - B) \log V_{t-1} = a_0 B + a_1 B C_{t-1} + v \tag{8}$$

which can be expressed as:

$$\log V_t = m_0 + m_1 C_{t-1} + m_2 \log V_{t-1} + v. \tag{8'}$$

this equation is fitted by least squares, yielding the parameters of equation (7) thus:

$$a_0 = m_0/(1 - m_2); \quad a_1 = m_1/(1 - m_2); \quad \text{and} \quad B = 1 - m_2.$$

Fitting (8') by least squares to the Chilean data yields a coefficient of determination of .621, which is considerably higher than that found using the actual rate of inflation, and supports the idea that there is a lagged relationship between velocity and the rate of inflation.

The series used to weigh price changes decreases exponentially into the past, at a rate determined by the parameter, B. In this test B had a value .48, at which 95 per cent of all possible weights in the weighting function are used up in four and a half years. This implies that money-holders in Chile acted as if they formed expectations of future rates of inflation almost entirely on the basis of price changes in the previous four and a half years.

Phillip Cagan, in his study of hyperinflations,[25] found a weighting pattern of about the same length for the Austrian inflation of 1921–22. Although this was one of the mildest inflations he studied, a price rise of 234 per cent occurred in one month during its course. This is gigantic compared with a maximum of 9.1 per cent a month that occurred during the twenty-five-year period before December 1955 in Chile. In all the other hyperinflations, the weighting pattern—in which over 95 per cent of the weights were used—was shorter than four years. This suggests that as inflations become more intense, money holders become more sensitive to changes in the rate of inflation. At lower rates of inflation less is at stake and reactions to changes in the rate are more sluggish. However, as will be seen in the next section, such a direct relationship between the rate of inflation and the statistical weighting period cannot be inferred from the Chilean data.

From equation (7) it is evident that the elasticity of demand for money is equal to $-a_1C*$.[26] The estimates of the coefficients of equation (8′) give a transformed value to a_1 of 1.05, indicating a mean elasticity of money demand of $-.127$. In concrete terms, a rise in the expected annual rate of inflation from 10 per cent to 20 per cent would induce about 13 per cent decrease in the demand for real cash balances. As will be seen in the next section, this is very close to the cost elasticities obtained with a more complex model.

The results from these tests may be summarized as follows:

1. Velocity (and real cash balances) in Chile is significantly related to the cost of holding money, measured by the actual rate of inflation. Velocity is even more closely related to the expected inflation cost, as estimated by a simple distributed lag model.

25. Cagan, "Monetary Dynamics," p. 43.

26. Subtracting $\log y$ from both sides of (7), reversing signs, and differentiating $\log M/P$ with respect to $C*$, we find

$$\frac{dM/P}{dC*M/P} = -a_1.$$

This, multiplied by $C*$, gives the expected cost elasticity of the demand for money. Where logarithms with a base x rather than e are used in the computations, then the elasticity is $-a_1C* \log_e x$.

2. In the annual data there is something over a one-year lag of velocity behind the actual rate of price change. The distributed lags model further reveals this lag, since it suggests that expectations of future price change may be formulated mostly within the previous four and a half years.

3. The inflation-cost elasticity, at a rate of inflation of about 10 per cent a year, is in the neighborhood of −.13.

Thus, even these fairly simple tests provide evidence that during inflations of moderate intensity people act as if they observed a definable demand schedule for money in terms of the cost of holding it.

However, data at one-year intervals may hide important changes. And it is not desirable to assume that income elasticity is always equal to one. So the following test, over the same period, was devised to overcome these faults.

C. HYPOTHESIS #2

The equations fitted in this section are of the following form:

$$\log M/P' = b_0 + b_1 C^* + b_2 \log y' + v, \tag{9}$$

where M/P' is the real stock of money per capita; C^* is the expected rate of change in the cost of living index (the expected rate of inflation); y' is the real per capita national income; b_0, b_1, and b_2 are constants; $b_1 C^*$ is the elasticity of demand for money in terms of the expected rate of change in prices; and b_2 is the income elasticity of demand for money. In the first test y' is real income per capita as it is usually measured. In the second test y' is computed as y'', the *expected* real income per capita. This is a statistical series designed to measure income levels regarded as normal over a short period of years by individuals and firms.[27]

The expected rate of inflation. The expected rate of change in the price level is obtained by the same method employed by Cagan in his study of hyperinflations,[28] and corresponds exactly to the method outlined above in section *A*.

The income variable. One purpose of this study is to estimate the income elasticity of the demand for money in Chile. The question arises whether

27. For the theory upon which this concept is based, see Milton Friedman's *A Theory of the Consumption Function* (Princeton, 1957). The application of this theory—an extension of the theory of consumption—is contained in Friedman's "The Demand for Money."

28. Cagan, "Monetary Dynamics," pp. 37–39. See note 22 above.

it is better to use current income or an expected income series, computed from the current income data in the same way as expected price change is computed from actual price change data. Properly measured, such a series would be, in Friedman's terminology, "permanent" income: income thought of as normal for a given period by individuals and firms. Permanent income would be more nearly proportional to wealth than would current income; for the latter contains elements which, by definition, are transitory and therefore not regarded as produced by one's stock of assets. So if money holdings are more a function of wealth than of current income, then permanent income is a better variable for the money demand equation than current income.

However, the transitory component of income may have some impact on the demand for money because outlets for saving, in an investment market or in the purchase of consumer durables, are poorly developed. If, as Friedman's study of money demand shows to be the case in the United States, transitory increments of income are generally saved, this may have quite a different impact on the demand for money in Chile than in the United States. The investment market in Chile is not as well developed as in the United States, and is accessible to a smaller proportion of money holders. Moreover, the market for consumer durables is proportionally much smaller, with a narrower selection of durable goods of intermediate and low cost, such as automobiles, household electrical equipment, and so on. With choices so limited, the additional savings accumulated from transitory income may be kept in the form of cash, assuming no change in the cost of holding money due to changes in the rate of inflation. Short-run rigidity in the investment and consumer durables markets could also lead to a somewhat higher proportion of the transitory component of income being consumed rather than saved.

This reasoning led me to use current income as an independent variable. But to test this assumption against the possibility that expected income is the appropriate variable, an expected income index was computed and fitted to equation (9) for the same set of periods as in the test using current income. I will discuss the result of this test after presenting the results of the test using current income data.

The shape of the data. Before examining the actual regressions it may be useful for me to comment on the data, shown in chart 3. Notice that income per capita and the real stock of money per capita have similar trends through 1946, and that both indices have a similar cyclical pattern. This suggests that income elasticity is not far from unity.

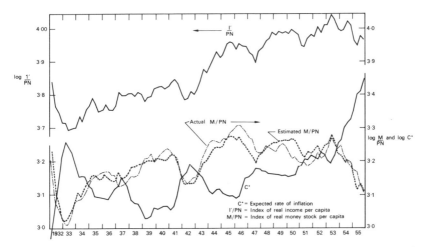

CHART 3. Per capita real income, per capita real total money stock, expected rate of inflation, and predicted total real money stock, Chile, 1932–55 (quarterly).

After 1946 the trends diverge and only the cyclical correspondence remains. The higher rate of inflation during the later period appears responsible for the downturn in cash balances, so the income elasticity could still be positive, though it looks low enough to pull down the average for the whole period.

The negative correlation between M/PN and C^* is quite obvious. Not only are the cyclical patterns inversely similar, but the trend is, in the case of M/PN, concave, and in the case of C^*, convex, to the time axis.

There are five complete cycles and one truncated cycle in both the series for money and the series for the expected price change. These cycles make it easy to break the data into periods in order to test whether there was an upward trend in the B coefficient, which determines the length of the weighting pattern. Such a trend would support the view that as the rate of inflation becomes more severe money holders tend to estimate future price changes more on the basis of price changes that are recent and less on those further in the past. If such a tendency were present, B would be smaller for those cycles when C^* was on a low absolute level than for those when C^* was on a high absolute level. Since the rate of inflation tends to increase over the period as a whole, the B's should be higher at the end than at the beginning of the period. As the results of the statistical test will show, B did not behave in this manner.

In the actual calculatiòns B was given the value $1 - e^{-\beta}$,[29] the length of the weighting pattern being governed by the value given to β. To facilitate comparison with Cagan's coefficient of expectations the following text will use the β notation.

The statistical results. Table 3 summarizes the results of the test. Chart 4 is a scatter showing the demand for cash balances in Chile as a function of the expected rate of inflation (holding income constant). In general the results support the money-demand hypothesis. All the coefficients of multiple determination except for the 1950–52 period are above .81; data for four of the six periods yielded positive and significant income elasticities, while the 1946–49 and 1953–55 periods yielded insignificant estimates of the parameters; all the estimates of the expected inflation cost parameters have the correct sign and are highly significant, except for the 1950–52 period in which the estimate is significant only at the 10 per cent level.

The relatively poor showing in 1950–52 is a reflection not on the

TABLE 3

Estimates of Parameters in Money-Demand Equation for Chile

$$\log M/P' = b_0 + b_1 C^* + b_2 \log y' + v$$

Period	R^2	b_0	b_1	b_2	β	$b_1\beta$	Mean Inflation Cost Elasticity[a]	Degrees of Freedom
1932–55	.852	.840	4.888 (.339)	.627 (.028)	.1	.489	−.155	92
1932–35	.935	1.640	2.706 (.407)	.404 (.136)	.2	.541	−.118	12
1936–40	.811	2.169	7.361 (.023)	.302 (.178)	.05	.368	−.320	16
1941–45	.968	1.280	2.763 (.400)	.511 (.063)	.3	.829	−.090	16
1946–49	.892	3.201	7.094 (.718)	.070 (.091)	.05	.355	−.185	12
1950–52	.596	1.752	1.039 (.568)	.371 (.151)	.3	.312	−.053	10
1953 55	.943	4.397	4.388 (.533)	.237 (.223)	.05	.219	−.249	10

a. Since the data were expressed as $\log_{10}$, and the elasticity is expressed as $b_1 C^*$ when the data are in natural logs, the statistical product of $b_1 C^*$ is multiplied by ($\log_e 10$).

29. The calculations were made using a notation in which the weights were expressed as $k \sum e^{-\beta t}$ rather than $B \sum (1 - B)^t$. Since each expression is equal to unity, $e^{-\beta} = (1 - B)$; hence, $B = 1 - e^{-\beta}$.

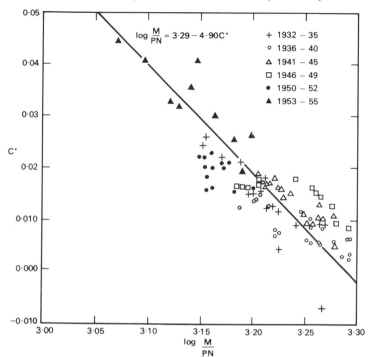

$$\log \frac{M}{PN} = 3\cdot29 - 4\cdot90C^{*}$$

+ 1932 – 35
o 1936 – 40
△ 1941 – 45
□ 1946 – 49
• 1950 – 52
▲ 1953 – 55

CHART 4. Scatter of expected rate of inflation against real per capita money stock corrected for differences in income.

NOTE: Income is assumed fixed at mean level over 1932–55 period.

hypothesis, but on the nature of the data. An examination of the relevant variables in chart 3 shows that the total variance, especially of C^{*} and M/P', is less during this period than during any other. Presumably the random, or unexplained, variance is just as great in absolute terms in this period; hence the ratio of the explained to the total variance must be smaller.

The b_1 coefficients, which are proportional to the elasticity of the inflation cost of holding money, differ considerably from period to period, with alternating highs and lows. Such differences correspond roughly to the lows and highs of the coefficient of expectations. As the β becomes higher, shortening the period over which expectations of price changes are formed, the C^{*} becomes more volatile, following more closely current changes in the price level. The greater volatility of C^{*} with the same changes in M/P' produces a lower inflation cost elasticity —and a lower b_1. Since β and b_1 tend to move in opposite directions, their product is more stable than either factor separately.

The coefficients of expectations determine the length of the weighting series. Cagan observed that inflation of higher intensity led to a shorter time span in which expectations of future price changes were formed.[30] This seems reasonable in view of the higher cost of making errors about price rises when inflation is very severe. However, in Chile the β's alternated mostly between .3 and .05, or between a four and a nineteen-year weighting pattern. This may be partly the result of Chile's very long history of inflation. The Chileans, within the range of inflations that took place between 1932 and 1955, may be as sensitive to inflation as they can get. But given this degree of sensitivity, they are influenced more by factors other than the intensity of inflation itself.

For instance, in 1938 Aguirre Cerda was elected on a platform that was generally understood to be inflationary—especially compared with the conservative policies of the Alessandri regime during the previous six years.[31] It is likely that when the reforms of the Popular Front were put through the public began to regard previous rates of inflation as poor indicators of the future trend. This could account for the fact that the β for the period 1941–46 was .3, rather than .05 as it was during the previous period, implying a weighting pattern of three years rather than nineteen years.

Similarly, in the period 1946–49 there may well have been a psychological letdown that affected expectations about inflation. A slower economic pace, reflected by a decline in real income per capita, and the absence of war may have created the impression that "normal" conditions would return, so that the more distant past was a relatively more reasonable indicator of future changes. This could explain why the β for this period implied a much longer weighting pattern than that of the preceding period.

The b_2 is an estimate of income elasticity. The basic data plotted in chart 4 suggest an overall income elasticity somewhat smaller than one; and the statistical estimate of the income parameter for the whole period is .627. Moreover, the estimates are even lower for the sub-periods, especially those after 1946. After 1946, only the 1950–52 cycle yielded a positive estimate of elasticity, significantly different from zero. These low elasticities imply that income velocity was rising

30. Cagan, "Monetary Dynamics." He also found that the longer the inflation lasted, even without reaching hyperinflation levels, the shorter the time period implied by the coefficient of expectations.

31. Gilbert J. Butland, *Chile* (London, 1953), p. 33.

independently of the rising cost of holding money.[32] On the basis of experience in the United States, one would not expect this result. So the question is, why should the income elasticity of demand for money be so low? Also, why should it be lower in the short than in the long periods?

There are two possible answers to these questions:

1. There may be substantial random errors in the income measurement. Such errors would be particularly damaging to the statistical fit in the short-cycle periods. They would be partly offset over the whole period by the trends in income and money.

2. Contrary to my original assumption, the relevant income variable may be permanent income rather than measured income; real cash balances in Chile may be uncorrelated with the transitory component of income. Over the long period this would have roughly the same effect as random errors in the income data (though, of course, the differences between permanent and measured income are not random). The elasticity coefficient would be mainly influenced by the trends in money and income.

But over a single cycle, the trend has slight effect. Permanent income is presumably above measured income during cyclical lows, and below measured income during cyclical highs, the difference being the transitory component of income. The errors thus introduced in the income variable would tend to overstate the movements in permanent income relative to those in the real money stock, and therefore to understate the permanent income elasticity of demand for money.

A test of the permanent income hypothesis. To test the possibility suggested in 2, above, an index was computed fitting the basic theoretical requirements of a permanent income series.[33] Computations were

---

32. If velocity is constant, we have, from $MV = Py$, that $dy/d(M/P) = V = y/(M/P)$. Hence,

$$\frac{d(M/P)}{M/P} \cdot \frac{y}{dy} = 1$$

= elasticity of income demand for money. If the elasticity should be greater than one, and assuming income is rising, then income rises more slowly than money and velocity falls. If the elasticity is less than one, this implies that income rises faster than money and velocity rises.

33. In calculating an expected series with a marked trend, it is desirable to include a trend parameter that will keep the expected series from deviating too far from the trend. The expected income series used here does not contain this parameter, but the trend is not sufficiently pronounced to induce a significant bias.

similar to those made on the first differences of prices to find the expected price-change series, C^*. A relatively large coefficient of expectations ($\beta = .3$) was used, implying a weighting pattern about four and a half years long. In order to ease the computing load the same β was used in the subperiods as over the whole period, and no effort was made to find the most appropriate β by testing various values to find that giving the highest R^2. Moreover, the expected price change variable, C^*, was calculated using the same coefficient of expectations for it as gave the best fit in the regressions using measured income, namely, $\beta = .1$.

There are several obvious shortcomings to this procedure. The results, summarized in table 4, are rather ambiguous.

All the estimates in these regressions are highly significant except those three that are indicated—the same three, in their respective equations, that were not significant in the test using measured income. Moreover, the R^2's are slightly lower than those in the previous test.

Otherwise, several tentative observations may be made about these results that bear on the permanent income hypothesis applied to the demand for real money stocks.

TABLE 4

Money-Demand Equation using Expected Income per Capita

$$\log M/P' = c_0 + c_1 C^* + c_2 \log y'' + v$$

Year	R^2	c_0	c_1	Expected Income Elasticity c_2	Mean Inflation-Cost Elasticity $c_1 C^* (\log_e 10)$	Difference in Elasticities in These Regressions Compared to Those Using Measured Income, for	
						C^{*b}	y''
1932–55	.741	.879	−5.219 (.472)	.617 (.039)	−.169	+.014	−.010
1932–35	.838	7.727	−11.089 (1.512)	−1.195 (.276)	−.486	+.368	−1.599
1936–40	.752	1.299	−7.162 (1.503)	.512 (.282)	−.314	−.006	+.210
1941–45	.921	.408	−6.330 (1.045)	.749 (.085)	−.207	+.117	+.238
1946–49	.834	3.900	−9.797 (1.222)	−.125[a] (.191)	−.249	+.064	−.195
1950–52	.589	−2.254	−.138[a] (1.251)	1.269 (.372)	−.005	−.048	+.898
1953–55	.948	5.058	−6.584 (1.074)	−.412[a] (.709)	−.334	+.085	−.175

a. Estimates not significant at 10% level. Estimates of corresponding parameters in regression using measured income were also not significant at the 10% level.

b. (+) means higher negative elasticity in this test than in the previous test.

1. If the estimates not significant at the 10 per cent level are not counted, then in three of the remaining four subperiods the expected income elasticity was substantially higher than the measured income elasticity. And in the 1950–52 period the expected income elasticity was well above one, while the measured income elasticity was far below one.

2. For the period as a whole the estimate of expected income elasticity was slightly lower than that for measured income elasticity. It was not anticipated that a large difference would occur in this parameter in either direction. However, if the β's had been chosen on the basis of numerous trials to find those giving the best fit, the estimate of income elasticity might have been higher.

3. One by-product of using expected income in the demand regressions was the generally higher (negative) estimates of cost elasticity, as can be seen in the next-to-last column of table 4. This is true for the period as a whole, and for four out of the five subperiods in which the estimates of the elasticity coefficients were significant.

Because of the arbitrary weighting pattern chosen to estimate the expected income variable, this test is inconclusive. When expected income is substituted for measured income in the demand equation, higher income elasticities are estimated for some subperiods, lower elasticities for others. And, except for the estimate for the 1950–52 period, these elasticities are still below unity. Further testing is required, in which the weighting patterns, instead of being given assumed values, are found by tests for those yielding the highest R^2's.

4. TIME DEPOSITS AS MONEY

In the last section time deposits were regarded as part of the money stock; they are highly liquid assets with many of the characteristics of demand deposits, and in Chile, as in most countries, they can be converted to cash on short notice. Furthermore, it is clear that in Chile during the twenty-seven years between 1928 and 1955 they must have had some liquidity value; for the inflation cost of holding such assets rose to several times the rate of interest paid on them, yet they did not disappear.

But during this period time deposits did fall substantially relative to other kinds of money. From 65 per cent of the total money stock in 1928—after several years of price stability—time deposits fell to only 11 per cent of the total money stock in 1955, when the rate of inflation was over 50 per cent a year. This raises two related questions: how good are time deposits as substitutes for other kinds of money? And, how much of the cost elasticity of the total money stock observed between 1932 and 1955 is due to the cost elasticity of time deposits alone?

The first question cannot be answered flatly. It is clear that a given rise in the cost of holding liquid assets due to inflation will have a greater effect on time deposits—assuming interest on them is constant —than on other kinds of money. This is so because the cost of holding time deposits is partly offset by the interest payments;[34] a given increment in the cost of holding liquid assets is added to a smaller base, producing a greater percentage increase.

Since the net cost of holding time deposits rises faster than the cost of holding cash, we would expect an increasingly severe inflation to result in a greater reduction in holdings of time deposits than of cash— how much greater would depend on the degree of substitutability between the two kinds of money. At one extreme, if they were perfect complements, the proportion between them would not change with changes in the relative cost of holding each. At the other extreme, if they were perfect substitutes, no one would hold cash or demand deposits, since they earn no interest. If they are a very good substitute they should constitute a large fraction of the total money stock during periods of little or no inflation, and a very small fraction during periods of relatively intense inflation. We have already seen that this has been the case. From constituting more than half the money stock in 1928 when there was no inflation, they fell to little more than one-tenth the money stock in 1955 after a period of rapid inflation.

Although we cannot measure with precision the degree of substitutability between time deposits and other kinds of money we can compare their cost elasticities of demand. Time deposits fell over the period, so we expect a higher elasticity for time deposits. To get a more exact measurement, I computed two least squares regressions, one on each of the two types of money, with income, y', and the expected inflation cost, C^*, as independent variables. The following results were obtained with the data for the 1932–55 period:

$$\log S/P' = 1.807 - 9.172\,C^* + .283 \log y', \quad R^2 = .932;$$
$$ (.29) (.04) \tag{10}$$

$$\log O/P' = -.535 - 1.476\,C^* + .937 \log y', \quad R^2 = .863. \tag{11}$$
$$ (.33) (.04)$$

---

34. If Y is the cost of holding cash, and i is the (constant) interest on time deposits, then $Y - i$ is the cost of holding time deposits. If K is the cost of holding cash relative to time deposits, $dK/dY = -i/(Y - i)^2$ which is negative

S/P' is time deposits per capita, O/P' is other kinds of money per capita. Estimates of the four main parameters in these regressions are highly significant, statistically. Moreover, the high cost elasticity of demand for time deposits (.29, at the mean rate of expected price rise), combined with the relatively low elasticity of demand for other kinds of money (.05), confirms the view that time deposits are good money substitutes.

Low income elasticities. But not all the results are so plausible. The low income elasticity for time deposits of .28 requires explanation. Two possibilities come to mind, apart from errors in the data:

1. The total real cost of holding money was defined as the expected rate of inflation plus the expected real rate of return on alternative forms of investment. The tests so far have been made on the assumption that the return on investments (R) was constant or varied in a random fashion about its mean. However, R might well be positively correlated with measured income. Changes in R, as changes in C^*, produce changes in the real money stock in the opposite direction. A high correlation of R with income would mean that in making least squares estimates, changes in the money stock that are caused by changes in R are attributed to changes in income, thus pulling down the income elasticity of demand for money. Put another way, a rise in income may induce a proportional or more than proportional rise in money stocks, other things being the same. But if, as income rises, the expected rate of return on capital also rises, this will have the effect of reducing money stocks. The net result will be a substantially less than proportional rise in money stocks with any given rise in income.

Since time deposits are far more sensitive to change in the cost of holding money than are demand deposits and cash, the result of omitting R from the cost variable will be to pull down the income elasticity of time deposits much more than it will pull down holdings of cash and demand deposits.

The only effective way to test this explanation of the low income elasticity is to find some index of the real return to capital, add it to the expected rate of inflation to measure the total cost of holding money, and see if using this variable in the demand regression raises the income elasticity coefficient. However, the data for such a test are not available.

2. A second possible cause of the very low income elasticity could be the use of measured instead of permanent income. Most of the discussion on this subject in the previous section is relevant here. However,

the distinction between the two kinds of money introduces an additional element.

The fact that time deposits are not perfect substitutes for other kinds of money may imply that the amount held is determined somewhat differently. Since part of the yield on time deposits is a pecuniary return, such deposits may be chosen entirely on the basis of permanent income—or wealth—and are thus completely uncorrelated with the transitory component of income. On the other hand, demand deposits and cash may be partially correlated with the transitory component, for reasons given in the previous section. Since the above regression relates time deposits to measured income, the correlated elements in measured income could mask the relationship between time deposits and the transitory component, and bring down the elasticity coefficient. Less distortion may have occurred in the regression with other kinds of money, if other kinds of money are more closely correlated with the transitory component of income.

This explanation of the low income elasticities is testable with the available data. Expected income series computed similarly to those for the previous chapter could be fitted independently to the time deposit and to the demand-deposit-plus-cash data. Higher income elasticities, particularly with respect to time deposits, would support the explanation, while lower elasticities would not.

An omitted variable. Some of the effects of omitting the expected real return on capital from the expected cost variable have already been discussed. Another effect of this omission would be that movements in time deposits (not accounted for by changes in income or the expected rate of inflation) would be correlated with movements in demand deposits and cash. To test whether this is so, the same regressions recorded in equations (10) and (11) were made, with the addition of one independent variable to each. Time deposits were added to the O/P' regression and other money added to the S/P' regression, giving the following results.

$$\log S/P' = 1.949 - 9.361\, C^* + .034 \log y' + .266 \log O/P'$$
$$ (.32) \qquad (.10) \qquad\quad (.09)$$
$$R^2 = .937$$

$$\log O/P' = -1.091 + 1.520\, C^* + .850 \log y' + .307 \log S/P'$$
$$ (1.09) \qquad (.05) \qquad\quad (.11)$$
$$R^2 = .874$$

The positive and significant elasticities of the two kinds of money with respect to each other—.266 and .307—indicate that if a variable was left out it affected both kinds of money in the same direction. By far the most likely candidate is the real return on capital.

If a variable was not left out, then either there are systematic errors in one of the included variables (such as the inclusion of the transitory component in the income variable), or there is some institutional tie between time deposits and other kinds of money. The latter effect could be produced if banks required a certain amount of time deposits be held for the privilege of receiving a bank loan. However, there is no evidence to suggest this kind of relationship in Chile.

It will be noted that the cost elasticity coefficient for demand deposits and cash is positive. This is an expression of the fact that as C^* rises the ratio of time deposits to other kinds of money falls. Normally a rise in C^* will produce a decrease in both kinds of money, but a much greater decrease in time deposits. In this regression the movements in the same direction are accounted for by the S/P' variable, so a rise in C^* produces a rise in O/P'—that is, a rise relative to S/P'.

The main conclusion to be drawn from this section is that time deposits, when counted as part of the money stock, introduce special problems because of the demand relationships between time deposits and other kinds of money. But because of the substantial degree of substitutability between time deposits and other money, it would clearly be a poor solution to exclude them. Analysis of the demand for each kind of money separately reveals a much higher cost elasticity of demand for time deposits than for other money.

5. CHILE'S TAX ON CASH BALANCES

Inflation imposes a real tax upon individuals and firms equal to the rate at which the level of prices is rising times the real value of their cash balances. It is the purpose of this section to show the size of Chile's inflation tax in terms of national income, to indicate the share of the tax that has been received by the government as revenue, and to show what fraction of total government revenue is derived from the tax.[35]

The inflation tax, 1929, 1955. The *rate* of the tax on cash balances for any period is equal to the average rate of inflation over that period. The

35. The theoretical development of this inflation tax problem can be found in Phillip Cagan's "Monetary Dynamics," and in Bailey's "Welfare Cost."

most useful and practical measure of such a rate is the instantaneous rate of change in a price index between the beginning and end of the period. The *base* of the tax is the average amount of money held by the public during the same period. The product of such yearly rates and the monetary tax base is the inflation tax. Table 5 shows this tax in Chile, based on the cost-of-living index, for the years 1929 to 1955. Note that in three years, 1930, 1931, and 1935, the tax was negative, that is, prices were falling. The tax varies widely from year to year, as a result primarily of changes in the rate of inflation. In the second column of the same table the nominal inflation tax figures have been deflated by a cost-of-living index to give the inflation tax in terms of constant prices. There has clearly been a consistent though unsteady rise in the real value of the tax.

TABLE 5

VALUE OF TAX ON CASH BALANCES IN CHILE
(In Millions of Pesos)

Year	Inflation Tax in Current Pesos	Inflation Tax in Pesos of 1930
1929.......	112	111
1930.......	−76	−76
1931.......	−17	−17
1932.......	299	283
1933.......	85	64
1934.......	94	72
1935.......	−21	−16
1936.......	294	203
1937.......	279	171
1938.......	62	36
1939.......	221	128
1940.......	368	189
1941.......	950	423
1942.......	1,269	450
1943.......	527	161
1944.......	1,150	314
1945.......	761	191
1946.......	2,909	630
1947.......	2,748	445
1948.......	2,407	330
1949.......	3,347	387
1950.......	3,285	330
1951.......	5,683	467
1952.......	3,510	236
1953.......	20,848	1,118
1954.......	36,591	1,139
1955.......	63,262	1,122

SOURCE: Prices from *Estadistica Chilena*, money stock compiled from data in *Boletin Mensual del Banco Central* and from *Estadistica Chilena*.

The inflation tax revenue. The inflation tax is a cost to the holder of money. It is also a source of revenue to those who create the new money. And this revenue is just equal to the real value of the new money that is created. Since it is both the government and the banking system that create money, the revenues are divided between them in the proportion in which they do so.

If prices were to rise at the same rate as the stock of money, the tax on cash balances would just equal the increase in the stock of money. However, prices may increase more or less rapidly than the stock of money, so that the real value of the stock of money falls or rises.

With a fall in the real stock of money, the public loses part of its money assets. In this case the inflation tax is larger than the revenue gained by the money creating authorities. It can be seen in column 3 of table 6 that between 1931 and 1945 the public increased its holdings of cash balances and, as a result, the tax was smaller than the direct revenues to the government and the banks.

On the other hand, if the stock of money rises faster than the price level, thus raising the real value of the total money stock, part of the new money goes to satisfy the public's desire for more money to hold. In this case the inflation tax is smaller than the value of the change in the money stock, and is thus smaller than the direct revenue of the

TABLE 6

BREAKDOWN OF AVERAGE ANNUAL TAX ON CASH BALANCES IN CHILE
(In Millions of Pesos of 1930)

	Tax on Cash Balances	Revenue to Banks and Their Borrowers	Revenue to Government	Discrepancy Due to Changes in Real Cash Balances	Statistical Error
	(1)	(2)	(3)	(4)	(5)
1929–30	17.5	−135.5	9.0	−140.0	4.0
1931–35	77.2	27.6	138.6	+87.4	−1.6
1936–40	145.4	157.6	41.0	+53.0	−.2
1941–45	307.8	330.6	47.8	+73.4	2.8
1945–50	424.4	259.8	88.4	−74.2	+2.0
1951–55	816.4	558.8	178.4	−71.2	8.0
Total 1929–55	8,891.0	6,401.0	2,489.0	+62.0	63.0

SOURCE: Inflation tax: see table 5; central bank's holdings of public debt, *Estadistica Chilena* and *Boletin Mensual del Banco Central*; bank's increase in the money stock is the difference between the increase in the total money stock and the government's deficit. The total money stock data were taken from the two sources mentioned above, in addition to data secured from the central bank of Chile by Martin Bailey.

NOTE: Col. 1 equals col. 2 plus col. 3 minus col. 4, plus col. 5. The totals in the bottom row are not totals of the averages in the columns, but totals of each number in the column times the number of years in the period.

government and banks supplying the new money. Again on table 6, it can be seen that in the first and last two periods the public decreased its holdings of cash. So the inflation tax was bigger than the direct revenues to the government and the banks.

Such changes in the real value of cash balances are likely to occur when there are changes in income and in the rate of inflation. It was shown in section 3 that in Chile a 10 per cent change in income tends to be accompanied by about a 6.5 per cent change in money holdings, while a 10 per cent change in the expected rate of inflation tends to be accompanied by about 1.5 per cent change (in the opposite direction) in money holdings. Both these factors have been at work between 1929 and 1954, and they have, over the period as a whole, just about offset each other. Thus, it is evident in column 4 of table 6 that though real balances rose and fell in different periods, over the whole twenty-five-year span real money balances increased by only 62 million pesos (at 1930 prices), compared with a total inflation tax of 8,891 million pesos.

The following statistical results will focus on the inflation tax and inflation revenue. Differences between these items are equal to the changes in the real value of the money stock and are labeled "discrepancy due to changes in the money stock."

Table 6 gives a breakdown of the tax into its components. Column 1 shows the growth in the value of the real tax during six periods since 1929. This summarizes the information from column 1 of table 5. Column 2 shows the direct inflation revenue of the banks, as measured by the increase in the total stock of money minus that which is created directly by the government through its deficits. The direct inflation revenue of the government, shown in column 3, is measured by the equivalent of the government's issue of money.[36] In Chile the equivalent of a government issue is its annual cash deficit. Not having these data at hand I have substituted the change in government indebtedness to the central bank.[37] Column 4 shows the discrepancy between the in-

36. The government does not issue money directly in Chile. But it achieves the same purpose by borrowing at rates of interest that are effectively zero or near to zero. The bulk of the government's deficits are financed through loans to the central bank. Although the loans bear interest, all but a small part of the proceeds are used to pay the regular expenses of the central bank (which may be regarded as a governmental function that should be paid for by regular taxation anyway) and are returned to the government as its share of the central bank's profits. Hence, we may consider the government's deficits as if they were financed by zero-interest loans, identical in effect to direct issues of fiat currency by the treasury.

37. This fails to account for several items, such as the government's indebtedness to the commercial banks and to the public (which should be added to my

flation tax and the direct inflation revenue—the change in the real stock of money. Except for the small statistical error, column 1 is equal to the sum of columns 2 and 3 minus column 4.

Absorption of total national income. In table 7 the information contained in table 6 has been reduced to percentages of the national income. Since 1928 the inflation tax has averaged 3.4 per cent of national income; and there has been an upward trend in this percentage running from .2 per cent during 1929–30 to 5.8 per cent during 1951–55. In the last three years, 1953, 1954, and 1955, the tax averaged 7.3 per cent of national income. This is equivalent to about two-thirds of the fraction of income devoted to gross capital formation. Even the 3.4 per cent average is substantial, being somewhat higher than the income share of the construction and utilities industries combined.

It is noteworthy that while the government's inflation tax revenue has been extremely erratic, even when measured on the basis of five-year averages, and shows very little growth trend, the banks have been able to capture a significant and growing fraction of national income through the tax on cash balances. Despite the losses during the period

TABLE 7

TAX ON CASH BALANCES AS PER CENT OF NATIONAL INCOME IN CHILE
1929–55

Period	Total Tax	Revenue to Banks and Their Borrowers	Revenue to Government	Discrepancy due to Changes in Real Cash Balances
	(1)	(2)	(3)	(4)
1929–30......	.22	−1.67	.11	−1.79
1931–35......	1.18	.42	2.11	+1.35
1936–40......	1.79	1.94	.50	+.65
1941–45......	3.31	3.35	.51	+.55
1946–50......	3.79	2.32	.78	−.69
1951–55......	5.78	3.86	1.26	−.66
Weighted average	3.38	2.44	.95	+.02

SOURCE: See table 6. Income data, *Statistics of National Income and Expenditures,* United Nations, September 1, 1955.

total) and changes in the government's holdings of cash in the banking system (additions to these holdings should be subtracted, and reductions should be added to my total). But these accounts are not large for those years for which I have data. The central bank is by far the largest creditor of the government, and it is not likely that my percentages would be significantly different—say 10 per cent instead of 6 per cent—if I could make the desired corrections.

1929–30 and the low revenues during the second period, the banks have managed to receive inflation tax revenue amounting to 2.44 per cent of national income over the whole period.

Significance of inflation tax to government. The government's inflation revenue, as measured by its cash deficit, has been a small percentage of the total inflation tax over the twenty-seven-year period, and although the percentage was large during the first twelve years the total tax was quite a small fraction of national income at that time. Since 1940 the tax, both absolutely and relative to national income, has been more important, but the fraction received by the government has been considerably less than in the earlier years. Thirty per cent of the aggregate inflation tax imposed during the twenty-seven-year period was received by the government, 70 per cent by the banks.

As the ratio of government inflation revenue to the total inflation tax fell during the late 1930s, the ratio corresponding to the banks and to that part of the public to which they extended credit rose. The very slow rise in the interest rates during the period under observation suggests that although the banks absorbed some fraction of the inflation revenue in higher profits, they passed on most of it to their borrowers. This implies that the inflation tax has provided substantial subsidies to bank borrowers. Over the whole period, as much as two-thirds of the inflation revenue may have been in the form of such subsidies.

Very little of the government's total expenditures were financed by its inflation revenues. An examination of column 2 of table 8 reveals

TABLE 8

GOVERNMENT INFLATION REVENUE IN CHILE, 1929–55

Period	Revenue to Government as Percentage of Total Inflation tax	Revenue to Government as Percentage of Total Government Revenue from All Sources
	(1)	(2)
1929–30	51.43	.74
1931–35	179.53	13.65
1936–40	28.20	4.04
1941–45	15.53	3.29
1946–50	20.83	4.44
1951–55	21.85	6.03
Weighted average ..	27.99	5.70

SOURCE: See table 6.

that the highest percentage of such expenditures covered in this way for any five-year period occurred between 1931 and 1935, during which time approximately 13.6 per cent of the budget was so covered; the average for the whole period was only about 5.7 per cent of the budget. This shows that the government has been able, by means of the inflation tax, to secure a somewhat larger fraction of resources than it obtained by its regular tax receipts alone. But it is equally clear that if the government had been the sole creator of money, and had created it at the rate at which the total stock actually rose, it could have obtained much more revenue, or substantially reduced other taxes.

APPENDIX A
INDEX OF CHILEAN NATIONAL INCOME
1932–1955

The *Corporacion de Fomento*, an agency of the Chilean government, has made estimates of Chile's national income, on an annual basis, for the years since 1940. However, in order to complete the study of money demand, it was desirable to obtain data going back to 1932, and to have all the data on a quarterly basis. Thus it was necessary to find an annual index that could be used to represent national income for the 1932–40 period, then to obtain a quarterly index—bench-marked to the annual data—for the whole period from 1932 to 1955.

The bench-mark series. For the period 1940–55, aggregate national income at market prices, as estimated by CORFO, was obtained from their publication, *Cuentas Nacionales de Chile, 1940–1954* (Santiago, 1957). For the period 1932–40, an index computed by Raul Simon, and recorded in the December 1943 issue of the *Estadistica Chilena*, was linked to the CORFO data. This index is an unweighted composite of a number of annual indices covering the output of a considerable range of industrial, agricultural, and mineral products, and including an index of the nation's wage bill and freight car loadings. Such an index is far from ideal. It omits much of the service sector, and its weighting is arbitrary, both because the various indices all carry unitary weights, and because several of the series overlap in coverage. However, this index should correspond fairly well to the overall output of goods and services in the country. In any case, nothing else was available and it did not seem worth going back to reexamine the original data in an effort to come up with a better but still indefensible index.

The quarterly income series. A quarterly production index is constructed from a composite of four monthly time series: mining production, industrial production, the wage bill, and ton-kilometers of rail freight. These indices, obtained from various issues of the *Estadistica Chilena*, are the only relevant monthly statistics covering as far back as the early 1930s. Combined, they provide a continuous index for the twenty-three years covered in this study, though data were obtained starting with 1929.

For the 1932–43 period the four indices are weighted equally, while for the 1943–55 period they are weighted differently. The index for the 1943–55 period was computed first. At the time, I attempted to pick weights that seemed reasonable: .43 for industrial production, .22 for mineral production, .18 for the wage bill, and .17 for the ton-kilometer index. Later, in extending this index back to 1932, I was less certain about the desirability of trying to weight the component indices, and therefore I did not. Although there is no satisfactory justification for this procedure, I doubt that it has a great effect on the month-to-month changes in the synthetic index within a year, apart from

TABLE 9

Log_{10} OF INDEX OF REAL PER CAPITA NATIONAL INCOME IN CHILE
QUARTERLY

1932	I	.83254	1940	I	.82409	1948	I	.93984
	II	.76523		II	.82425		II	.96002
	III	.74380		III	.81859		III	.96615
	IV	.71601		IV	.82249		IV	.98626
1933	I	.71423	1941	I	.83819	1949	I	.97929
	II	.69240		II	.84884		II	.98834
	III	.69693		III	.83183		III	.98526
	IV	.70097		IV	.80689		IV	.98907
1934	I	.73824	1942	I	.78252	1950	I	.98240
	II	.72129		II	.78824		II	.99325
	III	.75329		III	.80909		III	.98826
	IV	.76614		IV	.80167		IV	.97856
1935	I	.79009	1943	I	.81620	1951	I	.94804
	II	.77276		II	.84113		II	.94513
	III	.74727		III	.87319		III	.96870
	IV	.75293		IV	.86575		IV	.97713
1936	I	.77286	1944	I	.88106	1952	I	.97503
	II	.75329		II	.90476		II	1.00197
	III	.75275		III	.92787		III	.98628
	IV	.76608		IV	.92140		IV	1.00983
1937	I	.80985	1945	I	.91942	1953	I	1.00979
	II	.79825		II	.95035		II	1.04113
	III	.79626		III	.95929		III	1.02714
	IV	.80120		IV	.95704		IV	.99781
1938	I	.80252	1946	I	.93421	1954	I	.99128
	II	.79689		II	.95440		II	.99662
	III	.80731		III	.94774		III	1.02277
	IV	.80172		IV	.94517		IV	1.00841
1939	I	.77952	1947	I	.92397	1955	I	.96329
	II	.79038		II	.91986		II	.94359
	III	.79563		III	.89256		III	.97595
	IV	.82022		IV	.93180		IV	.96823

differential seasonal patterns which should be largely taken care of by a seasonal adjustment made on the final series. Moreover, the direction of change in the weights from the earlier to the later period is undoubtedly in the right direction: industrial production became more important, mining and rail freight less important in the Chilean economy.

The monthly synthetic index obtained from these four time series is bench-marked to the annual series in the following way: the arithmetic average of the synthetic series is assumed to correspond in time to the annual bench-mark data, and both of these to correspond to the end of June. Thus the bench-marking brings the June synthetic figure up (or down) by the percentage the bench mark is in excess of (or falls below) the annual average synthetic figure. Whether the bench-marked June figure is above or below the actual bench mark depends on whether the synthetic June figure is above or below the synthetic average for the year.

The monthly bench-marked data correspond approximately to mid-month, for they deal with aggregate monthly accumulations rather than the level of stocks. In order to make them correspond to my end-month money data it was necessary for me to convert the data to an end-month basis. I did this by finding the arithmetic mean of the mid-month data for each two consecutive months and considering this the end-month value of the first month in each pair.

The resulting end-month data were converted to logarithms, collapsed to quarters, and seasonally adjusted. From this final log income series, the log of population and the log of the cost-of-living index were subtracted, to give the log of real per capita income index shown in table 9.

APPENDIX B

THE CHILEAN MONEY DATA
1931–1955

Table 11, at the end of this appendix contains the basic money data used in the thesis. It is a continuous series containing three hundred end-month observations. In terms of computation—though not of difficulty—it stands midway between the crude money data and the final time series for "deflated money stock per capita" used to compute the demand elasticities in section 3. To advance to the final series, the data in this table were converted to logarithms, collapsed to centered quarterly geometric averages, seasonally adjusted, deflated by a seasonally adjusted cost-of-living index, and divided by population. This final series is given in table 11.

However, these notes will concentrate on the more difficult task of converting over fifty fragments of time series data into the continuous and fairly consistent set of numbers shown in table 11. Section A will outline the money data problem and indicate the framework on which the total money series was built. Section B will describe the data fragments used to construct a crude money index and indicate how it was bench marked to more sophisticated yearly observations.

A. THE DATA PROBLEM

There are two major difficulties in working with Chilean monetary statistics, particularly those published for the years before 1950.

1. Time series of money components are not always fully defined. Sometimes the only definition available is the title heading on a column of numbers.

2. There are serious discontinuities in basic time series. This difficulty was enhanced by the fact that none of the three basic sources for monetary statistics was available to me in an uninterrupted monthly or yearly series between 1931 and 1955.

Either of these deficiencies by itself would produce hazards in interpretation; combined, they could produce an appalling confusion.

53

At the time the first general monetary statistics became available, in 1928, it is unlikely that anyone in Chile had a firm idea of what "money" should consist of, other than currency. At any rate, there was no effort to bring the various elements of the money stock into a consistent framework until after World War II.

It was not until 1949 that the first generally complete compilation of the monetary liabilities of the banking system was published. This account developed by the *Banco Central* was placed in a table with the title *Total del Dinero Circulante*, and has appeared monthly in both the *Estadistica Chilena* and the *Boletin Mensual del Banco Central* since 1949. This table (referred to after this as the "1949 account") is very useful and is the main pillar supporting the final money series in table 11. The compilers carried the data in this series back monthly to June 1948.

The bench mark. The problem was to connect the hodgepodge of disconnected money series for the period before December 1948 to the relatively consistent series for the period after that date. Fortunately, when the new accounts were made up the figures for each year-end since 1928 were also computed, using the same definition as for the later monthly data. I used these year-end figures to construct a bench-mark for the earlier monthly series.

The bench-marked data are precisely consistent with the post–December 1948 data only at each end-year. However, it is reasonable to suppose that month-to-month fluctuations in the actual data correspond roughly to those that would appear in the bench-mark series if it had been computed for the intervening months of each year.

The bench-mark series for the total money stock is not identical to the total money supply as given in the 1949 accounts. Table 10 summarizes the difference.

There are five aspects of the bench-mark series that require comment:

First, float is excluded from demand and sight deposits. Float consists of uncollected cash items of the commercial banks. Most of it arises because of time involved in clearing checks. It is a noncash asset of the collecting bank. It is also a deposit liability of the drawee bank, though the transfer of the deposit from the check drawer to the collecting bank is only implicit.

The reason for excluding float from the money supply is the same as that for excluding inter-bank balances. An uncollected check, like an inter-bank deposit, is a claim against one bank by another. (And if the banks are loaned up, an increase in uncollected items, like an increase in inter-bank lending, restricts private credit and reduces publicly held

TABLE 10

1949 Accounts	Bench Mark
1. Demand and certain sight deposits in commercial banks. Includes float and deposits of the government and semi-fiscal agencies. Excludes inter-bank deposits, except time deposits due in more than 30 days.	1*. Same, but excludes float and government deposits.
2. Non-bank deposits in central bank. Includes deposits of government and semi-fiscal agencies.	2. Same.
3. Currency outside banks. Includes deposits of government and semi-fiscal agencies.	3. Same.
4. No time or savings deposits included in money.	4*. All time and savings deposits in commercial banks. Includes deposits of government and semi-fiscal agencies.
5. Total money stock is equal to: 1 + 2 + 3.	5*. Total money stock is equal to: 1* + 2 + 3 + 4*.

deposits.) Therefore they are removed from the deposit figure to give a more correct valuation to the public's *drawable* deposits. Inclusion of float, as in the 1949 account, could only be justified if depositors tend to regard deposits as still their own—even after drawing checks on them—until the moment their checks are collected.

The time lag in check clearing results in float. It also makes possible check kiting—drawing a check on a nonexistent deposit but re-depositing to cover the check just before it is collected. Obviously the value of kited checks cannot exceed float. And since there is a presumption that most checks are drawn on existing deposits, kiting must equal a small fraction of float. If during the 1932–55 period as much as 10 per cent of the float consisted of kited checks, it would have constituted less than .5 per cent of the total money stock.

After 1955 float rose more swiftly than check clearings, which lends support to the contention that kiting was encouraged and abetted by the banks to circumvent quantitive lending restrictions by the government.[38] It should be noted, however, that this could only increase total credit available—and deposits—providing the lending restrictions prevented the banks from being fully loaned up. Collusive kiting, as this might be called, would be a way for banks to use up excess reserves they could not otherwise legally employ.

Second, government deposits—including those in the central bank— are subtracted from total demand deposits. Since some government

38. Martin J. Bailey, "The Creation of New Money in Chile, 1943–56" (unpublished manuscript).

deposits are time deposits it would be desirable to subtract the latter from the time deposit category. Unfortunately the data required to do this are not available in the regular statistical publications.

Third, certain sight deposits are included in demand deposits. It could be argued that these deposits should be put with other non-checking accounts since they earn some interest and are less readily converted to cash than demand deposits. However, the amount involved is small and the problem academic since the required numbers are not available.

Fourth, currency held by government and semi-fiscal agencies is included in the currency figure, but there are no regularly published data from which these holdings can be derived. Since all currency is a liability of the central bank rather than the treasury, and since nearly all payments by the government are made by check, this inclusion is probably of little importance.

Fifth, inter-bank time deposits due in less than thirty days are *not* excluded from time deposits. I could find no figures on total inter-bank balances. Although it seems doubtful that more than a small fraction of such balances are in the time deposit category, I have no evidence that this is so. The regular monetary statistics on deposits contain two sets of tables, one for the *Caja Nacional de Ahorro* (CNA), and one for the consolidated commercial banks. One set of deposit tables gives a break-down by type of deposit, but does not indicate ownership. The tables giving a breakdown of ownership do not distinguish between different types of deposits. There is no way of deducing from these tables the inter-bank time deposits.

Despite some of the deficiencies of this bench-mark series, it has the advantage over the 1949 accounts of eliminating government deposits and float. Moreover, the addition of time deposits is useful despite the fact that inter-bank time deposits cannot be identified. The main problem arose in putting the monthly data fragments together for the years before 1949 and applying this annual bench mark.

B. APPLICATION OF THE BENCH MARK

In general the bench-marking was done in this way: the crude data for the monetary components selected for any year were added up for each month. Each monthly observation was then multiplied by a factor computed to bring (end) December figures to the level of the end-year bench-marks. Each component of the basic monthly money series was also bench-marked to the corresponding end-year bench-mark series.

From July 1948 on, the 1949 accounts are available monthly. However, the monthly figure for government deposits between that date and December 1950 seemed less reliable than another that was available only for each year-end until January 1951, after which it was available on a monthly basis. Therefore, the data for the period between June 1948 and January 1951 were bench-marked also. This adjustment raised the observations .3 per cent or less for these years.

The following paragraphs will describe the crude money series used between the more important points of discontinuity.

January 1931 to June 1944

Time and savings deposits: This category includes privately held deposits in commercial banks and the *Caja Nacional de Ahorros* (CNA). It also includes deposits of the government and semi-fiscal agencies. The data in this category are the sums of four time series: time deposits in the commercial banks, savings deposits in the commercial banks, time deposits in the CNA, and savings deposits in the CNA. They were taken from the *Anuario Estadistico: Finanzas, Bancos, y Cajas Sociales* and the *Estadistica Chilena*. Each had tables showing the same data, and the lack of one issue of one of the publications could be made up with the corresponding issue of the other.

Demand deposits: This category is a residual. It consists of all deposits of the public and of semi-fiscal agencies in the commercial banks and the CNA, *minus* time and savings deposits described above. This accounting makes demand deposits too small by the amount of government-held time deposits. The best alternative to this method was to take total demand and sight deposits including those of the government. But on the reasonable assumption that the government's holdings of demand and sight deposits were larger than its holdings of time deposits, this alternative was rejected in favor of the method used.

Total deposit figures were also obtained from four time series: total deposits in commercial banks, (minus) deposits of the government in commercial banks, total deposits in the CNA, (minus) deposits of the government in the CNA. These were taken from the same sources as indicated for time deposits.

Currency: This category contains all currency outside banks, plus all nonbank deposits in the central bank. This is undesirable. It would have been preferable to add the nonbank deposits in the central bank—exclusive of government deposits—to the demand deposit category. This could have been done, since the series containing this category was accompanied by another that contained only the nonbank holdings of currency. The difference is the nonbank holdings of deposits in the central bank.

When these data were collected I did not expect to need a monthly breakdown of the various kinds of money. In order to avoid seemingly superfluous adding and subtracting of these elements, I lumped all the nonbank monetary liabilities of the central bank together under the heading of currency.

It should be noted that this does not affect the total money figure, nor does it disturb the division of money stock which I use in section 4, viz., time and savings deposits versus all other kinds of money.

This time series was taken from the *Boletin Mensual*.

July 1944 to June 1947

Time and Savings Deposits: Same as above.

Demand Deposits: These are calculated as a residual, as they were for the previous period. However, the data are different. The new series was adopted because the tables from which the data for the preceding period were taken were discontinued in the *Estadistica Chilena* and could not be duplicated for all the succeeding years from either the *Boletin* or the *Anuario*. However, there were seven months of overlap in 1944.

The only deposits excluded from this series were inter-bank liabilities. Hence, they contain deposits of the government as well as of the public and of semi-fiscal institutions. From the months of overlap it is apparent that the new deposit figures exceed the old by an amount that is one-third greater than the bench-mark figure for government deposits. The one-third discrepancy can probably be attributed to government deposits in the central bank, which were excluded from the old series.

The monthly series for government deposits that is subtracted from this new deposit series was obtained in Chile by Martin Bailey. It is somewhat smaller than the bench-mark figure, but is close enough to be useful.

Currency: This series is defined in the *Boletin Mensual* as notes and coins in the hands of individuals, firms, and semi-fiscal agencies. It only excludes notes and coins in banks and currency held by the government. The bench-mark figures include government holdings, so they should be somewhat greater. Yet they are 10 to 12 per cent greater—which seems to imply an excessive amount of government-held cash. It seems probable that there is some other discrepancy in the definitions that cannot be explained from the information in the tables.

July 1947 to November 1948

Time and Savings Deposits: Same as above to January 1948. After that date the old series is graduated by monthly increments to a new series beginning in July 1948. The new series at this point is 4.7 per cent greater than the old.

The definition of the new series remains the same through December 1955 and is equivalent to the bench mark. The principal differences between it and the old series is that the new series contains inter-bank time deposits due in less than thirty days. There may be other differences, since the remaining elements of the new series may be calculated in a different way. Published definitions are inadequate to tell if this is so.

Demand Deposits: This series is also computed as a residual. Total deposits include those of the public in the commercial banks and in the CNA. Deposits of semi-fiscal agencies are added from independent series found in the *Boletin Mensual* in a table on deposits of the government and all affiliated agencies. However, government deposits are not included.

Currency: Same as for previous period.

December 1948 to December 1949

Time and Savings Deposits: Same as new series described above.

Demand and Sight Deposits: All demand and sight deposits (except sight savings deposits) in commercial banks and the CNA held by the public, and by the government and semi-fiscal agencies. From this total, float and government deposits are subtracted. Government deposits are taken from tables showing deposits of the consolidated commercial banks and deposits of the CNA, appearing in the *Boletin Mensual*. Except for the government deposit figures which come from a different source, this definition is identical with the bench-mark definition of demand deposits.

January 1950 to December 1951

All series during this period are the same as those in the bench mark itself. However, of the two series on government deposits available, the preferred series does not begin on a monthly basis until January 1951. Therefore the monthly data for 1950 are bench-marked to the preferred series.

From January 1951 to the end of the series in December 1955 no bench-marking is necessary, since the monthly data is defined identically with the bench-mark series.

TABLE 11
MONEY STOCK IN CHILE*
(In Millions of Pesos)

	Cash	Demand Deposits	Time Deposits	Total Money Stock
1931				
Jan.	250	352	798	1,400
Feb.	253	321	790	1,364
March.	247	321	782	1,350
Apr.	239	292	759	1,290
May	237	261	731	1,229
June.	232	215	718	1,165
July	241	208	707	1,156
Aug.	233	203	692	1,128
Sept.	238	221	659	1,118
Oct.	221	338	629	1,188
Nov.	219	383	603	1,205
Dec.	224	354	588	1,166
1932				
Jan.	229	262	591	1,082
Feb.	236	296	582	1,114
March.	227	337	570	1,134
Apr.	237	373	552	1,162
May	254	388	552	1,194
June.	289	392	545	1,226
July	283	441	538	1,262
Aug.	296	516	536	1,348
Sept.	313	574	534	1,421
Oct.	329	597	536	1,462
Nov.	357	652	547	1,556
Dec.	349	692	558	1,599
1933				
Jan.	332	716	569	1,617
Feb.	344	736	575	1,655
March.	371	767	577	1,715
Apr.	362	785	572	1,719
May	365	796	584	1,745
June	351	800	603	1,754
July	344	807	620	1,771
Aug.	340	786	630	1,756
Sept.	324	803	638	1,765
Oct.	319	805	643	1,767
Nov.	326	867	645	1,838
Dec.	349	899	651	1,899

NOTE: For sources see Appendix B.
* Not seasonally adjusted.

1934

Jan.	340	913	654	1,907
Feb.	350	954	664	1,968
March.	368	985	673	2,026
Apr.	385	1,032	669	2,086
May	363	1,047	675	2,085
June.	357	1,048	684	2,089
July	356	1,080	695	2,131
Aug.	351	1,042	692	2,085
Sept.	358	1,056	695	2,109
Oct.	365	1,079	705	2,149
Nov.	389	1,087	700	2,176
Dec.	400	1,093	720	2,213

1935

Jan.	413	1,117	772	2,302
Feb.	418	1,104	774	2,296
March	426	1,125	765	2,316
Apr.	415	1,189	774	2,378
May	415	1,182	814	2,411
June.	425	1,096	840	2,361
July	445	1,092	851	2,388
Aug.	442	1,083	852	2,377
Sept.	430	1,146	844	2,420
Oct.	440	1,173	855	2,468
Nov.	441	1,148	878	2,467
Dec.	487	1,128	895	2,510

1936

Jan.	458	1,163	905	2,526
Feb.	465	1,154	930	2,549
March.	492	1,297	913	2,702
Apr.	495	1,300	941	2,736
May	496	1,327	917	2,740
June.	498	1,316	931	2,745
July	502	1,280	944	2,726
Aug.	517	1,302	946	2,765
Sept.	510	1,338	933	2,781
Oct.	516	1,194	1,046	2,756
Nov.	521	1,268	1,056	2,845
Dec.	565	1,255	1,070	2,890

1937

Jan.	553	1,269	1,054	2,876
Feb.	582	1,285	1,042	2,909
March.	620	1,375	1,067	3,062
Apr.	639	1,401	1,110	3,150
May	627	1,434	1,114	3,175
June.	620	1,370	1,142	3,132
July	616	1,346	1,173	3,135
Aug.	618	1,295	1,198	3,111
Sept.	620	1,291	1,202	3,113
Oct.	610	1,274	1,183	3,067
Nov.	616	1,281	1,169	3,066
Dec.	630	1,221	1,202	3,053

TABLE 11—*Continued*

	Cash	Demand Deposits	Time Deposits	Total Money Stock
1938				
Jan..........	664	1,199	1,223	3,086
Feb..........	666	1,215	1,217	3,098
March........	679	1,248	1,213	3,140
Apr..........	683	1,275	1,207	3,165
May.........	684	1,235	1,256	3,175
June.........	661	1,213	1,279	3,153
July.........	637	1,177	1,289	3,103
Aug..........	652	1,219	1,293	3,164
Sept.........	659	1,241	1,286	3,186
Oct..........	697	1,190	1,325	3,212
Nov..........	665	1,243	1,322	3,230
Dec..........	719	1,247	1,328	3,294
1939				
Jan..........	762	1,182	1,337	3,281
Feb..........	783	1,232	1,321	3,336
March........	818	1,300	1,335	3,453
Apr..........	820	1,294	1,334	3,448
May.........	852	1,411	1,330	3,593
June.........	808	1,381	1,327	3,516
July.........	764	1,482	1,334	3,580
Aug..........	787	1,456	1,313	3,556
Sept.........	783	1,481	1,312	3,576
Oct..........	772	1,460	1,349	3,581
Nov..........	777	1,510	1,308	3,595
Dec..........	862	1,449	1,312	3,623
1940				
Jan..........	859	1,558	1,284	3,701
Feb..........	881	1,664	1,301	3,846
March........	929	1,773	1,309	4,011
Apr..........	956	1,846	1,310	4,112
May.........	939	1,832	1,329	4,100
June.........	937	1,840	1,345	4,122
July.........	994	1,746	1,378	4,118
Aug..........	1,005	1,711	1,383	4,099
Sept.........	989	1,758	1,422	4,169
Oct..........	927	1,853	1,372	4,152
Nov..........	934	1,929	1,354	4,217
Dec..........	1,034	1,808	1,366	4,208

1941

Jan...........	1,038	1,793	1,362	4,193
Feb...........	1,076	1,855	1,409	4,340
March........	1,089	1,912	1,440	4,441
Apr...........	1,109	1,967	1,458	4,534
May..........	1,086	1,962	1,455	4,503
June.........	1,097	1,988	1,460	4,545
July.........	1,083	2,165	1,491	4,739
Aug..........	1,084	2,238	1,504	4,826
Sept.........	1,089	2,213	1,511	4,813
Oct..........	1,100	2,126	1,527	4,753
Nov..........	1,111	2,164	1,550	4,825
Dec..........	1,310	2,171	1,532	5,013

1942

Jan...........	1,363	2,150	1,463	4,976
Feb...........	1,340	2,139	1,564	5,043
March........	1,412	2,233	1,582	5,227
Apr...........	1,430	2,318	1,591	5,339
May..........	1,436	2,269	1,613	5,318
June.........	1,457	2,367	1,625	5,449
July.........	1,447	2,360	1,797	5,604
Aug..........	1,466	2,394	1,802	5,662
Sept.........	1,495	2,547	1,807	5,849
Oct..........	1,520	2,423	1,799	5,742
Nov..........	1,628	2,551	1,795	5,974
Dec..........	1,700	2,527	1,797	6,024

1943

Jan...........	1,775	2,585	1,787	6,147
Feb...........	1,794	2,640	1,777	6,211
March........	1,831	2,941	1,803	6,575
Apr...........	1,853	3,125	1,833	6,811
May..........	1,842	3,175	1,864	6,881
June.........	1,944	3,298	1,894	7,136
July.........	1,930	3,220	1,980	7,130
Aug..........	1,959	3,234	2,011	7,204
Sept.........	1,954	3,320	1,980	7,254
Oct..........	1,915	3,453	1,990	7,358
Nov..........	1,988	3,588	2,000	7,576
Dec..........	2,100	3,504	2,067	7,671

1944

Jan...........	2,118	3,659	2,106	7,883
Feb...........	2,151	3,799	2,139	8,089
March........	2,196	3,874	2,159	8,229
Apr...........	2,237	3,896	2,132	8,265
May..........	2,206	4,022	2,225	8,453
June.........	2,200	4,120	2,251	8,571
July.........	2,199	4,191	2,312	8,702
Aug..........	2,205	4,164	2,337	8,706
Sept.........	2,262	3,946	2,350	8,558
Oct..........	2,229	3,936	2,365	8,530
Nov..........	2,240	4,014	2,407	8,661
Dec..........	2,390	3,904	2,488	8,782

TABLE 11—*Continued*

	Cash	Demand Deposits	Time Deposits	Total Money Stock
		1945		
Jan..........	2,446	4,056	2,536	9,038
Feb..........	2,517	4,071	2,602	9,190
March........	2,517	3,930	2,623	9,070
Apr..........	2,543	3,978	2,666	9,187
May.........	2,546	4,230	2,663	9,439
June.........	2,507	4,271	2,677	9,455
July.........	2,511	4,264	2 775	9,550
Aug..........	2,520	4,333	2,833	9,686
Sept..........	2,600	4,285	2,854	9,739
Oct..........	2,608	4,411	2,854	9,873
Nov..........	2,506	4,606	2,902	10,014
Dec..........	2,682	4,583	3,018	10,283
		1946		
Jan..........	2,722	4,703	3,044	10,469
Feb..........	2,827	4,784	3,181	10,792
March........	2,897	4,769	3,242	10,908
Apr..........	2,938	5,227	3,312	11,477
May.........	2,914	5,417	3,345	11,676
June.........	2,895	5,601	3,431	11,927
July.........	2,900	5,604	3,558	12,062
Aug..........	2,925	5,748	3,647	12,320
Sept..........	3,120	5,766	3,572	12,458
Oct..........	3,020	6,292	3,582	12,894
Nov..........	3,109	6,060	3,392	12,561
Dec..........	3,170	6,009	3,243	12,422
		1947		
Jan..........	3,257	6,135	3,288	12,680
Feb..........	3,349	6,631	3,305	13,285
March........	3,471	6,941	3,250	13,662
Apr..........	3,556	7,165	3,254	13,975
May.........	3,574	7,334	3,214	14,122
June.........	3,526	7,275	3,266	14,067
July.........	3,509	6,861	3,352	13,722
Aug..........	3,494	6,734	3,187	13,415
Sept..........	3,619	6,954	3,190	13,763
Oct..........	3,499	6,820	3,165	13,484
Nov..........	3,528	6,956	3,125	13,609
Dec..........	3,677	7,338	3,247	14,262

1948

Jan..........	3,836	7,294	3,244	14,374
Feb..........	3,920	7,307	3,241	14,468
March........	4,009	8,162	3,253	15,424
Apr..........	4,068	8,490	3,325	15,883
May..........	4,207	8,391	3,418	16,016
June.........	4,169	8,316	3,531	16,016
July.........	4,114	8,103	3,587	15,804
Aug..........	3,965	8,259	3,634	15,858
Sept.........	3,959	8,579	3,655	16,193
Oct..........	4,039	8,431	3,674	16,144
Nov..........	4,004	8,586	3,660	16,250
Dec..........	4,316	8,328	3,580	16,224

1949

Jan..........	4,191	8,436	3,640	16,267
Feb..........	4,374	8,591	3,891	16,856
March........	4,419	9,301	4,015	17,735
Apr..........	4,680	9,526	4,065	18,271
May..........	4,535	9,801	4,141	18,477
June.........	4,606	9,893	4,205	18,704
July.........	4,645	9,650	4,672	18,967
Aug..........	4,525	9,572	4,757	18,854
Sept.........	4,665	9,810	4,811	19,286
Oct..........	4,662	9,739	4,794	19,195
Nov..........	4,546	9,719	4,796	19,061
Dec..........	5,208	9,781	4,786	19,775

1950

Jan..........	4,898	9,721	4,678	19,297
Feb..........	5,072	9,942	4,550	19,564
March........	5,077	10,092	4,605	19,774
Apr..........	5,324	10,052	4,644	20,020
May..........	5,070	10,233	4,668	19,971
June.........	5,122	10,093	4,708	19,923
July.........	5,064	10,241	4,675	19,980
Aug..........	5,351	10,476	4,767	20,594
Sept.........	5,629	10,791	4,800	21,220
Oct..........	5,547	10,863	4,941	21,351
Nov..........	5,511	10,914	5,076	21,501
Dec..........	6,318	11,484	5,136	22,948

1951

Jan..........	5,911	12,102	5,125	23,138
Feb..........	6,118	12,461	5,199	23,778
March........	6,435	12,942	5,286	24,663
Apr..........	6,653	14,111	5,290	26,054
May..........	6,386	14,087	5,360	25,833
June.........	6,682	14,174	5,508	26,364
July.........	6,414	13,910	5,626	25,950
Aug..........	6,517	14,098	5,611	26,226
Sept.........	7,350	14,157	5,605	27,112
Oct..........	7,138	14,539	5,801	27,478
Nov..........	7,037	14,633	5,889	27,559
Dec..........	7,969	14,954	6,146	29,069

TABLE 11—*Continued*

	Cash	Demand Deposits	Time Deposits	Total Money Stock
		1952		
Jan..........	7,461	16,011	6,072	29,544
Feb..........	7,823	16,072	6,126	30,021
March.......	7,920	17,168	6,152	31,240
Apr..........	8,122	17,650	6,173	31,945
May.........	8,408	17,995	6,216	32,619
June.........	9,295	18,999	6,299	34,593
July.........	9,086	19,273	6,426	34,785
Aug..........	9,960	19,455	6,444	35,859
Sept.........	9,755	20,241	6,604	36,600
Oct..........	10,236	19,321	6,630	36,187
Nov..........	10,319	19,350	6,740	36,409
Dec..........	11,497	19,511	7,102	38,110
		1953		
Jan..........	11,270	16,894	7,331	35,495
Feb..........	12,022	22,173	7,480	41,675
March.......	12,120	24,296	7,635	44,051
Apr..........	12,999	25,190	7,785	45,974
May.........	13,205	25,843	7,941	46,989
June.........	13,492	26,617	7,998	48,107
July.........	13,117	27,450	8,146	48,713
Aug..........	13,431	27,530	8,322	49,283
Sept.........	13,659	27,797	8,809	50,265
Oct..........	14,164	27,610	9,093	50,867
Nov..........	14,106	28,823	9,215	52,144
Dec..........	16,660	29,932	9,316	55,908
		1954		
Jan..........	16,771	31,929	9,800	58,500
Feb..........	17,704	35,905	10,041	63,650
March.......	16,875	37,224	10,107	64,206
Apr..........	18,653	38,147	10,351	67,151
May.........	18,806	39,793	10,650	69,249
June.........	18,774	40,057	11,586	70,417
July.........	18,095	41,524	11,532	71,151
Aug..........	18,095	42,311	11,820	72,226
Sept.........	19,208	43,340	11,726	74,274
Oct..........	19,902	43,893	11,719	75,514
Nov..........	19,095	45,115	11,382	75,592
Dec..........	22,753	47,008	11,289	81,050

1955

Jan..........	23,739	49,685	11,435	84,859
Feb..........	24,978	53,716	12,390	91,084
March........	26,851	57,712	12,846	97,409
Apr..........	29,217	61,653	13,280	104,150
May.........	29,222	65,455	13,900	108,577
June.........	30,137	69,280	14,096	113,513
July.........	32,103	67,674	14,536	114,313
Aug..........	31,327	66,837	14,639	112,803
Sept.........	32,021	71,640	14,689	118,350
Oct..........	32,388	73,163	15,062	120,613
Nov..........	32,985	73,982	14,984	121,951
Dec..........	40,028	74,440	15,100	129,568

II

Money and Prices in Argentina, 1935–1962

ADOLFO CESAR DIZ

Money and Prices in Argentina, 1935–1962

INTRODUCTION

THIS study investigates the behavior of money and prices in Argentina from 1935 to 1962.

The period has been chosen for a variety of reasons. The year 1935 marks the establishment of the central bank. This is also the year of origin for many important economic time series. During this period the Argentine economy was subject to substantial and fluctuating rates of inflation, output showed a time pattern of unstable growth, and there were important changes in the nature of economic policies and in the underlying institutional framework (section 1). Such characteristics of the period suggest overall variability of economic magnitudes and allow one to entertain high expectations about statistical results.

Section 2 deals with the nominal stock of money, its rates of change through time, and the fraction of these changes that can be attributed to changes in each one of its proximate determinants. Among them, the reserve-deposit ratio of commercial banks is further analyzed.

The demand for money in real terms is the subject of section 3. The first part is devoted to the aggregate demand for money and an attempt is made to explain the observed variations in real per capita money holdings, for two definitions of money, in terms of changes in the expected rate of change in prices, real measured and permanent income, and the variance of inflation rates. The second part deals with the demand functions for components of the money stock, also in real terms, and the behavior of the ratio of currency to demand deposits and the ratio of savings and time deposits to demand deposits through time.

This paper is based on my "Money and Prices in Argentina, 1935–1962" (unpublished Ph.D. dissertation, University of Chicago, 1966). I owe a great intellectual debt to Milton Friedman and Arnold Harberger for their encouragement, suggestions, and criticisms at every stage of the work. David Meiselman and Larry Sjaastad also offered useful comments on earlier drafts. This work was made possible by the generous financial support given to me by the University of Tucuman (Argentina) and the Ford Foundation.

In section 4 the attention is turned to the dynamic behavior of prices in the Argentine inflationary process. In this section an attempt is made to estimate both the responses of the rate of change in prices to changes in the rates of change in money and other "policy" variables, and the time structure of those responses when they involve lags.

In the last section the main conclusions of the study are summarized.

1. THE INSTITUTIONAL BACKGROUND

From 1935 on, the central bank charter and the banking law have been the most important legal instruments governing the organization and functioning of monetary and banking institutions in Argentina. Three different versions of these instruments have been enacted and each has drastically transformed the monetary institutional arrangements of the economy.

The central bank charter of 1935. The creation of the Argentine Central Bank in May 1935 was the outcome of a long discussion beginning at the end of the nineteenth century, though the precise timing was largely the consequence of the problems raised for the existing banking structure by the economic crisis of the early 1930s.

The bank had the following main objectives:

a. To concentrate enough foreign exchange and gold reserves to moderate the consequences of export fluctuations and foreign capital movements on money, credit, and commercial activities, in order to maintain the value of money.

b. To regulate the quantity of credit and means of payments, adapting them to the actual volume of business.

c. To promote the liquidity and the appropriate functioning of the commercial banking system.

The principal tools of financial management given to the new institution were rediscounting and the fixing of the rediscount rate, open market operations (subject to certain limits), short-term advances to the commercial banks and to the treasury, regulation of new entry into banking, and control over the structure of banks' assets and liabilities. Differentiated minimum reserve requirements were established for demand, savings, and time deposits at levels fixed by law. Interest payments on these categories of deposits were not forbidden but were limited to maximum rates linked to the rediscount rate.

The bank was required to hold a minimum 25 per cent reserve in gold and foreign exchange against its notes and sight liabilities. The law also provided for convertibility to gold (a minimum of 400 Troy ounces), but this provision was suspended and never became effective.[1]

The 1935 charter and banking law ruled the Argentine monetary system for eleven years. The national and international economic developments during this period were quite different from those that had preceded—and to a certain degree influenced—this legislation. Inflation, not deflation, was the danger and the problem. Successively favorable balances of payments before, and particularly during, the World War II years meant that the bank's reserve requirements did not set very close limits on the quantity of money. The authorities used open market operations extensively but their effectiveness was impaired by the limits imposed on the bank's holdings of securities and concern over "the maintenance of an orderly market for government securities," especially during the last years of the period. Contrary to expectations in 1935, little use was made of rediscounting or the rediscount rate which was set at 3.5 per cent in 1936 and remained constant during ten years, with the exception of eighteen months in 1940–41.

The charter reforms of 1946 and 1949. The nationalization of the bank in 1946 and the technical reforms that complemented this measure were the means by which the institution was to accomplish the new, additional objective of

> promoting, orienting and carrying on adequate economic policies to maintain a high degree of activity in order to obtain the maximum level of employment of disposable human and material resources and the orderly expansion of the economy, so that the growth of the national wealth will allow the raising of the standards of living of the population.[2]

Thus the purpose and functioning of the bank were expanded to encompass control over the general economic policy of the country.

Since bankers "do not use their own but others' capital to obtain profits," it was felt necessary to insure depositors against the "inherent risks" of the banking business; hence, all deposits were transferred to and guaranteed by the central bank, commercial banks acting from then on as mere agents of the former. The law also provided for continuous "rediscounting" apportioned according to the "needs of

1. The preceding enumeration of objectives and tools is a summary of the main provisions of Argentine Laws 12155, 12156, and 12160, and of Executive Decrees 61126 and 65227, all of 1935.

2. Executive Decree 14957/46, enacted by Law 12962, section III, article 3.

business" and the bank's promotional objectives. These operations were implemented by discriminatory quantitative limitations imposed on individual banks and by a complex of rediscount rates to be charged according to the type of loan to which the funds were to be applied. To permit "a more efficient monetary regulation and that of the securities market" the maximum limits for open market operations were enlarged and the bank was allowed to issue its own securities.

The law provided for complete regulation by the bank of all interest rates charged on loans or paid by banks on savings and time deposits. Interest payments on demand deposits were forbidden. All banking expenses incurred in the handling of deposit accounts, including interest payments, were to be paid by the central bank. Minimum reserve requirements in gold and foreign exchange were set at 25 per cent of the bank's notes held by the public plus other sight liabilities, not including the transferred deposits.

The 1946 legislation gave the authorities a "sufficient" set of tools but no rule or guiding principle except, perhaps, that they should "regulate means of payments according to the needs of business in order to maintain the purchasing power of money." Private creation of money through the commercial banking system practically ceased. Rediscounting was an instrument with a different meaning. Open market operations were aimed at regulating the securities market, not the quantity of money. Selective credit controls became widely used in order to offer a "rational" allocation of credit, and to provide some rationing criteria for loans that, given the level of interest rates chosen by the bank and the ongoing inflation, were granted at negative real interest rates.

In 1949 a constitutional amendment brought about an administrative reform by which the bank's broad economic policy functions were transferred to a newly created National Economic Council. The new legislation also suspended indefinitely the minimum gold and foreign exchange reserve requirements for the central bank, because "monetary issues have to be linked to the national income and metallic and foreign exchange reserves to the balance of payments." A few months later the bank could not have met these requirements.

The central bank charter of 1957. The bank charter, as modified in October 1957, together with the 1957 banking law, regulated the banking structure of the country up to February 1969.[3]

3. Toward the end of 1967 the appropriateness of the regulations was under discussion, and a new and more comprehensive banking law was being drafted.

Deposits were returned to commercial banks (about ninety of them), but continued to be guaranteed in the sense that the central bank was ready to advance the funds to pay all deposits in case of any bank's failure.

The objectives of the transformed institution were stated as follows:

a. To regulate the volume of credit and means of payments so as to maintain the purchasing power of money . . . and stimulate the orderly and persistent growth of national income with the maximum employment of productive resources.

b. To concentrate and mobilize gold and foreign exchange reserves so as to moderate the effects of balance of payments fluctuations on the value of money and economic activity.

c. To promote the liquidity and the appropriate functioning of the commercial banking system.[4]

The bank was given "all necessary instruments to conduct the credit and monetary policy" of the country. These included all the original (1935) tools of financial management plus the additional power to establish and modify minimum reserve requirements for commercial banks according to the type of deposit and region of the country, and to impose additional marginal requirements on incremental deposits after given dates. The bank was also allowed to establish penalty rates on shortages of required reserves and to authorize banks to hold these reserves in the form of special kinds of bonds.

The law again provided for minimum gold and foreign exchange reserve requirements for the central bank and convertibility of its own notes, but these provisions have not been enforced.

The period 1957–62 was characterized by the use of variations in reserve requirements and selective credit controls as the major tools of monetary management.

2. The Money Supply Mechanism

This section presents an analysis of the changes in the stock of money in Argentina during the period 1935–62. First there is a description of the relationship between variations in the monetary "base" and in the

---

According to its proponents the main purpose of such reform would be to correct inadequacies of the existing legislation in the light of developments in the Argentine financial sector during the preceding 10 years, and to extend central bank control to nonbanking financial intermediaries whose growth was considered to be particularly significant. This new law was enacted February 1969.

4. Executive Decree 13126 of 1957, article 1.

quantity of money. Then the statistical behavior of the base multiplier and the quantitative influence of each of its proximate determinants is examined. Finally, one of these determinants, the reserve ratio, is further analyzed. The behavior of the ratio of currency to demand deposits and of savings and time deposits to demand deposits is discussed at the end of section 3.

Changes in the money supply, the monetary base, and the base multiplier. The expression

$$M = mB \tag{1}$$

expresses the quantity of money, M, as a product of the "base multiplier," m, and the monetary "base" or "high-powered money," B.[5] Chart 1 shows the behavior of these three variables during the period under consideration.[6] Their numerical values are given in tables 21 and 22 in the appendix.

Table 1 shows the average annual percentage rate of change of the annual averages of these three variables for the whole period 1935–62 and for each of three subperiods defined on the basis of their institutional characteristics, as explained in section 1.

These figures give an idea of the relative importance of the components of the total change in the quantity of money. They indicate that the changes in B have been quantitatively the most important but that the observed changes in m are not to be neglected: During 1935–45 the negative average rate of change in m "sterilized" a substantial part of the change that would have occurred in M in view of the average rate of increase in B. During 1958–62 the average expansion of m explains of more than a quarter of the average relative change in M, which thus reaches the highest level for the whole period despite the observed deceleration of B.

5. Where $M = C + D + T$ so that the total quantity of money includes currency, C, demand deposits, D, and savings and time deposits, T, held by the public, and where $B = C + R$ so that the monetary "base" includes the amount of currency held by the public and the banking reserves, R, composed of vault cash and deposits of the commercial banks with the central bank. Dividing one equality by the other and taking B to the right side of the equation,

$$M = \frac{C + D + T}{C + R} B, \tag{2}$$

which is the expanded version of equation (1).

6. The amount of high-powered money during 1946–57 is not shown in this figure because of the institutional characteristics of the subperiod, as explained in section 1 above.

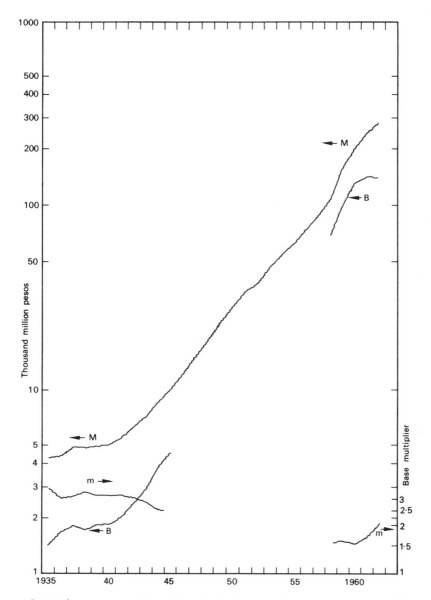

CHART 1. Annual averages of the stock of money, the monetary base, and the base multiplier, 1935–62.

SOURCES: Tables 21 and 22.

TABLE 1

AVERAGE ANNUAL PERCENTAGE RATES OF CHANGES IN THE
STOCK OF MONEY, THE MULTIPLIER, AND THE MONETARY BASE
(RATES OF CHANGE CONTINUOUSLY COMPOUNDED)

PERIOD	ANNUAL PERCENTAGE RATE OF CHANGE OF		
	M	*m*	*B*
1935–45........	8.45	−3.09	11.63
		(−.36)	(1.36)
1945–58........	18.45	−2.56	21.01
		(−.14)	(1.14)
1958–62........	24.03	6.21	17.82
		(.26)	(.74)
1935–62......	15.61	−1.45	17.06
		(−.09)	(1.09)

SOURCE: Tables 21 and 22.

NOTE: The average annual rate of change of a given series over a period of time is the difference between the natural logarithms of the terminal and initial values of the series divided by the number of years included in the period.

The figures in parentheses below the rates corresponding to *m* and *B* indicate the fraction of the total relative change in *M* that each one of them represents.

For both the initial and the last subperiods the analysis was also made in terms of the quarterly rates of change corresponding to these three variables.[7] These quarterly series (given numerically in tables 28 and 29) offer some interesting information which can be summarized by reference to their averages, the characteristics of their sequence, and the distribution of their values in absolute terms. The geometric means of the quarterly rates of change of *M*, *B*, and *m* provide an estimate of the contributions of the changes in *m* and *B* to the growth of the stock of money which is basically similar to that of the annual series.[8] The sequence of these quarterly changes show that those corresponding to

7. When considering discrete intervals of time we must make the analysis of the total rate of change in money in terms of first differences:

$$\frac{\Delta M}{M} = \frac{\Delta m}{m} + \frac{\Delta B}{B} + \frac{\Delta m}{m}\frac{\Delta B}{B}. \tag{3}$$

The last, additional term represents the interaction of changes in *m* and in *B* if they have taken place simultaneously through the period.

8. These geometric means are the quarterly rates of change compounded at quarterly intervals. During 1935–46 the fraction of total relative change in *M* accounted for by the relative changes in the multiplier and the monetary base were −.48 and 1.49, respectively. The interaction term had a value of −.01. During 1958–62 the corresponding figures were .23, .76, and .01.

B varied widely around a declining trend from 1935 to about 1939–40 and much less widely around an upward trend during the World War II years. During the period 1958–62 these relative changes in B showed a markedly negative trend. The relative changes in m during 1935–45 showed a weak negative trend after 1937 and were quantitatively less important than those of B. Their variability increased during the years 1958–62, but they do not show any definite trend. Table 2 shows the

TABLE 2

NUMBER OF RELATIVE QUARTERLY CHANGES IN THE MULTIPLIER
(CLASSIFIED ACCORDING TO THEIR INTENSITY IN ABSOLUTE VALUE)

$\left|\dfrac{\Delta m}{m}\right|$	ABSOLUTE, RELATIVE, AND CUMULATIVE RELATIVE FREQUENCIES						
	1935–45		1958–62		1935–45 and 1958–62		
%	Number of Changes	%	Number of Changes	%	Number of Changes	%	Cumulative Upward Frequencies
0–2......	19	42	9	45	28	43	100
2–4......	13	29	5	25	18	28	57
4–6......	7	16	2	10	9	14	29
6–8......	4	9	1	5	5	8	15
8–10.....	—	—	1	5	1	1	7
10+......	2	4	2	10	4	6	6
Total.....	45	100	20	100	65	100	—

SOURCE: Table 30.

frequency distribution of the quarterly rates of changes in the multiplier, in absolute value, during both subperiods. These figures indicate that throughout both subperiods, in approximately one out of three quarters the multiplier has been subject to relative changes of at least 4 per cent.

The next step in this study is an attempt to explain the observed variation in the multiplier and to quantify the contribution of each one of its proximate determinants.

The expression

$$m = \frac{\dfrac{C}{D} + \dfrac{T}{D} + 1}{\dfrac{C}{D} + \dfrac{R}{D+T}\left(1 + \dfrac{T}{D}\right)} \tag{4}$$

indicates that the observed changes in the multiplier through time can be explained by changes in the ratios C/D, T/D, and $R/(D + T)$.[9]

The total quantity of money has been roughly about twice the monetary base. This multiplying effect reflects the fractional reserve nature of the Argentine commercial banking institutions. Since, in addition, minimum reserve requirements differentiated by kind of deposits have been established, the size of the multiple depends not only on the distribution of high-powered money between the public and the banks but also on the relative amounts of different kinds of deposits in existence. These are the influences that work through the ratios mentioned above.

If we let the letters c, t, and r represent the corresponding ratios, their individual contribution to the change in m can be approximately measured in the following way:

$$\Delta m = \frac{\partial m}{\partial c} \Delta c + \frac{\partial m}{\partial t} \Delta t + \frac{\partial m}{\partial r} \Delta r + \text{Interaction} \tag{5}$$

where the increments in m, c, t, and r are those actually observed during each quarter, the partial derivatives are evaluated at the beginning of each quarter, and the value of the interaction is obtained as a residual.[10]

TABLE 3

CONTRIBUTION OF EACH RATIO TO THE CHANGES IN THE MULTIPLIER
(AVERAGE QUARTERLY VALUES IN PERCENTAGE)

Subperiod	Δm	$\frac{\partial m}{\partial c} \Delta c$	$\frac{\partial m}{\partial t} \Delta t$	$\frac{\partial m}{\partial r} \Delta r$	Interaction
1935–45.....	−2.85	.48 (.17)	−1.04 (−.36)	−3.03 (−1.06)	.74 (.25)
1958–62.....	2.39	−.89 (−.37)	.12 (.05)	2.52 (1.05)	.64 (.27)

SOURCE: Tables 29 and 33.

NOTE: The figures in parentheses indicate the fraction of the total change in the multiplier accounted for by changes in each of the ratios c, t, and r, and their interaction.

9. Expression (4) is derived from (2) by dividing numerator and denominator of m by D and then multiplying and dividing the last term of the new denominator by $(D + T)$. The new equation thus keeps T/D as a separate variable for analytical purposes but maintains the reserves held by banks as a fraction of total bank deposits.

10. The three partial derivatives are

$$\frac{\partial m}{\partial c} = -\frac{(1 + t)(1 - r)}{[c + r(1 + t)]^2}; \quad \frac{\partial m}{\partial t} = \frac{c(1 - r)}{[c + r(1 + t)]^2}; \text{ and } \frac{\partial m}{\partial r} = -\frac{(1 + t)(c + t + 1)}{[c + r(1 + t)]^2}$$

Table 3 shows, for each subperiod, the average quarterly value of each component of multiplier change. The table shows that the movements in the reserve ratio have been quantitatively the most important during both subperiods. Next in importance were the negative changes in T/D during the first subperiod and the positive changes in C/D (also with negative influence on the multiplier) during the last subperiod.

A. THE RESERVE-DEPOSITS RATIO OF COMMERCIAL BANKS

This section contains a brief summary of the Argentine regulations regarding banks' reserves, a description of the analytical framework used in explaining variations in the reserve ratio, and the empirical results. The C/D and T/D ratios are analyzed at the end of section 3.

Regulations concerning banks' reserves. The banking legislation of 1935 established minimum reserve requirements of 16 per cent for demand and 8 per cent for savings and time deposits for all banks. These requirements were fixed by law. Banks' deposits with the central bank and their holdings of gold and currency could be added to meet legal reserves. For each institution the requirements were computed on the basis of monthly averages of daily balances of aggregate reserves and deposits in all its branches.

The law did not provide for punitive interest to be charged in case of shortages of legal reserves. The central bank was empowered to waive the requirements transitorily for individual banks, but in such cases the bank involved could not pay dividends without the central bank's authorization. If within two years the requirements were not met, or at least a plan to do so in the future was not approved by the central bank, the bank was subject to liquidation.

The 1957 laws gave the central bank the power to use variations in reserve requirements as a tool of monetary management. The possibilities included modifications of basic or average requirements without limitations, the differentiation of requirements for different kinds of deposits, the definition of regions of the country and the differentiation of requirements according to the banks' location, the establishment and modification of additional reserve requirements on incremental deposits

---

where c and $t > 0$, and $1 > r > 0$. For simplicity, the last partial derivative does not take into account that r is itself a function of t. The signs that precede the values of each derivative indicate the direction of the impact on the multiplier of changes in c, t, and r, since all three numerators are positive. The derivatives also show the interdependence between all three ratios.

after a given date with an upper 100 per cent limit, and all their possible combinations. The central bank was also allowed to define the set of assets to be counted as reserves, which could include bonds, in addition to commercial banks' deposits with the central bank and vault cash.

During 1958–62 the authorities did not include bonds in the definition of legal reserves but made intensive use of almost every other possibility open to them for varying legal requirements. Most of those regulations and modifications were coexistent so that a great but unknown number of different legal requirements were in force throughout the country at any point in time.

The 1957 laws gave the central bank the power to establish and modify the penalty rate applicable to shortages of legal reserves and the length of the reserve period. The former was set at 7 per cent in December 1957 and was raised three times before the end of 1962, when it stood at 30 per cent. The length of the reserve period, set at fifteen days in 1957, was also changed to one month in April 1961.

The analytical framework. The main hypothesis of this study is that the observed variation in the reserve ratio of commercial banks can be explained by a simple model which takes institutional and behavioral considerations into account, thus incorporating the policy influences of the monetary authorities as well as the reactions of banks to certain variables which affect their decisions to hold reserves.

A different hypothesis, often made, is that variables other than legal reserve ratios are irrelevant either because it is assumed that banks keep a constant ratio of precautionary reserves to deposits above those requirements, or because the precautionary ratio is assumed to be proportional to the legal ratio, implying a reserve ratio proportional to the legal ratio, or because the precautionary ratio is considered to be a highly volatile and unpredictable magnitude, subject to a large number of influences very difficult to identify. The first two versions of this hypothesis are clearly rejected by the evidence of the first period when, even with constant legal reserve requirements, the reserve ratio showed great variability. This study provides a test for the hypothesis in its third version.

The reserve ratio can be viewed as the sum of the legal reserve ratio plus an excess, precautionary, or usable reserve ratio.[11] A discussion of each of these components and their determinants follows.

11. An alternative approach is to consider the reserve ratio as a weighted average of the ratios of individual banks or groups of banks. This may be an additional and fruitful way of analyzing the Argentine experience, where government-owned commercial banks, foreign banks, and other differentiated groups

When there is statistical information on the amount of legal reserves through time, it is easy to see how variations in this component affect the total reserve ratio. The question of why this component varies may still be interesting, depending on the institutional arrangements and the purposes at hand, but it does not seem to be crucial for the explanation of movements in the total reserve ratio. When this information is not available, as in Argentina, the questions about why and how much this component varies, if at all, become important in trying to explain the behavior of the total reserve ratio.

The sources of variation in the aggregate legal reserve ratio can be easily understood from the following definition:

$$l_t = \sum_{i=1}^{n_t} d_{it} r_{it}^l + \sum_{i=1}^{n_t} \left(\frac{D_{it} - D_{io}}{D_t} \right) m_{it}^l, \qquad (6)$$

where n_t is the total number of legal categories of deposits at each time t, r_{it}^l and m_{it}^l are the average and marginal coefficients applicable to the ith category of deposits at time t, D_{it} and d_{it} are the amount of the ith category of deposits and the fraction of total deposits they represent at time t, D_{io} is the amount of the ith category of deposits at the time $(t = 0)$ when marginal requirements are established, D_t is the total amount of deposits at time t, and $D_{it} > D_{io}$. The first term of expression (6) represents the usual situation, without marginal reserve requirements, in which the aggregate legal reserve ratio is an average of the required coefficients applicable to different kinds of deposits weighted by the fraction of total deposits that each kind represents. The second term represents the additional influence of marginal requirements on incremental deposits after a certain date $(t = 0)$.

Expression (6) shows that the legal ratio can vary through time because of changes in the average and marginal coefficients, the legal classification of deposits and the definition of $t = 0$, which are pure "policy" variables, and also because of changes in the public's preferences for different kinds of deposits which affect their relative importance and their particular rates of growth through time, and which may be independent of any central bank decision.[12]

During 1935–45 the existence of legally fixed but differentiated average requirements for demand and savings and time deposits made

---

operate. The paucity and poor quality of published disaggregated data prevented a full exploration of this alternative.

12. The central bank may influence the desired composition of deposits by controlling interest payments on different kinds of deposits, by varying their operational nature (particularly for savings and time deposits), etc.

changes in d_{it} the only source of variation in the aggregate legal reserve ratio. During the period 1958–62 the sources of variation in the aggregate legal reserve ratio included changes in the "policy" variables as well as in the structure of deposits.

The excess or precautionary reserve ratio is the difference between the actual and the legal reserve ratio. The hypothesis made here is that, given the legal reserve ratio, the value of the excess reserve ratio through time is determined by the commercial banks' demand for precautionary reserves and by the rate at which the central bank injects or withdraws total reserves.[13]

The first part of the hypothesis requires a theory of the banks' demand for excess reserves. The hypothesis is that, given the legal reserve ratio and the total amount of reserves, the banks' desired excess or precautionary reserve ratio is a function of the cost of holding those reserves and the composition of deposits. When banks hold reserves they incur a cost in the form of the foregone yield on earning assets they could substitute for those reserves, so that increases or decreases in those yields can be expected to lower or raise the desired excess reserve ratio. The composition of deposits may be expected to influence banks' expectations about clearing drains and thereby also to affect desired positions. Finally, if those expectations are also subject to other typical intra-year influences, they may introduce seasonal fluctuations in the demand for excess reserves.

The second part of the hypothesis implies that the central bank can interfere with the process by which banks adjust to their desired positions. Given the legal reserve ratio and the composition of deposits, any observed combination of a cost of holding reserves and an excess reserve ratio not on the banks' stock demand curve implies that they are changing the excess reserve ratio toward the desired level. But if the central bank is at the same time injecting or withdrawing reserves, it can offset the banks' intentions by keeping them in a position of secondary equilibrium where the excess reserve ratio remains constant.

When both parts of the hypothesis about the excess reserve ratio are put together they imply the following: If the rate of change in total reserves is constant, either because total reserves are constant or because they are changing at a constant positive or negative rate, changes in the cost of holding money will bring about changes of opposite sign in the ratio. When the rate at which the central bank injects reserves

13. This hypothesis was developed by Meigs in his study of free reserves in U.S. banks. See Alexander J. Meigs, *Free Reserves and the Money Supply* (Chicago: Univ. of Chicago Press, 1962).

into the system rises, or the rate at which it withdraws reserves falls, the banks' excess reserve ratio will rise provided the cost of holding reserves does not increase. If it does, the ultimate result will be the sum of two offsetting influences whose net effect on the excess reserve ratio cannot be determined a priori. When the rate of increase in total reserves declines or the withdrawal rate increases, the opposite would be true.

Nothing has been said up to this point about the speed with which banks adjust to desired positions. The hypothesis made here is that banks react not only to contemporaneous changes in the cost of holding reserves or the rate at which the central bank injects or withdraws total reserves, but that they operate with a longer horizon which also takes into account the behavior of these variables in the recent and more distant past.

The preceding discussion about the determinants of variations in the legal and excess reserve ratios leads to the formulation of the following hypothesis for explaining the behavior of the aggregate reserve ratio through time:

$$ r = f\left(r^l, d, i, \frac{1}{R}\frac{dR}{dt}, S, u\right), \tag{7} $$

where r^l is a "policy" variable representing the level of legal reserve coefficients, d stands for the amount of demand deposits relative to time deposits, i represents the actual or expected opportunity cost of holding reserves, the fourth variable is the actual or expected flow of total reserves, S is a dummy variable representing seasonal factors working through the legal or the excess reserve components, and u represents other influences on the reserve ratio which have not been considered in the preceding discussion.[14]

14. One such variable is the rediscount rate. The reason for not mentioning borrowing and the rediscount rate in the preceding paragraphs is empirical rather than theoretical. During the first period, as mentioned in section 1, the rediscount rate was constant, and rediscounting or other forms of borrowing were non-existent, except for a period of eighteen months during 1940–41. This exception lacks significance since it was a mere experiment (as it was officially described), or an exercise on the eligibility of paper, rather than a change in central bank policy or in the banks' attitudes toward borrowing. During the second period rediscounting was performed and may have had some influence on the banks' reserve holdings. The reason why no explicit allowance was made for this factor during this period is my belief that nonprice considerations and the use of a great deal of discretion by the central bank have been the most important factors. The rediscount rates' structure was very complicated and unstable through time and some extremely detailed and ad hoc regulations applied to certain operations.

The empirical results. The variables in expression (7) are quantitatively defined as follows.

The reserve ratio is the total amount of reserves that banks hold in the form of deposits with the central bank or in the form of vault cash divided by their total deposit liabilities (net of inter-bank deposits). Total deposits include all demand, savings, and time deposits held by the nonbanking public and the government. The values used in the regressions are the end-of-quarter percentages for the periods 1935–45 and 1958–62, without seasonal adjustment, and are graphed in chart 2 (and given numerically in tables 34 and 35).

The index of legal reserve coefficients is used only in the regressions dealing with the period 1958–62. Changes in required reserve coefficients are always announced through central bank circular letters to all commercial banks, and they show that requirements for different classes of deposits tend to move together through time. Under these circumstances the value of only one coefficient applicable to a particular kind of deposit seems to be a good proxy variable to represent changes in the whole spectrum of legal rates. The values of this variable are the end-of-quarter total (average plus marginal) effective percentage rates applicable to demand deposits in Buenos Aires banks, and are given in table 35.

The index of deposit composition is the end-of-quarter ratio of

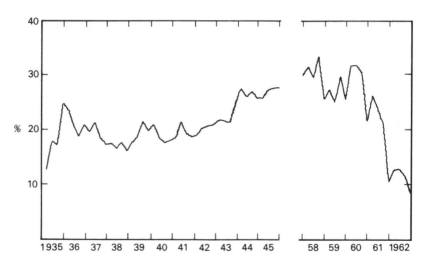

CHART 2. End-of-quarter reserve ratio of commercial banks, 1935–45 and 1958–62.
SOURCES: Tables 34 and 35.

demand to savings and time deposits.[15] During 1935–45 this was the only relevant legal differentiation of deposits, and during 1958–62 it was the most persistent in the sense that it was kept even in the context of other criteria (like region, provincial level of income, etc.). Since the difference between the average legal coefficients for demand and for savings and time deposits was greater during the second than the first period and since, in addition, marginal requirements were imposed only on demand deposits, it was expected that the changes in this variable would have a greater effect on the required reserve ratio during the second period.

The cost of holding reserves is represented by the end-of-quarter interest rates on 90-day certificates of consolidated treasury bonds (1935–45) and on 90-day treasury bills (1958–62). The actual values and several permanent versions of these variables, involving simple moving averages of these rates with an increasing number of terms, are used in different regressions. The results corresponding to the three- and five-term moving averages are reported here; they are approximate measures of the average yields during the semester and the year preceding the observed value of the reserve ratio, respectively. These variables in percentage form and their reciprocals are linearly introduced in the regressions to experiment with alternative forms.

The rate of change in total reserves is the first difference of the natural logarithms of total reserves at the end of quarters t and $t - 1$. This gives the quarterly percentage rate of change, continuously compounded, at which total reserves have been changing during the quarter immediately preceding the observed value of the reserve ratio. Several simple moving averages of these rates of flow with a different number of terms are used in the regression.

Seasonal factors are represented by a set of three dummy variables. An additional dummy variable is introduced in the regressions corresponding to the first period, with a value of unity for all quarters from the end of the second quarter, 1943, to the end of 1945 and zero otherwise. The data on the reserve ratio show a marked upward shift toward the end of 1943, and from then to the end of the period the level of the ratio fluctuates around this new and higher level. In the absence

---

15. Central bank reserve requirements differentiate only between demand and time deposits. Government deposits in commercial banks should then be subject to either requirement according to their nature. Since no statistical information is available on this subject, the assumption was made that all government deposits were demand deposits and were included, together with privately owned deposits, in the numerator of the index of deposit composition.

of any major changes in banking regulations or central bank policies, it is plausible to think that this shift may have been connected with the June 1943 military revolution which overthrew the existing constitutional government. By causing banks to expect greater economic instability, the new set of circumstances may have led banks to increase their precautionary reserve ratios, other things being equal.[16]

The preceding variables are used in two different sets of regressions corresponding to both subperiods, according to the following:

for 1935–45,

$$r = a + b_1 d + b_2 i_j^* + b_3\left(\frac{1}{R}\frac{dR}{dt}\right)_k^* + b_4 D + b_5 S_1 + b_6 S_2 + b_7 S_3 + u_1;$$

(8)

for 1958–62,

$$r = a + b_1 d + b_2 i_j^* + b_3\left(\frac{1}{R}\frac{dR}{dt}\right)_k^* + b_4 r^l + b_5 S_1 + b_6 S_2 + b_7 S_3 + u_2;$$

(9)

where $j = 1, 3, 5$, and $k = 1, 2, 3$. The variables in these equations have the same meaning as in expression (7); D is the shift dummy variable used during the first period, and j and k stand for the number of terms included in the moving averages used in those versions dealing with the cost and flow of total reserves defined as "permanent" magnitudes and denoted by the asterisks. Tables 4 and 5 show the estimated regression coefficients. The seasonal dummy variables were excluded in the regressions reported in these tables because in all cases their coefficients were not significantly different from zero, implying that no unexplained seasonal variation was left after all other variables were introduced in the regressions. The effective numbers of observations are 38 and 16, respectively.

The results in these tables tend to confirm the hypothesis made about the banks' behavior toward reserve holdings. The variables used explain a large fraction (roughly .90) of the observed variability of the reserve ratio and the standard errors of estimate range from about 6 to about 10 per cent of the mean value of the dependent variables, which are equal to 21.13 and 22.05 for the first and second periods, respectively.

16. The shift is not contemporaneous with the occurrence of the revolution but it may very well reflect a lag in response on the part of the banks or the lag involved in the formulation and announcement of the first major economic policies of the new government, which did not begin to take definite shape until several months after the revolution.

TABLE 4

THE RESERVE RATIO DURING THE PERIOD 1935–45
(ESTIMATED REGRESSION COEFFICIENTS FOR THE RESERVE RATIO WITH
ALTERNATIVE DEFINITIONS OF THE COST OF HOLDING RESERVES AND THE
FLOW OF TOTAL RESERVES)

Version j k		Constant	d	$1/i_j^*$	$\left(\frac{1}{R}\frac{dR}{dt}\right)_k^*$	D	R^2	$S_{y.x}$
1	1	15.643*	4.343	1.729	.0884*	2.941*	.862	1.382
		(1.372)	(3.046)	(1.004)	(.0277)	(.974)		
3	1	15.517*	4.243	2.138*	.0884*	2.598*	.867	1.356
		(1.298)	(2.811)	(1.020)	(.0269)	(.998)		
5	1	15.260*	4.222	2.766*	.0879*	2.122*	.874	1.319
		(1.227)	(2.587)	(1.082)	(.0260)	(1.028)		
1	2	16.343*	2.954	1.770	.136*	3.119*	.862	1.382
		(1.450)	(3.223)	(1.006)	(.043)	(.977)		
3	2	16.609*	1.512	2.751*	.155*	2.601*	.876	1.309
		(1.347)	(2.993)	(1.024)	(.041)	(.963)		
5	2	16.208*	1.860	3.311*	.152*	2.103*	.883	1.273
		(1.258)	(2.720)	(1.072)	(.040)	(.992)		
1	3	16.715*	2.535	1.468	.185*	3.284*	.865	1.364
		(1.471)	(3.214)	(.974)	(.055)	(.970)		
3	3	17.541*	−.616	3.056*	.233*	2.617*	.889	1.240
		(1.352)	(3.022)	(.983)	(.053)	(.912)		
5	3	17.215*	−.620	3.836*	.238*	2.014*	.899	1.178
		(1.234)	(2.713)	(1.016)	(.050)	(.918)		
Means:			.655	.877	3.150			
				.845	2.938			
				.801	2.811			

SOURCE: Tables 27, 29, and 34.

NOTE: The figures in parentheses under the regression coefficients are their standard errors of estimate, and the asterisks indicate that the corresponding coefficients are significantly different from zero at the 5 per cent level.

For the period 1935–45 (table 4) the reciprocal of the cost variable has the expected positive sign implying that, other things being equal, an increase in the yield on certificates of consolidated treasury bonds has tended to reduce the reserve ratio.[17] Changes in the contemporaneous yields do not significantly affect reserve holdings but when successively more comprehensive moving averages of the interest rates are introduced, the explanatory power of this variable improves up to the point where an annual or five-term average is used, implying an average length of six months for the weighting pattern. The coefficients of the actual and expected rate of change in total reserves also shows the

17. The results for the first period are considerably improved when the hypothesis of linearity in the reciprocal of the interest rate is used.

expected positive sign and are significantly different from zero in all cases. When alternative definitions of the expected variable are successively introduced, their explanatory power is increased up to the point where a three-term moving average is used, with an implicit average length of the weighting pattern of four and one-half months. The coefficients of the index of deposit composition show the expected signs but they are not significant in any of the regressions in table 4.

For the period 1958–62 (table 5) the coefficients of the variables representing the opportunity cost of holding reserves have the expected signs and are significant in all the regressions. The five-term moving average of current and past interest rates is, again, the one that best explains variations in the reserve ratio. The coefficients of the

TABLE 5

THE RESERVE RATIO DURING THE PERIOD 1958–62
(ESTIMATED REGRESSION COEFFICIENTS FOR THE RESERVE RATIO WITH
ALTERNATIVE DEFINITIONS OF THE COST OF HOLDING RESERVES AND THE
FLOW OF TOTAL RESERVES)

Version j k	Constant	d	i^*_j	$\left(\dfrac{1}{R}\dfrac{dR}{dt}\right)^*_k$	r^l	R^2	$S_{y.x}$
1 1	−36.754* (9.235)	25.056* (6.265)	−1.183* (.470)	.0764* (.032)	.508 (.365)	.906	2.909
3 1	−37.924* (7.426)	23.273* (4.941)	−1.397* (.356)	.0675* (.026)	.639* (.294)	.938	2.358
5 1	−34.121* (6.675)	22.859* (4.360)	−1.490* (.313)	.0584* (.023)	.563* (.260)	.952	2.087
1 2	−35.349* (13.801)	24.446* (7.396)	−1.257* (.561)	.0827 (.0772)	.510 (.476)	.870	3.429
3 2	−39.880* (11.900)	22.671* (6.155)	−1.511* (.459)	.0475 (.0684)	.730 (.411)	.904	2.938
5 2	−37.516* (10.485)	22.403* (5.436)	−1.670* (.407)	.0215 (.0622)	.690 (.363)	.925	2.603
1 3	−19.635 (11.250)	24.442* (5.640)	−1.035* (.431)	.259* (.082)	.084 (.382)	.924	2.618
3 3	−25.748* (10.574)	22.703* (5.024)	−1.179* (.394)	.203* (.081)	.329 (.360)	.936	2.399
5 3	−24.374* (9.375)	22.443* (4.495)	−1.319* (.356)	.173* (.075)	.315 (.321)	.949	2.153
Means:		1.819	5.661 5.370 5.079	−2.535 −1.940 −1.016	39.594		

SOURCE: Tables 27, 29, and 35.

NOTE: The figures in parentheses under the regression coefficients are their standard errors of estimate and the asterisks indicate that the corresponding coefficients are significantly different from zero at the 5 per cent level.

variables representing the actual and expected flow of total reserves also have the expected positive sign and significant values, except for the two-term moving average. The ratio of demand to time deposits has significant coefficients of the expected positive sign in all the regressions. The differential behavior of this variable during both periods can be found in the central bank practice toward differential reserve requirements mentioned above and, perhaps, in a different response of the banks' holdings of precautionary reserves to changes in this variable in a period of relatively low and falling excess reserves.

The index of legal reserve coefficients has the expected positive sign in all the regressions but fails to achieve significance in some of them. The variable has significant coefficients in the regressions including expected cost and current rate of change in total reserves, but this significance is lost as lagged flows of total reserves are taken into account. The statistical reason for this result is the existence of positive correlation between the current value of this "policy" variable and the lagged values of the flow of total reserves. One economic interpretation of these results can be that the central bank during this period has tended to move reserve requirements in such a way as to offset changes in total reserves and that it has done so with certain lag. When only the current flow of total reserves is considered, the index of legal coefficients is significant because it is a good proxy variable for past changes in total reserves. But when those changes are in turn taken into account, the current variations in legal reserve requirements tend to lose their significance because, in a way, they have already been expected by the banks. During this period a serious attempt was made to stabilize the level of prices, and the average of the rate of change in total reserves shows a negative value. If the preceding interpretation is correct, then it suggests that the central bank was altering reserve requirements in such a way as to offset part of its previous actions; it provides an explanation for the large number of changes in reserve requirements that the bank felt necessary to introduce during the period and shows that, by these actions, the policy variable was rendered largely ineffective to explain the observed variation in the reserve ratio.

3. The Demand for Money

From 1935 to 1962 the annual average nominal stock of money in Argentina was growing at an annual rate of either 15.5 or 17.8 per cent depending on whether "money" is defined inclusive or exclusive of savings and time deposits, respectively. During the same period population was increasing at about 1.9 per cent per year and the average annual rates of increase of the different series of price indexes available (GNP deflator, "cost of living," wholesale prices, and "cost of living" exclusive of the housing component) ranged from 15.3 to 16.1 per cent. Consequently, the rate of change of the real per capita money supply ranged from −2.5 to .6 per cent per year, depending on the definition of money chosen and the price index used for deflation.[18]

The composition of the stock of money shows important changes. As table 6 shows, currency doubled from 1935 to 1962 as a fraction of the more inclusive money stock, while savings and time deposits fell from nearly three-fifths of the total to only about one-fifth. As a fraction of income currency rose a trifle, demand deposits fell a trifle, and savings and time deposits fell drastically.

The movements of these series through time has not been smooth or even monotonic. On the contrary, they generally exhibit high variability.

TABLE 6

Components of Money Expressed as Fraction of Net National Income and of Total Money Supply

	1935			1962		
Component	As Fraction of			As Fraction of		
	NNI	M_1	M_2	NNI	M_1	M_2
C—Currency outside banks.....	.1210	.50	.21	.1312	.57	.44
D—Demand deposits..........	.1202	.50	.21	.0994	.43	.34
T—Savings and time deposits ..	.3282	—	.58	.0667	—	.22
$M_1 = C + D$.................	.2412	1.00	—	.2306	1.00	—
$M_2 = C + D + T$...........	.5694	—	1.00	.2974	—	1.00

Source: Tables 20 and 24.

This section analyzes the observed variation in the per capita real quantity of money and its composition in Argentina, during the period 1935–62, in terms of the theory of the demand for money. The first part deals with the aggregate demand for money, and the second part with the composition of the money stock.

A. THE AGGREGATE DEMAND FOR MONEY

During the period under study the Argentine economy was subject to substantial and fluctuating rates of inflation, important variations in real per capita income, and drastic changes in its monetary institutions.

Under such a set of generally unstable circumstances it is only

18. All rates of change used in this section assume continuous compounding.

natural that many will be led to think that monetary velocity or the amount of real cash balances in the hands of the public may have been responding passively to numerous influences difficult to isolate and identify, or that their variations showed mainly changes in tastes or even erratic behavior. An alternative hypothesis—and the one that is pursued in this analysis—is that even in such an environment a sizable fraction of the observed variability of real per capita money holdings can be explained by a few variables that have played a strategic role in people's behavior. Phillip Cagan's[19] study of relatively short hyperinflations in several European countries, and John Deaver's[20] of the Chilean "intermediate" case of less severe though still substantial inflation over a longer period of time and with fluctuating income, have among others provided strong evidence in support of this hypothesis under similar and even more abnormal circumstances.

The particular version of the demand for money hypothesis used in this study is that the real quantity of money demanded is a function of real per capita income, population, and the cost of holding money, and that this function is homogeneous of first degree in population.

Two quantitative definitions of "money" are used in this study. The first, M_1, consists of currency outside banks and demand deposits in commercial banks (net of inter-bank deposits, government deposits, and items in process of collection). The second, M_2, adds savings and time deposits in commercial banks to M_1. The behavior of these deposits during 1935–62 implies differential behavior of the two monetary totals through time. A decision was made to use both definitions in this study and to analyze them separately. The corresponding annual series are graphed in chart 3 and given numerically in table 21.

The cost of holding money in an inflationary environment is equal to the real rate of return on alternative forms of holding wealth plus the rate at which money holdings depreciate in purchasing power, that is, the rate of change in prices minus any interest paid on money. Unfortunately, there are no data on relevant interest rates in Argentina covering the whole period under consideration. However, the level and variability of the rate of inflation have been so high that this component probably dominates changes in the total cost of holding money. Hence, it has been used as an index of this cost.

19. Phillip Cagan, "The Monetary Dynamics of Hyperinflation," in *Studies in the Quantity Theory of Money*, ed. Milton Friedman (Chicago: Univ. of Chicago Press, 1956).

20. John V. Deaver, "The Chilean Inflation and the Demand for Money," above.

A further hypothesis is that people react not to the actual or measured rate of inflation but to some concept of the anticipated rate of change in prices. The particular model of expected rates of inflation used is similar to the one developed by Cagan and also used by Deaver. This model postulates the following basic relation:

$$\frac{dE(t)}{dt} = \delta[I(t) - E(t)] \quad \delta > 0 \tag{10}$$

Expectations of price changes are modified through time in proportion to the divergence between the observed inflation, $I(t)$, and the inflation that was expected, $E(t)$.

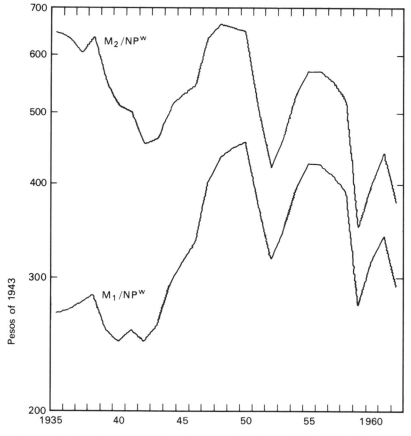

CHART 3. Annual averages of real per capita M_1 and M_2, 1935–62 (annual average wholesale price indexes used as deflators).
SOURCES: Tables 21, 23, and 24.

For discrete time intervals it is possible to approximate (10) by the following:

$$E_{t+1/2} - E_{t-1/2} = \delta\left[I_t - \frac{E_{t+1/2} + E_{t-1/2}}{2}\right]. \tag{11}$$

Lagging half a period and rearranging terms,

$$E_t = \left(\frac{2\delta}{2+\delta}\right)I_{t-1/2} + \left(\frac{2-\delta}{2+\delta}\right)E_{t-1},$$

or

$$E_t = \delta'I_{t-1/2} + (1 - \delta')E_{t-1} \quad \text{by making} \quad \delta' = \frac{2\delta}{2+\delta}.$$

This, in turn, yields the following expression:

$$E_t = \sum_{i=0}^{\infty} \delta'(1 - \delta')^i I_{t-i-1/2}, \tag{12}$$

where $I_{t-1/2}$ represents the annual rate of inflation centered at the beginning of year t and is approximated by the natural logarithm of the ratio of the annual averages of the wholesale price index for the years t and $t-1$. Expression (12) yields different weighted averages of past rates of inflation with weights declining geometrically toward the past and varying according to the particular coefficient of price expectations, δ, used.[21]

Real per capita net national income is the income variable used in the regressions. The corresponding series appear in table 24. As for the cost of holding money, several versions of a "permanent" concept of income are also introduced in different experiments. This variable is defined in terms of a geometrically declining weighted average of contemporaneous and past measured real per capita levels of income, and yields different series according to the value of the coefficient of income expectations, ϵ, used in the weighting procedure.

Next, the estimated coefficients of the following demand for money function are presented and discussed:[22]

$$\log\left(\frac{M_i}{NP^w}\right)_t = \alpha + \beta E_t^{(\delta)} + \gamma \log\left(\frac{Y}{NP^a}\right)_t^{(\epsilon)} + u_t, \tag{13}$$

21. The number of terms included in these averages, for a given δ, was truncated on the basis of a sum of original weights equal to or greater than .95. A subsequent proportional adjustment of these original weights made their sum equal to unity.

22. In the early stages of the work some experimentation was performed with 25 different values of δ, ranging from .05 to 1, and 6 values of ϵ, ranging from .02

where

$i = 1, 2$
$\delta = .2 \,(.1)\, .7,$ and 1
$\epsilon = .2 \,(.1)\, .4,$ and 1
$t = 1938(1)1962$

and where

$M_i =$ Annual average nominal stock of two definitions of "money,"
  $i = 1, 2$
$N_t =$ Population at the middle of year t
$P_t^w =$ Annual average wholesale price index
$E_t^{(\delta)} =$ Actual $(\delta = 1)$ or expected $(\delta \neq 1)$ annual rate of change in wholesale prices for the year ending at the middle of year t
$Y_t =$ Nominal net national income
$P_t^d =$ GNP deflator in year t
$\delta =$ Coefficient of price expectations
$\epsilon =$ Coefficient of income expectations

and where $\beta < 0$ and $\gamma > 0$ on theoretical grounds.

This function was estimated on the basis of twenty-five annual observations for the period 1938–62.[23]

Tables 7 and 8 show the results of the regressions for M_1 and M_2, respectively. In each table the regression coefficients are reported for alternative values of the coefficient of expectations for prices (rows) and income (columns). In general the results tend to confirm the hypothesis

---

to 1. In this chapter the results for several values of δ and ϵ are shown, in addition to those that maximize the coefficient of correlation, and including δ and $\epsilon = 1$, but they have been collapsed to a much smaller and more manageable subset.

23. Even when all the necessary data were available since 1935, the computational requirements of the expected income variable forced 1938 as the initial date. In order to use expected series of similar length without losing much valuable information on the other series, a value for the expected per capita real income for the year 1934 $[y_{34}^{(\epsilon)}]$ was estimated on the basis of linear extrapolations of several corresponding series computed with all the available data, and was used as the initial value in the equation

$$y_t^{(\epsilon)} = \epsilon y_t + (1 - \epsilon) y_{t-1}^{(\epsilon)}, \quad \text{where} \quad y_0^{(\epsilon)} = y_{34}^{(\epsilon)}.$$

defined for several ϵ coefficients. Finally, the first three values estimated with these equations were dropped to lessen the influence of possible errors in the estimated initial value. No similar problem arose in connection with the expected rate of change in prices because the data on prices went back as far as necessary.

that the demand for per capita real money balances in Argentina, during 1935–62, was a stable function of the cost of holding money and real per capita income, and that these two variables alone explain a high fraction of the observed variability of those balances. The signs of the coefficients coincide with those expected on theoretical grounds. The tables also show that the expectational variables for changes in prices and in real income tend to improve the results relatively to those obtained with immediately past inflation and current measured income. The tables also show that the two definitions of money behave somewhat differently in these and some other connections.

Table 7 shows that holdings of real M_1 per capita do not respond significantly (at the 5 per cent significance level) to changes in the current or expected cost of holding money when current measured income is used in the regressions, but that both variables have highly significant coefficients when a "permanent" concept of income is used in the regressions.[24]

The table also shows that for a given coefficient of income expectation, the R^2's show little response to changes in the coefficient of price expectations, so that not much confidence can be put on any particular value of δ as representing the "true" implicit speed of adjustment for price expectations. The R^2's vary much more in general, as the coefficient of income expectation changes. The particular values of the expectations coefficients which maximize R^2 are δ and $\epsilon = .3$.

The results of table 8 show that when savings and time deposits in commercial banks are included in the definition of money, the cost of holding money in terms of immediately past inflation and current measured real income per capita are both statistically significant at the 5 per cent level but can only explain less than half of the observed variability in per capita money holdings. The introduction of permanent versions of these variables significantly improves the results. The values of R^2 are responsive to changes in the coefficients of expectations and reach absolute maxima at $\delta = .2$ and $\epsilon = .3$.[25]

The results in tables 7 and 8, using comparable values of δ and ϵ, show that the estimated equations for M_2 consistently have higher cost coefficients (in absolute terms) and lower income coefficients than those

24. Actually, the estimated response to cost changes is close to the critical region and when all 28 observations are used the coefficients of actual and expected cost of holding money achieve significance even with measured income in the regressions.

25. The values of R^2 for $\delta = .1$ (not shown in table 8) show a marked decline as compared with those that correspond to $\delta = .2$.

TABLE 7

The Demand for M_1

(Estimated Coefficients of the Cost of Holding Money and Real Income Per Capita for Different Coefficients of Price and Income Expectations)

Coefficient of Price Expectations δ	Coefficient of Income Expectations ε											
	1.0			.4			.3			.2		
	Cost	Income	R^2 $S_{y.x}$	Cost	Income	R^2 $S_{y.x}$	Cost	Income	R^2 $S_{y.x}$	Cost	Income	R^2 $S_{y.x}$
1.0	−.195 (.113)	1.708* (.162)	.836 .086									
.7	−.264 (.142)	1.713* (.161)	.838 .085	−.679* (.092)	2.034* (.111)	.939 .053	−.745* (.114)	2.039* (.137)	.910 .064	−.823* (.170)	2.058* (.212)	.812 .092
.6	−.302 (.156)	1.718* (.160)	.840 .085	−.783* (.091)	2.064* (.100)	.951 .047	−.881* (.111)	2.091* (.121)	.932 .056	−1.000* (.173)	2.147* (.196)	.845 .084
.5	−.340 (.174)	1.725* (.160)	.841* .085*	−.901* (.096)	2.097* (.093)	.958 .044	−1.044* (.108)	2.150* (.106)	.949 .048	−1.223* (.177)	2.253* (.180)	.877 .075
.4	−.377 (.198)	1.737* (.162)	.840 .085	−1.036* (.110)	2.136* (.095)	.958* .043*	−1.245* (.109)	2.226* (.095)	.962 .042	−1.520* (.181)	2.396* (.163)	.907 .065
.3	−.398 (.238)	1.754* (.168)	.834 .087	−1.215* (.148)	2.205* (.111)	.948 .048	−1.537* (.131)	2.351* (.098)	.964** .041**	−2.008* (.196)	2.642* (.152)	.932 .055
.2	−.364 (.281)	1.763* (.177)	.826 .089	−1.305* (.216)	2.258* (.145)	.920 .060	−1.779* (.196)	2.477* (.131)	.944 .050	−2.591* (.230)	2.972* (.161)	.942* .051*

NOTE: The figures in parentheses under each coefficient correspond to its estimated standard deviation. An asterisk in the coefficients indicates significance at the 5 per cent level. An asterisk in the coefficient of determination (R^2) and in the standard error of estimate ($S_{y.x}$) indicates maximum and minimum column values, respectively, and a double asterisk indicates maximum and minimum column *and* row values, respectively.

TABLE 8

The Demand for M_2

(Estimated Coefficients of the Cost of Holding Money and Real Income Per Capita for Different Coefficients of Price and Income Expectations)

| Coefficient of Price Expectations δ | Coefficient of Income Expectations ϵ | | | | | | | | | | | |
| | 1.0 | | | .4 | | | .3 | | | .2 | | |
	Cost	Income	R^2 $S_{y.x}$	Cost	Income	R^2 $S_{y.x}$	Cost	Income	R^2 $S_{y.x}$	Cost	Income	R^2 $S_{y.x}$
1.0	−.602* (.171)	.635* (.245)	.445 .130									
.7	−.914* (.189)	.663* (.213)	.580 .113	−1.060* (.201)	.735* (.241)	.575 .114	−1.049* (.216)	.624* (.260)	.521 .121	−1.009* (.238)	.444 (.298)	.451 .130
.6	−1.090* (.188)	.687* (.193)	.656 .103	−1.275* (.196)	.802* (.214)	.669 .101	−1.276* (.216)	.713* (.236)	.618 .108	−1.247* (.244)	.565 (.277)	.544 .118
.5	−1.300* (.187)	.722* (.173)	.728 .091	−1.536* (.189)	.880* (.184)	.760 .086	−1.558* (.212)	.819* (.207)	.714 .094	−1.552* (.249)	.712* (.254)	.640 .105
.4	−1.560* (.184)	.782* (.150)	.797 .079	−1.868* (.173)	.985* (.150)	.847 .068	−1.928* (.199)	.961* (.173)	.811 .076	−1.970* (.249)	.913* (.225)	.741 .089
.3	−1.914* (.187)	.900* (.131)	.849 .068	−2.359* (.151)	1.172* (.113)	.920 .050	−2.497* (.180)	1.204* (.135)	.898 .056	−2.661* (.248)	1.263* (.193)	.840 .070
.2	−2.233* (.201)	1.051* (.127)	.869* .063*	−2.827* (.148)	1.385* (.099)	.945* .041*	−3.098* (.159)	1.500* (.107)	.945** .041**	−3.547* (.219)	1.759* (.153)	.923* .049*

Note: See Table 7, n.

of M_1. This, in turn, implies that savings and time deposit holdings in Argentina have been more responsive to cost and less responsive to income variations than either or both currency and demand deposit holdings.[26]

The values of δ which maximize R^2 in the regressions using both definitions of money, namely, $\delta = .3$ and $.2$, imply an average length of the weighting pattern of about two and one-half and four years, respectively.[27] This seems to be a rather extended horizon in the case of a country subject to substantial and prolonged inflation.

The particular distributed lag model used imposes a single δ for the whole period. However, it seems conceivable that the actual coefficient might have increased through time either according to the length or duration of the inflationary period, or according to the level of the inflation itself. To test these further hypotheses about δ, the data were divided into two subperiods of approximately equal length (1938–50 and 1951–62), and separate demand for money functions were estimated for each subperiod.[28] The results of these regressions (not reported here) were puzzling because, if anything, they showed a tendency for the "best" values of δ to be *lower* during the second than during the first subperiod. These results led to further analysis of the data and it was found that, since the variability of the rates of inflation was also greater during the second subperiod, they were consistent with a third hypothesis, namely, that the value of δ may inversely respond to changes

26. At the time this study was being completed both the National Development Council (CONADE) and the central bank made available a revised set of product and income series for Argentina. Unfortunately the new series had several characteristics which diminished their potential usefulness and made a decision to substitute them for the old series used in this study extremely difficult. First, they only covered the period since 1950 and thus created the problem of appropriate grafting with the figures of the old series for the earlier years. Second, the two sets of new figures showed divergences between themselves raising the additional problem of choice in the face of no information about the nature of their discrepancies. Finally, the plotting of the relative rates of change of the annual real per capita income figures corresponding to each of the new series showed a very high degree of correlation with those of the old series and corresponding regression coefficients not significantly different from one, a result which tended to make the effort of substitution and the dangers of grafting less worthwhile incurring than would have otherwise been the case.

27. An explanation is provided, in the second part of this section, for the lower value of δ when savings and time deposits are included in the definition of money.

28. The trouble with the Argentine experience, however, is that the rates of inflation show a rising trend in the period 1935–62, so that a problem of identification of hypothesis was bound to arise.

in the variance of inflation, since a greater variability may lead people to trust recently observed rates less and to look for more extensive evidence on which to base their expectations.

A different approach was then taken to analyze the influence of the variance of the rate of inflation upon the demand for money. A new variable, representing the variance of inflation, was introduced in the demand function together with the expected cost and real per capita income. This new function was defined as follows:

$$\log \left(\frac{M_i}{NP^w}\right)_t = \alpha + \beta E_t^{(\delta)} + \gamma \log \left(\frac{Y}{NP^d}\right)_t^{(\epsilon)} + \lambda V_t^{(\delta)} + v_t \qquad (14)$$

where

$$V_t^{(\delta)} = \sum_{i=0}^{\infty} \delta(1 - \delta)^i [I_{t-i-1/2} - E_{t-i}^{(\epsilon)}]^2 \qquad (15)$$

and where E_t was defined according to expression (12). The value of λ was expected to be positive on the assumption that an increase in uncertainty—as measured by the degree to which expectations have been frustrated in the past—would lead people to hold more real cash balances than otherwise.

TABLE 9

THE DEMAND FOR MONEY
(ESTIMATED COEFFICIENTS OF REGRESSIONS INCLUDING THE VARIANCE OF
THE RATE OF INFLATION AS AN ADDITIONAL EXPLANATORY VARIABLE)

MONEY DEFINITION	COEFFICIENT OF EXPECTATIONS		EXPLANATORY VARIABLE			R^2 $S_{y.x}$
	Price δ	Income ϵ	Cost	Income	Variance†	
M_1	.4	.4	−1.284* (.179)	2.198* (.098)	1.950 (1.143)	.964* .0416*
	.3	.3	−1.928* (.228)	2.456* (.105)	2.163 (1.066)	.970** .0380**
M_2	.2	.4	−3.555* (.279)	1.592* (.111)	3.499* (1.195)	.961* .0353*
	.2	.3	−4.050* (.276)	1.784* (.112)	4.292* (1.112)	.968** .0320**

NOTE: See note to Table 7.
† Variance of the rate of inflation.

The results of these regressions are reported in table 9 only for those values of δ which maximize R^2, and they show that the coefficients of the new variable have the expected signs and are clearly significant (at the 5 per cent level) for M_2, but that they do not quite reach significance in the case of M_1.

Table 10 provides a comparison of the results of this study with those of Cagan[29] and Deaver[30] for Austria and Chile, respectively.

The values of δ imply an average length for the weighting pattern of price expectations of about eleven quarters for Chile, ten quarters for Argentina,[31] and seven quarters for Austria.

The values of ε for Chile and Argentina cannot be properly compared because Deaver did not attempt to estimate the "best" income expectations coefficient.

The results for Chile show lower cost elasticities than those for Argentina and Austria. The results for Chile also show that when savings and time deposits are excluded from the definition of money the cost elasticity decreases and the income elasticity increases, as in the Argentine case.

B. DEMAND FUNCTIONS FOR COMPONENTS OF THE QUANTITY OF MONEY

The study of demand functions for components of the money stock is important because it provides additional information on the behavior of the latter and because it allows some useful inferences in connection with the differential behavior of alternative definitions of "money" through time. In addition, by increasing our knowledge about the manner in which those components behave, they help us to understand the movements of certain relationships which play some role in the observed variations in the money supply, given differentiated fractional reserves for different kinds of deposits.

A good starting point is provided by the same demand function used to explain the observed variability of the aggregate money concepts; that is, by considering the per capita real amounts of currency, demand deposits adjusted, and savings and time deposits to be a function of the cost of holding money and the expected real per capita income. The results of these regressions, using a logarithmic transformation for the

29. Cagan, "Monetary Dynamics," p. 43. The Austrian demand function was chosen for this comparison because this was the mildest hyperinflation Cagan studied.

30. Deaver, "Chilean Inflation," above, pp. 34, 38, and 40.

31. The Argentine average takes δ = .3 as the "best" value, for reasons explained in the next section.

TABLE 10

Estimated Coefficients of the Demand for Money Function in Argentina, Chile and Austria

Money Definition	Country	Period	Number and Frequency of Observations	Coefficients of Expectations δ Price	Coefficients of Expectations ε Income	Explanatory Variable Cost	Explanatory Variable Income	R^2
M_1	Chile	1932–55	92 Quarterly	.10	1	−1.476 (.33) [−.050]	.937 (.04)	.863
	Argentina	1938–62	25 Annual	.075	.3	−1.537 (.131) [−.23]	2.351 (.098)	.964
M_2	Chile	1932–55	92 Quarterly	.10	1	−4.888 (.339) [−.155]	.627 (.028)	.852
	Chile	1932–55	92 Quarterly	.10	.3	−5.219 (.472) [−.169]	.617 (.039)	.741
	Argentina	1938–62	25 Annual	.05	.3	−3.098 (.159) [−.43]	1.500 (.107)	.945
	Austria	1921–22	20 Monthly	.15	—	−8.55 [−.35]	—	.989

Source: Phillip Cagan, "The Monetary Dynamics of Hyperinflation," in *Studies in the Quantity Theory of Money*, ed. Milton Friedman (Chicago: Univ. of Chicago Press, 1956), p. 43; John Deaver, "The Chilean Inflation and the Demand for Money," above pp. 34, 38, and 40; my tables 7 and 8.

Note: The figures in parentheses under the regression coefficients are their standard error of estimate. The figures in brackets indicate the cost elasticities and are equal to βE. The δ's are all converted to a quarterly basis.

TABLE 11

DEMAND FUNCTIONS FOR COMPONENTS OF AGGREGATE MONEY SUPPLY
(ESTIMATED COEFFICIENTS OF THE COST OF HOLDING MONEY AND EXPECTED
REAL PER CAPITA INCOME ($\epsilon = .3$) FOR THREE ALTERNATIVE VALUES OF
THE PRICE EXPECTATIONS COEFFICIENT)

MONEY SUPPLY COMPONENTS AND AGGREGATES	COEFFICIENT OF PRICE EXPECTATION δ	EXPLANATORY VARIABLE		R^2 $S_{y,x}$
		Cost	Expected Income	
Using M_1 value of δ				
Currency................	.3	−.954* (.366)	2.913* (.274)	.856 .1135
Demand deposits..........	.3	−2.111* (.383)	1.804* (.286)	.673 .1189
M_1.....................	.3	−1.537* (.131)	2.351* (.098)	.964 .0406
Using M_2 value of δ				
Currency................	.2	−.892 (.469)	2.899* (.315)	.838 .1204
Demand deposits..........	.2	−2.674* (.431)	2.077* (.289)	.717 .1107
Savings and time deposits...	.2	−6.013* (.334)	.117 (.224)	.961 .0856
M_2.....................	.2	−3.098* (.159)	1.500* (.107)	.945 .0409
Values of δ free				
Currency................	.6	−.680* (.214)	2.810* (.234)	.870 .1076
Demand deposits..........	.1	−3.423* (.497)	2.245* (.282)	.753 .1033
Savings and time deposits...	.1	−7.538* (.311)	.433* (.177)	.978 .0646

NOTE: The first two sets of estimated coefficients correspond to the values of δ which maximize R^2 in the aggregate demand equations corresponding to M_1 and M_2 (reproduced here to facilitate comparisons). The last set shows the coefficients of the demand for each component for those values of δ which *individually* maximize R^2. The figures in parentheses and the starred coefficients have the same meaning as before (see note to table 7).

dependent variable and for the expected ($\epsilon = .3$) income variable and covering the period 1938–62, are presented in table 11. The annual series of components of the money stock are given in table 20 and the per capita real amounts are graphed in chart 4.

The estimates in the first two sets of equations in table 11 show that in both cases the currency reaction to changes in the expected rate of change in prices is lower (and even nonsignificant) than the reaction of deposits and that savings and time deposits show a much greater reaction than demand deposits. The regressions also show a relatively

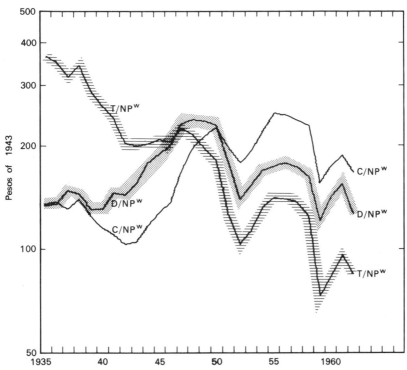

CHART 4. Annual averages of real per capita currency, demand deposits, and savings and time deposits, 1935–62 (wholesale price index used as deflator).
SOURCES: Tables 20, 23, 24.

high expected income elasticity for currency as compared to that of demand deposits and a nonsignificant expected income elasticity for savings and time deposits. In the light of this additional information about the behavior of components, it is easier to explain the differences between the coefficients corresponding to the two aggregate money concepts. The estimates in the third set of equations show that the demand for currency seems to imply a faster reaction to past inflation than the demand for either demand or savings and time deposits.

Finally, the results show that the simple expected inflation and real income model explains a sizable fraction of the observed variations in the real amounts of per capita components of money holdings, but they also suggest that there is still ample room for improvement, particularly in connection with the currency and demand deposits equation. For this purpose several additional variables were considered. A brief discussion of each one of them follows.

When one considers the demand for particular components of money, it is necessary to take into consideration their money returns, because the cost of holding any component with respect to each of the alternative components is the difference between the money return on the former and the money return on each one of the alternative components. The money return on currency is typically zero. The money return on demand deposits is positive if interest is paid and negative if there are service charges or other money costs involved. For the period 1935–62 it is possible to treat demand deposits as if their money rates of return have been constant and to exclude any explanatory variable in this connection.[32] Savings and time deposits yield a money return in the form of interest paid on them by the commercial banks. These rates have been subject to strict maximum regulations during 1935–62 and there are no data on the amounts of actual interest payments. However, actual payments have been generally close to maximum limits and both maximum rates have moved together. Hence the maximum rate of interest on savings deposits is a good approximation to the actual average money returns on these deposits.

Changes in the distribution of income may affect the demands for money components if individuals within different income groups have differential preferences for these components.[33] During the period 1935–62 the fraction of total income going to the labor sector had marked variations in Argentina. If low income groups derive their incomes mainly from labor, then the fraction of total income going to labor can be used as an index of distribution of income.

The spread of banking facilities and the accessibility to banking services might explain some changes in the amounts of desired currency and deposit holdings. The number of persons per bank office was

32. Interest payments on demand deposits were forbidden in Argentina in May 1946. During 1935–46 commercial banks were allowed to pay interest on these deposits up to a maximum of one-half of one percentage point, but no data are available on the amount of interest payments, if any. Service charges have been forbidden in Argentina, but a nominal tax has been applied to each check.

33. For instance, if income levels are related to educational levels and they in turn condition money holding practices, then a change in the income distribution may affect the demands for components. Also a redistribution of income may affect the composition of aggregate consumption expenditures and if there are differences in the amounts of currency used per unit of consumption expenditures for different categories of expenditures then the redistribution may affect the partial demands for money. For certain low income groups, currency hoarding may be the only financial means of holding wealth, etc.

the variable used in the regressions in an attempt to capture these effects.[34]

The preceding variables (whose numerical values are given in table 26) were introduced as additional explanatory variables in the demand functions for components of money, after a logarithmic transformation, with the last variable mentioned not being included in the savings and time deposits equation. The results of the new regressions are shown in tables 12, 13, and 14.

TABLE 12

THE DEMAND FOR CURRENCY
(ESTIMATED COEFFICIENTS OF THE COST OF HOLDING CURRENCY, EXPECTED PER CAPITA REAL INCOME ($\epsilon = .3$) AND OTHER VARIABLES FOR THOSE VALUES OF THE PRICE EXPECTATIONS COEFFICIENT WHICH MAXIMIZE R^2)

Coefficient of Price Expectations δ	Cost	Expected Income	Interest on Savings	Income Distribution	Persons Per Bank	R^2 $S_{y.x}$
.6	−.680* (.214)	2.810* (.234)				.870 .1076
.3	−1.820* (.354)	3.137* (.218)	.239* (.059)			.918 .0873
.3	−1.616* (.305)	2.208* (.349)	.215* (.050)	.875* (.280)		.945 .0733
.3	−1.607* (.302)	2.432* (.398)	.269* (.069)	.691* (.321)	.409 (.359)	.949 .0728

NOTE: The estimates in the first row are the same as those in the last set of results in table 11 and are reproduced here to facilitate comparisons. In each row only the results for those values of δ which maximize R^2 are presented.

In general, the results of these tables tend to confirm the a priori expectations as to the direction in which these additional variables would operate in the demand functions for components of money and the increased explanatory power of a more elaborate model. The results, however, also show some puzzling findings difficult to explain.

The currency equations show significant and consistently positive coefficients for the variable representing interest rates paid on savings

34. In some earlier versions of this work the fraction of aggregate national income represented by the revenue from direct taxes (income, capital gains, extraordinary benefits, etc.) and a dummy variable representing the existence of generalized price controls in the economy were also introduced as explanatory variables, but their coefficients turned out to be consistently nonsignificant and the variables were excluded in the regressions reported here.

TABLE 13

THE DEMAND FOR DEMAND DEPOSITS
(ESTIMATED COEFFICIENTS OF THE COST OF HOLDING DEMAND DEPOSITS,
EXPECTED REAL PER CAPITA INCOME ($\epsilon = .3$) AND OTHER VARIABLES, FOR
THOSE VALUES OF THE PRICE EXPECTATION COEFFICIENT WHICH MAXIMIZE
R^2)

Coefficient of Price Expectations δ	Cost	Expected Income	Interest on Savings	Income Distribution	Persons Per Bank	R^2 $S_{y.x}$
.1	−3.423* (.497)	2.245* (.282)				.753 .1033
.3	−1.347* (.410)	1.607* (.252)	−.210* (.069)			.774 .1012
.3	−1.653* (.289)	2.998* (.331)	−.175* (.048)	−1.311* (.266)		.898 .0696
.3	−1.660* (.289)	2.805* (.380)	−.222* (.066)	−1.152* (.307)	−.353 (.343)	.903 .0695

NOTE: See table 12, note.

TABLE 14

THE DEMAND FOR SAVINGS AND TIME DEPOSITS
(ESTIMATED COEFFICIENTS OF THE COST OF HOLDING SAVINGS AND TIME
DEPOSITS, EXPECTED REAL INCOME PER CAPITA ($\epsilon = .3$) AND OTHER
VARIABLES FOR THOSE VALUES OF THE PRICE EXPECTATIONS COEFFICIENTS
WHICH MAXIMIZE R^2)

Coefficient of Price Expectations δ	Cost	Expected Income	Own Interest	Income Distribution	Trend	R^2 $S_{y.x}$
.1	−7.538* (.311)	.433* (.177)				.978 .0646
.1	−8.672* (.567)	.787* (.223)	.147* (.064)			.982 .0591
.1	−8.815* (.562)	1.141* (.328)	.162* (.063)	−.314 (.218)		.984 .0576
.3	−3.043* (.246)	1.880* (.460)	.195 (.094)	−.689* (.223)	−.047* (.0075)	.985 .0571

NOTE: See table 12, note.

and time deposits. These results are contrary to expectations, since they would indicate that, other things being equal, an increase in the rates paid on savings deposits would tend to increase the amount of real currency holdings. The results are even more puzzling because the variable operates with the appropriate and significant signs in both deposits equations. The income distribution index is significant in the currency and demand deposits equations and operates with the expected signs. The coefficient of this variable is not significant in the savings and time deposits equations. The introduction of this variable also changes the point estimates of the expected income elasticities in all three regressions, lowering that corresponding to currency and increasing those corresponding to both deposits. The average number of persons per bank shows coefficients with the appropriate positive sign for currency and negative sign for deposits, but the variable does not reach statistical significance.

Finally, these results provide some additional information on the behavior of the price expectation coefficient. When the additional variables are introduced in the demand functions for components, the values of the δ coefficients maximizing R^2 for currency and demand deposits are the same in both cases and the difference noticed in the third set of regression results of table 11 disappears. Yet, the corresponding value of δ in the savings and time deposits equations remains the same, namely, $\delta = .1$. Since a lower value of δ implies a smoother time series for the expected rate of change in prices, a plausible statistical explanation for this disparity may be that the variable is picking up the effect of the noticeable declining trend in the real per capita holdings of savings and time deposits. In order to test this hypothesis, I introduced an additional trend variable in the equations dealing with these deposits. The results, reported in the last row of table 14, show that when the trend is included, the value of δ maximizing R^2 becomes .3, as in the equations for currency and demand deposits, and the cost response is drastically reduced.

The behavior of the C/D and T/D ratios. The preceding analysis of the demand for components of the stock of money provides the basis for an explanation of the behavior of the C/D and the T/D ratios, during 1935–62. The corresponding annual series are graphed in chart 5 and given numerically in table 25.

The C/D ratio shows a declining trend from 1935 to around the end of World War II, followed by a long upward trend which levels off around 1955. From this date to the end of the period, the ratio shows

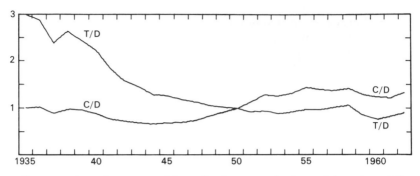

CHART 5. Annual averages of the ratio of currency to demand deposits and the ratio of savings and time deposits to demand deposits, 1935–62.
SOURCE: Table 25.

a slow decline. The estimated coefficients of the demand functions for C and D (tables 12 and 13) imply that the C/D ratio can be expected to react negatively to income changes and positively to changes in the share of income going to labor and interest rates paid on savings deposits. Changes in the expected rate of inflation cannot be expected to affect the ratio because the individual responses are very similar. On the basis of this and the movements observed in the explanatory variables, it is possible to say that the increase in permanent income seems to be the main factor behind the initial decline in the ratio. The sharp increase after the Second World War seems to have been mainly a response to the important increases in the share of income going to labor which took place during those years. The slow decline after 1955 seems to reflect the influence of two forces operating with opposite signs on the ratio, namely, a decline in permanent income and also a decline in the share of income going to labor.

The T/D ratio shows a long and sharp decline from 1935 to about 1952. From this date to 1958 the series shows a slow increase in the ratio. During the last four years the ratio first declines to an absolute low level in 1960 and then rises toward 1962. The coefficients of the partial demands for T and D (tables 13 and 14) show that the ratio would respond negatively to changes in the expected rate of change in prices and in real per capita permanent income, and positively to changes in interest rates paid on savings deposits and changes in the share of income going to labor. Combining this with the observed movements in the explanatory variables, it is possible for me to explain the initial decline mainly in terms of the increase in the expected rate of change in prices and in permanent income. The share of income going to labor also increased toward the end of this first subperiod but its influence was not very important when compared with that of the other two variables. The small rising trend of the ratio during most of the 1950s can be explained by a deceleration and even a decline of the expected rate of change in prices, and of the permanent real per capita income. The increase in the maximum rates of interest allowed to be paid on savings deposits during this period also explains part of the observed increase in the ratio. The increase in the expected rate of change in prices and the decline in the share of income going to labor seem to be the most important influences explaining the fall in the level of the ratio from 1958 to 1960. The subsequent increase seems to have been induced by declining expectations of inflation and permanent real income and by an important increase in the maximum rate of interest that the central bank allowed banks to pay on savings and time deposits.

4. THE DYNAMICS OF INFLATION

The magnitude of the Argentine inflationary process together with the failure of repeated anti-inflationary efforts have produced heated and prolonged debate on the causes of inflation, the role of some important economic variables, and the alleged effects of alternative measures aimed at decelerating the trend of prices. Unfortunately, a corresponding amount of energy and resourcefulness has not been applied to a careful and systematic analysis of the available evidence in Argentina or in other Latin American countries under similar conditions, except for the work done for Chile by Professor Arnold C. Harberger.[35]

This section presents an analysis of the dynamic responses of prices to changes in some of the variables considered to be important in order to estimate their individual contributions to the rate of change in prices. This analysis follows the line of Harberger's study of the Chilean inflation and covers the years 1935–62, with the empirical results for the whole period and for the subperiod 1946–62 being reported separately.

The starting point is a relationship that links the relative rate of change in prices during a given period to the contemporaneous and past rates of change in the quantity of money, under the assumption that

35. Arnold C. Harberger, "The Dynamics of Inflation in Chile" in *Measurement in Economics: Studies in Mathematical Economics and Econometrics in Memory of Yehuda Grunfeld*, ed. Carl F. Christ (Stanford, Calif.; Stanford Univ. Press, 1963). Also Carlos F. Diaz Alejandro, *Exchange Rate Devaluation in a Semi-industrialized Country: The Experience of Argentina, 1955–61* (Cambridge: M.I.T. Press, 1965).

they affect the level of prices through a process of adjustment that involves time.

$$\Delta \log P_t = a_1 \Delta \log M_t + a_2 \Delta \log M_{t-1} + a_3 \Delta \log M_{t-2} + \cdots. \quad (16)$$

Several comments are in order about this relationship.[36] First, on theoretical grounds, one should expect that, other things being equal, an upward and sustained shift in the rate of monetary expansion would, after a while, bring about a similar increase in the rate of price changes. This implies that the sum of the a coefficients should be expected to add up to unity when all the relevant lags are taken into consideration. Second, according to the theory of the demand for money, and the empirical results reported in the preceding section, one should expect a lower level of real cash balances to be consistent with the new and higher rate of change in prices after the above shift has fully worked its effects in the economy. This, in turn, implies that some overshooting will occur in the path of the rate of change in prices during the adjustment period, in order for real cash balances to decline to their lower desired level. Under these circumstances it may be possible to observe some partial sums of the a coefficients to be greater than unity and some of them to be negative, while the total sum approaches unity as the whole adjustment process comes to an end. Third, nothing definite can be said on theoretical grounds about the number of the a coefficients or their individual values, since they depend on the speed of adjustment and on the particular periods chosen for the analysis.[37]

From an empirical point of view the above relationship presents some difficult problems, particularly for choosing the appropriate number of lagged changes in money. The stepwise inclusion of lagged values of the independent variable cannot be terminated on the basis of a sum of the coefficients equal to one, or the lack of statistical significance of the last estimated coefficient, because the overshooting of prices might produce both effects before all relevant lags are included. In addition, multicollinearity will almost surely become a

36. The logarithmic first differences in expression (16) indicate relative rates of change, continuously compounded, for the price level, the contemporaneous and the lagged values of the stock of money, provided e is the base of these logarithms.

37. These two characteristics have, however, an enormous importance from a policy point of view, since they may imply, for instance, that even a cessation of a monetary expansion that has been taking place at a certain rate may not work its full effects on prices until several quarters, or semesters, or even years have elapsed.

problem in an estimation which may include many values of the same variable at successive points in time, if the adjustment is not a rapid one. All this does not mean that some valuable information cannot be obtained from a relationship of this kind. It provides a test for the assumption of lagged response in prices; it allows comparisons of response patterns between different price indexes and alternative definitions of money; and even when it may prove to be impossible to obtain a good idea of the whole pattern of the lags involved, it may still give useful information about the structure of the reaction of prices to money changes for a given number of lags.

The study attempts to explain the relative rates of change in the quarterly averages of the wholesale and the cost-of-living indexes of prices. The money variables used were the semiannual relative rates of change for two definitions of money, with the first term including the change in the average stock of money from quarter $t - 2$ to quarter t, and so on.[38] The use of quarterly and semiannual rates of change for the dependent and independent variables, respectively, also means that the sum of the coefficients should approach one-half rather than one, as the adjustment process comes to an end.

Table 15 shows the estimated coefficients of expression (16) for the period 1935–62 and 1946–62, using both price indexes and M_1 and M_2 as alternative definitions of money. These results tend to confirm the basic hypothesis of the existence of lagged response in prices to changes in money.[39] They also reveal initial overshooting and a later significant deceleration of prices which takes place approximately during the third semester following the acceleration of money. The sum of the coefficients generally falls short of the expected norm of .5 except in those regressions involving the cost-of-living index and the whole period. This seems to provide some evidence that the total adjustment period may take longer than the two years included in these regressions.

The second step in the analysis involves the consideration of further variables which may also affect the behavior of prices. In particular, it seems necessary to consider the role of expectations, real income,

38. This may tend to increase the degree of multicollinearity for a given number of lagged money terms, but it allows the length of the reaction period analyzed to be doubled for a given number of terms.

39. The R^2's are still relatively low but they indicate a remarkable improvement over those corresponding to a set of simple regressions (not reported here), involving the same dependent variables and the contemporaneous quarterly rates of change in money, that ranges from .09 to .19 for the four different combinations of prices and money definitions.

TABLE 15

REACTION OF PRICES TO MONEY CHANGES
(ESTIMATED COEFFICIENTS OF REGRESSIONS OF QUARTERLY RATES OF
INFLATION ON LAGGED SEMESTERLY RATES OF CHANGE IN MONEY)

Price Index	Definition of Money	$\dot{M}_t$	$\dot{M}_{t-2}$	$\dot{M}_{t-4}$	$\dot{M}_{t-6}$	R^2 $S_{y.x}$
Period 1935–62 ($N = 101$)						
Wholesale........	M_1	.594* (.078)	.060 (.076)	−.336* (.076)	.011 (.077)	.414 .042
	M_2	.739* (.102)	.044 (.103)	−.480* (.103)	.032 (.101)	.380 .043
Cost of living.....	M_1	.420* (.084)	.184* (.082)	−.078 (.082)	−.008 (.083)	.288 .046
	M_2	.541* (.105)	.211* (.106)	−.168 (.106)	−.018 (.104)	.311 .045
Subperiod 1946–62 ($N = 63$)						
Wholesale........	M_1	.629* (.110)	.088 (.103)	−.445* (.104)	−.043 (.114)	.443 .045
	M_2	.701* (.136)	.054 (.126)	−.546* (.128)	−.051 (.140)	.400 .047
Cost of living.....	M_1	.500* (.117)	.224* (.109)	−.252* (.111)	−.126 (.122)	.343 .048
	M_2	.563* (.145)	.214 (.134)	−.317* (.136)	−.139 (.149)	.299 .050

NOTE: The figures in parentheses under each coefficient denote their standard errors, and the asterisks, significance at the 5 per cent level. R^2 and $S_{y.x}$ indicate the estimated values of the coefficient of multiple determination and the standard errors of estimate, respectively. N indicates the effective sample size.

other policy variables like the exchange rate and wages, and the possibility of seasonal factors affecting the quarterly rates of inflation.

It has been shown in the preceding section how people's expectations as to the degree of inflation prevailing in the economy influence their desire to hold money. A transformation of the logarithmic stock demand for money allows one to express the relative rate of change in prices in terms of the relative rate of change in money and in real income and the change in expectations. There thus seem to be good grounds for including the changes in expectations in a relationship which attempts to explain the rate of inflation, although some important practical problems must be solved before doing so.

This expectational variable is defined in terms of past rates of change in prices and, according to expression (16), incorporates some influences of past rates of change in money. This problem was solved through a two-stage estimating procedure. First, a multiple regression was run, in which the dependent variable was the change in the expected rate of change in prices from quarter $t - 2$ to quarter $t - 1$ and where the independent variables were the four corresponding semi-annual rates of change in the stock of money and the quarterly rates of change in the official rate of exchange. The residuals of this regression provided an estimate of the exogenous changes in expectations which could not be accounted for by changes in previous policy variables used in the final regression. Secondly, these residuals were introduced as an explanatory variable in the final regressions under the assumption that they represented exogenous changes in expectations and also served as a proxy variable for still more lagged values of the rate of change in money.[40]

The role that changes in real income play in explaining the variations of the rate of inflation seems clear and needs no further elaboration. The difficulties here arise out of the lack of quarterly data and the inadequacy of some other quarterly series which could have been used as good proxy variables for these changes. A quarterly series was constructed by linearly interpolating the values of real income corresponding to each quarter, subject to the constraint that their sum will add up to the true annual figure. The series appear in table 32.

I also explored the role that devaluations and a centralized (governmental or unionized) wage policy may have played in the Argentine inflationary process, by introducing the rates of change in the official rate of exchange and an index of nominal wages. The basic series appear in table 36.

All these variables were linearly introduced in a relationship of the following type.

$$
\begin{aligned}
\Delta \log P_{i,t} = \; & a_1 \Delta \log M_{j,t} + a_2 \Delta \log M_{j,t-2} \\
& + a_3 \Delta \log M_{j,t-4} + a_4 \Delta \log M_{j,t-6} + b \Delta RE^{(\delta)}_{i,t-1} \\
& + c \Delta \log Y_t + d \Delta \log X_t + e \Delta \log W_t + f S_t + u_t, \quad (17)
\end{aligned}
$$

where

$\Delta \log P_{i,t} =$ Quarterly rate of change of average price index i from quarter $t - 1$ to quarter t.

$\Delta \log M_{j,t-k} =$ Semiannual rate of change of average stock of money j from quarter $t - k - 2$ to quarter $t - k$, for $k = 0$, 2, 4, and 6.

40. For the period 1946–62 this two-stage procedure also incorporated the current and lagged value of the rate of change of an index of nominal wages in the first regression.

$\Delta RE^{(\delta)}_{i,t-1} =$ "Exogenous" changes in price expectations from quarter $t - 2$ to quarter $t - 1$. The basic expected rate of change in prices is defined on the basis of price index i, with a quarterly price adjustment coefficient δ. The values of this variable are the residuals of multiple regressions of $\Delta E^{(\delta)}_{i,t-1}$ on all the other variables included in the final regressions (except for the change in real income and seasonal dummy), lagged one quarter.

$\Delta \log Y_t =$ Quarterly rate of change of average real income from quarter $t - 1$ to quarter t.

$\Delta \log X_t =$ Quarterly rate of change of official exchange rate for the U.S. dollar from the middle of quarter $t - 1$ to the middle of quarter t.

$\Delta \log W_t =$ Quarterly rate of change of an index of nominal wages from the middle of quarter $t - 1$ to the middle of quarter t.

$S_t =$ A set of three seasonal dummy variables.

and where i indicates either the wholesale or the cost-of-living price indexes; j indicates M_1 or M_2; and the values of δ are .1, .2, and .3. All the rates of change assume continuous compounding.[41] The results for the period 1935–62 are presented in table 16, where the wholesale price index is used, and table 17, where a cost-of-living index is used. Results for the period 1946–62 are found in tables 18 and 19.

The results show that, in general, the introduction of the additional explanatory variables significantly increases the fraction of total variation in the rates of inflation being explained. The coefficients of the successively lagged changes in money supply reveal approximately the same structure of price responses as mentioned before, with some interesting differences between price indexes and money definitions.[42]

41. The variable $\Delta \log W$ was not included in the regressions dealing with the whole period 1935–62 because the available wage series starts in 1946.

42. For the regressions covering the whole period wholesale prices seem to have a faster initial adjustment (and even overshooting), within the first semester, than those implicit in the cost-of-living index, while there seem not to exist substantial differences between their sums toward the end of the first year. During the second year wholesale prices also seem to decelerate more rapidly so that the total sum of their coefficients is lower than that corresponding to the cost-of-living index which approaches the theoretical norm of one-half after four lagged changes in money are included. In both cases the initial acceleration and subsequent deceleration seems to be more marked for the more inclusive definition of money.

TABLE 16

Estimated Coefficients of Multiple Regressions for the Rate of Change of the Wholesale Price Index
(Period 1935–62)

Money Definition	Coefficient of Price Expectations δ	$\dot{M}_t$	$\dot{M}_{t-2}$	$\dot{M}_{t-4}$	$\dot{M}_{t-6}$	RE	$\dot{Y}$	$\dot{X}$	S_1	S_2	S_3	R^2 $S_{y \cdot x}$
M_1.......	.1	.487* (.074)	.062 (.079)	−.298* (.078)	.043 (.068)	3.194* (.938)	−.550* (.173)	.101* (.023)	.027 (.015)	.024 (.012)	.027* (.009)	.685 .032
	.2	.495* (.076)	.058 (.080)	−.299* (.079)	.045 (.069)	1.387* (.475)	−.580* (.174)	.100* (.023)	.025 (.015)	.023 (.013)	.027* (.010)	.675 .032
	.3	.499* (.076)	.055 (.082)	−.299* (.080)	.046 (.070)	.778* (.318)	−.609* (.176)	.100* (.023)	.024 (.015)	.022 (.013)	.026* (.010)	.667 .033
M_2.......	.1	.548* (.093)	.080 (.097)	−.420* (.097)	.073 (.085)	3.879* (.933)	−.445* (.175)	.106* (.023)	.034* (.014)	.028* (.012)	.026* (.010)	.661 .033
	.2	.559* (.095)	.073 (.099)	−.422* (.099)	.076 (.087)	1.715* (.472)	−.480* (.177)	.105* (.024)	.032* (.014)	.027* (.013)	.025* (.010)	.648 .034
	.3	.564* (.096)	.069 (.101)	−.423* (.101)	.078 (.088)	.994* (.318)	−.511* (.179)	.105* (.024)	.031* (.014)	.026* (.013)	.025* (.010)	.636 .034

NOTE: See table 15, note.

TABLE 17

ESTIMATED COEFFICIENTS OF MULTIPLE REGRESSIONS FOR THE RATE OF CHANGE OF THE COST-OF-LIVING PRICE INDEX
(PERIOD 1935–62)

Money Definition	Coefficient of Price Expectation δ	$\dot{M}_t$	$\dot{M}_{t-2}$	$\dot{M}_{t-4}$	$\dot{M}_{t-6}$	RE	$\dot{Y}$	$\dot{X}$	S_1	S_2	S_3	R^2 $S_{y.x}$
M_1	.1	.321* (.080)	.185* (.086)	−.056 (.084)	.039 (.074)	3.127* (.924)	−.748* (.184)	.091* (.025)	.005 (.016)	.029* (.013)	.001 (.010)	.616 .035
	.2	.332* (.081)	.178* (.086)	−.054 (.085)	.039 (.074)	1.483* (.471)	−.747* (.186)	.090* (.025)	.003 (.016)	.028* (.014)	.001 (.010)	.610 .035
	.3	.339* (.082)	.173* (.087)	−.054 (.086)	.041 (.075)	.897* (.318)	−.759 (.188)	.091* (.025)	.002 (.016)	.027 (.014)	.002 (.010)	.602 .035
M_2	.1	.398* (.095)	.207* (.098)	−.107 (.100)	.032 (.087)	3.430* (.906)	−.716* (.178)	.087* (.024)	.004 (.014)	.028* (.013)	−.0003 (.010)	.631 .034
	.2	.411* (.096)	.198 (.101)	−.109 (.101)	.034 (.088)	1.598* (.464)	−.720* (.181)	.087* (.024)	.003 (.014)	.027* (.013)	−.0002 (.010)	.622 .034
	.3	.417* (.098)	.195 (.103)	−.111 (.102)	.037 (.089)	.947* (.315)	−.735* (.183)	.088* (.014)	.002 (.014)	.026* (.013)	.0002 (.010)	.611 .035

NOTE: See table 15, note.

TABLE 18

Estimated Coefficients of Multiple Regressions for the Wholesale Price Index
(Subperiod 1946–62)

Money Definition	Coefficient of Price Expectations δ	$\dot{M}_t$	$\dot{M}_{t-2}$	$\dot{M}_{t-4}$	$\dot{M}_{t-6}$	RE	$\dot{Y}$	$\dot{X}$	$\dot{W}$	S_1	S_2	S_3	R_2 $S_{y.x}$
M_1	.1	.462* (.105)	−.022 (.108)	−.217* (.103)	−.079 (.092)	4.536* (1.196)	−.514* (.234)	.097* (.024)	.033 (.043)	.006 (.022)	.017 (.019)	.045* (.012)	.760 .031
	.2	.474* (.109)	−.032 (.112)	−.219* (.107)	−.071 (.095)	1.999* (.623)	−.580* (.239)	.093* (.025)	.038 (.044)	.004 (.023)	.015 (.020)	.044* (.013)	.744 .033
	.3	.479* (.112)	−.037 (.115)	−.220* (.110)	−.064 (.097)	1.159* (.427)	−.643* (.242)	.091* (.025)	.039 (.046)	.002 (.023)	.015 (.020)	.043* (.013)	.731 .033
M_2	.1	.539* (.129)	−.085 (.131)	−.260* (.126)	−.091 (.110)	4.792* (1.238)	−.535* (.240)	.099* (.024)	.026 (.044)	.004 (.023)	.012 (.020)	.045* (.012)	.745 .032
	.2	.550* (.133)	−.094 (.135)	−.261* (.130)	−.080 (.114)	2.117* (.640)	−.613* (.244)	.094* (.026)	.032 (.046)	.002 (.023)	.012 (.021)	.043* (.013)	.728 .033
	.3	.546* (.136)	−.095 (.138)	−.261 (.133)	−.071 (.116)	1.224* (.435)	−.682* (.246)	.093* (.026)	.035 (.047)	.001 (.024)	.012 (.022)	.042* (.013)	.715 .034

Note: See table 15, note.

TABLE 19

Estimated Coefficients of Multiple Regressions for the Cost-of-Living Price Index
(Subperiod 1946–62)

Money Definition	Coefficient of Price Expectations δ	$\dot{M}_t$	$\dot{M}_{t-2}$	$\dot{M}_{t-4}$	$\dot{M}_{t-6}$	RE	$\dot{Y}$	$\dot{X}$	$\dot{W}$	S_1	S_2	S_3	R^2 $S_{y.x}$
M_1..........	.1	.307* (.120)	.153 (.123)	−.090 (.118)	−.109 (.105)	3.398* (1.229)	−.731* (.264)	.076* (.027)	.074 (.049)	−.014 (.025)	.043 (.022)	.011 (.014)	.679 .036
	.2	.319* (.120)	.145 (.124)	−.091 (.118)	−.103 (.105)	1.624* (.617)	−.753* (.264)	.075* (.027)	.079 (.049)	−.015 (.025)	.042 (.022)	.011 (.014)	.675 .036
	.3	.323* (.122)	.140 (.125)	−.091 (.119)	−.098 (.106)	.997* (.413)	−.789* (.265)	.074* (.028)	.082 (.050)	−.016 (.025)	.042 (.022)	.011 (.014)	.669 .036
M_2..........	.1	.371* (.145)	.117 (.147)	−.096 (.141)	−.121 (.124)	3.654* (1.252)	−.771* (.269)	.077* (.027)	.066 (.050)	−.018 (.025)	.038 (.023)	.011 (.014)	.667 .036
	.2	.384* (.146)	.108 (.148)	−.098 (.142)	−.113 (.124)	1.736* (.626)	−.803* (.269)	.075* (.027)	.072 (.050)	−.019 (.025)	.038 (.023)	.011 (.014)	.662 .037
	.3	.384* (.148)	.106 (.150)	−.098 (.144)	−.105 (.126)	1.055* (.417)	−.845* (.267)	.074* (.028)	.076 (.051)	−.020 (.026)	.038 (.023)	.011 (.014)	.654 .037

NOTE: See table 15, note.

These coefficients lend some support to the idea that the adjustment process may be about two years for the cost-of-living index and somewhat longer for wholesale prices, when the exchange rate is held constant.

The variable representing exogenous changes in expectations has the expected positive and significant coefficients in all regressions, and the value of δ which maximizes R^2, namely, δ = .1, is compatible with the value of δ = .3 found as the most appropriate for the stock demand equation using annual observations.[43]

The changes in real income also show significant coefficients of the expected negative sign. These results seem to be quite good when account is taken of the quality of the original quarterly series.[44]

The coefficients of the exchange rate variable show a positive value of about .10, indicating that the direct effect of a 10 per cent devaluation will be about 1 per cent on the wholesale and about .9 per cent on the cost-of-living indexes. This is a surprising result in the light—or, should I say, the heat—of the discussion on the inflationary effects of devaluations in Argentina.[45] Lagged values of this variable have tended to be nonsignificant and to have negative signs in a different set of regressions not reported here.

The regressions corresponding to the subperiod 1946–62 tell basically the same story with some differences in the money coefficients and additional information given by the presence of the wage variable.

The wage variable has a nonsignificant coefficient which ranges from about .03 to about .07 in the regressions for the wholesale and the cost-of-living price indexes, respectively. This, again, is a remarkable figure in connection with the debate on the role of wages in the Argentine inflation, particularly when the period covered by the data is the one most frequently mentioned in the discussion of the alleged wage-push inflation.[46] As in the case of exchange rates the lagged value of

43. These coefficients are compatible in the sense that δ = .3 with annual data and δ = .1 with quarterly data imply an average length of the weighting pattern of approximately 2.5 years and 11 quarters, respectively.

44. The results should not be taken with much enthusiasm, however, because errors in measuring prices would introduce spurious negative correlation between changes in prices and in nominal income deflated by an index of prices and may thus account for some fraction of the explanatory power of this variable.

45. There is no doubt that this is a lower limit for the true potential effect, given the fact that most big devaluations have been accompanied by an elaborate scheme of witholding taxes on exports but, at any rate, it is a smaller number than the figure implicit or explicit in most discussions.

46. It can be granted that these coefficients measure only the current direct

this variable was also introduced in some experiments not explicitly reported here. In the case of the wholesale prices the lagged change in the wage rate was consistently nonsignificant. The coefficients showed some significant values in those regressions dealing with the cost-of-living index with a sum of both coefficients never greater than .17.

Conclusions

From 1935 to 1962 the Argentine stock of money, inclusive of savings and time deposits in commercial banks, increased at an average rate of about 15 per cent per year. Most of this increase can be attributed to increases in the monetary base (high-powered money), but the contribution of the changes in the base multiplier to variations in the stock of money around its growth trend has been substantial. The observed variations in the base multiplier can, in turn, be attributed to changes in the ratio of banks' reserves to deposits (quantitatively the most important of its proximate determinants), to changes in the ratio of currency to demand deposits, and to changes in the ratio of savings and time deposits to demand deposits.

The behavior of the reserve ratio of commercial banks in Argentina during the periods 1935–45 and 1958–62 can be explained mainly in terms of variations in the expected flow of total reserves and in the expected opportunity cost of holding reserves. The effects of changes in the composition of deposits on the reserve ratio are significant only during the second period. Changes in reserve requirements during 1958–62 do not seem to have affected the reserve ratio significantly, mainly because those changes seem to have been passive responses to previous central bank actions affecting the flow of total reserves.

The behavior of the currency-demand deposits ratio from 1935 to 1962 can be explained mainly in terms of variations in permanent income and in the fraction of income going to labor. In particular, the increase of this ratio during the late 1940s and early 1950s appears to have been mainly induced by changes in the distribution of income.

The behavior of the ratio of savings and time deposits to demand deposits in the period 1935–62 can be explained in terms of variations

---

impact of an increase in wages and that the indirect effects may be hidden in the money and perhaps the exchange rate coefficients (if the authorities have, for instance, increased money as a consequence of the potential unemployment that might have arisen because of the increase in wages, or have devalued because of the "loss of competitive position in the world markets" also as a consequence of the wage increase), but even then, the magnitude of the direct effect appears much smaller than that implied by those discussions.

in the expected rate of change in prices, the level of permanent income, and the rate of interest paid on savings and time deposits. In particular the long and marked decline in this ratio from 1935 to about 1952 can be explained by a combination of increasing expectations of inflation and virtually constant rates of interest paid on savings and time deposits.

The study of the demand for money in Argentina during the period 1935–62 reveals that variations in the expected rate of change in prices and in the expected per capita real income explain a very high fraction of the observed variation in per capita real money holdings. This conclusion is independent of the inclusion or exclusion of savings and time deposits in the definition of money. The values of the estimated coefficients show that the cost elasticity increases and the income elasticity decreases when savings and time deposits in commercial banks are included in the definition of money. The results also show that an increase in uncertainty—as measured by the degree to which inflationary expectations have been frustrated in the past—tends to increase desired money holdings, and that this effect is more significant for the more inclusive definition of money.

The analysis of the demand functions for components of the stock of money shows that, in addition to those variables mentioned in the preceding paragraph, variations in the share of income going to labor and in the rate of interest paid on savings and time deposits significantly affect the desired real per capita holdings of currency, demand, and savings and time deposits. The coefficients of these variables are significant in all equations, and, with one exception, they have the expected signs. The exception is the positive coefficient of the rate of interest paid on savings deposits in the currency demand function, which implies significant complementarity rather than substitutability between these two financial assets.

From 1935 to 1962 the changes in the rate of change in money significantly affected the behavior of the rate of inflation, through a process of adjustment which involved considerable time. The results indicate that the adjustment of prices to an acceleration of money seemed to require no less than two years and that it involved initial overshooting and later deceleration of prices. Changes in the expected rate of change in prices and real income also affected significantly the rate of inflation. The role of devaluations and wage increases in the Argentine inflationary process was also analyzed, but the results show that their influence on the rate of inflation failed to achieve the levels and significance usually attributed to them.

APPENDIX
SOURCES AND DESCRIPTION OF THE DATA

The annual and quarterly series appearing in the tables at the end of this appendix can be classified as follows: Money data, price data, income data, and other data.

THE MONEY DATA

The annual and quarterly monetary data consist of a set of basic series (currency outside banks, different kinds of deposits at commercial banks, and banks' reserves), and another set of series derived from them (quantity of money, monetary base, base multiplier, reserve ratio, etc.). The basic series consist of annual averages or end-of-quarter figures derived from end-of-month series based on central bank publications. The description of those monthly series and the way in which published figures were used for the periods before and after June 1940 follows.

The period June 1940 to December 1962. In April 1963, the central bank published a revision of the principal end-of-month monetary series, covering the period from June 1940 to December 1960, in a supplement to its *Boletín Estadístico* of June 1962. The revised data for the years 1961 and 1962 were published in the regular monthly issues of the *Boletín Estadístico* after December 1961. These two sets of data were used, without modification, as the monthly data for the period after May 1940.

The annual basic series appearing in table 20 and in the first column of table 22 are annual averages centered on June 30 of each year. These averages were computed by adding the twelve monthly values of each year plus the value of the previous December and dividing the resulting sum by thirteen. The end-of-quarter series, which appear in table 27 and the first column of table 29, reproduce the end-of-month figures for March, June, September, and December of each year. A description of each basic series follows.

Currency (Amount of currency outside banks). This is a residual series obtained by subtracting commercial banks' holdings of central bank notes and coin from the total amounts issued. Before 1946, when the issue of treasury currency (five- and one-peso bills plus all coins) was discontinued, the figures include the amount of treasury currency outside the central bank and commercial banks. The figures in this series include currency held by the government and semi-fiscal agencies. For many purposes this is undesirable but there are no data from which these holdings can be derived.

Demand deposits (Amount of commercial banks' demand deposits held by the nonbanking public). This series excludes inter-bank deposits, government deposits, and items in process of collection.

Savings deposits (Amount of commercial banks' savings deposits held by the nonbanking public).

Other deposits (Amount of "other deposits of little mobility" [as they are officially described] held by the nonbanking public). The figures include deposits held in commercial banks in connection with judicial processes, some international trade operations, etc. They also include deposits in foreign currencies during the few and short subperiods in which they were allowed by the central bank.

Government deposits (Amount of commercial banks' demand and time deposits held by the national, provincial, and local governments; and by semi-fiscal agencies).

Bank reserves (Amount of reserves held by commercial banks in the form of gold, currency, and deposits with the central bank). Before 1946 the series also includes the amount of treasury currency held by commercial banks.

The period December 1934 to May 1940. From 1935 to 1948 the central bank published end-of-month figures for the basic series described above. These series were published in the bank's *Revista Económica* (until July 1937), the *Suplemento Estadístico de la Revista Económica* (from August 1937 to April 1946), and the *Boletín Estadístico* (from May 1946 to April 1948). The figures in these series were the aggregates obtained from twenty-three reporting banks whose deposits and reserves represented, in 1935, approximately "ninety-three per cent of all deposits and reserves of the commercial banking system."

Since the banks in the sample remained the same throughout the period, the increase in the number of banks and the probable change in the distribution of deposits between banks made the sample aggregates a declining but unknown fraction of total deposits and reserves through time. It follows that some correction was needed in order to link these old series with the new series, corresponding to the period after May 1940, which were based on information from all the existing banks.

During the period 1940 to 1948 the new and the old series overlapped so that, for each of the basic series, they provided pairs of observations on the same phenomena. Separate regressions of the values of the new series on the values of the old series were run for each of the basic series. These regressions provided estimates of the parameters of lineal functions that were then used to extrapolate the values of the new series for the period 1935–40 on the basis of the information provided by the old series.[47]

The resulting end-of-month corrected figures were then used to construct the annual averages and the end-of-quarter basic series by the same procedure used with the monthly data for the period after June 1940.

47. The estimated functions were the following:

	r^2
$C^n = 96.43 + .9943\ C^o$ $(6.07)\quad(.0027)$	.9993
$s^n = -243.19 + 1.2671\ s^o$ $(15.00)\quad(.0053)$	.9984
$t^n = -3.07 + 1.1305\ t^o$ $(5.63)\quad(.0194)$	.9739
$O^n = -21.35 + 1.0835\ O^o$ $(12.51)\quad(.0253)$	.9527

where C^n, s^n, t^n, and O^n indicate the values of currency, savings deposits, time deposits and other deposits in the new series; C^o, s^o, t^o, and O^o indicate the corresponding values in the old series; and r^2 is the coefficient of determination. The number of observations was 93. Since the series corresponding to demand deposits in the old series (D^o) included government deposits (G^o), the following procedure was followed:

$D^n = -141.43 + .9179\ D^o$ $(15.67)\quad(.0042)$	.9981
$(D + G)^n = -201.44 + 1.0837\ D^o$ $(16.09)\quad(.0043)$	.9986

and subtracting the first from the second

$$G^n = -60.01 + .1658\ D^o.$$

Finally, the function for the stock of reserves

$R^n = -57.65 + 1.1120\ R^o$ $(10.28)\quad(.0069)$	.9974

was estimated on the basis of 70 overlapping observations for the period June 1940 to April 1946.

The way in which the remaining monetary series were derived from the basic series is explained in the corresponding tables.

Two annual and two quarterly series of price indexes are shown in this appendix. The annual series (table 23) correspond to wholesale prices and the GNP deflator; the quarter series (table 31) to the wholesale prices and the cost-of-living index of prices. A description of the sources and procedures followed to construct these series follows.

Wholesale prices. The basic information for the construction of the annual and quarterly series for the period 1935–62 was taken from four monthly series: first, a wholesale price index (1926 = 100) compiled by the *Banco de la Nación Argentina* and the central bank from 1926 to 1948 and published by the central bank in the monthly issues of the *Suplemento Estadístico de la Revista Económica* and the *Boletín Estadístico* from 1937 to 1948; second, two wholesale price indexes compiled by the central bank and covering the periods 1939–53 (1939 = 100) and 1953–56 (1953 = 100). These two series were not published by the central bank until September 1962, when they appeared in its *Boletín Estadístico*. The last is a wholesale price index (1956 = 100) compiled by the *Dirección Nacional de Estadística y Censos* and published in its *Boletín Mensual de Estadística*. All these were linked by the regression method using the overlapping monthly observations, and were then converted to a common base, 1943 = 100.

The figures for the period 1913–25 in table 23 correspond to those of a wholesale price index compiled by the *Banco de la Nación Argentina*, covering the period 1913–27 (1913 = 100) and published in the monthly issues of the *Revista de Economía Argentina*. The figures for the period 1907–12 in table 23 are based on a wholesale price index compiled by the *Sociedad Rural Argentina*, covering the period 1907–27, also published in the *Revista de Economía Argentina*. These two series were linked by the ratio method to the previously mentioned series (1935–62) by using the overlapping information corresponding to 1926–27 and 1913–27, respectively.

Cost-of-Living Index. The figures for the period 1943–62 on table 31 are the quarterly averages of the monthly series published by the *Dirección Nacional de Estadística y Censos* in its *Boletín Mensual de Estadística*. The figures for the period 1935–42 are based on a previous cost-of-living index compiled by the *Dirección Nacional del Trabajo*, covering the period 1933 to 1948, and published in the *Revista de*

Economía Argentina. The overlapping information of the two series was then used to link them by the ratio method.

GNP Deflator. The annual series from 1935 to 1952 was published by the *Secretaría de Asuntos Económicos* in its *Producto e Ingreso de la República Argentina.* The figures from 1953 to 1962 are based on the series of nominal GNP and GNP at constant prices published by the central bank in its *Boletín Estadístico.*

THE INCOME DATA

The annual figures for the net national income at current prices which appear in table 24 are taken from *Producto e Ingreso de la República Argentina* (1935 to 1952), *Boletín Mensual de Estadística* (1953 to 1955), and the central bank's *Boletín Estadístico* (1956 to 1962).

The quarterly series for real net national income in table 32 was derived from the annual series deflated by the GNP implicit price index. The quarterly figures, expressed in annual rates, are the result of linear interpolation of the annual series, subject to the condition that their sum for each year should add up to four times the corresponding annual value.[48]

OTHER DATA

Several additional annual and quarterly series are presented in this appendix. A brief description of their sources follows.

Population. The population series, table 24, is taken from the *Boletín Mensual de Estadística.* In those cases in which the basic information was available only for end-of-year dates, the figures for June 30 were obtained by linear interpolation.

Interest Rates. The maximum rates of interest paid on savings deposits (table 26) from 1935 to 1945 are derived from the rediscount

---

48. Let y_t denote real income in year t and $q_{i,t}$ the corresponding value for quarter i of year t. The quarterly figures were obtained as follows:

$$q_1 = \frac{4y_t}{\sum q_i}\left[y_{t-1} + \frac{7.5}{12}(y_t - y_{t-1})\right]$$

$$q_2 = \frac{4y_t}{\sum q_i}\left[y_{t-1} + \frac{10.5}{12}(y_t - y_{t-1})\right]$$

$$q_3 = \frac{4y_t}{\sum q_i}\left[y_t + \frac{1.5}{12}(y_{t+1} - y_t)\right]$$

$$q_4 = \frac{4y_t}{\sum q_i}\left[y_t + \frac{4.5}{12}(y_{t+1} - y_t)\right].$$

rate (3.5 per cent) and the existing regulations which did not allow them to be greater than the rediscount rate minus one percentage point. For the period after 1945 the rate is taken from information published in the *Suplemento Estadístico de la Revista Económica* (until 1948) and unpublished information obtained from the central bank's statistical office.

The interest rates on consolidated treasury bonds, table 34, are taken from the central bank's annual report and the *Suplemento Estadístico de la Revista Económica*.

The interest rates on treasury bills, table 35, are taken from the central bank's *Boletín Estadístico*.

Labor Income. The series on the share of income going to labor, table 26, are taken from *Producto e Ingreso de la República Argentina* (for the years 1935–52), the *Boletín Mensual de Estadística* (1953 to 1955) and the central bank's *Boletín Estadístico* (1956 to 1962).

Number of Banking Offices. This series (table 26) was obtained from the central bank's *Guía Bancaria* by the following procedure. The *Guía* listed all existing banking offices in Argentina in 1962. Additional information was obtained from the central bank about the date at which each of the existing banking offices started operations. A time series of new banking offices was then constructed and from this a cumulative series of existing banking offices through time. Since bank failures have been negligible in Argentina the figures of this series did not differ significantly from information available in the central bank about banking offices in the last years of the period under consideration.

Index of legal reserve requirements. The series (table 35) was constructed on the basis of average and marginal reserve requirements on demand deposits for Buenos Aires banks according to the central bank's circular letters, the recorded amounts of demand deposits in Buenos Aires' banks, and their increases after the dates of application of marginal requirements.

Exchange rates. The figures in table 36 represents the monthly averages of the official rates of exchange for the United States dollar in the months of February, May, August, and November of each year. This gives the monthly average rates at the middle of each quarter. The figures correspond to the rates applied to imports. During the periods in which multiple rates were in effect the rate applicable to the widest range of imports was chosen. From 1959 on, the figures correspond to the average selling rates published by the central bank in its *Boletín Estadístico*.

Wage index. Since 1946 the *Dirección Nacional de Estadística y*

Censos has published in its *Boletín Mensual de Estadística* monthly series of three indexes corresponding to (*a*) number of workers; (*b*) number of hours worked per worker; and (*c*) total amount of wages paid. The figures in table 36 are the ratios of the values of series (*c*) to the product of series (*a*) and (*b*). The three basic series were published with two different bases (1943 and 1952). These two series were linked by a proportional adjustment on the basis of the overlapping information for the years 1952 and 1953 and expressed on a 1943 basis.

Annual Series

TABLE 20

CURRENCY OUTSIDE BANKS AND DEPOSITS OF COMMERCIAL BANKS, 1935–62
(ANNUAL AVERAGE STOCKS IN MILLIONS OF PESOS)

YEAR	CURRENCY OUTSIDE BANKS (1)	DEPOSITS OF COMMERCIAL BANKS, ADJUSTED				
		Demand (2)	Savings (3)	Time (4)	Others (5)	Government (6)
1935....	861.0	855.1	1,763.5	571.1	226.5	119.9
1936....	911.6	897.9	1,794.6	554.8	232.5	127.6
1937....	1,017.8	1,149.5	1,970.2	505.7	264.0	173.1
1938....	1,030.5	1,062.4	2,046.7	488.6	265.7	157.4
1939....	1,083.4	1,132.8	2,045.8	452.8	266.1	170.1
1940....	1,084.1	1,231.0	2,044.2	402.2	296.1	190.4
1941....	1,154.2	1,525.1	2,119.6	405.6	299.6	237.7
1942....	1,379.4	1,918.5	2,315.3	400.1	321.9	285.9
1943....	1,567.4	2,301.8	2,610.4	375.4	347.7	418.3
1944....	1,914.1	2,896.4	2,988.9	337.9	395.6	540.5
1945....	2,318.5	3,425.3	3,482.7	309.7	511.1	572.5
1946....	2,932.4	4,265.3	4,178.1	219.6	643.0	612.6
1947....	3,817.4	5,236.6	4,996.4	67.2	836.8	939.3
1948....	5,231.4	6,361.4	5,733.6	41.7	928.2	1,559.1
1949....	7,152.1	7,950.3	6,586.8	32.0	1,441.4	3,383.3
1950....	9,375.6	9,534.7	7,514.0	27.2	1,904.6	3,460.2
1951....	12,578.3	11,380.6	7,977.2	42.9	2,305.1	4,293.0
1952....	15,167.6	11,935.7	8,807.1	48.8	2,191.6	5,021.1
1953....	18,675.3	14,897.2	10,905.4	45.3	2,025.9	5,825.7
1954....	22,339.7	17,099.0	13,248.5	69.4	2,192.9	7,718.4
1955....	27,016.0	18,864.7	15,198.2	31.1	2,796.4	10,143.1
1956....	31,455.7	22,706.0	17,849.3	9.9	3,941.3	14,000.4
1957....	36,616.4	26,802.2	21,168.0	10.5	5,889.8	16,801.1
1958....	45,031.7	31,965.8	24,513.2	140.2	8,925.0	19,785.7
1959....	66,251.3	51,619.5	30,639.9	522.0	12,153.0	26,329.1
1960....	86,273.5	70,211.2	39,514.8	1,879.4	11,335.4	37,422.4
1961....	101,748.9	84,143.4	47,181.7	5,345.5	15,666.3	45,061.3
1962....	118,808.3	90,056.2	52,972.1	7,473.3	19,848.5	37,224.4

TABLE 21

STOCK OF MONEY, 1935–62, FOR THREE DEFINITIONS OF MONEY
(ANNUAL AVERAGE STOCKS IN MILLIONS OF PESOS)

Year	M_1 (1)	M_2 (2)	M_3 (3)
1935.....	1,716.1	4,050.7	4,277.2
1936.....	1,809.5	4,158.9	4,391.4
1937.....	2,167.3	4,643.2	4,907.2
1938.....	2,092.9	4,628.2	4,893.9
1939.....	2,216.2	4,714.8	4,980.9
1940.....	2,315.1	4,761.5	5,057.6
1941.....	2,679.3	5,204.5	5,504.1
1942.....	3,297.9	6,013.2	6,335.2
1943.....	3,869.3	6,855.1	7,202.9
1944.....	4,810.5	8,137.4	8,533.0
1945.....	5,743.7	9,536.2	10,047.3
1946.....	7,197.7	11,595.5	12,238.5
1947.....	9,054.0	14,117.6	14,954.4
1948.....	11,592.8	17,368.1	18,296.3
1949.....	15,102.4	21,721.3	23,162.6
1950.....	18,910.3	26,451.5	28,356.1
1951.....	23,958.9	31,979.0	34,284.1
1952.....	27,103.4	35,959.2	38,150.8
1953.....	33,572.6	44,523.2	46,549.2
1954.....	39,438.7	52,756.7	54,949.5
1955.....	45,880.6	61,109.9	63,906.3
1956.....	54,161.7	72,020.8	75,962.2
1957.....	63,418.6	84,597.1	90,486.9
1958.....	76,997.5	101,650.9	110,575.9
1959.....	117,870.8	149,032.7	161,185.7
1960.....	156,484.7	197,878.9	209.214.3
1961.....	185,892.3	238,419.6	254,085.9
1962.....	208,864.5	269,309.9	289,158.4

NOTE: M_1 includes currency outside banks and demand
deposits of commercial banks (col. [1] plus col. [2] of table
20); M_2 includes M_1 plus savings and time deposits of
commercial banks (M_1 plus cols. [3] and [4] of table 20);
and M_3 includes M_2 plus "other" deposits of commercial
banks (M_2 plus col. [5] of table 20).

TABLE 22

BANK RESERVES, MONETARY BASE AND BASE MULTIPLIER, 1935–45
AND 1958–62
(ANNUAL AVERAGES)

Year	Bank Reserves (Millions of Pesos) (1)	Monetary Base† (Millions of Pesos) (2)	Base Multiplier‡ (3)
1935.....	576.0	1,437.0	2.976
1936.....	780.9	1,692.5	2.595
1937.....	806.0	1,823.8	2.691
1938.....	709.7	1,740.2	2.812
1939.....	774.9	1,858.3	2.680
1940.....	788.0	1,872.1	2.702
1941.....	892.2	2,046.4	2.690
1942.....	1,054.4	2,433.8	2.603
1943.....	1,352.8	2,920.2	2.467
1944.....	1,886.4	3,800.5	2.245
1945.....	2,227.6	4,596.1	2.186
. . .	. . .	. . .	. . .
1958.....	25,556.0	70,587.7	1.567
1959.....	34,641.9	100,893.2	1.598
1960.....	48,041.4	134,314.9	1.558
1961.....	43,711.7	145,460.6	1.747
1962.....	25,157.6	143,965.9	2.009

† The monetary base is defined as the amount of currency outside banks plus the amount of bank reserves (col. [1], table 20, plus col. [1], table 22).

‡ The base multiplier is equal to the money supply, M_3, divided by the monetary base (col. [3], table 21, divided by col. [2], table 22).

TABLE 23

PRICE INDEXES

(ANNUAL AVERAGES, 1943 = 100)

Year	Wholesale Prices (1)	Year	Wholesale Prices (1)	GNP Deflator (2)
1907.........	31.6	1935.......	48.6	74.6
1908.........	31.6	1936.......	49.9	75.8
1909.........	35.1	1937.......	57.4	77.6
1910.........	35.1	1938.......	53.4	80.3
1911.........	34.1	1939.......	61.9	82.1
1912.........	35.4	1940.......	66.0	83.6
1913.........	37.8	1941.......	72.3	86.0
1914.........	38.3	1942.......	90.8	94.9
1915.........	41.1	1943.......	100.0	100.0
1916.........	46.4	1944.......	108.2	102.1
1917.........	57.4	1945.......	117.9	117.3
1918.........	63.2	1946.......	136.5	141.5
1919.........	64.9	1947.......	141.3	169.9
1920.........	68.0	1948.......	163.2	198.2
1921.........	54.2	1949.......	200.8	249.9
1922.........	49.4	1950.......	241.3	298.5
1923.........	51.0	1951.......	359.9	407.8
1924.........	54.9	1952.......	472.2	500.9
1925.........	55.6	1953.......	526.9	530.4
1926.........	50.3	1954.......	536.2	572.8
1927.........	49.2	1955.......	564.3	640.3
1928.........	49.5	1956.......	652.9	793.7
1929.........	48.2	1957.......	775.3	981.2
1930.........	45.8	1958.......	968.5	1,319.7
1931.........	44.0	1959.......	2,065.0	2,629.3
1932.........	44.4	1960.......	2,362.2	3,258.8
1933.........	42.1	1961.......	2,544.5	3,629.3
1934.........	49.3	1962.......	3,271.8	4,584.2

TABLE 24

POPULATION AND NATIONAL INCOME, 1935–62

Year	Population (Thousands) (1)	Net National Income (Million Pesos) (2)	Real Income Per Capita (1943 Pesos) (3)
1935.......	13,043.8	7,114	731.1
1936.......	13,259.8	7,699	766.0
1937.......	13,490.0	8,870	847.3
1938.......	13,724.5	8,750	794.0
1939.......	13,947.6	8,937	780.5
1940.......	14,169.2	9,190	775.8
1941.......	14,401.5	10,006	807.9
1942.......	14,637.5	11,489	827.1
1943.......	14,877.4	12,298	826.6
1944.......	15,129.5	14,012	907.1
1945.......	15,390.0	15,669	868.0
1946.......	15,653.6	21,330	963.0
1947.......	15,943.8	30,027	1,108.5
1948.......	16,309.8	37,762	1,168.2
1949.......	16,740.3	44,483	1,063.3
1950.......	17,191.8	51,939	1,012.1
1951.......	17,638.8	72,310	1,005.3
1952.......	18,042.7	82,811	916.3
1953.......	18,399.3	94,597	969.3
1954.......	18,748.8	106,306	989.9
1955.......	19,118.6	125,581	1,025.9
1956.......	19,497.6	150,909	975.2
1957.......	19,876.7	190,163	975.0
1958.......	20,252.5	271,162	1,014.6
1959.......	20,605.8	492,309	908.7
1960.......	20,955.4	626,006	916.7
1961.......	21,318.6	745,552	963.6
1962.......	21,684.6	905,563	911.0

TABLE 25

The Ratios of Currency to Demand Deposits, Savings and Time Deposits to Demand Deposits, and Reserves to Deposits, 1935–62
(Ratios of Annual Averages)

Year	$\dfrac{C}{D}$ † (1)	$\dfrac{T}{D}$ ‡ (2)	$\dfrac{R}{D+T}$ § (3)
1935.......	1.0069	2.9952	.1686
1936.......	1.0153	2.8755	.2244
1937.......	.8854	2.3836	.2072
1938.......	.9700	2.6365	.1837
1939.......	.9564	2.4406	.1988
1940.......	.8807	2.2279	.1983
1941.......	.7568	1.8522	.2051
1942.......	.7190	1.5832	.2128
1943.......	.6809	1.4483	.2401
1944.......	.6609	1.2852	.2850
1945.......	.6769	1.2564	.2947
1946.......	.6875	1.1818	. . .‖
1947.......	.7290	1.1268	. . .
1948.......	.8224	1.0538	. . .
1949.......	.8996	1.0138	. . .
1950.......	.9833	.9907	. . .
1951.......	1.1052	.9073	. . .
1952.......	1.2708	.9256	. . .
1953.......	1.2536	.8711	. . .
1954.......	1.3065	.9071	. . .
1955.......	1.4321	.9555	. . .
1956.......	1.3853	.9601	. . .
1957.......	1.3662	1.0099	. . .
1958.......	1.4087	1.0504	.3899
1959.......	1.2835	.8391	.3649
1960.......	1.2288	.7510	.3908
1961.......	1.2092	.8104	.2869
1962.......	1.3193	.8916	.1477

† The values of the ratio of currency to demand deposits are obtained from table 20 by dividing column (1) by column (2).

‡ The values of the ratio of savings and time deposits to demand deposits are obtained from table 20 by dividing the sum of columns (3) to (5) by column (2).

§ The values of the reserve-deposits ratio are obtained by dividing column (1) of table 22 by the sum of columns (2) to (5) of table 20.

‖ The figures for the period 1946–57 are omitted because of the institutional characteristics of the period.

TABLE 26

ADDITIONAL EXPLANATORY VARIABLES IN THE DEMAND FUNCTIONS FOR
COMPONENTS OF MONEY SUPPLY

Year	Rate of Interest on Savings Deposits (Percentage) (1)	Share of Income Going to Labor (Percentage) (2)	Number of Banking Offices (3)
1935.....	2.50	46.1	638
1936.....	2.50	46.0	650
1937.....	2.50	43.9	663
1938.....	2.50	46.2	675
1939.....	2.50	46.3	687
1940.....	2.50	46.4	698
1941.....	2.50	45.7	711
1942.....	2.50	43.5	726
1943.....	2.50	44.4	743
1944.....	2.50	45.2	764
1945.....	2.50	46.7	793
1946.....	2.00	46.8	821
1947.....	1.91	47.9	838
1948.....	1.98	52.4	850
1949.....	1.91	59.4	860
1950.....	2.19	60.9	872
1951.....	2.03	56.7	890
1952.....	2.88	61.0	909
1953.....	2.88	59.2	927
1954.....	2.85	60.7	952
1955.....	2.87	57.9	975
1956.....	2.78	57.0	991
1957.....	5.00	55.8	1,013
1958.....	5.00	56.9	1,058
1959.....	5.00	50.6	1,128
1960.....	5.00	50.3	1,216
1961.....	5.00	52.5	1,327
1962.....	8.00	52.5	1,433

Quarterly Series

TABLE 27

CURRENCY OUTSIDE BANKS AND DEPOSITS AT COMMERCIAL BANKS, 1935–62
(END-OF-QUARTER FIGURES IN MILLIONS OF PESOS)

YEAR	QUARTER	CURRENCY OUTSIDE BANKS (1)	DEPOSITS OF COMMERCIAL BANKS, ADJUSTED				
			Demand (2)	Savings (3)	Time (4)	Others (5)	Government (6)
1934...	IV	852.5	878.5	1770.0	566.2	220.4	124.1
1935...	I	837.8	927.9	1775.4	583.9	228.4	133.0
	II	861.8	837.6	1774.8	585.2	229.7	116.8
	III	858.5	843.8	1751.0	560.1	223.9	117.9
	IV	912.1	836.2	1759.1	556.3	213.5	116.5
1936...	I	901.3	866.8	1784.4	578.7	233.5	122.1
	II	890.8	887.6	1794.6	546.1	239.7	125.8
	III	919.6	901.6	1807.9	544.6	237.1	128.4
	IV	1005.0	1041.3	1853.4	557.6	228.0	153.6
1937...	I	1004.5	1182.9	1955.5	506.3	268.3	179.1
	II	1020.8	1189.1	1961.1	512.0	268.8	180.3
	III	1035.5	1160.9	2010.7	484.1	277.3	175.2
	IV	1080.7	1145.4	2050.0	473.3	246.9	172.4
1938...	I	1036.3	1099.2	2062.2	502.5	266.8	164.0
	II	1011.5	1032.6	2059.8	499.4	266.9	152.0
	III	1022.2	1035.1	2033.4	486.9	264.8	152.4
	IV	1075.6	1063.2	2042.0	472.2	254.2	157.5
1939...	I	1091.5	1107.1	2028.2	460.9	262.4	165.4
	II	1077.1	1131.9	2054.0	456.8	271.1	170.0
	III	1076.6	1169.0	2047.5	450.0	272.0	176.6
	IV	1101.6	1218.6	2035.1	418.9	260.1	185.6
1940...	I	1080.3	1242.9	2039.6	416.7	268.9	189.9
	II	1071.3	1292.5	2055.3	390.3	297.5	192.5
	III	1037.5	1218.8	2058.2	396.6	312.4	189.4
	IV	1127.6	1303.9	2053.5	372.0	334.6	192.5
1941...	I	1108.8	1467.7	2081.7	397.0	311.1	215.8
	II	1125.7	1559.1	2123.8	421.8	289.4	250.9
	III	1168.1	1586.0	2159.9	430.2	287.7	262.4
	IV	1327.8	1771.1	2185.0	382.3	287.5	238.4
1942...	I	1348.1	1872.9	2252.8	401.3	316.7	241.2
	II	1360.9	1956.6	2337.0	399.7	331.4	301.1
	III	1393.9	1932.8	2365.8	407.2	340.0	313.8
	IV	1510.6	2120.4	2440.4	399.2	328.0	345.5
1943...	I	1470.0	2267.5	2541.3	403.8	348.6	385.1
	II	1548.1	2330.6	2642.5	387.0	354.9	449.9
	III	1613.6	2266.5	2650.1	352.8	355.1	417.2
	IV	1770.0	2578.5	2761.1	339.0	346.9	457.1

TABLE 27—*Continued*

YEAR	QUARTER	CURRENCY OUTSIDE BANKS (1)	DEPOSITS OF COMMERCIAL BANKS, ADJUSTED				
			Demand (2)	Savings (3)	Time (4)	Others (5)	Govern-Ment (6)
1944...	I	1813.3	2830.4	2879.6	341.5	364.2	584.4
	II	1902.5	2940.0	3001.4	341.3	407.3	563.1
	III	1991.9	3026.0	3102.5	334.5	411.8	535.7
	IV	2197.5	3180.0	3242.5	327.9	449.3	549.9
1945...	I	2218.4	3190.4	3345.8	318.3	491.0	590.0
	II	2307.3	3422.7	3481.4	312.3	514.0	594.0
	III	2384.7	3541.8	3608.4	296.6	547.4	574.0
	IV	2639.9	3831.6	3743.0	293.1	518.4	505.6
1946...	I	2712.1	3852.8	3878.4	286.0	557.9	615.6
	II	2906.4	4150.3	4012.0	267.1	625.2	500.2
	III	3041.9	4602.0	4516.4	139.8	753.4	575.8
	IV	3581.6	4879.0	4700.9	103.2	720.6	770.0
1947...	I	3476.5	5291.4	4920.3	79.6	779.5	951.8
	II	3778.3	5211.2	4982.0	60.9	885.4	998.5
	III	3966.7	5231.3	5088.0	51.5	884.5	832.0
	IV	4771.9	5475.1	5244.7	47.1	856.0	1168.5
1948...	I	4684.2	6171.8	5618.3	44.7	857.9	1052.0
	II	5137.0	6405.9	5729.6	41.7	950.5	1058.0
	III	5501.8	6730.5	5897.3	41.1	994.4	1699.8
	IV	6736.6	7034.8	6093.6	36.4	974.7	3064.7
1949...	I	6561.4	7821.7	6406.0	32.5	1024.7	3354.1
	II	6943.1	8053.1	6565.6	32.8	1753.4	3450.3
	III	7399.7	8005.0	6787.3	29.1	1848.2	3804.9
	IV	9066.4	8511.1	6992.2	25.8	1800.8	3285.3
1950...	I	8710.2	9274.4	7425.8	27.7	1852.2	3423.8
	II	9044.6	9544.3	7647.6	26.7	1846.2	3435.7
	III	9698.9	9931.0	7633.6	28.7	1964.8	3373.6
	IV	11912.1	10136.6	7664.4	26.1	2071.1	3480.1
1951...	I	11649.7	11736.3	8019.8	28.2	2135.8	3737.0
	II	12493.2	11325.1	7968.5	34.5	2341.9	4587.2
	III	12997.9	11633.2	8027.9	59.9	2566.4	4870.1
	IV	15363.0	11381.6	8014.7	63.8	2466.3	4283.1
1952...	I	14263.4	12237.3	8489.0	50.3	2385.0	4663.6
	II	14779.7	11907.4	8723.7	41.1	2215.9	5293.7
	III	15227.6	11986.5	9145.0	31.1	2006.2	5475.1
	IV	18258.2	12157.5	9604.1	52.3	1960.4	4516.7
1953...	I	17752.7	15230.3	10547.2	43.5	2031.3	5080.6
	II	18415.3	14972.3	10911.8	41.2	2017.7	6439.1
	III	18922.4	15684.0	11357.0	39.5	2071.8	6429.8
	IV	22065.2	15666.8	11912.9	70.3	2055.2	6035.2
1954...	I	21228.9	17538.9	12981.1	77.3	2155.8	6903.0
	II	21607.0	17294.0	13292.1	66.0	2194.7	7892.2
	III	22665.5	17350.1	13633.5	66.4	2258.0	8440.4
	IV	26744.2	17135.1	14199.2	74.1	2372.8	8828.9

TABLE 27—*Continued*

1955...	I	25916.5	19575.6	15230.1	47.7	2568.0	9038.1
	II	26344.5	18747.7	15190.6	9.6	2884.9	10452.4
	III	27694.0	18461.7	15225.0	16.8	3029.6	10711.2
	IV	31825.6	19786.9	15844.3	16.4	3135.0	10675.5
1956...	I	30597.7	23144.5	17311.4	10.6	3786.3	11714.9
	II	30881.8	22397.1	17802.5	9.5	3962.2	12496.3
	III	31851.1	22857.9	18430.8	7.8	4263.2	16503.2
	IV	36143.4	24094.5	19524.7	7.9	4692.8	16163.1
1957...	I	35963.2	28072.1	21042.0	7.9	5496.5	15638.4
	II	36460.8	27271.4	21394.1	7.3	6082.3	16790.9
	III	36517.1	27079.7	21506.6	6.9	6727.8	17334.1
	IV	41813.0	25770.5	22080.7	49.0	6437.7	17555.3
1958...	I	40712.7	31220.5	22726.8	79.0	8551.1	18363.2
	II	42254.3	30214.7	24113.5	117.3	7645.2	18599.7
	III	46343.6	33842.2	25580.4	195.6	10537.8	20593.3
	IV	60278.4	38548.8	27122.4	262.3	12774.7	23553.7
1959...	I	61327.6	47724.7	29876.7	223.2	11546.1	22485.2
	II	61909.1	61081.5	29074.9	279.4	16719.3	21825.0
	III	68735.1	52717.7	31604.1	686.6	11715.5	29189.5
	IV	84414.6	57742.2	34586.7	1105.1	8947.5	30452.3
1960...	I	82637.1	67602.6	38128.5	1147.6	10208.1	30773.3
	II	84269.8	73644.3	39814.8	1781.1	11461.7	36658.0
	III	87298.2	75049.9	41158.3	2212.6	12096.1	42066.0
	IV	105361.5	73278.4	43166.9	3572.1	13102.9	43528.2
1961...	I	99440.8	84682.2	46452.8	4448.5	14759.8	42719.2
	II	99333.2	86894.0	47146.8	5580.6	15599.8	45473.8
	III	101385.7	85932.5	47919.9	6387.0	16420.1	48437.5
	IV	121684.8	83759.9	50469.2	6354.4	17755.9	41036.1
1962...	I	119466.2	90124.8	52652.2	5585.2	22414.8	38238.3
	II	115840.8	94756.3	51529.6	6434.8	19633.0	37220.7
	III	119162.9	89571.0	53799.7	9111.8	20460.4	36066.0
	IV	135379.0	84284.3	56951.8	10531.6	17456.0	34761.9

TABLE 28

STOCK.OF MONEY, 1935–62, FOR THREE DEFINITIONS OF MONEY
(END-OF-QUARTER FIGURES, IN MILLIONS OF PESOS)

Year	Quarter	M_1 (1)	M_2 (2)	M_3 (3)
1934.......	IV	1,731.0	4,067.2	4,287.6
1935.......	I	1,765.7	4,125.0	4,353.4
	II	1,699.4	4,059.4	4,289.1
	III	1,702.3	4,013.4	4,237.3
	IV	1,748.3	4,063.7	4,277.2
1936.......	I	1,768.1	4,131.2	4,364.7
	II	1,778.3	4,119.0	4,358.7
	III	1,821.2	4,173.7	4,410.8
	IV	2,046.3	4,457.3	4,685.3
1937.......	I	2,187.4	4,649.2	4,917.5
	II	2,209.9	4,683.0	4,951.8
	III	2,196.4	4,691.2	4,968.5
	IV	2,226.1	4,749.4	4,996.3
1938.......	I	2,135.5	4,700.2	4,967.0
	II	2,044.1	4,603.3	4,870.2
	III	2,057.3	4,577.6	4,842.4
	IV	2,138.8	4,653.0	4,907.2
1939.......	I	2,198.6	4,687.7	4,950.1
	II	2,209.0	4,719.8	4,990.9
	III	2,245.6	4,743.1	5,015.1
	IV	2,320.2	4,774.2	5,034.3
1940.......	I	2,323.2	4,779.5	5,048.4
	II	2,363.8	4,809.4	5,106.9
	III	2,256.3	4,711.1	5,023.5
	IV	2,431.5	4,857.0	5,191.6
1941.......	I	2,576.5	5,055.2	5,366.3
	II	2,684.8	5,230.4	5,519.8
	III	2,754.1	5,344.2	5,631.9
	IV	3,098.9	5,666.2	5,953.7
1942.......	I	3,221.0	5,875.1	6,191.8
	II	3,317.5	6,054.2	6,385.6
	III	3,326.7	6,099.7	6,439.7
	IV	3,631.0	6,470.6	6,798.6
1943.......	I	3,737.5	6,682.6	7,031.2
	II	3,878.7	6,908.2	7,263.1
	III	3,880.1	6,883.0	7,238.1
	IV	4,348.5	7,448.6	7,795.5

NOTE: M_1 includes currency outside banks and demand deposits of commercial banks (col. [1] and col. [2] of table 27); M_2 includes M_1 plus savings and time deposits of commercial banks (M_1 plus cols. [3] and [4] of table 27); and M_3 includes M_2 plus "other" deposits of commercial banks (M_2 plus col. [5] of table 27).

TABLE 28—*Continued*

1944.......	I	4,643.7	7,864.8	8,229.0
	II	4,842.5	8,185.2	8,592.5
	III	5,017.9	8,454.9	8,866.7
	IV	5,377.5	8,947.9	9,397.2
1945.......	I	5,408.8	9,072.9	9,563.9
	II	5,730.0	9,523.7	10,037.7
	III	5,926.5	9,831.5	10,378.9
	IV	6,471.5	10,507.6	11,026.0
1946.......	I	6,564.9	10,729.3	11,287.2
	II	7,056.7	11,335.8	11,961.0
	III	7,643.9	12,300.1	13,053.5
	IV	8,460.6	13,264.7	13,985.3
1947.......	I	8,767.9	13,767.8	14,547.3
	II	8,989.5	14,032.4	14,917.8
	III	9,198.0	14,337.5	15,222.0
	IV	10,247.0	15,538.8	16,394.8
1948.......	I	10,856.0	16,519.0	17,376.9
	II	11,542.9	17,314.2	18,264.7
	III	12,232.3	18,170.7	19,165.1
	IV	13,771.4	19,901.4	20,876.1
1949.......	I	14,383.1	20,821.6	21,846.3
	II	14,996.2	21,594.6	23,348.0
	III	15,404.7	22,221.1	24,069.3
	IV	17,577.5	24,595.5	26,396.3
1950.......	I	17,984.6	25,438.1	27,290.3
	II	18,588.9	26,263.2	28,109.4
	III	19,629.9	27,292.2	29,257.0
	IV	22,048.7	29,739.2	31,810.3
1951.......	I	23,386.0	31,434.0	33,569.8
	II	23,818.3	31,821.3	34,163.2
	III	24,631.1	32,718.9	35,285.3
	IV	26,744.6	34,823.1	37,289.4
1952.......	I	26,500.7	35,040.0	37,425.0
	II	26,687.1	35,451.9	37,667.8
	III	27,214.1	36,390.2	38,396.4
	IV	30,415.7	40,072.1	42,032.5
1953.......	I	32,983.0	43,573.7	45,605.0
	II	33,387.6	44,340.6	46,358.3
	III	34,606.4	46,002.9	48,074.4
	IV	37,732.0	49,715.2	51,770.4
1954.......	I	38,767.8	51,826.2	53,982.0
	II	38,901.0	52,259.1	54,453.8
	III	40,015.6	53,715.5	55,973.5
	IV	43,879.3	58,152.6	60,525.4
1955.......	I	45,492.1	60,769.9	63,337.9
	II	45,092.2	60,292.4	63,177.3
	III	46,155.7	61,397.5	64,427.1
	IV	51,612.5	67,473.2	70,608.2

TABLE 28—*Continued*

Year	Quarter	M_1 (1)	M_2 (2)	M_3 (3)
1956.......	I	53,742.2	71,064.2	74,850.5
	II	53,278.9	71,090.9	75,053.1
	III	54,709.0	73,147.6	77,410.8
	IV	60,237.9	79,770.5	84,463.3
1957.......	I	64,035.3	85,085.2	90,581.7
	II	63,732.2	85,133.6	91,215.9
	III	63,596.8	85,110.3	91,838.1
	IV	67,583.5	89,713.2	96,150.9
1958.......	I	71,933.2	94,739.0	103,290.1
	II	72,469.0	96,699.8	104,345.0
	III	80,185.8	105,961.8	116,499.6
	IV	98,827.2	126,211.9	138,986.6
1959.......	I	109,052.3	139,152.2	150,698.3
	II	122,990.6	152,344.9	169,064.2
	III	121,452.8	153,743.5	165,459.0
	IV	142,156.8	177,848.6	186,796.1
1960.......	I	150,239.7	189,515.8	199,723.9
	II	157,914.1	199,510.0	210,971.7
	III	162,348.1	205.719.0	217,815.1
	IV	178,639.9	225,378.9	238,481.8
1961.......	I	184,123.0	235,024.3	249,784.1
	II	186,227.2	238,954.6	254,554.4
	III	187,318.2	241,625.1	258,045.2
	IV	205,444.7	262,268.3	280,024.2
1962.......	I	209,591.0	267,828.4	290,243.2
	II	210,597.1	268,561.5	288,194.5
	III	208,733.9	271,645.4	292,105.8
	IV	219,663.3	287,146.7	304,602.7

NOTE: M_1 includes currency outside banks and demand deposits of commercial banks (col. [1] and col. [2] of table 27); M_2 includes M_1 plus savings and time deposits of commercial banks (M_1 plus cols. [3] and [4] of table 27); and M_3 includes M_2 plus "other" deposits of commercial banks (M_2 plus col. [5] of table 27).

TABLE 29

BANK RESERVES, MONETARY BASE, AND BASE MULTIPLIER, 1935–45
AND 1958–62
(END-OF-QUARTER FIGURES)

Year	Quarter	Bank Reserves (Millions of Pesos) (1)	Monetary Base† (Millions of Pesos) (2)	Base Multiplier‡ (3)
1934.......	IV	402.5	1,255.0	3.416
1935.......	I	464.4	1,302.2	3.343
	II	635.2	1,497.0	2.865
	III	602.4	1,460.9	2.900
	IV	862.5	1,774.6	2.410
1936.......	I	846.3	1,747.6	2.498
	II	746.2	1,637.0	2.663
	III	675.6	1,595.2	2.765
	IV	801.0	1,806.0	2.594
1937.......	I	801.4	1,805.9	2.723
	II	876.5	1,897.3	2.610
	III	762.0	1,797.5	2.764
	IV	709.3	1,790.0	2.791
1938.......	I	722.3	1,758.6	2.824
	II	666.3	1,677.8	2.903
	III	701.5	1,723.7	2.809
	IV	643.9	1,719.5	2.854
1939.......	I	712.4	1,803.9	2.744
	II	769.4	1,846.5	2.703
	III	889.7	1,966.3	2.551
	IV	816.1	1,917.7	2.625
1940.......	I	877.7	1,958.0	2.578
	II	783.8	1,855.1	2.753
	III	736.2	1,773.7	2.832
	IV	771.3	1,898.9	2,734
1941.......	I	835.5	1,944.3	2.760
	II	1,001.8	2,127.5	2.595
	III	918.8	2,086.9	2.699
	IV	911.5	2,239.3	2.659
1942.......	I	971.8	2,319.9	2.669
	II	1,088.4	2,449.3	2.607
	III	1,115.0	2,508.9	2.567
	IV	1,186.8	2,697.4	2.520
1943.......	I	1,299.9	2,769.9	2.538
	II	1,338.4	2,886.5	2.516
	III	1,294.9	2,908.5	2.489
	IV	1,613.4	3,383.4	2.304

TABLE 29—*Continued*

Year	Quarter	Bank Reserves (Millions of Pesos) (1)	Monetary Base† (Millions of Pesos) (2)	Base Multiplier‡ (3)
1944.......	I	1,929.3	3,742.6	2.199
	II	1,894.2	3,796.7	2.263
	III	2,010.2	4,002.1	2.216
	IV	2,006.5	4,204.0	2.235
1945.......	I	2,052.5	4,270.9	2.239
	II	2,278.4	4,585.7	2.189
	III	2,383.6	4,768.3	2.177
	IV	2,470.5	5,110.4	2.158
1946.......	I	2,576.4	5,288.5	2.134
...	...	...	...	...
1957.......	IV	21,706.3	63,519.3	2.514
1958.......	I	25,723.3	66,436.0	1.555
	II	23,966.8	66,221.1	1.576
	III	30,322.5	76,666.1	1.520
	IV	26,257.5	86,535.9	1.606
1959......,.	I	30,738.4	92,066.6	1.637
	II	32,535.5	94,444.6	1.790
	III	37,393.7	106,128.8	1.559
	IV	34,090.3	118,504.9	1.576
1960.......	I	47,281.2	129,918.3	1.537
	II	52,339.3	136.609.1	1.544
	III	53,044.8	140,343.0	1.552
	IV	38,090.6	143,452.1	1.662
1961.......	I	51,077.8	150,518.6	1.659
	II	47,950.3	147,283.5	1.728
	III	43,515.8	144,901.5	1.781
	IV	21,022.4	142,707.2	1.962
1962.......	I	26,990.3	146,456.5	1.982
	II	27,383.5	143,224.3	2.012
	III	24,449.7	143,612.6	2.034
	IV	17,503.3	152,882.3	1.992

† The monetary base is defined as the amount of currency outside banks plus the amount of bank reserves (col. [1], table 27, plus col. [1], table 29).

‡ The base multiplier is equal to the money supply, M_3, divided by the monetary base (col. [3], table 28, divided by col. [2], table 29).

TABLE 30

CHANGES IN THE STOCK OF MONEY, THE MONETARY BASE, AND THE
BASE MULTIPLIER, 1935–45 and 1958–62
(PERCENTAGE RELATIVE RATES OF CHANGE WITHIN QUARTERS)

Year	Quarter	$\frac{\Delta M_3 \dagger}{M_3}$ (1)	$\frac{\Delta m \ddagger}{m}$ (2)	$\frac{\Delta B \S}{B}$ (3)	Interaction ‖ (4)
1935......	I	1.53	−2.14	3.76	−.08
	II	−1.48	−14.30	14.96	−2.14
	III	−1.21	1.22	−2.41	−.03
	IV	.94	−16.90	21.46	−3.63
1936......	I	2.04	3.65	−1.52	−.06
	II	−.14	6.60	−6.33	−.42
	III	1.20	3.83	−2.55	−.10
	IV	6.22	−6.18	13.21	−.82
1937......	I	4.96	4.97	.00	.00
	II	.70	−4.15	5.06	.00
	III	.34	5.90	−5.26	−.31
	IV	.56	.98	−.42	.00
1938......	I	−.59	1.18	−1.75	−.02
	II	−1.95	2.80	−4.59	−.13
	III	−.57	−3.24	2.74	−.09
	IV	1.34	1.60	−.24	.00
1939......	I	.87	−3.85	4.91	−.19
	II	.82	−1.49	2.36	−.04
	III	.48	−5.62	6.49	−.36
	IV	.38	2.90	−2.47	−.07
1940......	I	.28	−1.79	2.10	−.04
	II	1.16	6.79	−5.26	−.36
	III	−1.63	2.87	−4.39	−.13
	IV	3.35	−3.46	7.06	−.24
1941......	I	3.36	.95	2.39	.02
	II	2.86	−5.98	9.42	−.56
	III	2.03	4.01	−1.91	−.08
	IV	5.71	−1.48	7.30	−.11
1942......	I	4.00	.38	3.60	.01
	II	3.13	−2.32	5.58	−.13
	III	.85	−1.53	2.43	−.04
	IV	5.57	−1.83	7.51	−.14
1943......	I	3.42	.71	2.69	.02
	II	3.30	−.87	4.21	−.04
	III	−.34	−1.07	.76	−.01
	IV	7.70	−7.43	16.33	−1.21
1944......	I	5.56	−4.56	10.62	−.48
	II	4.42	2.91	1.44	.04
	III	3.19	−2.08	5.41	−.11
	IV	5.98	.86	5.04	.04

TABLE 30—*Continued*

Year	Quarter	$\frac{\Delta M_3\dagger}{M_3}$ (1)	$\frac{\Delta m\ddagger}{m}$ (2)	$\frac{\Delta B\S}{B}$ (3)	Interaction‖ (4)
1945.......	I	1.77	.18	1.59	.00
	II	4.95	−2.23	7.37	−.16
	III	3.40	−.55	3.98	−.02
	IV	6.23	−.87	7.17	−.06
1946.......	I	2.37	−1.11	3.48	−.04
...	...	...	...	...	...
1958.......	I	7.42	2.71	4.59	.12
	II	1.02	1.35	−.32	.00
	III	11.65	−3.55	15.77	−.56
	IV	19.30	5.66	12.87	.73
1959.......	I	8.43	1.93	6.39	.12
	II	12.19	9.35	2.58	.24
	III	2.13	−12.90	12.37	−1.60
	IV	12.90	1.09	11.66	.13
1960.......	I	6.92	−2.47	9.63	−.24
	II	5.63	.46	5.15	.02
	III	3.24	.52	2.73	.01
	IV	9.49	7.09	2.22	.16
1961.......	I	4.74	−.18	4.93	.00
	II	1.91	4.16	−2.15	−.10
	III	1.37	3.07	−1.62	−.05
	IV	8.52	10.16	−1.51	−.15
1962.......	I	3.65	1.02	2.63	.03
	II	−.70	1.51	−2.21	−.03
	III	1.36	1.09	.27	.00
	IV	4.28	−2.06	6.45	−.13

† From table 28, column (3).
‡ From table 29, column (3).
§ From table 29, column (2).
‖ Product of columns (2) and (3).

TABLE 31

Year	Quarter	Wholesale Prices (1)	Cost of Living (2)	Year	Quarter	Wholesale Prices (1)	Cost of Living (2)
1935....	I	48.7	75.2	1945....	I	114.3	113.6
	II	48.2	77.7		II	117.1	120.2
	III	48.0	80.1		III	118.4	121.3
	IV	49.5	84.6		IV	121.8	122.5
1936....	I	49.4	84.1	1946....	I	129.8	134.5
	II	49.0	86.3		II	137.9	140.2
	III	50.2	87.8		III	139.9	141.3
	IV	50.8	86.2		IV	138.5	145.8
1937....	I	54.5	86.4	1947....	I	138.7	150.1
	II	58.3	89.5		II	140.2	159.1
	III	59.1	88.6		III	142.1	163.3
	IV	57.9	89.1		IV	144.3	165.7
1938....	I	56.5	87.5	1948....	I	150.6	167.7
	II	53.8	88.4		II	158.9	175.0
	III	51.7	87.6		III	168.1	184.3
	IV	51.5	87.9		IV	175.1	194.8
1939....	I	59.7	87.7	1949....	I	186.5	207.1
	II	59.7	89.0		II	195.6	231.9
	III	61.7	89.1		III	205.8	244.3
	IV	66.6	91.0		IV	215.3	262.6
1940....	I	67.4	91.8	1950....	I	222.2	269.4
	II	67.5	92.3		II	230.1	289.3
	III	66.2	91.3		III	244.7	303.7
	IV	63.0	89.3		IV	268.1	325.2
1941....	I	64.3	89.2	1951....	I	305.2	332.7
	II	69.5	91.6		II	343.9	389.6
	III	76.6	95.1		III	383.9	433.1
	IV	78.9	98.5		IV	406.4	467.7
1942....	I	83.9	98.2	1952....	I	439.2	521.4
	II	90.9	99.5		II	461.9	575.9
	III	93.2	98.7		III	485.8	567.5
	IV	95.4	99.3		IV	501.8	586.9
1943....	I	97.1	101.9	1953....	I	521.2	602.8
	II	100.3	102.9		II	528.2	579.7
	III	101.6	97.3		III	528.2	579.4
	IV	101.0	97.9		IV	530.1	579.2
1944....	I	103.7	98.7	1954....	I	526.4	572.5
	II	108.2	98.4		II	529.7	586.8
	III	109.1	100.3		III	524.8	613.6
	IV	111.6	101.4		IV	546.0	656.9

TABLE 31—*Continued*

Year	Quarter	Wholesale Prices (1)	Cost of Living (2)	Year	Quarter	Wholesale Prices (1)	Cost of Living (2)
1955....	I	552.0	664.3	1959....	I	1,659.4	2,062.0
	II	559.0	676.7		II	2,009.7	2,627.3
	III	566.3	685.8		III	2,277.6	3,002.7
	IV	579.8	702.5		IV	2,313.2	3,165.1
1956....	I	612.3	715.4	1960....	I	2,366.1	3,362.3
	II	647.1	766.7		II	2,339.4	3,443.9
	III	671.4	790.7		III	2,373.5	3,475.9
	IV	680.8	822.6		IV	2,369.9	3,535.4
1957....	I	704.4	855.6	1961....	I	2,405.2	3,580.6
	II	752.4	930.5		II	2,459.7	3,838.2
	III	813.0	1,014.8		III	2,617.3	4,053.2
	IV	831.3	1,059.3		IV	2,695.7	4,212.1
1958....	I	823.6	1,055.5	1962....	I	2,747.6	4,348.2
	II	887.8	1,183.8		II	3,088.1	4,800.9
	III	1,007.9	1,336.5		III	3,537.5	5,355.7
	IV	1,154.9	1,503.8		IV	3,714.0	5,579.9

TABLE 32

QUARTERLY REAL NET NATIONAL INCOME
(ANNUAL RATES IN TENS OF MILLIONS OF PESOS AT 1950
PRICES)

Year	Quarter	Real Income	Year	Quarter	Real Income
1935....	I	2,822.6	1945....	I	3,951.1
	II	2,822.6		II	3,924.1
	III	2,845.6		III	3,973.5
	IV	2,891.6		IV	4,099.3
1936....	I	2,937.9	1946....	I	4,276.2
	II	2,983.9		II	4,403.6
	III	3,054.1		III	4,563.7
	IV	3,148.5		IV	4,756.5
1937....	I	3,334.7	1947....	I	5,029.6
	II	3,431.8		II	5,225.5
	III	3,460.0		III	5,375.2
	IV	3,419.5		IV	5,478.6
1938....	I	3,292.6	1948....	I	5,630.1
	II	3,253.1		II	5,734.4
	III	3,233.1		III	5,739.1
	IV	3,232.4		IV	5,644.4
1939....	I	3,246.5	1949....	I	5,422.1
	II	3,245.8		II	5,329.7
	III	3,249.4		III	5,268.3
	IV	3,257.5		IV	5,238.3
1940....	I	3,250.2	1950....	I	5,211.5
	II	3,258.2		II	5,181.5
	III	3,286.1		III	5,178.9
	IV	3,333.9		IV	5,203.7
1941....	I	3,408.8	1951....	I	5,313.7
	II	3,457.0		II	5,338.9
	III	3,498.3		III	5,306.2
	IV	3,533.1		IV	5,215.6
1942....	I	3,570.8	1952....	I	4,975.4
	II	3,605.6		II	4,887.5
	III	3,630.4		III	4,891.1
	IV	3,644.8		IV	4,986.4
1943....	I	3,604.0	1953....	I	5,198.8
	II	3,618.4		II	5,296.3
	III	3,678.2		III	5,372.1
	IV	3,783.4		IV	5,426.4
1944....	I	4,002.8	1954....	I	5,446.5
	II	4,111.1		II	5,500.4
	III	4,151.2		III	5,566.7
	IV	4,123.3		IV	5,645.2

TABLE 32—*Continued*

Year	Quarter	Real Income	Year	Quarter	Real Income
1955....	I	5,797.7	1959....	I	5,705.5
	II	5,877.2		II	5,571.5
	III	5,894.4		III	5,522.3
	IV	5,849.1		IV	5,558.0
1956....	I	5,706.3	1960....	I	5,648.7
	II	5,661.8		II	5,684.7
	III	5,653.1		III	5,752.3
	IV	5,680.4		IV	5,851.1
1957....	I	5,714.7	1961....	I	6,061.3
	II	5,742.0		II	6,162.0
	III	5,798.9		III	6,182.6
	IV	5,885.6		IV	6,123.0
1958....	I	6,114.1	1962....	I	5,955.3
	II	6,202.8		II	5,896.7
	III	6,177.9		III	5,867.4
	IV	6,039,2		IV	5,867.4

TABLE 33

RATIOS OF CURRENCY TO DEMAND DEPOSITS AND SAVINGS AND TIME
DEPOSITS TO DEMAND DEPOSITS
(End-of-Quarter Figures)

Year	Quarter	C/D† (1)	T/D‡ (2)
1934........	IV	.9704	2.9102
1935........	I	.9029	2.7888
	II	1.0289	3.0918
	III	1.0174	3.0043
	IV	1.0908	3.0243
1936........	I	1.0398	2.9956
	II	1.0037	2.9075
	III	1.0200	2.8722
	IV	.9651	2.5343
1937........	I	.8492	2.3080
	II	.8585	2.3059
	III	.8920	2.3879
	IV	.9435	2.4185
1938........	I	.9428	2.5760
	II	.9796	2.7369
	III	.9875	2.6907
	IV	1.0117	2.6038
1939........	I	.9859	2.4853
	II	.9516	2.4577
	III	.9210	2.3691
	IV	.9040	2.2272
1940........	I	.8692	2.1926
	II	.8289	2.1223
	III	.8512	2.2704
	IV	.8648	2.1168
1941........	I	.7555	1.9008
	II	.7220	1.8184
	III	.7365	1.8145
	IV	.7497	1.6119
1942........	I	.7198	1.5862
	II	.6955	1.5681
	III	.7212	1.6106
	IV	.7124	1.4939
1943........	I	.6483	1.4526
	II	.6642	1.4522
	III	.7119	1.4816
	IV	.6864	1.3368
1944........	I	.6407	1.2667
	II	.6471	1.2755
	III	.6583	1.2719
	IV	.6910	1.2641

TABLE 33—*Continued*

Year	Quarter	C/D† (1)	T/D‡ (2)
1945.........	I	.6953	1.3024
	II	.6741	1.2586
	III	.6733	1.2571
	IV	.6890	1.1887
1946.........	I	.7039	1.2257
. . .	. . .	. . .	. . .
1957.........	IV	1.6225	1.1085
1958.........	I	1.3040	1.0044
	II	1.3985	1.0550
	III	1.3694	1.0730
	IV	1.5637	1.0418
1959.........	I	1.2850	.8726
	II	1.0135	.7543
	III	1.3038	.8348
	IV	1.4619	.7731
1960.........	I	1.2224	.7320
	II	1.1443	.7205
	III	1.1632	.7391
	IV	1.4378	.8166
1961.........	I	1.1743	.7754
	II	1.1432	.7863
	III	1.1798	.8231
	IV	1.4528	.8904
1962.........	I	1.3256	.8949
	II	1.2225	.8189
	III	1.3304	.9308
	IV	1.6062	1.0078

† From table 27, column (1) divided by column (2).

‡ From table 27, sum of columns (3) to (5) divided by column (2).

TABLE 34

RESERVE RATIO AND INTEREST RATES ON CONSOLIDATED
TREASURY BONDS, 1935–45
(END-OF-QUARTER PERCENTAGES)

Year	Quarter	Reserve Ratio† (1)	Interest Rate (2)	Year	Quarter	Reserve Ratio† (1)	Interest Rate (2)
1935....	I	12.73		1941...	I	18.68	2.38
	II	17.92	2.88		II	21.57	2.38
	III	17.23	2.75		III	19.44	1.25
	IV	24.77	2.75		IV	18.74	1.17
1936....	I	23.60	2.57	1942...	I	19.11	1.15
	II	20.76	2.02		II	20.44	1.00
	III	18.67	1.99		III	20.80	.97
	IV	20.89	1.97		IV	21.07	.95
1937....	I	19.58	1.88	1943...	I	21.86	.95
	II	21.32	1.89		II	21.71	.95
	III	18.55	1.85		III	21.43	.98
	IV	17.35	1.72		IV	24.89	.85
1938....	I	17.64	2.02	1944...	I	27.56	.64
	II	16.61	2.25		II	26.12	.48
	III	17.66	2.37		III	27.13	.45
	IV	16.14	2.38		IV	25.89	.47
1939....	I	17.70	2.38	1945...	I	25.87	.53
	II	18.84	2.38		II	27.37	.57
	III	21.62	2.38		III	27.82	.71
	IV	19.82	2.38		IV	27.78	.85
1940....	I	21.11	2.38	...	...	...	...
	II	18.54	2.38	...	...	...	...
	III	17.63	2.38	...	...	...	...
	IV	18.12	2.38	...	...	...	...

† The values of the reserve ratio are obtained by dividing the values of column (1), table 29, by the sum of those of columns (2) to (6), table 27.

TABLE 35

THE RESERVE RATIO AND RELATED VARIABLES, 1958–62
(END-OF-QUARTER PERCENTAGES)

Year	Quarter	Reserve Ratio† (1)	Treasury Bill Rate (2)	Index of Reserve Requirement (3)
1957.......	IV	30.19	1.49	17.9
1958.......	I	31.78	1.49	22.7
	II	29.70	1.49	20.0
	III	33.41	1.49	20.0
	IV	25.68	1.49	22.1
1959.......	I	27.48	1.49	38.4
	II	25.23	1.49	41.1
	III	29.70	5.47	39.3
	IV	25.66	7.58	41.1
1960.......	I	31.98	7.08	43.5
	II	32.04	6.27	45.6
	III	30.74	6.10	46.2
	IV	21.56	6.10	41.5
1961.......	I	26.46	6.02	40.4
	II	23.89	6.10	40.4
	III	21.22	6.15	37.0
	IV	10.54	6.15	33.0
1962.......	I	12.91	6.15	35.0
	II	13.07	6.14	37.0
	III	11.70	6.14	37.0
	IV	8.58	6.15	37.0

† See table 34, note.

TABLE 36

EXCHANGE RATE AND WAGE INDEX
(MONTHLY AVERAGES CORRESPONDING TO THE MONTH IN THE
MIDDLE OF EACH QUARTER)

Year	Quarter	Exchange Rate (Pesos/ U.S. Dollars) (1)	Wage Index (1943 = 100) (2)	Year	Quarter	Exchange Rate (Pesos/ U.S. Dollars) (1)	Wage Index (1943 = 100) (2)
1935...	I	3.47		1945...	I	4.23	
	II	3.47			II	4.23	
	III	3.42			III	4.23	
	IV	3.45			IV	4.23	
1936...	I	3.40		1946...	I	4.23	139.6
	II	3.42			II	4.23	124.9
	III	3.39			III	4.23	126.0
	IV	3.47			IV	4.23	143.1
1937...	I	3.26		1947...	I	4.23	184.3
	II	3.24			II	4.23	198.9
	III	3.21			III	4.23	278.8
	IV	3.20			IV	4.23	291.8
1938...	I	3.19		1948...	I	4.23	215.7
	II	3.22			II	4.23	219.0
	III	3.28			II	4.23	212.1
	IV	3.57			IV	4.23	243.9
1939...	I	3.63		1949...	I	4.23	299.1
	II	3.63			II	4.23	292.7
	III	3.69			III	4.23	301.5
	IV	4.23			IV	6.09	333.1
1940...	I	4.23		1950...	I	6.09	397.7
	II	4.23			II	6.09	345.2
	III	4.23			III	6.09	368.5
	IV	4.23			IV	7.50	414.5
1941...	I	4.23		1951...	I	7.50	475.4
	II	4.23			II	7.50	470.6
	III	4.23			III	7.50	484.9
	IV	4.23			IV	7.50	525.0
1942...	I	4.23		1952...	I	7.50	572.4
	II	4.23			II	7.50	605.1
	III	4.23			III	7.50	597.6
	IV	4.23			IV	7.50	681.5
1943...	I	4.23		1953...	I	7.50	757.3
	II	4.23			II	7.50	693.7
	III	4.23			III	7.50	667.9
	IV	4.23			IV	7.50	702.7
1944...	I	4.23		1954...	I	7.50	796.0
	II	4.23			II	7.50	690.9
	III	4.23			III	7.50	858.5
	IV	4.23			IV	7.50	817.3

TABLE 36—*Continued*

Year	Quarter	Exchange Rate (Pesos/ U.S. Dollars) (1)	Wage Index (1943 = 100 (2)	Year	Quarter	Exchange Rate (Pesos/ U.S. Dollars) (1)	Wage Index (1943 = 100) (2)
1955...	I	7.50	984.9	1959...	I	65.96	3,123.4
	II	7.50	826.3		II	85.42	3,050.6
	III	7.50	779.9		III	84.02	3,294.2
	IV	18.00	841.8		IV	82.83	3,699.7
1956...	I	18.00	963.6	1960...	I	82.92	4,611.7
	II	18.00	932.6		II	83.09	4,338.4
	III	18.00	910.1		III	82.79	4,749.6
	IV	18.00	1,086.0		IV	82.92	5,019.7
1957...	I	18.00	1,443.8	1961...	I	82.70	5,762.2
	II	18.00	1,304.5		II	82.93	5,774.4
	III	18.00	1,236.2		III	82.74	6,322.9
	IV	18.00	1,261.4		IV	83.04	6,911.4
1958...	I	18.00	1,449.6	1962...	I	83.04	7,775.1
	II	18.00	1,776.4		II	105.44	7,176.9
	III	18.00	1,969.1		III	123.60	7,786.7
	IV	18.00	2,061.2		IV	146.93	8,817.3

III

Monetary Policy and the Business Cycle in Postwar Japan

MICHAEL W. KERAN

Monetary Policy and the Business Cycle
in Postwar Japan

1. INTRODUCTION

THE postwar growth of Japan is an authentic economic miracle. Since recovering her prewar levels of per capita production and income in 1953, Japan has had a growth rate which in real terms has averaged close to 10 per cent a year. This performance is by far the most impressive of any of the major industrial countries in the world. Even the Japanese business cycle has been relatively mild, reflecting mainly variations in a positive growth rate. Optimists have speculated that the Japanese-type business cycle is what may be in store for many industrial countries in the future because the economic policy tools necessary to prevent major economic declines have been developed.

The object of this study is to analyze the postwar cyclical experience of Japan which has taken place, within the context of rapid secular growth in real income. I will do this by developing a business-cycle model which uses as one of its assumptions the modern quantity theory of money. This will not be a monetary business-cycle theory in the usual sense because disturbances from sources other than money can trigger the cycle.

Modern business-cycle models have typically been constructed on the basis of assumptions about interaction among various components of the national income accounts. The Keynesian income-expenditure framework is usually the static equilibrium limit.[1] Most of the initial work in this area was concentrated on specifying alternative lags and analyzing their effects on the cycle. Lloyd Metzler (1948) postulated that there are "three lags in the circular flow of income." The major segments of the circular flow and the possible sources of lags suggested by Metzler are as follows:

Production $\xrightarrow{(1)}$ Income $\xrightarrow{(2)}$ Consumption (sales) $\xrightarrow{(3)}$ Production.

1. Some business-cycle model building has been based on the assumption that the economy was in unstable equilibrium. The best known of these is perhaps the Hicks-Domar growth model, with its knife's edge equilibrium growth path.

The first lag between production and income was not considered important because the largest component of income, wages and salaries, is paid with a very short lag, usually weekly or biweekly. The second lag between income and consumption was incorporated in Samuelson's (1939) "Interactions between Multiplier Analysis and Principle of Acceleration." The third lag between sales and production was used by Metzler (1941) in his "The Nature and Stability of Inventory Cycles." [2]

Such lagged endogenous business-cycle models (given realistic values of the parameters) are analogous to the operation of a defective thermostat. If the thermostat is working properly, it can keep the actual temperature in a room very close to the desired temperature. However, if the thermostat is defective in the sense that it transmits signals to the furnace with a lag, then the actual temperature will fluctuate around the desired temperature. The reason is fairly obvious. If the actual temperature rises above the desired temperature, the defective thermostat will not signal the furnace to turn off immediately. Conversely, if the actual temperature falls below the desired temperature, the defective thermostat will not signal the furnace to turn on immediately. In business-cycle models the lags in behavioral responses lead to similar deviations between desired and actual income.

The business-cycle model developed in this study follows in the footsteps of these earlier models. Its cyclical properties are based on highly simplified assumptions about lagged behavior of decision-making units in the economy.

Eight variables are considered in this model: real and nominal variables for income, money, international reserves, and imports. All are measured as quarterly rates of change: [3]

2. The earliest work incorporating dynamic properties into the Keynesian system was contemporaneous with the publication of the *General Theory*. D. H. Robertson considered the second type of lag in "Some Notes on Mr. Keynes' General Theory of Employment," *Quarterly Journal of Economics* 51 (1936): 168–91. Erik Landberg considered the third type of lag in *Studies in the Theory of Economic Expansion* (London, 1937), chap. 9.

3. Because of the impressive growth Japan has enjoyed over the period of this study, virtually all of the economic series considered here have a strong upward time trend. To estimate meaningful behavioral relations under this circumstance requires recognition of this time trend. Various techniques are possible, such as scaling, deviation from trends, or first differences. In this study, scaling was not considered feasible and deviations from trends were not reliable. Thus, first differences in the form of rates of change were employed.

The general convention for computing rates of change at period t is to base it on the difference between period $t - 1$ and t:

$\dot{Y}$ = Nominal gross national product.

$\dot{X}$ = Index of industrial production.

M = Nominal money stock. Currency in the hands of the nonbank public plus designated monetary deposits of the banking system.

M^* = Real money stock. The nominal money stock divided by the GNP implicit price deflator.

$\dot{R}$ = Nominal international reserves. The foreign exchange special account of the ministry of finance, government of Japan. (This series is exclusive of changes in reserves which arise from transactions with foreign central banks or international organizations.)

$\dot{R}^*$ = Real international reserves. Nominal international reserves divided by the import price index.

$I\dot{m}$ = Nominal imports on a customs clearance basis.

$I\dot{m}^*$ = Real imports. Nominal imports divided by the import price index.

The first assumption of this model is that the modern version of the quantity theory of money provides an accurate determination in the short run of the level of national income. Given a predictable and quantifiable link between the money stock and money income, there will also be a predictable and quantifiable link between changes in the money stock, $\dot{M}$, and changes in money income, $\dot{Y}$. Therefore,

$$\dot{Y}_t = \alpha_0 + \alpha_1 \dot{M}_{t-m} + v_1. \tag{1}$$

The second assumption of this model is that variations in the money supply represent a discretionary policy tool in the hands of the monetary

---

$$\dot{Y}_t = \frac{Y_t - Y_{t-1}}{Y_{t-1}}.$$

However, it would be equally reasonable to compute the change at t as the difference between t and $t + 1$:

$$\dot{Y}_t = \frac{Y_{t+1} - Y_t}{Y_t}.$$

Either alternative would be the rate of change *between* periods and not the rate of change *for* a period. To more closely approximate a smooth rate of change at a point of time, this paper employs a modified form of the central difference theorem used by John Kareken and Robert Solow in "Research Study One, Lags in Monetary Policy" *Stabilization Policies* (Englewood Cliffs, N.J.: Prentice-Hall, 1963), p. 18. The rate of change for any period t equals:

$$\dot{Y}_t = \frac{\dfrac{Y_t - Y_{t-1}}{Y_{t-1}} + \dfrac{Y_{t+1} - Y_t}{Y_t}}{2}.$$

authorities. As such, the money stock can be manipulated in such a way as to achieve some target policy goal. In the case of Japan, this goal is postulated to be attainment of "external stability"; that is, reducing variations in the growth of international reserves, $\dot{R}$. When $\dot{R}$ declines, monetary policy becomes "tighter," and when $\dot{R}$ increases, monetary policy becomes "easier." This is a statement about the behavior of the policy authorities and, as such, is capable of theoretical analysis and statistical verification in the same way as statements about behavior of other elemental decision-making units in the economy. In this sense money stock is an endogenous variable.

$$\dot{M}_t = \beta_0 + \beta_1 \dot{R}_{t-n} + v_2. \tag{2}$$

The third assumption is that variations in international reserves, $\dot{R}$, are largely dependent upon variations in imports rather than upon variations in exports or capital movements.

$$\dot{R}_t = \rho_0 + \rho_1 I\dot{m}_{t-p} + v_3. \tag{3}$$

This unusual assumption about the behavior of international reserves will be considered in some detail in section 4C.

The final assumption in this model is that variations in imports are dependent upon variations in income.

$$I\dot{m}_t = \gamma_0 + \gamma_1 \dot{Y}_t + v_4. \tag{4}$$

The dynamic process of adjustment implied by these statements about behavior can be described as follows: [4] Assume an initial condition of equilibrium growth in income, money, international reserves, and imports. Some exogenous event occurs which causes a deceleration in international reserves. The authorities react with a restrictive monetary policy. $\dot{M}$ decreases, causing money income and imports to decelerate. The decline in $\dot{Y}$ and $I\dot{m}$ will lead to a reversal of the deceleration in international reserves. An increase in $\dot{R}$ will allow the authorities to ease monetary policy and $\dot{M}$ will increase. The resulting rise in $\dot{Y}$ and $I\dot{m}$ will eventually lead to a decline in $\dot{R}$ and the whole process will be repeated again.

4. Previous work linking money, income, and the balance of payments was done by J. J. Polak (1957, 1960). He makes roughly the same set of behavioral assumptions as in this paper. However, the Polak study differs from this one in several important respects. The statistical testing in that study compared average values and ratios of important time series with the underlying theoretical relationship to determine the long-run effect of money on the balance of payments. The present study utilizes regression techniques and difference equations to measure the short-term effect of money on international reserves and income.

It can be observed that increases in income in one period will lead to decreases in income in a future period. The transmission mechanism can be illustrated as follows:

$$\uparrow \dot{Y} \rightarrow \uparrow I\dot{m} \rightarrow \downarrow \dot{R} \rightarrow \downarrow \dot{M} \rightarrow \downarrow \dot{Y}.$$

The implications can be seen more formally by a simple process of algebraic substitution. The four equations (1) through (4) can be reduced to one equation of the following form:

$$\dot{Y}_t = A_0 + A_1(\dot{Y})_{t-z} \tag{5}$$

where

$$A_0 = \alpha_0 + \alpha_1\beta_0 + \alpha_1\beta_1\rho_0 + \alpha_1\beta_1\rho_1\gamma_0,$$
$$A_1 = \alpha_1\beta_1\rho_1\gamma_1,$$

and

$$z = m + n + p.$$

The change of income in period $t - z$ will lead to a predictable change in income in period t. The direction and degree of the change will depend upon the size and sign of A_1.

In section 2, a brief summary of postwar Japanese economic history is presented, including a description of the Japanese financial structure and of the four business cycles from 1953 to 1966. Section 3 discusses the mechanism by which central bank actions affect the money stock. In section 4, the behavioral relations which link income, money, international reserves, and imports are considered. Finally, in section 5, the underlying difference equation is analyzed and the effects of alternative monetary policy actions on the business cycle are considered. The study is closed with a summary and suggestions for future research.

2. The Japanese Economy, 1946–66

The postwar economic history of Japan can be separated into two periods: (1) an immediate postwar period of reconstruction and attainment of prewar levels of per capita output (1946–52), and (2) a later period of rapid but fluctuating growth in output and income (1953–66). In order to set the stage for a description of Japanese financial institutions and the business cycles which emerged in the latter period, it would be useful to review briefly the early postwar years.

A. economic reconstruction, 1946–52

From 1946 until 1952 Japan was in a period of reconstruction from the devastation suffered during World War II. At the beginning of 1946

Japan was a broken nation, with over 20 per cent of its capital stock destroyed, its people dispersed to the countryside, and its business organization in chaos.

A sudden termination of the war in August 1945 led to a drastic decline in industrial production to one-third of the 1944 level. As this reflected a termination of war production, it had little effect on the civilian population which had already experienced a sharp reduction in consumption in the last year of the war. The average level of production in 1946 was only about one-half of the 1945 level, as the effects of terminating war production continued to unwind and civilian production did not grow. Only a relatively good agricultural harvest in the summer of 1946 plus the massive infusion of food aid from the United States maintained consumption above starvation levels.

During 1947 industrial production hit its postwar trough and started to rise: by 22 per cent in that year, by 46 per cent in 1948, and by 30 per cent in 1949. In spite of these growth rates, however, industrial production in 1949 was only 71 per cent of the 1934–36 average. In this context economic recovery had not been impressive.

The decline in production in 1946 and the relatively slow recovery through 1949 can be attributed in part to the disorganized state of Japanese business and its inability to adjust to the new conditions of civilian production. A major factor in this disorganization was the maldistribution of resources due to a price inflation which averaged 247 per cent per year from 1945 to 1948. These increases were partially due to the elimination of price controls and thus reflected de jure the inflationary pressure built up in the last years of the war. The price increase from 1945 to 1946 was 365 per cent.

The price increases in 1946–48, which averaged 180 per cent per year, were due largely to the very easy monetary policy pursued by the early postwar government. On top of a tripling of the money stock in 1945,[5] the money stock grew at an average annual rate of 90 per cent in 1946

5. A major factor in the rise of the money stock in 1945 was the action of the Japanese government at the very end of the war. They paid off all of the long-term government debt in cash, doubling the money stock in one stroke. This is a very curious and perhaps unique experience in modern monetary history and would be worth further detailed investigation. It is curious in that the government thought that it was doing the bond holder a favor by substituting a non–interest-bearing note for an interest-bearing bond. Perhaps the government was afraid that the occupation authorities would repudiate the war debt and thus leave the bond holders with worthless pieces of paper. But even if this action protected the bond holders, it hurt the rest of the Japanese people by adding to price inflation and thereby leaving everyone with less valuable financial assets.

through 1948. The expansionary policy, which received the support and encouragement of the United States occupation authorities, was designed to channel resources into what the government considered high-priority basic industries necessary for reconstruction.[6]

In the latter part of 1948, increasing concern was expressed regarding the effects of rising prices on the distribution of resources and the possible adverse effect this was having on industrial recovery. This concern led to a major shift in monetary policy. Growth in the money stock was virtually stopped in 1949 largely because the government sector shifted from substantial deficit in 1948 to a moderate surplus in 1949. Rather surprisingly, this sudden shift in policy seems to have had only a moderately depressing effect on the growth in industrial production in 1949. Although prices increased by 60 per cent in 1949, the rate was only one-third of the two previous years. In 1950 the price rise slowed to 18 per cent.

Japan was fortunate in picking this time to put her financial house in order, because she was then able to take effective advantage of the great increase in export demand stemming from the Korean War which started in June 1950. By the middle of 1951 Japan was a major workshop and arsenal in direct support of United Nations troops in Korea. This favorable status resulted in substantial increases in exports. By 1952 this source was almost two-thirds the size of all other forms of exports combined. From the end of 1950 to the end of 1952 foreign exchange reserves increased 100 per cent, from $560 million to $1,138 million.

At the end of 1952 a formal peace treaty with Japan had been signed and the allied occupation was about to terminate (April 19, 1953). Industrial production was 126 per cent of the 1934–36 level, and per capita income was approaching its prewar peak. Traditional foreign markets were again opening up, prices had been stabilized, and some sense of confidence had been restored to the Japanese people.

With the end of the allied occupation, full control of the levers of economic policy-making was returned to Japanese hands. This is the most appropriate point at which to begin the analysis of Japanese business cycles.

The remainder of this section will consider briefly the institutional structure in which monetary policy operated, and will describe the four business cycles Japan experienced between 1953 and 1966.

6. Economic Stabilization Board, annual *Economic Survey of Japan,* 1951–52 (July 1952).

B. THE FINANCIAL STRUCTURE OF JAPAN

The institutional underpinning of Japan's financial structure is different from that of the United States and Western European countries. This difference is even deeper than can be presented in a simple quantitative framework. Japan is strongly influenced by the Oriental culture in which the role of the individual is subordinated to the role of the group in the decision-making process. Therefore, business transactions in Japan are substantially different than in the West. These quantitative and qualitative differences would seem to imply that the transmission mechanism by which changes in the financial sector lead to changes in the real sector would be different, and yet this does not seem to be the case. A major implication of this study is that the highly generalized statement of economic behavior embedded in the quantity theory of money is a useful tool of analyzing short-term fluctuations in income in a wide variety of institutional environments.

There are two important features to consider in the institutional structure of Japanese finance: (1) the dependence of the corporate business sector on the banking system for external financing, and (2) the dependence of the banking system on the central bank for reserves. Neither of these conditions is, of course, unique to Japan. What is unique is their extent and how they operate.

Corporate dependence on the banking system. The dependence of corporations on the banking system for a large share of their financing is due to the very rapid rate of growth in corporate investment which has outstripped the rate of growth in corporate profits and retained earnings. This forced corporations to rely heavily on external rather than internal sources of financing. The banking system is the major financial intermediary through which corporations borrow because of the underdeveloped structure of alternative markets.

By the standards of other industrialized nations (or Japan before World War II), the share of internal financing by Japanese business is quite small. Net worth is only one-third of total liabilities plus net worth. In the United States and Western Europe and in prewar Japan, net worth was about two-thirds of liabilities plus net worth.[7] Most of this external financing is done through the banking system.

7. Hugh T. Patrick, *Monetary Policy and Central Banking in Contemporary Japan* (Bombay: University of Bombay Press, 1962), p. 28. The description of Japanese financial institutions in this study draws heavily on Professor Patrick's work.

The immediate postwar chaos in the Japanese economy, combined with the allied occupation policy of destroying the prewar economic power centers which were believed to have contributed to the expansionist military policy, led to the destruction of the equity structure of the major segments of Japanese business. The inflation of the middle and late 1940s also wiped out most of the bonded debt of Japanese corporations.[8]

As a result, the corporate cash flow in the form of retained earnings and depreciation allowances was small relative to the need to finance corporate investment and meet liquidity needs. Corporations were forced to rely heavily on external sources of funds.

TABLE 1

Sources of Funds for Nonfinancial Corporations
(Share of Total)

	1953	1955	1957	1959	1961	1963
External sources......	.68	.61	.66	.66	.65	.68
Internal sources......	.32	.39	.34	.34	.35	.32
Retained profit.....	(.18)	(.18)	(.14)	(.15)	(.16)	(.12)
Dep. allowance.....	(.14)	(.21)	(.20)	(.19)	(.19)	(.20)

Source: Economic Planning Agency, Government of Japan.

Note: As demonstrated by Meiselman (1967), there are serious conceptual problems in the uses of flow of funds data in economic analysis because of the difficulty of arriving at meaningful gross flow data. Thus, tables 1 and 2 should be interpreted as only a very rough measure of the financing conditions of Japanese nonfinancial corporations.

Institutionally, domestic loans from commercial banks were the most important external source of financing. Alternative sources had not developed to sufficient size or flexibility to meet the financing needs of business. The bond market provided an insignificant 3 to 6 per cent of total external financing. It was badly hit by the early postwar inflation, and attempts at recovery were handicapped by government policy of pegging interest rates at a relatively low level. No effective device seems to have been developed to increase the real interest rate sufficiently to make bonds attractive to the investing public. Of the modest amount

8. When serious recovery started in 1948–49, many corporations had no real financial ties with the past, The only continuity was personal ties and a strong sense of identity with the organization. It is interesting to note that although many firms were forced to change their names as a part of the general occupation policy of breaking up the Zaibatsu structure, they reverted to something closely approximating their prewar names only a few months after the effective date of the Peace Treaty in April 1953.

issued, 80 to 90 per cent were purchased by the banking system.[9]

The stock market has grown rapidly since it was reopened in 1949, but it is a relatively expensive source of funds. Traditionally, new stock issues are offered at par value to old stockholders. As the market price is generally several times the par value, corporations consider that the effective annual interest cost of acquiring funds through stock issues is about 25 per cent. In addition, there are substantial tax advantages to acquiring funds by issuing debt rather than equity instruments. Thus, the incentives are great for corporations not to raise funds through the stock market.[10]

In the years just after the war, governmental financial institutions provided an important source of external funds to private corporations. However, over the period considered in this study there has been a steady decline in the importance of this source. Foreign borrowing is also a marginal source of funds. The banking system, on the average, provides two-thirds of the external funds to nonfinancial corporations. (See table 2.)

Dependence of the banking system on the central bank. In general, the loan policy of the banking system can be strongly influenced by central bank actions which affect bank reserves. This influence is enhanced in the case of Japan by the substantial and continuous debt of the banking system with the central bank. The natural sources of reserves for the banking system are from government deficits financed by the central bank and balance of payments surpluses. The banking system uses reserves to meet the demand for currency by the nonbanking public. In Japan, the natural sources of reserves have not been sufficient to meet this demand. The central bank had to meet this deficiency through extensions of central bank credit. From 1953 to 1966 the cumulative increase in central bank credit to the banking system was ¥1,969 billion ($5.5 billion). During the same period the cumulative

9. Since 1962, bonds of the largest corporations held by commercial banks have been eligible for discounting with the Bank of Japan.

10. In the late 1950s and early 1960s there was great interest on the part of the small investor in the stock market. The peak was reached in 1961 when investment trusts, which are purchased exclusively by small investors, received over $1.5 billion in new funds. In September 1961, the market broke and the price fell by more than one-third in less than a year. This collapse in stock prices brought to light the most flagrant form of market manipulations practiced by the security companies, which dominate the market and which are virtually free of supervision. There followed a massive decline in small-investor participation in the market, and investment trusts received only $140 million in new funds by 1963 and no new funds in 1964

TABLE 2

EXTERNAL SOURCES OF FUNDS FOR NONFINANCIAL CORPORATIONS
(Share of Total)

| | TOTAL (Billions of Yen) | PRIVATE DOMESTIC SOURCES | | | GOVERNMENT SOURCES | FOREIGN SOURCES |
		Banking System	Stock Market	Bond Market		
1953....	966	66	17	4	13	—
1954....	637	57	19	2	19	2
1955....	844	65	10	4	12	9
1956....	1,805	70	13	4	6	6
1957....	1,612	75	15	2	10	−2
1958....	1,729	71	12	5	9	4
1959....	2,418	65	14	6	8	7
1960....	3,631	64	14	9	6	7
1961....	4,236	61	22	4	6	6
1962....	5,090	73	14	2	6	4
1963....	5,831	71	11	3	6	8
*1964...	5,274	70	12	3	9	6

SOURCE: Economic Planning Agency, Government of Japan.
* Estimated.

increase in the reserves of the banking system was ¥525 billion ($1.4 billion).

The major device for extending Bank of Japan credit is through loans and discounts on commercial paper held by the banks. Starting in the fall of 1962, central bank credit was expanded to include what the Bank of Japan calls open-market operations. These operations do not differ substantially from loans and discounting of commercial paper except that the eligible instruments are long-term bonds rather than short-term bills and notes. In each open-market transaction the seller must agree to repurchase the bond at the option of the Bank of Japan. This option can be exercised only on certain stipulated dates, usually three months apart, and has substantially the same impact on commercial banks as discounting regular commercial paper with a ninety-day due date.

Because central bank loans and discounts and open-market operations are essentially identical instruments, they are treated here as one instrument and called central bank credit. Tools other than central bank credit are unimportant. Official reserve requirements have been applied since 1959, but they average only one-half of one per cent of deposits.[11]

11. The use of a single policy variable makes appraisal of central bank policy easier than if a variety of tools were utilized. With more than one central bank tool, one is faced with the important methodological difficulty which is generally referred to as the index number problem. For instance, how does one determine

The Bank of Japan did not regulate its credit extension to the banking system through the price mechanism. The discount rate plus penalty charges were the cheapest marginal sources of funds. Thus, a nonprice rationing technique called *madoguchi shido*, or window guidance, was used. The operational mechanism of window guidance has evolved over the years. Each commercial bank is given a ceiling beyond which it may not borrow from the central bank. The exact formula for determining the height of this ceiling is a well-kept secret of the Bank of Japan. However, according to Patrick (1962) who has closely investigated the institutional structure of Japanese monetary policy, it is generally geared to the amount of deposits held by each bank. There are only twelve major "city" banks which, under normal conditions, are allowed to borrow from the Bank of Japan.[12]

In the early years of window guidance, central bank credit in excess of ceiling amounts was made available to individual banks at a special penalty rate, and then only on the promise of the affected bank that it would restrict the growth of the loans outstanding. However, as these penalty rates were lower than the cost of alternative marginal sources of funds, the banking system was not discouraged from borrowing, and many of the promised reductions in bank loans were not realized. As the Bank of Japan seemed unwilling to make the penalty rate high enough to discourage borrowing, this technique was gradually reduced in importance and finally abolished in 1962. It was replaced by a system in which banks which requested central bank credit in excess of their ceiling allotment were told to meet their needs in the inter-bank call market. This market, which was quite small prior to 1955, grew to substantial proportions by 1961. Interest rates in the call market are highly sensitive to changes in demand. Peak interest rates in the call market reached 20 per cent per annum in 1957 and 1961 and 13 per cent

the relative importance of a 1 per cent change in the discount rate versus ¥100 billion change in open-market operations? When this problem arises, it is frequently necessary to construct an indirect test of central bank policy before appraising monetary actions. See Kareken and Solow, "Lags in Monetary Policy," p. 78.

12. Each of the "city" banks has a nation-wide system of branches, and all but two are headquartered in Tokyo. The fastest growing corporations are also headquartered in Tokyo and acquire most of their external financing from the city banks. There are 64 local banks which are restricted by law to doing business only with corporations in their prefectures. Thus, city banks have greater demand than supply of funds from deposits, while the local banks are in the opposite position. This creates the condition where city banks are not only the dominant borrowers from the Bank of Japan, but also major borrowers from the local bank through the call market.

in 1963. This expensive marginal source of funds put a more effective profit squeeze on the banking system than the central bank penalty interest rates, which never were more than 9.5 per cent.

Under this revised system, window guidance procedures also changed. Not only were commercial banks given a ceiling beyond which they could not borrow from the central bank; they were also given a ceiling beyond which they were asked not to extend loans, which was usually stated in the form of a fixed per cent increase in loans outstanding over some base period, for example, a 10 per cent increase over the same quarter in the previous year. Those banks which succeeded in maintaining their outstanding loans close to the target figures established by the Bank of Japan were allowed to replenish their reserve deficiencies from the relatively low-cost central bank credit. Those banks which exceeded their ceiling loan target were denied central bank credit and forced to meet their reserve needs from the high-cost call market.[13]

One of the costs of nonprice rationing of central bank credit was that the commercial banks which were more expansionist and innovating were unable to increase their share of the market. These banks were the first to approach their central bank borrowing ceilings and the first to exceed the central bank's suggested ceiling on new loan commitments to the public. Banks which were less expansionary and less innovating were less likely to exhaust their borrowing ceilings from the central bank and were less likely to exceed their suggested loan ceilings.

The Bank of Japan's window guidance techniques tended to keep the growth rates of the member banks relatively even with one another, irrespective of differences in management or efficiency. Table 3 illustrates this result. The twelve major city banks are listed in order of the size of their deposits as of March 31, 1956. The same ordering of banks was also true as of March 31, 1961, and March 31, 1965, the only exception being that bank number eight moved temporarily ahead of bank number seven in the March 31, 1961, observation. This stability in the ordering of Japan's major banks is probably a necessary condition for their acceptance of nonprice rationing of central bank credit. Whatever its inherent logic it is generally accepted that a fair rule for accepting nonprice rationing is that each participant maintains his same relative position in the group.

13. Many banks attempted to hide the fact that their loans exceeded the recommended ceiling. This was typically done by repayment of the loan on the statement day at the end of the month and re-loaning on the next day. These hidden loans were estimated to be over $500 million in early 1962.

TABLE 3

DEPOSITS OF JAPAN'S MAJOR CITY BANKS
(Billions of Yen)

	March 31, 1956		March 31, 1961		March 31, 1965	
Fuji............	319	(1)	745	(1)	1,354	(1)
Miysubishi......	302	(2)	712	(2)	1,311	(2)
Sanwa..........	286	(3)	686	(3)	1,288	(3)
Sumitomo.......	280	(4)	674	(4)	1,274	(4)
Tokai..........	203	(5)	486	(5)	1,029	(5)
Dai-Ichi........	187	(6)	457	(6)	914	(6)
Mitsui..........	184	(7)	433	(8)	846	(7)
Kangyo.........	181	(8)	435	(7)	829	(8)
Kyowa.........	156	(9)	318	(9)	592	(9)
Daiwa..........	130	(10)	308	(10)	555	(10)
Kobe..........	102	(11)	228	(11)	479	(11)
Hokhaido.......	91	(12)	187	(12)	353	(12)

SOURCE: *Economic Statistics of Japan*, 1965, Bank of Japan.

NOTE: Numbers in parentheses refer to cardinal ordering of banks in each period according to value of deposits.

C. CYCLICAL EXPERIENCE, 1953–66

Each of Japan's four cyclical declines in production was induced by restrictive government policy to correct a decline in international reserves. The Japanese authorities initially experimented with a variety of techniques for implementing this restrictive policy. In the first cycle they employed a wide range of small restrictions, hoping to prevent the effects from being concentrated in any one segment of the economy. Government spending was to be reduced by stretching out some programs and terminating others; special credit facilities to importers were eliminated, and the Bank of Japan initiated a form of rationing central bank credit to the banking system.

It soon became clear that planned restrictions in government spending could not be realized because of the intense political pressures for increased spending from inside the coalition of special interest groups which made up the party in power. For example, in the first restrictive period although government spending was planned to be reduced by 2 per cent, spending actually increased 17 per cent. In succeeding periods when restrictive actions were called for, no serious effort was made to restrict the increase in government spending or to increase taxes.

With most of the weight for restrictive actions imposed on monetary policy, the authorities gradually moved from emphasis on particular credit restrictions to generalized credit restrictions. In the early stages it was believed that if restrictions were needed to correct a deterioration in the balance of payments, then a policy which directly discouraged imports and encouraged exports would be the most useful. However, experience with such policies convinced the authorities that the only effective way to reduce imports and encourage exports was to impose generalized restrictions.[14]

Japan has not employed the orthodox monetary measures to achieve generalized credit restrictions. Reserve requirements did not exist in law or custom until 1959, and since then they have only been used moderately; open-market operations were unfeasible because the appropriate market structure did not exist, and the basic central bank discount rate was either not raised at all or not raised sufficiently to discourage the borrowing demands of the banking system.

The emergence of tight money occurred in substantially the same way in all four cycles. In the late boom phase of the cyclical upswing, the government's cash debt to the Bank of Japan was reduced as tax and other receipts exceeded government spending. At the same time, imports accelerated, causing international reserves to decline. Both of these actions tended to reduce the reserves of the banking system, causing them to increase their borrowings from the central bank. Precisely at the time when the central bank was considering the need to impose restrictive monetary policy because of a decline in international reserves, the amount of central bank credit was growing faster than at times when restrictive monetary policy was not being considered. Tight money policy consisted of insuring that the increase in central bank credit was not sufficient to offset completely the reserve losses of the banking system from government surpluses and balance-of-payments deficits.

This set of circumstances made it politically easier for the authorities to implement a restrictive monetary policy. The initial loss of reserves of the banking system did not come from any overt action of the monetary authorities. As a matter of fact, the authorities permitted a substantial increase in central bank credit to ease the reserve loss. This kept the monetary authorities in a strong position to implement

14. The commitment to general rather than particular credit restrictions did not prevent the authorities from attempting to shield certain preferred industries from the effects of the credit restrictions. Basic industries, such as iron and steel whose long-term growth was considered an important national goal, were supposed to receive sufficient funds to insure that their investment plans were not curtailed. There is, however, little evidence to indicate that the preferred industries were any less adversely affected by tight money than was industry as a whole.

effective restrictions through the window guidance technique, while at the same time appearing to be quite generous in providing credit to the banking system. Therefore the monetary authorities were able to follow a restrictive policy even when the political authorities were not completely in favor of it.

First cycle, 1953–56.[15] Japan entered 1953 with abundant foreign exchange reserves and an optimistic business community eager to modernize its plant and equipment. Investment in fixed capital was 21 per cent larger in 1953 than in 1952, which had also been a year of rapid growth in investment. In addition, consumer spending increased 20 per cent as the fruits of the first postwar wave of prosperity were enjoyed by the individual Japanese household. Although the overall increase in nominal demand was 15 per cent, the increase in output was less than 8 per cent. Consequently, prices increased 7.5 per cent, and imports increased 21 per cent. Because of the termination of the Korean War, exports showed no increase. The current account of the balance of payments deteriorated $500 million and, because capital movements were insignificant, there was a similar deterioration in international reserves.

In this first postwar balance-of-payments problem the authorities planned moderately restrictive fiscal and monetary policies. The general account budget expenditures for 1954 were planned to be 2.5 per cent below 1953. But, because of pressures from within the Liberal Democratic Party, which was in power throughout this period, spending actually increased 17 per cent over 1953. The result was a relatively large cash deficit.

With respect to monetary policy, there was no increase in the central bank discount rate because of fear that higher interest costs would weaken the competitive position of Japanese exporters.[16] Other monetary actions were taken. The special credit facilities available to importers since the Korean War period were terminated; in addition, importers were required to make advance deposits with commercial

15. Most business cycle analysts date turning points on the basis of the peaks and troughs in the *level* of business activity. However, because this study concentrates on rates of change, the timing of each cycle is based on peaks and troughs in the rate of change of business activity. As would be expected, turning points in the level of business activity generally occur after turning points in the rate of change in business activity because a deceleration generally occurs before a decline.

16. Patrick, *Monetary Policy and Central Banking*, p. 270.

banks at the time the import contracts were signed. Finally, the Bank of Japan initiated window guidance (*madoguchi shido*), a form of credit rationing discussed above.

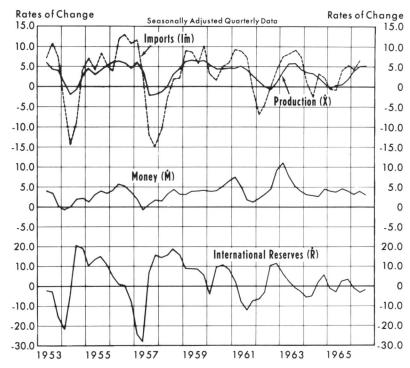

CHART 1. Japan: International reserves, money, production, and imports
SOURCE: Bank of Japan.

These money and credit restrictions were initially imposed in September 1953, and gradually tightened and expanded until they were fully in effect by April 1954. The effects of this policy were felt quickly as the money stock stopped growing in the fourth quarter of 1953 and declined slightly in the first and second quarters of 1954. This had a prompt effect on industrial production and imports; they both stopped growing in the first quarter of 1954 and declined in the second and third quarters. Exports in 1954, responding to a cyclical upswing in the United States and to some dismantling of import controls in Europe, increased at an 8 per cent rate. The sharp decline in imports and the resumption of normal growth in exports permitted international reserves to recover rapidly from the second half of 1954. This improvement continued through the end of 1955.

Second cycle, 1956–58. Starting in the second quarter of 1956, the quarterly growth in imports more than doubled from the average of the previous six quarters because continued growth in industrial production in excess of 5 per cent per quarter required an accelerated use of imported materials. The acceleration in imports caused international reserves to decelerate in the first three quarters of 1956 and to decline sharply in the fourth quarter.

The decline in international reserves triggered a debate within the Japanese government as to whether policy should become restrictive. One group in the ministry of finance insisted that a tight policy was not necessary.[17] It considered that the increase in imports was mainly due to speculative materials imports and that foreign exchange was simply being turned into industrial materials inventories. Their policy prescription was to wait out the speculators, and import demand would soon decline to a more normal level.

Another group in the Bank of Japan contended that the increase in imports was induced by the high level of domestic demand and would continue as long as demand was not curtailed.[18]

In public, the politically more powerful ministry of finance group had apparently won the debate, as no official monetary restrictions were introduced in late 1956 or early 1957. Moreover, a government budget calling for a large increase in spending passed the Diet (parliament) in early 1957. But later events did not support the contentions of the winning group. During the first half of 1957 international reserves declined 55 per cent because of a continued sharp rise in imports. By early May, it was obvious that corrective steps had to be taken immediately.

The discount rate was increased on May 8 from 7.67 to 8.40, and window-guidance procedures originally developed in the first cycle were again applied. No selective credit controls were used, and there was no increase in tariffs or other particular restrictions on imports. However,

17. See Osamu Shimomura, "Tomen no Keizai Kyokumen o Tsuranuku Kihon Dōkō." (The Fundamental Tendencies of the Immediate Economic Situation), *Kinyū Zaisei Jijō*, vol. 8 (February 11 and 18, 1957.)

18. See Yonosuke Goto, "Keiki Dōkō to Junkan Kyokumen no Rikai no tame ni" (Understanding the Tendency of Economic Activity and the Business Cycle), *Kinyū Zaisei Jijō*, vol. 8 (February 25, March 4, 1957).

more preferential treatment was given to exporters with a reduction in the central bank rate on export bills.

Although the Bank of Japan seemed to have lost the policy fight, in fact the money stock had started to decelerate three quarters before the public announcement of tight money and had reached its trough in the second quarter of 1957, when the tight money policy was officially announced. Government cash surpluses and balance-of-payments deficits had drained reserves out of the banking system. The Bank of Japan had been able to take appropriate monetary action even in the face of a publicly stated rejection of tight money policy.

The effects of the monetary restraints were felt promptly. The rate of growth in industrial production and imports reached its cyclical peak in the first quarter of 1957, decelerated moderately in the second quarter, and fell in absolute amount in the third and fourth quarters. An impressive turnaround in international reserves followed, from a 28 per cent decline in the second quarter of 1957 to an 8 per cent increase in the third quarter, and to a 15 per cent increase in the fourth quarter. The growth in international reserves continued at a very rapid rate through 1958 and at a decelerated rate into 1960.

Third cycle, 1958–62. In the period from 1958 to 1961 Japan enjoyed the most rapid growth in her history, perhaps the most rapid growth any country had ever experienced. Real output increased at an average annual rate of 14 per cent, while prices increased at a rate of only 3 per cent. This experience affected the outlook of the Japanese businessmen, who became very optimistic about the future.

The policy authorities were also caught up in this optimistic mood. Some believed that their major contribution to stimulating growth was to provide an easy monetary and fiscal environment. The political leader most thoroughly committed to this point of view was Mr. Hayato Ikeda, who had been finance minister during the 1957–58 cycle. The Ikeda group was brought into power in July 1960 because of a political incident. In the summer of 1960 there were massive student riots against the Japanese–United States Military Security Treaty and the visit of President Eisenhower to Japan. Because the government of Prime Minister Kishi could not control the rioters or guarantee the safety of the president, the visit was cancelled, resulting in the downfall of the Kishi government.

Because Prime Minister Kishi's main mistakes were considered to have been an overly aggressive foreign policy and a domestic policy of riding roughshod over the opposition Socialist Party, it was deemed advisable to bring in a new face who would take a "low posture" on these sensitive political issues.[19] Ikeda was made prime minister in July 1960 on this basis. His interests were largely economic; indeed, he considered himself an economist, and took an active interest in the implementation of monetary policy. In the spring of 1961 he presented a plan to the public which was designed to double national income in one decade, 1960–70.

To implement this plan, Ikeda intended to follow an expansionist monetary policy. As indicated in table 4, during the four-year period

TABLE 4

COMPARISON OF IKEDA AND PRE-IKEDA PERIODS

Per Cent Change in	1956-III to 1960-III	1960-III to 1964-III
Money......................	60	120
Industrial Production.......	70	70
Consumer price index.......	5	26
Import value..............	37	65
Export value..............	66	63
International reserves.......	72	−10
Employment...............	6	5

NOTE: The beginning and terminal dates for each period were all in the late boom phase of the business cycle.

of the Ikeda administration the money stock increased at a rate twice as fast as in the previous four-year period. On the other hand, industrial production and employment increased at the same rate, while prices rose five times faster and imports rose almost twice as fast. Exports increased at the same rate in both periods. The expansionary Ikeda policies did not increase the rate of real growth but only added to price inflation and balance of payments problems.

Ikeda initiated an expansionary policy as soon as he came into office. The rate of growth of the money stock, which had been at an average quarterly rate of about 4 per cent from the middle of 1958 to the middle of 1960, increased to 5.5 per cent in the third quarter of 1960, 7 per cent in the fourth quarter, and 7.5 per cent in the first quarter of 1961. The acceleration in the money stock led to an increase in aggregate demand, causing imports to accelerate and breaking the price stability which had characterized the Japanese economy since 1954.

19. "Low posture" is a direct translation of the Japanese phrase which conveyed the intention not to take political actions which would trigger strong opposition.

International reserves decelerated in the first quarter of 1961 and fell during the next five quarters. As in the previous cycle, a public debate ensued between the Bank of Japan which proposed a policy of restraint, and the ministry of finance which proposed a policy of continued expansion. Publicly the issue was again settled in favor of the ministry of finance.

The stated policy of the Bank of Japan remained expansionary. The discount rate, which was acknowledged as the official expression of policy, was reduced in August 1960 and again in January 1961. Only towards the end of July 1961, when international reserves had declined by nearly 20 per cent in six months in spite of a large short-term capital inflow, did the Ikeda administration introduce a tight monetary policy.

On July 22 the discount rate was raised from 6.57 to 6.94, and window-guidance procedures reinstituted. On September 29 the discount rate was raised again to 7.30 and the window-guidance procedures tightened. However, as in the 1957–58 downturn, the deceleration in the money stock actually started earlier. Growth in the money stock reached a peak in the first quarter of 1961 and decelerated rapidly through the fourth quarter of 1961.

The deceleration in the money stock was followed by a deceleration in production and imports starting in the third quarter of 1961. However, the rate of deceleration in production was slower than in the two previous downturns. The business community was aware that the tight-money policy was in response to balance-of-payments considerations and would be eased when international reserves started to recover. Past experience had taught them that if they maintained their investment projects through the period of tight money, they would be in better position to take advantage of new and profitable sales opportunities when monetary policy was eased. Thus, a great deal of private effort was put into reducing imports rather than production.

International reserves showed gradual improvement from late 1961; the money stock accelerated moderately during the first three quarters of 1962 and accelerated rapidly in late 1962 and early 1963.

Fourth cycle, 1962–66. The deceleration in production which took place in 1962 was moderate compared with previous downturns. As a result, the margin of unused capacity created was also smaller than in previous downturns. When the growth in production was resumed in the fourth quarter of 1962, the margin of unused capacity was quickly eliminated. This led to the emergence of domestic bottlenecks in certain sectors of the Japanese economy and caused a sharper acceleration in imports in

1963 than had taken place in previous periods of early cyclical upswing. The acceleration in imports pushed the current account into deficit in 1963, even with strong growth in exports. A large short-term capital inflow was not sufficient to prevent international reserves from declining moderately ir the last half of 1963.

In reaction to this deceleration in international reserves, the money stock was gradually decelerated from the high levels reached in the first half of 1963 to a growth rate of about 3.5 per cent in the middle of 1964. By previous cyclical standards, such a growth in the money stock would have been consistent with moderately expansionary monetary policy. However, rising prices had induced an increase in the transactions demand for money which absorbed the 3.5 per cent rate of growth in nominal cash balances. Thus production also decelerated slowly through early 1965.

Given the large growth in exports which was taking place in 1963 and 1964, it was apparently the hope of the government that only a moderately restrictive monetary policy would correct the decline in international reserves. This expectation proved correct. By the third quarter of 1964 international reserves started to increase. As in previous cycles, this was the signal to end tight mon⌃y.

In November 1964, Ikeda resigned as prime minister for health reasons. He left the Japanese business community in what was generally referred to as a "recession mood." It was called a mood because the aggregate economic data indicated that this downturn had been much smaller and more gradual than previous cyclical downturns. And yet the optimism of the business community about the future had been impaired, as reflected in the statistics on new investment which did not show the prompt recovery that had been true of previous periods of monetary ease.

Prior to the fourth cycle, Japanese businessmen had enjoyed three to four years of prosperous growth in sales and profits between periods of tight money. Such a spacing of cyclical downturns allowed businesses to pass through a period of tight money with no impairment of their view of real long-term growth prospects. The Japanese business practice of increasing capacity in excess of short-term expectations of increase in sales had paid off handsomely in these cycles. Even though the fourth cyclical decline in production was relatively moderate, profits had not recovered and inventories had not been worked down from the third cycle just two years before.[20]

20. There were two reasons for the rise in inventories. First, the optimism of businessmen that the rise in inventories would only be temporary, as was the

The new prime minister, Mr. Eisaku Sato, was faced with a serious economic policy dilemma. Should the government take drastic and immediate monetary and fiscal actions which would be necessary to turn the economy around quickly in the face of the "recession mood," or should the government follow a less expansionary policy which might provide a more stable growth in production. The Sato administration chose the latter policy, holding the average quarterly growth in the money stock to around 4 per cent during 1965 and 1966.[21]

Although the recovery in production was somewhat slower than in previous cyclical upswings, problems with the balance of payments were avoided, permitting growth in production to be sustained for a longer period.

3. Central Bank Actions and Monetary Policy

This section will consider two questions. First, the link between the monetary policy variable (money stock) and the monetary target variable (international reserves), and second, how central bank actions affect the money stock. The latter can be broken down into two subsidiary questions. How does central bank action affect high-powered money, and how does high-powered money affect the money stock?

A. MONETARY POLICY AND MONETARY TARGETS

In the late nineteenth century, most advanced monetary systems were on a gold standard. This meant that gold coins and warehouse receipts for gold bars circulated freely with domestically issued paper to form the basis for the money stock. Because gold was also the international medium of exchange, the money stock was automatically

---

case in previous cycles. Second, given the lifetime employment tradition in Japan, the permanent production workers are not laid off unless there is a permanent reduction in the work force.

21. The major factor in the moderate monetary response was to avoid the expansionist excesses of the previous administration. However, a secondary factor was that international reserves showed no consistent growth in 1965 and 1966. Although the current account registered a large surplus because of a moderate growth in imports and very rapid growth in exports, there was a large capital outflow. The easing of monetary policy and the weakness in business investment pushed Japanese interest rates down just at a time when rates were rising to new historic highs in the United States and money was generally tight in Europe. This caused a substantial shift in trade financing from foreign to domestic sources and made Euro-dollars a less attractive source of funds to Japanese banks. At the same time, the U.S. interest equalization tax (July 1963) and the president's "voluntary" program to support the United States balance of payments (February 1965) reduced the long-term capital in flow.

linked to the balance of payments and to the level and rate of change in international reserves. A balance-of-payments deficit meant a decline in international reserves, an outflow of gold, and a decline in the domestic money stock. A balance-of-payments surplus meant an increase in international reserves, an inflow of gold, and an increase in the domestic money stock.

This automatic link between money and international reserves is now considered broken because gold is no longer a component of the domestic money stock.[22] The monetary authorities have the ability to achieve any desired money stock through expansion and contraction of central bank credit. With the automatic link between international reserves and money broken, the monetary authorities can direct monetary policy toward achieving any monetary target variable they desire, such as a target level of prices, unemployment, or international reserves.

The most generalized method of presenting the link between a target variable and a policy variable is in a stock adjustment mechanism. It is generally recognized that Japanese monetary policy is sensitive to changes in international reserves.[23] If the target level of international reserves is different from the actual level of international reserves, then monetary policy will be adjusted accordingly. If the actual level is less than the target level, policy will be restrictive. If the actual level is greater than the target level, policy will be easy. The stock adjustment mechanism is consistent with a wide range of observed behavior. For example, an acceleration in international reserves could be associated with a restrictive policy if the level of reserves is below the target, while a deceleration in international reserves could be associated with an expansionary policy if the level of reserves is above the target.

The observed behavior of the Japanese monetary authorities is that when international reserves decline, monetary policy in the form of

22. Domestic gold stocks may affect the supply of money even if they are not directly measured in the stock of money. If the central bank must hold a certain stock of gold as a reserve against central bank notes or deposits outstanding, an outflow of gold could theoretically affect the domestic money supply. However, in Japan, central bank notes are backed by full faith and credit of the government and not by gold or any other internationally liquid assets. Only Belgium, The Netherlands, and Switzerland have a legal requirement for gold backing to control central bank note issue. The United States ceased its gold backing on March 15, 1968.

23. See Hugh T. Patrick, *Monetary Policy and Central Banking*, p. 24; Miyoshi Shinohara, *Growth and Cycles in the Japanese Economy* (Tokyo: Kenkyusha Printing Co., 1962); *Money and Banking in Japan* (Research Department, Bank of Japan, 1964), p. 51.

chang€s in the money stock is restrictive, and when international reserves increase, monetary policy is expansionary. This behavior is consistent with a specific form of the international reserve target which says that if international reserves are falling, the target level is greater than the actual level of reserves. If international reserves are rising, the target level is equal to the actual level of reserves.

The monetary authorities are sensitive to changes in international reserves because of the relatively low level of international reserves held by Japan and the rapidity with which these reserves can be drawn down during periods of balance-of-payments difficulties. The ratio of international reserves (gold plus convertible currencies) to imports has fallen from one-third in 1954 to one-fourth in 1964 and to one-fifth in 1966. The ratio of international reserves to imports of the European Economic Community (Common Market) countries, which Japan resembles in terms of industrial development and absence of reserve currency status, has increased from 41 per cent in 1954 to 44 per cent in 1966. The rate of growth in Japanese reserves from 1954 to 1964 has been about 60 per cent of the rate of growth in imports. For common market countries the rate of growth in reserves has been close to 110 per cent of the rate of growth in imports.[24]

The cost of this slow growth in international reserves is the large potential decline in reserves in a short period of time. In the first two periods of balance-of-payments weakness, Japan's reserves declined 40 per cent and 55 per cent in six months. In the last two periods reserves declined 35 per cent and 15 per cent in nine months.[25]

The observed policy relations between changes in the money stock and changes in international reserves can be stated as follows:

$$\dot{M}_t = \beta_0 + \beta_1 \dot{R}_{t-n}. \tag{6}$$

An increase in $\dot{R}$ will lead to an increase in $\dot{M}$, and conversely a decrease in $\dot{R}$ will lead to a decrease in M. The only difference between this

24. See *International Financial Statistics*, February 1967, published by the International Monetary Fund.

25. Japan had a relatively modest decline in reserves during the last two periods because she was able to tap the international short-term capital market to a significant extent. The absolute size of Japan's current account deficit was actually much larger in 1964 than in 1954. Although the inflow of short-term capital had increased the apparent stability of the official international reserves position in the third and fourth cycle, it had also increased claims against these reserves. For example, Euro-dollar deposits in Japanese commercial banks (which have an average maturity of 45 days) were about $150 million at the end of 1960 and about $1,250 million at the end of 1964.

hypothesis and others which attempt to explain economic behavior is that there is only one decision-making unit in this case, which is generally and vaguely referred to as the "monetary authorities."

Although the monetary authorities are sensitive to changes in international reserves, the degree of sensitivity varies, depending upon the importance which they attach to other goals. Japanese monetary policy can be divided into two subperiods on the basis of differing sensitivity to changes in international reserves; the first period from 1953 to the middle of 1960, and the second period from 1960 to the end of 1964.

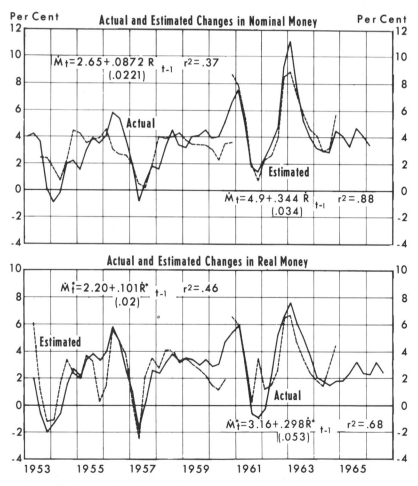

CHART 2. Japan: Actual and estimated changes in nominal money; actual and estimated changes in real money.

Monetary policy in 1965 and 1966 was essentially a reversion to the first period.

There were three prime ministers during the first period: Mr. Yoshida, Mr. Ishibashi, and Mr. Kishi. None of these men had any immediate interest in the day-to-day operation of monetary policy, leaving most decisions to the finance minister, the planning agency director, and the central bank governor. Thus, policy during most of this period was conducted by a committee with no strong personality dominating the decision-making process. Although individual members of this ad hoc committee changed during the period, the collective nature of the decision-making process kept policy relatively uniform in terms of the international reserve constraint.

In July 1960, Mr. Kishi was forced to resign and Mr. Ikeda (finance minister on two former occasions) was made prime minister. Ikeda took over the day-to-day direction of economic policy and the committee approach to policy formulations was abandoned.[26] In an attempt to accelerate the growth in the Japanese economy, Mr. Ikeda initiated a substantially more expansionist monetary policy than did his predecessors. This policy continued over four years until Mr. Ikeda resigned in November 1964.

The increased emphasis on growth during the Ikeda period did not mean that the international reserve constraint was ignored. It meant that the policy coefficients relating changes in international reserves to changes in the money stock were different in these two subperiods. To determine the value of the coefficients, regressions were run on the money and international reserve time series for each subperiod:[27]

26. There are no parliamentary obstacles to the prime minister's controlling the levers of monetary policy if he wishes. The Japanese cabinet is structurally similar to the United Kingdom parliamentary ministerial system. The prime minister appoints the minister of finance and the director of the Economic Planning Agency. The governor of the Bank of Japan is accountable to the minister of finance and can be removed at the discretion of the finance minister. Although this has never been done, it is a powerful potential threat.

27. A statistical test of the relationship between two variables where only one decision-making unit is involved may have greater systematic variation between observed and estimated values of the dependent variable than when a large number of decision-making units are involved. For example, the estimated movement in $\dot{M}$ was greater than the observed movement in late 1954 and early 1955, and less than the observed movement in late 1956. These discrepancies between observed and actual movements in $\dot{M}$ are not as apparent when the decision-making unit looks at real rather than nominal variables.

Subperiod 1953-II to 1960-IV [28]

$$\dot{M}_t = 2.65 + .087\dot{R}_{t-1}, \qquad r^2 = .37. \tag{7}$$
$$(.022)$$

Subperiod 1960-IV to 1964-IV:

$$\dot{M}_t = 4.9 + .344\dot{R}_{t-1}, \qquad r^2 = .88. \tag{8}$$
$$(.034)$$

These two equations illustrate the wide range of discretionary monetary policies which can be accommodated within an international reserves constraint in the short run.[29] With no change in the reserve level, monetary policy in the second period was almost twice as expansionary as in the first period (4.9 per cent per quarter versus 2.6 per cent per quarter). For every 10 per cent acceleration in international reserves, there was a 3.4 per cent acceleration in the money stock during the expansionary subperiod and a .9 per cent acceleration in the money stock in the nonexpansionary subperiod. Conversely, deceleration in international reserves led to a sharper deceleration in the money stock in the expansionary subperiod than in the nonexpansionary subperiod. Given Japan's slim foreign exchange reserves, this pattern of behavior is reasonable. A monetary policy which, on the average, is more expansionist must also be more sensitive to declines in international reserves. Whether an expansionary policy with such implications for $\dot{M}$ is desirable will be considered explicitly in section 5.

This study considers real as well as nominal business-cycle move-

28. The lags reported here and in the rest of this study are of the single non-distributed type. Alternative lags were tested and the one with the lowest standard error and highest r^2 was used. This procedure was used whenever lagged relationships were tested statistically.

29. During the last half of 1960 and the first half of 1961, neither equation (7) nor (8) provides an accurate estimate of the actual changes in money. This period can be considered a transition from a less to a more expansionary monetary policy. As a result, (7), my policy equation for pre-Ikeda years, underestimates the growth in this period, while (8), the policy equation for the Ikeda period, overestimates changes in money in this period. This pattern is quite reasonable and reminds us that great caution must be used in applying policy equations in the early period of any new political administration. The Sato administration, which came into power in November 1964, abandoned the expansionist monetary policies of its predecessor. In the first five full quarters of the Sato administration the actual stock of money increased 20 per cent, while the growth in the money stock using the Ikeda policy equation would have been 27 per cent. The growth in money, using the pre-Ikeda policy equation, would have been 13 per cent. Before a realistic policy equation can be established for this new administration, it will probably be necessary to observe one cyclical decline in reserves.

ments; therefore, a structural equation relating real money stock to real reserves was also estimated. The money series was deflated by the implicit price deflator, and international reserves by the import price index:

Subperiod 1953-II to 1960-IV:

$$\dot{M}_t^* = 2.20 + .101\dot{R}_{t-1}^*, \qquad r^2 = .46.$$
$$(.020)$$

Subperiod 1960-IV to 1964-IV:

$$\dot{M}_t^* = 3.16 + .298\dot{R}_{t+1}^*, \qquad r^2 = .68.$$
$$(.053)$$

These results are substantially the same as above. The results are statistically significant and the values of the coefficients are larger in the expansionary subperiod than in the nonexpansionary subperiod.

B. CENTRAL BANK ACTIONS AND MONETARY POLICY VARIABLES

The central bank does not have direct control of the money stock; it can only vary the volume or price at which it extends credit to the banking system. The central bank is in a position similar to that of a monopolist because it can control the price and allow the quantity to vary, or it can control the quantity and allow the price to vary. The comparison is not exact, of course, because a monopolist is a profit maximizer and a central bank is not.

If the central bank wants to control the amount of credit it extends to the banking system, it has essentially two choices: (1) it can price its credit facilities at the rate which will keep commercial bank demand for this credit at the level desired by the central bank; or (2) it can allow the price of central bank credit to remain unchanged and ration the quantity directly. The advantage of the first approach is that rationing is done by market forces like most other commodities and keeps the central bank out of a difficult administrative process. The advantage of the second approach is that if the short-run demand for central bank credit is price inelastic, then a very high interest rate to ration credit by the price mechanism is avoided.

Traditionally, central banks have been unwilling to suffer the public criticism associated with high rates and have chosen nonprice rationing of their credit. Thus, the best measure of central bank action is the volume of credit extended rather than the price at which it is extended.

This generalization applies to Japan. The Bank of Japan has a penalty rate on top of its basic discount rate which is applied to those commercial banks which exceed their designated borrowing ceilings. Because most banks are above the ceiling during periods of tight money, the penalty rate is the operational rate. When the penalty rate is compared with the closest alternative market rate of interest, it is always lower. This differential widens during periods of tight money. Interest rates for call money have gone as high as 20 per cent, while the highest central bank penalty rate has been 9.5 per cent. Nonprice rationing of credit is the major monetary tool of the Bank of Japan.

To understand the effect of changes in central bank credit on the money stock requires consideration of the links which connect these two variables. One can do this by utilizing the analytical technique developed by Friedman and Schwartz.[30]

The money stock is defined as:

$$M = C + D, \tag{9}$$

where

M = Money stock,
D = Designated monetary deposits of the banking system,[31]

and

C = Currency in the hands of the public.

High-powered money is defined in two ways. The uses of high-powered money are:

$$H = C + BR, \tag{10}$$

where

H = High-powered money,

and

BR = Reserves of the banking system.

30. Milton Friedman and Anna Schwartz, *A Monetary History of the United States, 1867–1960* (National Bureau of Economic Research, 1964), Appendix B, pp. 776–808.

31. This is drawn from the money supply statistics of the Bank of Japan. Throughout this study references are made to the banking system when in fact other financial intermediaries such as agricultural cooperatives, mutual loan and savings banks, and credit associations also hold monetary deposits. This is done for simplicity in explanation and because commercial banks hold 80–85 per cent of all monetary deposits. These deposits include current deposits, ordinary deposits, deposits at notice, and special deposits. The only one against which checks can be drawn is current deposits. Other deposits pay interest and are similar to passbook savings in the United States. What the Bank of Japan calls time and savings deposits are excluded from the money supply. These are fixed maturity deposits similar to certificates of deposits (CD's) in the United States. Thus, the Japanese money stock concept is closer to M_2 than M_1. See *Money and Banking in Japan*, pp. 52–53.

The sources of high-powered money are:

$$H = B + R + G, \tag{11}$$

where

$B =$ Central bank credit to the banking system,

$R =$ International reserves,

and

$G =$ Government debt to the central bank.[32]

The money identity can be written in terms of high-powered money and a money multiplier based on the deposit-currency ratio, D/C, and the deposit-reserve ratio, D/BR:

$$M = H\left(\frac{D}{BR}\right)\left[\frac{1 + \dfrac{D}{C}}{\dfrac{D}{BR} + \dfrac{D}{C}}\right]. \tag{12}$$

Alternatively, the money identity can be written in terms of the sources of high-powered money, including central bank credit, and the money multiplier:

$$M = (B + R + G)\left(\frac{D}{BR}\right)\left[\frac{1 + \dfrac{D}{C}}{\dfrac{D}{BR} + \dfrac{D}{C}}\right]. \tag{13}$$

The central bank can only control B directly. The other influences on the money stock are determined by other decision-making units: R largely depends upon the decision of exporters and importers; G depends upon the fiscal policy decisions of the ministry of finance and the government; the deposit-currency ratio, D/C, depends upon the decision of the nonbank public with respect to the desired composition of their money holdings; the deposit-reserve ratio, D/BR, depends upon the desire of the banking system for excess reserves. It is useful to analyze the linkages between B and M in two stages: first, the link between B and H, and second, the link between H and M.

32. The Bank of Japan is the sole custodian of central government cash and supplier of credit to the government. Government receipts, including receipts for sales of bonds and notes to the public, less government payments to the public, are disposed of by changes in the government's current account with the Bank of Japan. An increase in this account is an increase in high-powered money, and a decrease in this account is a decrease in high-powered money. These transactions between the government and the Bank of Japan are in addition to those related to purchases and sales of international reserves. See *Money and Banking in Japan*, pp. 56–57.

The relation between B and H. The amount of high-powered money in circulation can be found in the balance sheet of the central bank. The uses are central bank notes and deposits of the banking system which are liabilities of the Bank of Japan.[33] The sources are found on the asset side of the balance sheet: central bank credit to the banking system, central bank credit to the government, and central bank holdings of foreign exchange.[34]

High-powered money in the form of currency reaches the nonbank public through the banking system. This is accomplished through the public's drawdown of deposits with the banking system. The banks maintain working balances of vault cash to meet the expected demands of the nonbank public for currency. These working balances must be restored continuously by acquisitions of additional central bank notes from the Bank of Japan. For the banking system as a whole, central bank notes can be acquired in only three ways: (1) selling foreign exchange to the central bank, which can only be generated by a surplus in the balance of payments;[35] (2) presenting a draft on the government's account with the Bank of Japan, which can be generated only by a government cash deficit; (3) borrowing from the Bank of Japan.

All increases in high-powered money, whether it stays in the banks or in the hands of the nonbank public, affect the balance sheet of the banking system. The first two sources of high-powered money reduce other assets of the banking system because foreign exchange assets and claims on the government are converted into high-powered money assets; the third source of high-powered money increases the banking system's liabilities by increasing the debt to the Bank of Japan.

An important institutional question with respect to the operation of monetary policy is whether the banking system responds differently to

33. Deposits of the banking system with the Bank of Japan are an insignificant use of high-powered money. Reserve requirements have existed in law since 1957 and have only been applied to banks since 1959. The range is from 0.25 per cent for banks with deposits of less than ¥20 billion, to 1.5 per cent for banks with deposits in excess of ¥100 billion. Total deposits of the banking system with the Bank of Japan were ¥89 billion as of December 31, 1966. On that same date central bank note issue was ¥2,914 billion, of which ¥477 billion was in the vaults of the banking system.

34. Another source of high-powered money is subsidiary coins issued by the treasury. However, the amount is trivial, adding less than 2 per cent to the value of central bank notes. Subsidiary coins are included with central bank notes in this study.

35. This assumes that commercial banks do not change their working balances of foreign exchange.

an increase in its liabilities than it does to a decrease in its other assets. This same issue arises in international financial discussions about the characteristics of a new international reserve asset; should it be in the form of borrowed reserves through the IMF which must theoretically be repaid, or in the form of owned reserves for which repayment is not even theoretically required? This issue also arises in financial discussions in the United States about whether federal reserve credit extended through the discount window is less expansionary than when extended through open market purchases of government securities. Some authors consider that United States commercial banks prefer to build their reserves on the sale of assets rather than on the basis of debt to the federal reserve system. It is postulated that American banks will reduce loans and take other restrictive actions to clear themselves of debt to the federal reserve as soon as possible.

In the case of Japan, virtually all central bank credit is in the form of direct increases in the debt of the banking system.[36] If Japanese banks treat such debt in the same way as American banks are postulated to treat borrowings from the federal reserve, it is quite possible that central bank credit would be a less expansionary source of high-powered money than, for example, sales of international reserves. However, the institutional factors surrounding central bank borrowing in Japan are different from those in the United States. The Bank of Japan, as a long-term policy, must increase the amount of credit provided to the banking system, because alternative sources of high-

TABLE 5

SOURCES OF HIGH-POWERED MONEY, 1953–66
(Billions of Yen)

	Cumulative Increase
High-powered money................	2,455
International reserves...............	432
Government debt to central bank.....	700
Other*...........................	−646
Central bank credit to banking system .	1,969

SOURCE: Bank of Japan, *Economic Statistics*, 1966.
* Mostly profits of the Bank of Japan.

36. It is interesting to note, however, that small prefectural banks in Japan do have a traditional reluctance to borrow from the central bank. This is because small banks as a whole are not subject to the same intense reserve pressures as the large city banks. Those small prefectural banks which do attempt to borrow are considered to have poor management policies.

powered money are not sufficient to meet demand, as illustrated in table 5. Only half of the growth in high-powered money between 1953 and 1966 was from international and government sources. The remainder was in the form of Bank of Japan credit to the private banking system.

Open-market transactions as a technique to extend central bank credit have not been used in Japan because the appropriate short-term financial markets have not been developed. As a result, the large commercial banks are constantly in direct and substantial debt to the central bank. The reluctance of the American commercial banker to be in debt to the federal reserve is not found among the managers of large Japanese commercial banks.[37] Central bank credit extended through the discount window is as expansionary a source of high-powered money as any other source. This is an important consideration, because it allows one to treat high-powered money as a homogeneous product which does not change in quality because of a change in the composition of its sources.

Although fluctuations in international reserves, the government debt with the central bank, and the level of central bank credit to the banking system do not change the quality of high-powered money, they quite obviously change the quantity of high-powered money. Because all sources of high-powered money are on its balance sheet, the Bank of Japan knows from day to day not only the amount of high-powered money in circulation, but also the changes in the various sources of high-powered money creation. As indicated in chart 3, there have been substantial variations in the sources of high-powered money creation. The "natural" sources of high-powered money fluctuated because of domestic economic conditions.

During periods of economic boom, tax receipts accelerate and the government tends to reduce its debt with the central bank; also imports accelerate, and international reserves of the central bank are reduced. The sharp decline in high-powered money that could result is prevented by an expansion of central bank credit to the banking system. Periods of domestic boom and inflation are associated with periods of the largest Bank of Japan credit extensions.

The same results apply during periods of slowdown in domestic activity. Imports decline and foreign exchange holdings of the central bank increase; tax receipts decline and the government's cash debt to the central bank increases. Both actions tend to increase the supply

37. *Money and Banking in Japan*, p. 123.

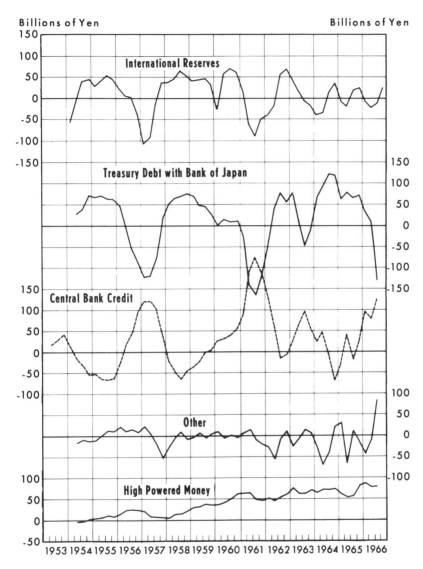

CHART 3. Japan: Changes in the sources of high-powered money
SOURCE: Bank of Japan.

of high-powered money. To prevent the full amount of the increase, the Bank of Japan reduces its credit to the banking system.

In order to have expansions and contractions in high-powered money consistent with monetary policy objectives, the central bank must take substantial action to break the "natural" expansions and contractions in high-powered money from international and government transactions.

High-powered money is a homogeneous financial asset which the Bank of Japan can control to any degree of accuracy it wishes. This is because it can know the level of high-powered money at any time by striking a balance sheet and because it can change the level at any time by changing central bank credit. Thus, the observed level of high-powered money and the target level of high-powered money are assumed to be the same at all times.

The relationship between H and M. High-powered money can be viewed as a pool banks dip into to meet reserve needs and the public draws on to meet currency needs. The banks and public are, in a sense, competing for use of the high-powered money which the central bank supplies. By definition ($H = BR + C$), the entire pool is always claimed. If the relation desired by the banking system for deposits to reserves, D/BR, and the relation desired by the public of deposits to currency, D/C, are known, then the money stock, M, can be determined given the amount of high-powered money, H.

The relationship between high-powered money and the total money stock can be seen by recalling equation (12):

$$M = \left(\frac{D}{BR}\right)\left[\frac{1 + \dfrac{D}{C}}{\dfrac{D}{BR} + \dfrac{D}{C}}\right]H.$$

The information needed to compute these ratios comes from the consolidated balance sheet of the banking system and is available only once a month with a four-week time lag. In contrast with H, which can be controlled quite closely, the monetary authorities could miss the money stock target by a substantial margin from month to month because of this information lag. If the time period for determining the target money stock is lengthened, this error will decline because of the decline in the relative importance of the information lag. In this study the time period for determining the money stock target is one quarter, which reduces the error from the information lag to moderate proportions. It is assumed that the observed quarterly money stock is a close approximation of the target money stock.

The deposit-currency ratio, D/C, and the deposit-reserve ratio, D/BR, jointly determine the value of the money multiplier. If these ratios are constant, the money multiplier will be constant and the link between high-powered money and the total money stock will also be constant. If these ratios vary over the cycle, the money multiplier will not be constant and the relationship between high-powered money and the total money stock will fluctuate.[38]

38. The reserves of the banking system are equal to required reserves established by the Bank of Japan and excess reserves of the banking system. There were no required reserves from 1953 to September 1959. During that period the deposit-reserve ratio remained relatively constant and exhibited no significant fluctuations over the cycle. After reserve requirements were imposed, there were sharp changes in the deposit-reserve ratio every time reserve requirements were changed. The ratio fell in the quarter reserve requirements increased, and rose in the quarter reserve requirements decreased. Each time the requirements were changed, finer distinctions were made with respect to the size and source of deposits and the type of bank. By April 1963, there were ten categories of reserve requirements. As requirements were changed for different categories of deposits at different times, variations in the deposit-reserve ratio had a strongly random character from 1959 to 1966.

To eliminate these random fluctuations in the deposit-reserve ratio, changes in reserves due to changes in requirements were eliminated. Only desired reserves of the banking system were used in computing the deposit-reserve ratio, which made the ratio consistent before and after September 1959. The ideal method of making this adjustment in reserves would be to compute the value of required reserves for each time period by multiplying the reserve requirement by the size of deposits by category. Unfortunately, the appropriate deposit data are not available to make this computation.

There is, however, another method of estimating required reserves. The law states that required reserves must be held as deposits with the Bank of Japan. Such deposits had existed prior to September 1959, when required reserves were enforced, but the amounts were small—between ¥2 billion and ¥6 billion. Rough estimates of required reserves in 1965 and 1966 indicate that amounts in excess of those required were about the same as in the 1953–59 period. As deposits in excess of required are less than 1 per cent of other reserves of the banking system, i.e., vault cash, a rough but reasonably accurate adjustment of total bank reserves could be achieved by subtracting all deposits of the banking system with the Bank of Japan from reserves.

This adjustment in reserves of the banking system means that the total uses of high-powered money have been reduced by an equal amount requiring that the sources of high-powered money also be reduced. Typically, the banking system has met increased needs for required reserves by increasing borrowings from the Bank of Japan. Thus, it seems reasonable to make the adjustment on the sources side in central bank credit.

The regression between rates of change in H and rates of change in M is:

$$\dot{M}_t = .60 + 1.01\dot{H}_t, \qquad r^2 = .51.$$
$$(.15)$$

For every 1 per cent change in H, there is a 1 per cent change in M. These results are statistically significant, but examination of the residuals in chart 4 indicates that there is a systematic cyclical discrepancy between actual and estimated M. The residuals fall in periods of tight money and rise in periods of easy money. In a purely definitional sense, this residual is explained by changes in the money multiplier and, underlying that, changes in the deposit-currency ratio and in the deposit-reserve ratio.

The deposit-reserve ratio, D/BR, is dependent on the level of desired reserves of the banking system as described in note 38. This ratio has a relatively stable value with no significant cyclical variations.

The deposit-currency ratio, on the other hand, showed substantial deviations from trend with a cyclical pattern which followed closely

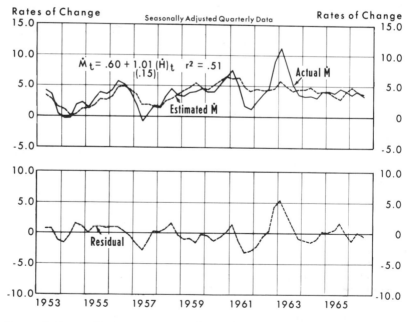

CHART 4. Japan: Estimated value of M due to changes in high-powered money. SOURCE: Bank of Japan.

the acceleration and deceleration of the money stock. During periods of tight money, deposits decrease sharply relative to currency, pushing the ratio down. During periods of easy money, deposits increase sharply relative to currency, pushing the ratio up. Regressing the rate of change of (D/C) and $\dot{H}$ on $\dot{M}$ yields the following results:

$$\dot{M}_t = -.169 + 1.02\dot{H}_t + .737(D/C)_t, \qquad r^2 = .94.$$
$$\phantom{\dot{M}_t = -.169 + } (.05) \qquad (.037)$$

This means that cyclical movements in high-powered money are reinforced by cyclical movements in the deposit-currency ratio. In some periods, movement in the deposit-currency ratio plays a more important role in changing the total money stock than does the rate of change in high-powered money.[39]

The aggregate deposit-currency ratio is a weighted average of the deposit-currency ratios of the subsectors of the economy, of which the household and business sectors are the most important. The cyclical fluctuations in the aggregate deposit-currency ratio can be explained by two factors: first, the deposit-currency ratio of the corporate business sector is much higher than that of the household sector; and second, the effects of tight money policy fall more heavily on the corporate business sector than on the household sector.[40]

39. Cagan observed the same results in his study of U.S. money stock.

High-powered money was the major determinant of the secular movement in the money stock, but the deposit-currency ratio was the major determinant of the cyclical movement in the money stock. See *Determinants and Effects of Changes in the U.S. Money Stock, 1875 to 1960.*

40. If the deposit-currency ratios maintained by each sector are constant but differ between themselves, then the aggregate ratio will vary if there is a change in the currency holdings between sectors.

The aggregate deposit-currency ratio can be expressed as follows:

$$(D/C)_a \equiv (D/C)_h(C_h/C_a) + (D/C)_b(C_b/C_a)$$
$$\equiv (D/C)_h(C_h/C_a) + (D/C)_b\frac{C_a - C_h}{C_a}$$
$$\equiv [(D/C)_h - (D/C)_b](C_h/C_b) + (D/C)_b$$

where subscript h stands for household sector, b for business sector, and a for aggregate ratio. Hence, if the sector deposit-currency ratio remains constant, the aggregate ratio can vary as follows:

$$\frac{d(D/C)_a}{dt} = [(D/C)_h - (D/C)_b]\frac{d(C_h/C_b)}{dt}.$$

If monetary policy primarily affects the business sector, there will be a proportionately larger decline in C_b than in C_h and the ratio C_h/C_b will rise. Because $[(D/C)_h - (D/C)_b]$ is negative, the value of $(D/C)_a$ will decline.

The business sector holds its money primarily as monetary deposits, while the household sector holds money primarily in the form of currency.[41] This phenomenon can be observed in the flow-of-funds data.[42] In the household sector, which includes nonincorporated business, for every ¥100 held in the form of currency, only ¥6 are held as deposits on the average. This ratio has been quite stable, ranging between 5 per cent and 7 per cent. In the case of the nonfinancial corporate business sector, for every ¥100 held in the form of currency, there has been about ¥340 held in the form of deposits. The deposit-currency ratios are strongly divergent between the household and business sectors.

The business sector is more affected by changes in monetary policy than is the household sector. The loans of the banking system are largely concentrated in loans to business, with virtually no loans to households. Household debt is not significant even in the mortgage market for single-family residences. Thus, a deceleration in bank loans has its initial effect on business. In attempting to adjust to the resulting liquidity squeeze, there is a strong incentive to economize on money stocks. Because business has a much higher deposit-currency ratio than households, a deceleration in money stocks of business will have a greater effect on deposits than on currency, with the result that the aggregate deposit-currency ratio will fall in periods of tight money and tend to rise in periods of easy money.

The Bank of Japan can come quite close to achieving its money stock target within a quarter time period because it can achieve its high-powered money target exactly and can estimate with a relatively short time lag the predictable cyclical movement in the deposit-currency ratio.

4. The Behavioral Link between Money, Income, Imports, and International Reserves

The model which ties this study together was presented in section 1. It can be summarized as follows: an acceleration in the money stock

---

41. The strongly divergent ratios in the personal sector and the corporate sector are due to the fact that individual household checking accounts are almost nonexistent in Japan. Only corporations which do extensive and continuous business with each other find settlement of bills through exchange of monetary deposits a convenient procedure. It is virtually impossible for private persons to transfer funds by check because, legally, a bad check is considered only a breach of contract, not a theft. Thus, the procedure for collecting on a bad check is more expensive and complicated in Japan than in countries where writing a bad check is a criminal offense.

42. Bank of Japan, *Economic Statistics of Japan*, 1966.

leads to an acceleration in income and imports which causes international reserves to decelerate. The policy response is to decelerate the money stock, which will decelerate income and imports and reverse the decline in international reserves. Monetary policy is then eased, which leads to a new acceleration in income and imports. In section 3, the behavior of the policy authorities, the determinants of the money stock, and the relation of the money stock to international reserves were considered. In this section the hypothesized behavior of the decision-making units which provide the other links in the model is investigated. There are three such links: the relation between money and income, between income and imports, and between imports and international reserves.

A. THE RELATION OF MONEY TO INCOME

The relationship hypothesized between money and income is derived from the quantity theory of money. It states that the level of income, Y, is dependently related to the stock of money, M; also, that variations in income, $\dot{Y}$, are dependently related to variations in money, $\dot{M}$. The existence of such a functional relationship does not imply that velocity, V, is constant. However, it does imply that it is functionally stable. This has been the case in Japan. Velocity has not been constant over time, but has exhibited two stable and independent characteristics.

The first was the secular tendency of velocity to rise in the first decade after the war and to decline in the second decade. The second was the cyclical tendency for velocity to rise during periods of tight money and fall during periods of easy money. The secular pattern of velocity may be attributed to the postwar price experience of Japan. Table 6 provides three indexes of prices: wholesale, consumer, and the GNP price deflator. Although the average rate of change in prices

TABLE 6

PRICE CHANGES

	AVERAGE ANNUAL PER CENT CHANGE IN:		
	Wholesale Prices	Consumer Prices	GNP Price Deflator
1946–48.....	180.0	93.6	
1948–53.....	22.5	8.6	
1953–60.....	0.0	1.9	2.0
1960–66.....	1.0	6.0	4.8

SOURCE: Bank of Japan, *Economic Statistics*, 1967.

measured by each of these indexes varies, they all show the same inflationary direction.

In the early postwar period, 1946 to 1948, the inflation was substantial. In the period 1948 to 1953 the inflation was sharply reduced, and in the period 1953 to 1960 there was virtually no inflation. The period 1960 to 1966 brought an emergence of new price increases.

According to Cagan (1956), desired real cash balances of money holders in periods of hyperinflation are inversely related to the expected rate of change in prices. An expectation of rapid price increases creates an incentive to reduce the value of real cash balances. When the expected rate of change in prices is small, the desire for real cash balances is unchanged or rising. Cagan's study dealt with relatively short time periods and with high average monthly rates of price increases.

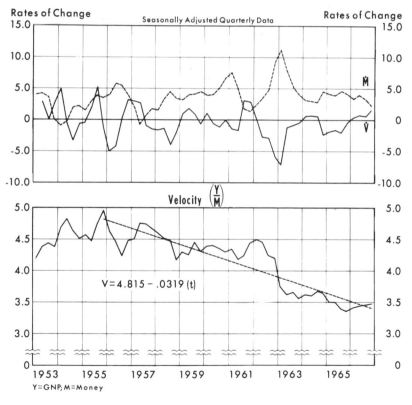

CHART 5. Japan: Money and velocity; velocity (Y/M)
SOURCES: Bank of Japan; Economic Planning Agency, Government of Japan.

When the analysis of real cash balances is conducted in a longer time period with lower price increases, changes in real income also affect the results. Deaver, in a companion study, considers this issue using Chilean data. His results indicate that as inflation becomes less intense, money holders become less sensitive to the rate of inflation. Because they have less at stake, their reactions to price changes are not as prompt. It seems to take several years for money holders to adjust their expectations to relatively moderate changes in inflation.

Deaver's results with respect to Chile seem to be supported by the Japanese case. The rise in velocity (the reciprocal of real cash balances), in the period 1946 to 1955, was in response to the rapid but decelerating inflation of the period 1946 to 1953. There was a gradual decline in velocity from 1955 to 1962, a sharp decline in velocity in 1963, and a continued gradual decline in velocity through 1965.

The decline in velocity from the middle of the 1950s until the early 1960s is consistent with the expectations of continued price stability which followed from 1953–60 price experience. Because the price rise from 1960 through 1966 was largely in consumer goods, it is not surprising that the response in the form of a rise in velocity was lagged. This is especially true considering that real income during this period was rising at a substantial rate. (See latter part of this section for further discussions of this issue.)

The cyclical tendency for velocity to rise during the early period of tight money and fall during the early period of easy money is consistent with rational behavior on the part of money holders. The deceleration in the money stock tends to create an excess demand for money, which pushes up short-term interest rates. The incentive of households and firms is to economize on cash balances, increasing velocity. At the same time reduced spending commitments affect inventories and later production and income. The deceleration in income slows the rise in velocity and in time reverses it.

The opposite process takes place when the stock of money accelerates. The temporary excess supply of money leads to a sharp decline in short-term interest rates, easing the incentive of money holders to economize on cash balances, causing velocity to decline. Associated increase in spending commitments reduces inventories and, after some time lag, leads to increased production and income, slowing the decline in velocity.[43]

43. In the United States, the cyclical pattern of velocity is similar to that of Japan, in spite of the fact that the secular trend of velocity has been just the opposite of Japan from 1955 to 1965.

In spite of this cyclical flexibility in the relationship between money and income, the fluctuations in velocity were not sufficiently large or long-lasting to prevent changes in money from dominating changes in income.

Comparing quarterly rates of change in money with quarterly rates of change in nominal GNP gave the following result:

$$\dot{Y}_t = 1.27 + .51\dot{M}_{t-2}, \qquad r^2 = .27. \qquad (14)$$
$$(.13)$$

The two-quarter lag in $\dot{M}$ gives the best statistical results, with a one-quarter lag being almost as good. The r^2's with alternative lags in $\dot{M}$ were as follows:

$$\dot{M}_t = .10,$$
$$\dot{M}_{t-1} = .26,$$
$$\dot{M}_{t-3} = .15.$$
$$\dot{M}_{t-4} = .03.$$

Even the best correlation of determination (r^2) is not especially high. One reason for this is that quarterly national income accounts in Japan are still in an experimental stage. And there are frequent changes in accounting practices, coverage, and reporting techniques. Thus, there is some uncertainty about the degree to which the sample is representative of the universe. Large sampling fluctuations result in a substantial amount of random variation in the GNP series.[44] When quarterly rates of change are taken, this random element is magnified, as can be seen in chart 6. A five-term moving average of the GNP series improves the relationship between $\dot{M}$ and $\dot{Y}$, which implies that measurement errors rather than specification errors were the source of irregularity. However imperfect the data, the only information available on nominal GNP is from the quarterly national income accounts.

This study is interested in considering the effects of alternative monetary policies on the business cycle measured not only in terms of nominal income, but also in terms of real income. There are several choices open for measuring the relationship between money and real income.

Consider a money–real-income relation expressed in log linear terms.

$$\log Y = \log \alpha_0 + \log \alpha_1 M_{t-2} \qquad (15)$$
where
$$\log Y = \log y + \log P,$$

44. See Adelman and Adelman, *Readings in Business Cycles* (Homewood, Ill.: Richard D. Irwin, 1965), pp. 290–91.

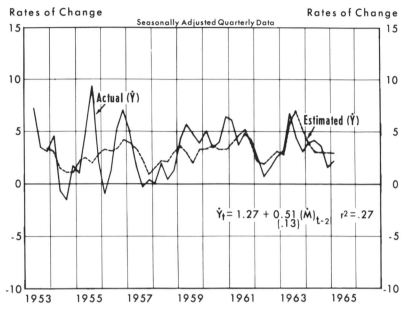

CHART 6. Japan: Actual and estimated changes in nominal GNP
SOURCE: Bank of Japan.

and

$$Y = \text{nominal GNP},$$
$$y = \text{real GNP},$$
$$P = \text{price index}.$$

So

$$\log y = \log \alpha_0 + \log \alpha_1 M_{t-2} - \log P_t. \tag{16}$$

In first differences:

$$\Delta \log y_t = \Delta \log \alpha_1 M_{t-2} - \Delta \log P_t. \tag{17}$$

Fitted to the statistical time series of real GNP, money and the price deflator measured as quarterly rates of change gives:

$$\dot{y}_t = 1.00 + .40\dot{M}_{t-2} - .18\dot{P}_t, \qquad r^2 = .19.$$
$$\quad\;\; (.13) \qquad\quad (.38)$$

The signs are as expected for both the money and the price variables. However, the analysis implies a price coefficient homogeneous to the first degree and an insignificant constant term. In fact, the constant term is large, and the price coefficient is closer to zero than to (-1.0). The fact that the price coefficient is not statistically significant is reassuring. In addition, the coefficient of determination is low. The reason has already been suggested. Nominal income as reported in the national income accounts has a large random element. Dividing through by the implicit price deflator to get real GNP does not reduce the random element. A meaningful statistical test of the underlying behavioral relation is therefore difficult using real GNP.

Fortunately, there is an alternative measure of real output—industrial production.[45] Movements in industrial production and real GNP are quite close when the random element in the real GNP series is accounted for by smoothing with a five-term moving average. The correlation coefficient between rates of change in industrial production and rates of change in real GNP is .78. The industrial production series has been collected for many years, is easily understood, and is relatively straightforward to calculate. Thus, random errors are reduced. In addition, because the quarterly figures are the average of three monthly figures, random variations are reduced further. Thus, industrial production exhibited relatively stable rates of change over time.

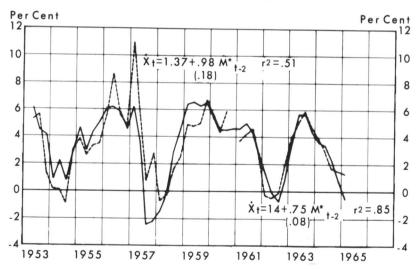

CHART 7. Japan: Actual and estimated changes in real product

45. The relation between industrial production, money, and consumer prices has a closer fit than when real GNP is used:

$$\dot{X}_t = .97 + .75\dot{M}_{t-2} - .46\dot{P}_t, \qquad r^2 = .39.$$
$$\quad\quad (.15) \quad\quad (.39)$$

However, the same statistical problems are evident: a large constant term and an absolute value of the price coefficient less this minus one (−1.0) which is statistically insignificant.

This study is concerned with the differing effects of monetary policy on real and nominal income, and not directly concerned with effects on prices. To handle the real output–money relation without the added complication of explicitly introducing prices into the model, two techniques were tried. First, coefficients relating observed changes in the nominal money stock to changes in industrial production were estimated separately for periods with different rates of change in prices. Second, the money series was deflated by the GNP price deflator and changes in real money compared with changes in industrial production.

With the first technique, the subperiod 1953 to 1960 (when prices increased at a moderate 2 per cent per year) was separated from the subperiod 1960 to 1964 (when prices rose 5 per cent per year). The coefficients estimated separately for each subperiod were:

$$\text{Subperiod 1953-II to 1960-IV:}$$
$$\dot{X}_t = -.07 + 1.21\dot{M}_{t-2}, \qquad r^2 = .59.$$
$$(.19)$$

$$\text{Subperiod 1960-IV to 1964-IV:}$$
$$\dot{X}_t = -.54 + .66\dot{M}_{t-2}, \qquad r^2 = .83.$$
$$(.08)$$

This split in the series corresponds to the one in section 3 relating changes in money, $\dot{M}$, to changes in international reserves, $\dot{R}$. The reasons for splitting this series in 1960 are substantially the same in both cases. The monetary policy followed from 1960 to 1964 by Prime Minister Ikeda was more expansionary than that of his predecessors in the years 1953–60.

It should be noted that the coefficient relating $\dot{M}$ to $\dot{X}$ in the period 1953 to 1960 is almost twice as large as the value of that coefficient during the period 1960 to 1964 (1.21 versus .66). Put another way, a 1 per cent increase in the money stock in the earlier period had almost twice as big an effect on real output as a 1 per cent increase in the money stock in the latter period. These results are reasonable under the circumstances. The average growth in real output over the long run is a function of the growth in real inputs of labor, capital, and technology. The average secular growth in the stock of money will not necessarily affect the secular growth in real output. Variations in the growth in the stock of money will, of course, have a major effect on the short-term growth in real output. If the secular growth in the stock of money increases, the coefficient relating the quarterly values of $\dot{M}$ to $\dot{X}$ would be expected to decrease roughly in proportion to the change in the average growth in nominal money stock. This is what happened in the case of Japan. The average quarterly value of M moved from 3.1 per cent per quarter in 1953–60 to 4.8 per cent per quarter in 1960–64 (an increase of 55 per cent), while the coefficient relating M to X moved from 1.21 to .66 in the same period (a decrease of 45 per cent).

The second method of adjusting for changes in prices was to compute coefficients relating changes in the real stock of money to changes in industrial production. The values of the coefficients were estimated for the whole period and also estimated separately for each of the policy subperiods:

Period 1953-II to 1964-IV:

$$\dot{X}_t = 1.23 + .77M^*_{t-2}, \qquad r^2 = .47.$$
$$(.12)$$

Subperiod 1953-II to 1960-IV:

$$\dot{X}_t = 1.37 + .98M^*_{t-2}, \qquad r^2 = .51.$$
$$(.18)$$

Subperiod 1960-IV to 1964-IV:

$$\dot{X}_t = .14 + .75\dot{M}^*_{t-2}, \qquad r^2 = .85.$$
$$(.08)$$

As with other measures of the money-income relation, the best fit was with a two-quarter time lag in money. The difference in the value of the coefficients between the two policy subperiods was just barely significant. The differences were smaller but in the same direction as in the nominal money–real output relationship. This implies that the amount of real money which households and firms were willing to hold increased in the 1960–64 period relative to the 1953–60 period. How was this possible in the face of an increase in inflationary pressure in 1960–64?

The reasons were suggested earlier in this section. The inflationary pressures in the early and middle 1960s were relatively moderate compared to the early postwar years and compared to the contemporaneous growth in real income. Under such circumstances money holders may not reduce their desired real cash balances.

The reasoning is analogous to substitution and income effects in price theory. An increase in the expected price level will cause the demand for real cash balances to decline,[46] while a rise in real income will cause the

46. A complete measure of the substitution effect would require taking account of the cost of holding money relative to the cost of holding alternative assets. One or more interest rate variables would be needed to measure the demand for

demand for real cash balances to increase. If, as some evidence suggests, the income elasticity of demand for real cash balances is greater than one,[47] then the simultaneous rapid increase in real income and moderate increase in prices could lead to an increase in observed real cash balances and a decline in velocity. Given Japan's rapid growth in real income and relatively mild price increases, the decline in velocity from 1961 to 1965 is not unreasonable.

B. THE RELATION OF INCOME TO IMPORTS

A popular saying is that "Japan must export to live." The truth in this phrase lies in the fact that Japan must *import* to live. Although the ratio of imports to income in Japan is lower than for many industrial nations, she lacks significant quantities of most raw materials required for industrial development. In 1964 she imported 96 per cent of her iron ore, 100 per cent of her raw cotton and wool, 60 per cent of her copper, 99 per cent of her petroleum, and 49 per cent of her industrial coal. With the third largest steel industry in the world, she must import 24 per cent of her steel scrap. In recent years there has also been a significant increase in food imports, as the Japanese diet has shifted towards Western eating patterns more rapidly than has Japanese food production.[48] Finally, Japan imports a wide range of sophisticated machinery and, with the recent trend towards import liberalization, a small but increasing amount of finished consumer goods.

The relationship between income and imports in Japan is substantially different when viewed in secular terms than when viewed in cyclical terms. The elasticity of nominal imports with respect to nominal GNP for the period 1953 to 1965 was not significantly different from 1.0. The elasticity of real imports with respect to industrial production was also not significantly different from 1.0. However, when the relationship between imports and income is computed on a quarter-to-quarter basis, the elasticity varied widely, with most observations in

---

money balances. The sharp quarter-to-quarter movements in short-term interest rates have affected the cyclical movement in velocity. But the long-term trend in interest rates has been stable, after adjustment for price expectations, and therefore probably played little role in the trend of velocity. Because most interest rate data for Japan are misleading, it is not possible to quantify this observation.

47. Milton Friedman, "The Demand for Money," *Journal of Political Economy* 67 (1959): 328–29.

48. The government's price support program for rice discourages shifting to production of other crops.

the range of -1 to $+4$ and some much larger in absolute value. This variation in elasticity is implicit in the following equations:

Nominal imports $(I\dot{m})$ to nominal GNP $(\dot{Y})$:

$$I\dot{m}_t = -3.16 + 1.91(\dot{Y})_t, \qquad r^2 = .39.$$
$$(.36)$$

Real imports $(I\dot{m}^*)$ to industrial production $(\dot{X})$:

$$I\dot{m}_t^* = -3.26 + 2.04(\dot{X})_t, \qquad r^2 = .76.$$
$$(.17)$$

The higher income elasticity of imports observed in the cyclical measure than in the secular measure is due to sharp cyclical movements in the imports of some commodities.

Table 7 illustrates the problem. The average experience during the

TABLE 7

RELATIONSHIP OF PRODUCTION AND IMPORTS TO CONSUMPTION
AND INVENTORIES OF SEMIPROCESSED MATERIALS
(Percentage Change in Four Quarters before and after Peak)

	Industrial Production	Consumption of Semiprocessed Materials	Consumption of Imported Semiprocessed Materials	Inventories of Imported Semiprocessed Materials	Total Imports
1st cycle peak 1954-I					
Before peak	22	20	60	59	32
After peak	1	6	-20	-13	-20
2d cycle peak 1957-II					
Before peak	26	18	48	49	58
After peak	-8	-10	-33	-28	39
3d cycle peak 1961-IV					
Before peak	19	16	53	25	33
After peak	1	-3	-41	-28	-12
4th cycle peak 1964-I					
Before peak	21	24	97	99	34
After peak	8	5	-11	-22	-1
Four cycle averages					
Before peak	22	20	65	58	39
After peak	0	1	-26	-23	-18

SOURCE: Bank of Japan, "Basic Data for Economic Analysis, 1965."

NOTE: Data for the table were available only through 1964-IV. As a result, the timing of the fourth cycle peak is only approximate.

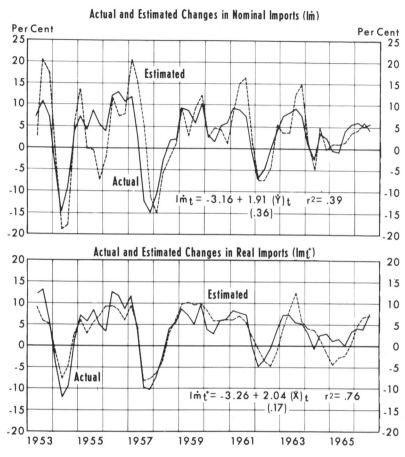

CHART 8. Japan: Actual and estimated changes in nominal imports; actual and estimated changes in real imports.

four business cycles was that the industrial consumption of all semi-processed materials rose and fell proportionately with the rise and fall in industrial production. However, the consumption of imported semi-processed materials tended in the last year of the upswing to rise three and one-fourth times as rapidly as total consumption of semiprocessed materials. In the downswing (four quarters following the peak), the consumption of imported semiprocessed materials declined on the average by 26 per cent, while total consumption was virtually un-changed. This pattern implies a strong cyclical shift between foreign and domestic sources of supply.

This dependence on imports as a marginal source of supply makes Japanese businessmen sensitive to their needs for inventories of such materials. A rise in the consumption of imported semiprocessed materials is associated with a correspondingly sharp rise in the stock of inventories of these materials. Conversely, a decline in the consumption of imported semiprocessed materials is associated with a decline in inventories. As a result, imported inventories have typically increased 58 per cent in the four quarters before the peak of the cycle when their consumption was rising 65 per cent. In the four quarters after the peak in the cycle, inventories of imported semiprocessed materials declined 23 per cent, while their consumption declined 26 per cent.

The dual impact of sharp changes in consumption and inventories of imported semiprocessed materials over the cycle plays a key role in the cyclical pattern of total imports.[49]

The observed cyclical shift between foreign and domestic sources of supply for these important industrial inputs is due to shifts in the relative cost of domestic versus foreign sources of supply. Although the market price of these domestic products does not exhibit a strong cyclical pattern, its nonmarket price does. The nonmarket price of a commodity may be defined as the indirect cost to the consumer of a given purchase. These indirect costs consist of such things as queuing, delays in delivery, and decline in quality of product or services. These nonmarket prices increase substantially during periods of acceleration in domestic demand and decline sharply in periods of deceleration in domestic demand. This creates the incentive to shift from domestic to foreign sources of supply during the late phase of the boom, and to shift from foreign to domestic sources of supply during the period of business decline.

C. THE RELATION OF IMPORTS TO INTERNATIONAL RESERVES

The change in international reserves for any time period can be defined as equal to the surplus or deficit in the balance of payments for that time period. For Japan this procedure presents no serious problems because its currency is not held as an international reserve asset

---

49. It is interesting to note that raw materials, which represent 60 per cent of Japan's total imports, make a relatively small contribution to the deviation of imports from its trend. The relatively modest cyclical pattern in the movement of raw material imports is due to Japan's almost complete dependence on foreign sources of supply. Therefore, shifts between domestic and foreign sources of supply do not play an important role in the quarter-to-quarter fluctuations in imports.

by other countries. The accounting definition of changes in international reserves is as follows:

$$\Delta R_t \equiv BP_t \equiv E_t - Im_t + K_t,$$
$$\Delta R = \text{change in international reserves,}$$
$$BP = \text{balance of payments,} \tag{18}$$
$$E = \text{exports of goods and services,}$$
$$Im = \text{imports of goods and services,}$$
$$K = \text{net capital receipts.}[50]$$

The relation hypothesized in the model is that the rate of change in international reserves is predictably related to the rate of change in imports.

$$\dot{R}_t = \rho_0 + \rho_1 I\dot{m}_{t-\rho}. \tag{19}$$

This relation is derived from the following transformation:

$$R_t \equiv R_{t-1} + K_t + E_t - Im_t. \tag{20}$$

Differentiating with respect to time,

$$\frac{dR_t}{dt} \equiv \frac{dR_{t-1}}{d(t-1)} \left(\frac{d(t-1)}{dt} \right) + \frac{dK_t}{dt} + \frac{dE_t}{dt} - \frac{dIm_t}{dt}. \tag{21}$$

Find the per cent change in reserves by dividing by R_{t-1} and restating other terms so they can be written in rate of change form.

$$\dot{R}_t \equiv \frac{1}{R_{t-1}} \left(\frac{dR_{t-1}}{dt} \right) + \frac{K_{t-1}}{R_{t-1}} \cdot \frac{1}{K_{t-1}} \left(\frac{dK_t}{dt} \right) + \frac{E_{t-1}}{R_{t-1}} \cdot \frac{1}{E_{t-1}} \left(\frac{dE_t}{dt} \right)$$
$$- \frac{Im_{t-1}}{R_{t-1}} \cdot \frac{1}{Im_{t-1}} \left(\frac{dIm_t}{dt} \right). \tag{22}$$

Replace t with $t-1$ in (21) and substitute into (22).

$$\dot{R}_t \equiv \frac{1}{R_{t-1}} \left[\frac{dR_{t-2}}{dt} + \frac{dK_{t-1}}{dt} + \frac{dE_{t-1}}{dt} - \frac{dIm_{t-1}}{dt} \right]$$
$$+ \frac{K_{t-1}}{R_{t-1}} (\dot{K}_t) + \frac{E_{t-1}}{R_{t-1}} (\dot{E}_t) - \frac{Im_{t-1}}{R_{t-1}} (I\dot{m}_t). \tag{23}$$

50. All international capital transfers are handled in either dollars or pounds sterling. The domestic currency is converted into one of the international currencies at a domestic bank which is authorized to deal in foreign exchange. These banks will match their international receipts and payments daily or weekly and make up the balance with either a purchase or a sale of foreign exchange from the Bank of Japan, which acts as an agent for the foreign exchange special account of the ministry of finance.

By repeated substitution of (21) into (22) until such point that dR_{t-n}/dt equals zero we get the following identity:

$$\dot{R}_t \equiv \frac{1}{R_{t-1}} \cdot \frac{dR_{t-n}}{dt} + \frac{1}{R_{t-1}} \left[\sum_{i=0}^{n-1} (K_{t-i-1})(\dot{K}_{t-i}) \right]$$

$$+ \frac{1}{R_{t-1}} \left[\sum_{i=0}^{n-1} (E_{t-i-1})(\dot{E}_{t-i}) \right] - \frac{1}{R_{t-1}} \left[\sum_{i=0}^{n-1} (Im_{t-i-1})(I\dot{m}_{t-i}) \right]. \tag{24}$$

The identity shows that the per cent change in reserves is a weighted sum of the per cent rate of change of past imports, exports, and capital back to some point in time when the rate of change in reserves was zero. To assert that this identity can be approximated solely by the lagged rate of change in imports, one must show that exports and net capital flows have grown at a relatively stable rate.

The identity (24) can be rewritten factoring out one lagged value of the rate of change of imports.

$$\dot{R}_t \equiv \frac{1}{R_{t-1}} \cdot \frac{dR_{t-n}}{dt} + \frac{1}{R_{t-1}} \left[\sum_{i=0}^{n-1} (K_{t-i-1})(\dot{K}_{t-i}) \right]$$

$$+ \frac{1}{R_{t-1}} \left[\sum_{i=0}^{n-1} (E_{t-i-1})(\dot{E}_{t-i}) \right] - \frac{1}{R_{t-1}} \left[\sum_{\substack{i=0 \\ i \neq p}}^{n-1} (Im_{t-i-1})(I\dot{m}_{t-i}) \right]$$

$$- \frac{Im_{t-p-1}}{R_{t-1}} (I\dot{m}_{t-p}). \tag{25}$$

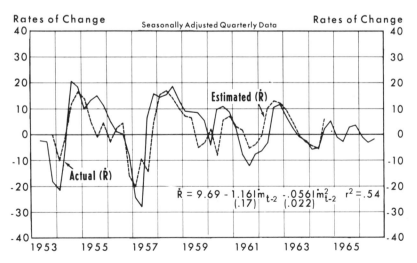

CHART 9. Japan: Actual and estimated changes in nominal international reserves.

SOURCE: Bank of Japan.

The best linear approximation of this identity is specified as follows: the term factored out of the import summation is the "active" term, since it is approximated by $\rho_1 I \dot{m}_{t-p}$ in the regression equation $\dot{R}_t = \rho_0 + \rho_1 I \dot{m}_{t-p}$. The sum of the other terms on the right-hand side is approximated by the constant term ρ_0. The lagged time index p is selected so as to minimize the variation in the terms represented by ρ_0. Conceptually, p should be the time lag that most closely synchronizes turning points in the rate of change of reserves to the negative of the turning points in the rate of change of imports.[51] A polynomial of the form $\dot{R}_t = \rho_0 - \rho_1 I \dot{m}_{t-p} - \rho_2 I \dot{m}_{t-p}^2 - \cdots - \rho_n I \dot{m}_{t-p}^n$ can be used to simulate the cyclical movements of the coefficient $-Im_{t-p-1}/R_{t-1}$ in the identity. In fact, the polynomial form gives the best regression fit and was incorporated into this model as a result.

The evidence presented to justify this form of the identity is of two types. First, exports and net capital flows exhibit a stable growth relative to imports and, second, regressions between rates of change in imports and reserves have reasonably good statistical fits. As the regression evidence is the most straightforward, it is given first.

A second-degree polynomial regression gave the best results.

Nominal imports and nominal reserves:

$$\dot{R}_t = 9.69 - 1.16 I \dot{m}_{t-2} - .056 I \dot{m}_{t-2}^2, \qquad r^2 = .54.$$
$$\quad\;\; (.17) \qquad\quad (.022)$$

Real imports and real reserves:

$$\dot{R}_t^* = 10.1 - 1.23 I \dot{m}_{t-2}^* - .056 I \dot{m}_{t-2}^{*2}, \qquad r^2 = .54.$$
$$\quad\;\; (.10) \qquad\quad\;\; (.027)$$

With respect to the first type of evidence, it can be noted that Japan has benefited substantially from the stable and prosperous inter-national economic environment which has existed in the postwar period.[52] Of course, the fact that Japan's export growth has been two

51. The assumption would be that the two time series would be out of phase by approximately one-quarter of a cycle. As analyzed in section 5, the cycle is ten quarters long. Therefore, the estimated lags between rates of change of imports and reserves of two quarters are quite consistent.

52. This raises some interesting questions about the international transmission of business cycles. This analysis implies that Japan has been relatively little affected by fluctuations from abroad in the postwar period. Thus, the popular saying that when the U.S. sneezes Europe catches cold and Japan is confined to its bed doesn't seem to hold. Of course, these observations are based on a quite mild business cycle pattern. If the fluctuations were more severe, the international transmission of cycles would probably be more apparent, as was the case in the 1930s.

to three times the growth in world trade is largely due to domestic considerations, such as a growing and sophisticated capital plant and well-trained and motivated work force, and an imaginative application of technology to the needs of world trade. None of these domestic factors is strongly influenced by the short-run Japanese business cycle.

As can be seen in chart 10, none of the four periods of decline in reserves can be attributed primarily to export considerations.[53] During

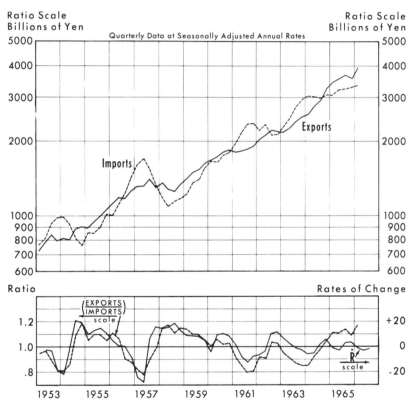

CHART 10. Japan: Current account of balance of payments

SOURCE: Government of Japan Economic Planning Agency.

NOTE: National income accounts basis.

53. Cyclical movements in the current account have been the major cause of fluctuations in foreign exchange reserves, with net capital movements playing a growing but secondary role. Since the mean import-reserve ratio has been close to one (.92), it is possible to illustrate the relative importance of current account

two periods, 1957 and 1963, Japanese exports were rising at a rate faster than average, and in the other two periods, 1953–54 and 1961, exports were rising at a rate slower than average. Each of the four decelerations in international reserves was associated with a rapid increase in imports; the acceleration in reserves was associated in the first two periods with a rapid decrease in imports, and the last two periods with a moderate decrease in imports.

Fluctuations in imports have played a major role not only in the timing of changes in international reserves, but also in the size of their deterioration and subsequent improvement. Notice in chart 10 that variations in imports in the first two cycles were larger than in the last two cycles, and also that fluctuations in international reserves were larger in the first two cycles than in the last two.

From 1953 to the middle of 1960, the ratio of exports to imports moved in a pattern and amplitude almost identical to that of the rate of change in international reserves. This implies not only that imports dominated the current account but also that capital movements were relatively unimportant in the Japanese balance of payments during this period. However, from the middle of 1960 until the end of 1964, the rate of change in international reserves was at a much higher average level than the ratio of exports to imports. This implies a heavy capital inflow during the period.[54]

The emergence of a heavy capital inflow from 1960 to 1964 is consistent with the previous analysis of monetary policy. It will be recalled that Prime Minister Ikeda (July 1960–November 1964) wished to push

---

and capital flows to the rates of change of reserves by superimposing the export-import ratio graph on the rate of change of reserves graph. Algebraically, the procedure is justified as follows:

$$\dot{R}_t = \frac{\Delta R_t}{R_{t-1}} = \frac{K_t + E_t - Im_t}{R_{t-1}} \equiv \frac{K_t}{R_{t-1}} + \frac{Im_t}{R_{t-1}}\left[\frac{E_t}{Im_t} - 1\right].$$

The mean import-reserve ratio is the factor of proportionality between the scale for the rate of change of reserves and the export-import ratio scale. In effect, the export-import ratio is used as a proxy for the measure of the rate of change of reserves due to net quantity flows of current account. The export-import ratio somewhat exaggerates rates of change in reserves due to current account flows, whenever the import reserve ratio is below the mean. The opposite case holds when the import reserve ratio is above the mean.

54. Consistent data on the Japanese capital account are not available during this whole period because of changes in the method of presentation. However, what data are available confirm this result. The sum of long- and short-term capital receipts between 1956 and 1959 was − $126 million; the sum of long- and short-term capital receipts between 1960 and 1964 was + $2.3 billion.

an expansionary monetary policy. Hoping to prevent such a policy from causing the balance of payments to deteriorate, the Ikeda administration substantially reduced restrictions on short-term capital imports and moderately liberalized long-term capital imports.[55] Because controls on export of capital by European countries were also being relaxed, and because the Japanese growth rate and domestic interest rates were considerably higher than in other industrial countries, the reductions of controls on capital led to an immediate and heavy inflow of foreign funds.

In spite of this capital inflow from 1960 to 1964, Japan's balance of payments was still dominated by fluctuations in imports. The capital inflow could only reduce the magnitude of the international reserve loss.[56]

55. A partial listing of the capital liberalization moves taken by the Ikeda administration include:

a. In July 1960 nonresidents of Japan were permitted to purchase yen accounts with foreign currency which were automatically reconvertible into foreign exchange. This permitted Japanese banks with branches in Europe to take advantage of the Euro-dollar market. Within less than three years Euro-dollar deposits in Japanese banks increased more than $1 billion.

b. In the fall of 1960, domestic Japanese banks were given increased freedom to refinance import trade credits with foreign banks. This permitted a substantial expansion in the amount of short-term credit which was available to Japan from foreign sources.

c. From 1960 to 1962, the Japanese government gradually eased restrictions on domestic business organizations' floating bonds abroad, permitted foreign purchasers of Japanese stocks to repatriate their income with only a minimum waiting period, and generally eased the government's administrative restrictions of Japanese corporations assuming foreign liabilities.

The purpose of these liberalization moves was to increase the amount of capital inflow, but because of the Japanese native suspicion of foreign influences, there was relatively little improvement in the attitude of the Japanese government regarding foreign direct investment. Such investment was, and still is, restricted to minority participation to insure that Japanese nationals control the decision-making process.

56. The relative stagnation in international reserves in the face of a strong current account surplus since the end of 1964 is mainly due to the cyclical decline in Japanese interest rates relative to those in the rest of the world. To a lesser extent, it is due to the "voluntary program" of the United States to correct its balance of payments problem, which was initiated on February 10, 1965. The decline in interest rates has hit short-term capital flows, while the voluntary program has primarily affected long-term capital flows. In 1965–66 there was net capital outflow of $1.3 billion from Japan.

The reemergence of boom conditions towards the end of 1965 took longer than usual to affect interest rates. But when rates started to rise toward the end of

5. MONETARY POLICY AND THE BUSINESS CYCLE

The four-equation model of the Japanese business cycle which was presented briefly in section 1 and considered in detail in sections 3–4 can be analyzed formally with the help of difference equations. The unique advantage of difference equations is that in its application to economics, the solution traces out a path over time. In this way the dynamic properties of the model can be analyzed.

A. THE SIMPLEST EXAMPLE

The structural equations which underlie this difference equation in their simplest form are as follows:

$$\dot{Y}_t = \alpha_0 + \alpha_1 \dot{M}_{t-2}, \tag{26}$$

$$\dot{M}_t = \beta_0 + \beta_1 \dot{R}_{t-1}, \tag{27}$$

$$\dot{R}_t = \rho_0 + \rho_1 I\dot{m}_{t-2}, \tag{28}$$

$$I\dot{m}_t = \gamma_0 + \gamma_1 \dot{Y}_t. \tag{29}$$

The lagged values are determined by the statistical results presented in sections 3 and 4.

The reduced form of this system of equations ([26] through [29]) is:

$$\dot{Y}_t = A_0 + A_1 \dot{Y}_{t-5},$$

where

$$A_0 = \alpha_0 + \alpha_1\beta_0 + \alpha_1\beta_1\rho_0 + \alpha_1\beta_1\rho_1\gamma_0, \tag{30}$$
$$A_1 = \alpha_1\beta_1\rho_1\gamma_1.$$

While this equation appears to be of the fifth order, it is in fact a system of five first-order equations, because all equations are of the form:

$$\dot{Y}_t = f(\dot{Y}_{t-h}).$$

Because h is a constant time interval, the equation can be handled as if it were of the first order. For example, instead of saying $t - 5$ (quarters), we can say $t - 1$ (5-quarter interval). To illustrate this, consider the following initial conditions,

$$\dot{Y}_{-4} = 9, \quad \dot{Y}_{-3} = 6, \quad \dot{Y}_{-2} = 1, \quad \dot{Y}_{-1} = 2, \quad \dot{Y}_0 = 5,$$

and the determining equation,

$$\dot{Y}_t = 1 - 2\dot{Y}_{t-5}.$$

1966, the capital outflow was reversed. In the first half of 1967 there was a net capital inflow of $244 million.

The sequence, including the initial conditions, that would be generated is:

$$\begin{Bmatrix} 9,\ 6,\ 1,\ 2,\ 5,\ -17,\ -11,\ -1,\ -3,\ -9, \\ 35,\ 23,\ 3,\ 7,\ 19,\ -63,\ -45,\ -5,\ -13,\ -37, \\ 125,\ 89,\ \ldots \end{Bmatrix}.$$

The original sequence can be decomposed into five separate subsequences which have no common elements. Each element of the original sequence with subscript t is placed in the corresponding ith ($i = 1,2,3,4,5$) subsequence when $i_t = (t + 5 - i)/5$ assumes an integral value. Each subsequence can be generated by a first-order difference equation of the form

$$\dot{Y}_{i_t} = 1 - 2\dot{Y}_{i_{t-i}}.$$

1. $\{9,\ -17,\ 35,\ -63,\ 125, \ldots\}$
2. $\{6,\ -11,\ 23,\ -45,\ 89, \ldots\ \}$
3. $\{1,\ -1,\ 3,\ -5, \ldots\ \ \ \ \ \ \ \ \ \}$
4. $\{2,\ -3,\ 7,\ -13, \ldots\ \ \ \ \ \ \ \}$
5. $\{5,\ -9,\ 19,\ -37, \ldots\ \ \ \ \ \ \}$

The elements of each subsequence are uniquely related to the initial condition (first element) of that subsequence. The "behavior" of any one subsequence is mathematically independent of the "behavior" of the other subsequences. However, as the initial conditions are drawn from consecutive observations of the Japanese economy, the subsequences are assumed to be consistently related to one another. Given these nonrandom initial conditions, it is not unreasonable to reassemble the five subsequences (generated from the first-order difference equations) to form the fifth-order difference equation, approximating the cyclical behavior of the Japanese economy.

Specifying the behavior of the first-order equation $\dot{Y}_t = A_0 + A_1\dot{Y}_{t-1}$ also specifies the behavior of the fifth-order equation $\dot{Y}_t = A_0 + A_1\dot{Y}_{t-5}$. For purposes of tracing out the solution of a first-order difference equation, the constant term A_0 can be omitted, as the value A_1 determines the cyclical properties of the model.[57]

If the value of A_1 is positive, then the rate of change in income, $\dot{Y}$, will not have a cyclical pattern. If A_1 is equal to one, income will grow at a constant rate each period and $\dot{Y}$ will be constant. If A_1 is less than one but greater than zero, income will grow at a constantly decreasing rate each period and $\dot{Y}$ will decrease. If A_1 is greater than one, income

---

57. See Baumol, *Economic Dynamics*, 2d ed. (New York: Macmillan Co., 1959), p. 162.

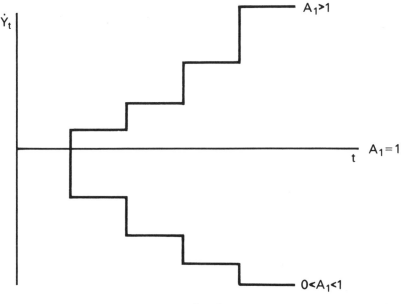

FIG. 1.

will grow at a constantly increasing rate each period and $\dot{Y}$ will increase (see fig. 1).

If, on the other hand, the value of A_1 is negative, the time path of $\dot{Y}$ will oscillate in a regular cyclical pattern. If the value of A_1 is equal to minus one, the cyclical path of $\dot{Y}$ will be of constant amplitude. If the value of A_1 is less than zero but greater than minus one, the cyclical path of $\dot{Y}$ will be damped. If A_1 is less than minus one (its absolute value is greater than one), the cyclical path of $\dot{Y}$ will be explosive (see fig. 2).

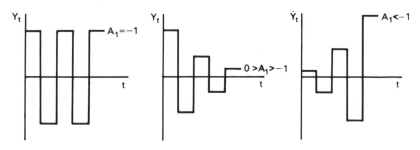

FIG. 2.

On a priori grounds we can postulate that the value of A_1 in this model of the business cycle is negative, because in equation (28) the value ρ_1 is negative; that is, an acceleration in imports will lead to a deceleration in international reserves. As the value of coefficients in the other three equations is positive, the product $A_1 = \alpha_1\beta_1\rho_1\gamma_1$ will be negative. Thus, the model has a built-in cyclical property.

These results can be seen intuitively. Consider the reduced-form equation:

$$\dot{Y}_t = A_0 + A_1\dot{Y}_{t-5}.$$

If A_1 is negative and the value of $\dot{Y}_{t-5}$ is positive, then the product of these two values will be negative. This means that the value of $\dot{Y}_t$ will be smaller than that of $\dot{Y}_{t-5}$. If the value of $\dot{Y}_{t-5}$ is negative and is multiplied by A_1 which is also negative, then the product will be positive and the value of $\dot{Y}_t$ will be larger than $\dot{Y}_{t-5}$. Thus, the value of $\dot{Y}_t$ over time is periodically larger and smaller.[58]

These relations can be viewed schematically.

$$\dot{M}_t \xrightarrow{(+)} \alpha_1\dot{Y}_{t+2} \xrightarrow{(+)} \gamma_1 I\dot{m}_{t+2} \xrightarrow{(-)} \rho_1\dot{R}_{t+4} \xrightarrow{(+)} \beta_1\dot{M}_{t+5}.$$

The arrow indicates the hypothesized direction of causality. The sign above the arrow indicates whether the relation is positive or negative. The time subscript indicates the number of quarters between the change in $\dot{M}_t$ and the change in the other variables. The sequence takes five quarters from peak to trough and ten quarters for the entire cycle.

An increase in $\dot{M}$ will increase $\dot{Y}$ and $I\dot{m}$ in about two quarters and reduce $\dot{R}$ in about four quarters. The monetary policy response will lead to a decline in $\dot{M}$ in about five quarters. The cyclical process could be equally well described starting with any of the other variables and would lead to the same results.

There are two major implications of this model. First, the built-in cyclical property is due to monetary policy responding exclusively to changes in international reserves and such changes are due to domestic considerations. Second, the more expansionary the monetary policy, the greater the cyclical fluctuations in income.

The first implication is derived directly from the structure of the model. Coefficient β_1 is a measure of the policy response to changes in

---

58. The value around which $\dot{Y}_t$ will fluctuate depends strongly on the value of A_0. If A_0 is large, the average value of $\dot{Y}_t$ will be high, and if A_0 is small or negative, the average value of $\dot{Y}_t$ will be low or negative. In one sense, A_0 can be considered as all the unexplained factors in the economy which contribute to its average growth rate, while A_1 represents all of the explicitly considered factors which explain the fluctuations in the growth rate.

international reserves. If monetary policy was not responsive to changes in international reserves, β_1 would be equal to zero. This implies that the product of $\alpha_1\beta_1\rho_1\gamma_1 = A_1 = 0$. In this case, money would grow at a steady rate, β_0, and income would grow at a steady rate $(\beta_0\alpha_1 + \alpha_0)$ subject only to random exogenous influences. Divorcing monetary policy from fluctuations in international reserves would also lead to increased stability in the growth of international reserves. This can be seen by solving the reduced form of the four structural equations for $\dot{R}$ rather than for $\dot{Y}$. The value A_1 would still be equal to the product of $\alpha_1\beta_1\rho_1\gamma_1$.

$$\dot{R}_t = A_{00} + A_1(\dot{R})_{t-5}.$$

If β_1 is zero, then A_1 is also zero and $\dot{R}$ will grow at a steady rate determined by the value A_{00} and random exogenous events.

The economic reasoning behind this is that fluctuations in international reserves are due to domestic factors, namely, variations in imports, and fluctuations in money lead to fluctuations in domestic income. The relationship is, in a sense, a closed loop, with increases in money causing increases in income, and *increases* in income causing *decreases* in money. If the money stock grows at a steady rate, this will lead to a steady rate of growth in income and imports and thereby reduce the variability in international reserves.[59]

The second implication of this model follows easily from the first implication. The more expansionary monetary policy leads to greater fluctuations in income because the more expansionary policy leads to a larger value for the coefficient β_1. As a result, the absolute value of A_1 is larger, which implies larger fluctuations in income.

B. THE ACTUAL DYNAMIC PROPERTIES

The actual set of structural equations used to estimate the behavior postulated in this model is somewhat more complicated than presented in the above example. The statistical estimation of the relation of $I\dot{m}$ to $\dot{R}$ was a second-degree polynomial:

$$\dot{R}_t = \rho_0 + \rho_1 I\dot{m}_{t-2} + \rho_2 I\dot{m}_{t-2}^2.$$

When this is substituted for equation (28) in the example, the reduced form of this system of four equations is as follows:

$$\dot{Y}_t = A_0 + A_1\dot{Y}_{t-5} + A_2\dot{Y}_{t-5}^2, \qquad (31)$$

59. Not all target growth rates in the money stock would be sustainable. If the target growth rate is too high, international reserves will decline and a restrictive monetary policy would have to be initiated. Judging by the 1953–66 experience, target growth rate of 3–4 per cent per quarter would be sustainable.

where

$$A_0 = \alpha_0 + \alpha_1\beta_0 + \alpha_1\beta_1\rho_0 + \alpha_1\beta_1\rho_1\gamma_0 + \alpha_1\beta_1\rho_2\gamma_0^2,$$
$$A_1 = \alpha_1\beta_1\rho_1\gamma_1 + 2\alpha_1\beta_1\rho_2\gamma_0\gamma_1,$$

and

$$A_2 = \alpha_1\beta_1\rho_2\gamma_1^2.$$

Equation (31) can be simplified into a first-order difference equation of the second degree by the same process described above. Thus, it can be rewritten as follows:

$$\dot{Y}_t = A_0 + A_1\dot{Y}_{t-1} + A_2\dot{Y}_{t-1}^2.$$

The implications for the time path of $\dot{Y}_t$ in this more complicated reduced form are not as straightforward mathematically or as intuitively understandable as in my previous example. However, in the range of values of A_1 and A_2 which are observed in the case of Japan (between 0 and -1), the results are the same as in the simple case and this can be shown by simulation.

This business-cycle model was tested for both real and nominal values. The values of the nominal coefficients are as follows:[60]

$$\dot{Y}_t = 1.27 + .51\dot{M}_{t-2}, \tag{32}$$

$$\dot{M}_t = 2.65 + .09\dot{R}_{t-1}, \qquad \dot{M}_t = 4.90 + .34\dot{R}_{t-1}, \tag{33}, (33a)$$

$$\dot{R}_t = 9.69 - 1.16I\dot{m}_{t-2} - .06I\dot{m}_{t-2}^2, \tag{34}$$

$$I\dot{m}_t = -3.16 + 1.91\dot{Y}_t. \tag{35}$$

Equations (33) and (33a) were estimated for separate periods of monetary policy response to the balance of payments. Therefore, the reduced form has two versions:

$$\dot{Y}_t = 3.19 - .068\dot{Y}_{t-5} - .009\dot{Y}_{t-5}^2, \tag{36}$$

$$\dot{Y}_t = 6.01 - .269\dot{Y}_{t-5} - .035\dot{Y}_{t-5}^2. \tag{37}$$

Equation (36) represents the period of less expansionary monetary policy between 1953 and 1960 and (37) the period of more expansionary monetary policy between 1960 and 1964. The results of simulating this equation over time are presented in chart 11. The initial conditions are the first five observations in 1953 and 1954. This chart confirms the implications of the simple example. A monetary policy which is responsive to changes in international reserves leads to an internally

---

60. These coefficients are drawn from sections 3 and 4 where each of the behavioral relations was discussed and the statistical results presented.

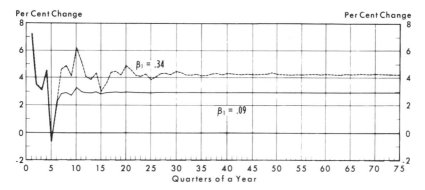

CHART 11. Japan: Simulation of nominal GNP with alternative monetary policies (β_1).

generated cycle in income, and when monetary policy is more expansionary ($\beta_1 = .34$), the fluctuations in nominal income are larger than when monetary policy is less expansionary ($\beta_1 = .09$).

Even though the more expansionary monetary policy leads to larger fluctuations, it also leads to a higher average growth in nominal income. Some fluctuation in the rate of growth of nominal income may seem a small price to pay for increasing the average growth rate. However, this result is illusionary. This we can see by looking at the real variant of the business-cycle model. The values of the real coefficients are given below: [61]

$$\dot{X}_t = 1.37 + .98\dot{M}^*_{t-2}, \qquad \dot{X} = .14 + .75\dot{M}^*_{t-2}, \qquad (38), (38a)$$

$$\dot{M}^*_t = 2.20 + .101\dot{R}^*_{t-1}, \qquad \dot{M}^*_t = 3.16 + .298\dot{R}^*_{t-1}, \qquad (39), (39a)$$

$$\dot{R}^*_t = 10.1 - 1.23I\dot{m}^*_{t-2} - .056I\dot{m}^*_{t-2}, \qquad (40)$$

$$I\dot{m}^*_t = -3.26 + 2.04\dot{X}_t. \qquad (41)$$

In the real version of the business-cycle model, there are two monetary policy subperiods as in the nominal version. Thus, in the reduced form, there are also two real variants, one for the period of moderate policy (1953–60) and one for the period of expansionary policy (1960–64):

$$\dot{X}_t = 4.86 - .175\dot{X}_{t-5} - .023\dot{X}^2_{t-5}, \qquad (42)$$

$$\dot{X}_t = 5.53 - .394\dot{X}_{t-5} - .052\dot{X}^2_{t-5}. \qquad (43)$$

When (42) and (43) are simulated in the same manner as in the nominal version, the same results are observed with respect to the effects of monetary policy on the business cycle. A policy responsive to changes

61. Sources of those coefficients are the same as in note 60.

in international reserves leads to cyclical movements in income, and the more expansionary policy ($\beta_1 = .298$) leads to greater fluctuation than the less expansionary policy ($\beta_1 = .101$). However, in this case the average rate of growth of real output is actually somewhat less in the expansionary period than in the nonexpansionary period. These results can be seen in chart 12.

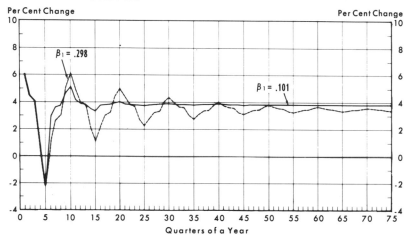

CHART 12. Japan: Simulation of real product with alternative monetary policies (β_1).

The different results in the nominal and in the real business-cycle models are reasonable. In the nominal business-cycle model, the more expansionary period is also one of rising prices, while the less expansionary period is one of relative price stability. Thus, one would expect that a business-cycle model utilizing nominal values would exhibit a higher average growth rate in periods of monetary expansion. One would also expect that a business-cycle model using real values would not necessarily show a higher average growth rate during expansionary periods. These results are consistent with the historic evidence. Nominal income grew more rapidly in the expansionary period (1960–64) than in the less expansionary period (1953–60). But real income grew at about the same rate in both periods.

C. THE SHOCKED DYNAMIC PROPERTIES

So far the cyclical properties of this model have been investigated under a very restrictive set of assumptions. The functional relationships have been treated as if they were exact. But, in fact, random elements are inherent in the statistical estimation of all the equations. By ignoring the random elements I have deliberately sacrificed much of the inherent cyclical properties of the model. As pointed out by Frisch (1933), the random elements alone could induce a cycle.

In spite of the limitation of treating the model as if each of the four equations were exact, the cyclical pattern of the model has been apparent. However, this cyclical pattern is both damped and highly regular in timing. Although the Japanese business cycle has shown some regularity in timing, its pattern has not been damped. Specifically recognizing the random element will eliminate the dampening observed in the simulation of the model.

Because the four structural equations which underlie this model are probabilistic, there is a random error term in each of the equations. These random error terms stem from specification errors, measurement errors, and exogenous factors such as strikes, natural calamities, etc., which temporarily distort the systematic behavioral relation among the variables, and represent sources of irregularity in estimating the original structural equations. The residuals of the four equations in this model can therefore be attributed to a number of different types of errors. Since there appears to be no a priori correlation among the individual sources of error, these residuals or error terms are assumed to be normally distributed.

These error terms have been utilized to introduce realistic random shocks into the model. For each of the structural equations, an additive random error term was specified. Using the same process of algebraic substitution which was used in solving the reduced form of the unshocked system, a new reduced form equation was constructed. In this equation several error terms appear as parameters analogous to lagged endogenous variables. The size and direction of these shocks are determined by selection of random numbers out of a normally distributed population based on the size of the error terms in each of the structural equations.

The results of simulating this model for both its real and nominal versions are shown in charts 13 and 14. It can be observed that the cyclical pattern of income is no longer damped nor as regular in timing as in the unshocked simulation of the model. It is a more realistic representation of the Japanese business cycle. It is interesting to note that the more expansionary policy leads to larger fluctuations in both nominal GNP and real product than does the less expansionary policy. This is true in spite of the fact that the error terms in the expansionary period are smaller.

It should be kept in mind that contrary to the dynamic properties of

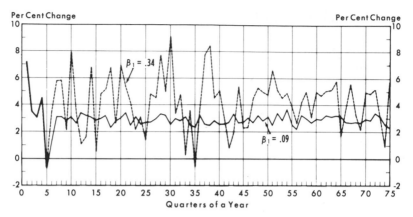

CHART 13. Japan: Shocked simulation of nominal GNP with alternative monetary policies (β_1).

more elaborate economic models which have been tested for the United States and elsewhere,[62] the cyclical fluctuations of this model are inherent in its dynamic properties. The application of random shocks to the system only makes the magnitude and timing of the cycles more in line with real-world observations.   ·

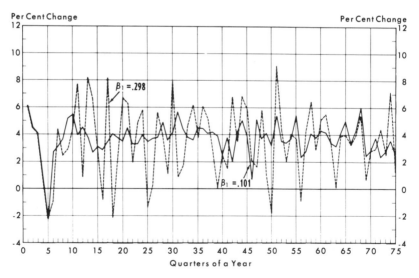

CHART 14. Japan: Shocked simulation of real product with alternative monetary policies (β_1).

62. Adelman and Adelman, *Readings in Business Cycles*, p. 252.

D. CONCLUSION

The Japanese business cycle can be understood reasonably well on the basis of the highly simplified model developed in this study. This model, as with any economic model, is useful only to the extent that its underlying assumptions remain valid. The statements that monetary policy is a function of fluctuations in international reserves and that changes in international reserves are a function of changes in imports are special assumptions which may not be applicable in the future.

The relatively stable international economic environment of post–World War II has led to the dismantling of exchange controls and steady expansion in world trade. In the short run each country's exports are largely a function of the growth and stability of world trade, so it is not unreasonable to attribute fluctuations in Japan's international reserves primarily to domestic factors. A useful direction for future research would be to see whether this same phenomenon can be observed in other countries. If it holds reasonably well, this model may have wider implications for analyzing business-cycle developments in other countries.[63]

The major conclusion of this study is that given the assumptions made, monetary policy directed at reducing fluctuation in international reserves will not only lead to greater fluctuations in income but also to greater fluctuations in international reserves. An important consideration in future research would be to see if alternative monetary policy targets, such as stable prices or reduced unemployment, led to the same results. The basic structural model underlying these alternative policy goals is similar to the one constructed in this study.

Consider the price stability target $(\dot{P}_t)$. The model could be as follows:

$$\dot{Y}_t = \alpha_0 + \alpha_1 \dot{M}_{t-m},$$

$$\dot{M}_t = \lambda_0 + \lambda_1 \dot{P}_{t-p},$$

$$\dot{P}_t = \delta_0 + \delta_1 \dot{Y}_{t-r}.$$

The reduced form of this series of equations is

$$\dot{Y}_t = A_0' + A_1' \dot{Y}_{t-(m+p+r)},$$

where $\dot{P}$ = rate of change in prices, and where $A_1' = \alpha_1 \lambda_1 \delta_1$.

63. There is some evidence to indicate that a model similar to that developed in this study could explain much of the postwar business cycle experience of the major western European countries. See Federal Reserve Bank of St. Louis, *Review*, November 1967, "Monetary Policy, Balance of Payments, and Business Cycles—The Foreign Experience," by Michael Keran.

A'_1 is negative because λ_1 is negative.

Consider the unemployment target (U_t):

$$\dot{Y}_t = \alpha_0 + \alpha_1 \dot{M}_{t-m},$$

$$\dot{M}_t = \theta_0 + \theta_1 U_{t-s},$$

$$U_t = \phi_0 + \phi_1 \dot{Y}_{t-v}.$$

The reduced form is:

$$\dot{Y}_t = A''_0 + A''_1 \dot{Y}_{t-(m+s+v)},$$

where U is the unemployment rate and $A''_1 = \alpha_1 \theta_1 \phi_1$. A''_1 is negative because ϕ_1 is negative.

The difference equations developed with respect to the price and unemployment targets are mathematically equivalent to the one developed in this study with respect to the international reserve target. And in each case there is a built-in cyclical bias in the application of monetary policy. Whether this bias is significant depends on how sensitive the policy-makers are to these various policy goals. If their response is relatively prompt, that is, the time lags are short, and if the response is relatively moderate, the value A_1 being closer to 0 than to -1, then cyclical bias may not be significant. Further research could usefully explore these issues.

Is it inevitable that monetary policy have a bias toward cyclical instability irrespective of the policy target chosen? There is one policy target which does not have the cyclical bias; that is, a policy of maintaining a steady growth in the stock of money.

APPENDIX

KEY

(Billions of Yen)

		Source
Y	Nominal GNP	(1)
Y^*	Real GNP	(2)
M	Nominal money supply	(2)
M^*	Real money supply	(2)
R	Nominal international reserves	(3)
R^*	Real international reserves	(3)
Im	Nominal imports (millions of U.S. $)	(2)
Im^*	Real imports (millions of U.S. $)	(2)
X	Industrial production (1960 = 100)	(2)
$\dot{X}$	Rate of change in series	

SOURCES:
1. *Annual Report on National Income Statistics*, 1967. Economic Planning Agency, Government of Japan.

2. *Basic Data For Economic Analysis, 1966*. Statistics Dept., Bank of Japan.

3. *Economic Statistics Monthly* (various issues). Statistics Dept., Bank of Japan.

TABLE 8

NOMINAL LEVELS
(Billions of Yen)

Year	Quarter	Y	M	R	Im (Millions of U.S. Dollars)
1953.........	I	6,403	1,525	332	521
	II	6,787	1,548	303	566
	III	7,357	1,657	317	640
	IV	7,276	1,661	285	698
1954.........	I	7,817	1,668	202	692
	II	7,943	1,656	173	633
	III	7,700	1,664	188	534
	IV	7,714	1,704	252	519
1955.........	I	7,956	1,735	276	556
	II	7,866	1,768	307	596
	III	8,719	1,845	358	624
	IV	9,400	1,894	411	698
1956.........	I	9,114	1,967	446	672
	II	9,225	2,070	455	752
	III	9,346	2,212	457	856
	IV	10,229	2,275	458	959
1957.........	I	10,701	2,373	382	1,056
	II	11,286	2,382	259	1,196
	III	11,076	2,346	197	1,090
	IV	11,212	2,394	226	914
1958.........	I	11,156	2,421	268	811
	II	11,219	2,488	301	730
	III	11,601	2,593	358	735
	IV	11,298	2,702	427	761
1959.........	I	11,905	2,764	462	789
	II	12,290	2,892	509	895
	III	13,292	2,990	550	912
	IV	13,462	3,124	600	1,003
1960.........	I	14,334	3,266	613	1,109
	II	14,852	3,370	649	1,063
	III	15,364	3,531	729	1,143
	IV	16,047	3,741	788	1,164
1961.........	I	17,311	4,010	851	1,292
	II	18,053	4,296	819	1,405
	III	18,711	4,414	728	1,529
	IV	19,810	4,491	641	1,595
1962.........	I	20,320	4,531	629	1,492
	II	20,867	4,652	562	1,406
	III	20,582	4,852	595	1,367
	IV	21,549	5,160	673	1,374

TABLE 8—*Continued*

1963	I	21,616	5,764	730	1,484
	II	22,953	6,305	759	1,622
	III	24,586	6,714	763	1,756
	IV	24,990	7,055	746	1,872
1964	I	26,128	7,214	727	1,989
	II	26,982	7,462	666	1,965
	III	28,340	7,716	662	1,929
	IV	28,944	7,980	714	2,044
1965	I	29,264	8,367	732	1,993
	II	30,209	8,605	701	2,060
	III	30,537	9,000	693	2,067
	IV	31,699	9,435	737	2,062
1966	I	32,738	9,760	738	2,232
	II	34,204	10,091	724	2,285
	III	35,909	10,569	694	2,431
	IV	36,909	10,773	700	2,592

TABLE 9

REAL LEVELS
(Billions of 1960 Yen)

Year	Quarter	*Y**	*M**	*R**	*Im** (Millions of U.S. Dollars)	*X* (1960 = 100)
1953....	I	7,902	1,960	264.8	415.5	36.3
	II	8,170	1,845	260.7	455.3	39.8
	III	8,534	1,933	256.7	521.6	41.5
	IV	8,464	1,881	214.6	580.7	43.6
1954....	I	9,011	1,986	171.0	585.9	44.2
	II	8,880	1,840	164.7	534.6	44.2
	III	8,700	1,895	199.7	453.7	42.9
	IV	8,558	1,850	235.0	437.2	43.5
1955....	I	9,006	2,034	256.9	465.3	44.8
	II	8,970	1,998	292.9	501.7	45.6
	III	9,818	2,094	333.6	520.4	47.8
	IV	10,544	2,068	375.3	590.0	49.8
1956....	I	10,117	2,264	396.6	571.9	51.9
	II	10,251	2,292	396.5	633.0	55.8
	III	10,226	2,436	399.3	724.2	59.5
	IV	10,964	2,380	357.2	789.3	62.8
1957....	I	11,329	2,591	265.4	854.4	65.0
	II	11,772	2,476	194.4	985.2	70.1
	III	11,556	2,457	185.8	920.6	69.5
	IV	11,724	2,455	224.1	803.2	67.3
1958....	I	11,826	2,634	267.4	742.7	66.7
	II	11,885	2,638	319.7	692.6	64.8
	III	12,313	2,779	383.5	704.7	66.3
	IV	11,908	2,791	443.1	746.1	69.0
1959....	I	12,470	2,947	489.1	782.7	72.6
	II	12,876	3,038	528.0	880.0	77.7
	III	13,726	3,118	574.4	898.5	82.3
	IV	13,781	3,140	595.4	971.0	88.1
1960....	I	14,613	3,370	575.0	1,080.9	92.5
	II	14,823	3,377	639.1	1,048.3	97.8
	III	15,258	3,542	718.7	1,144.1	101.9
	IV	16,245	3,646	786.1	1,174.0	106.9
1961....	I	16,962	3,939	795.0	1,292.0	111.9
	II	17,401	4,139	718.6	1,377.5	116.7
	III	17,706	4,216	631.4	1,499.0	122.7
	IV	18,388	4,124	590.5	1,585.5	127.1
1962....	I	18,613	4,161	557.9	1,502.5	129.8
	II	19,059	4,252	546.8	1,431.8	130.2
	III	18,583	4,435	608.2	1,402.1	129.0
	IV	19,552	4,632	680.0	1,413.6	128.4

TABLE 9—*Continued*

1963....	I	18,891	5,021	714.7	1,506.6	131.9
	II	19,932	5,473	721.7	1,623.6	138.0
	III	21,242	5,874	704.4	1,730.0	146.1
	IV	21,513	6,014	672.8	1,806.9	153.7
1964....	I	22,471	6,198	632.9	1,916.2	158.9
	II	22,942	6,361	608.8	1,917.1	165.0
	III	23,755	6,572	635.9	1,893.0	168.8
	IV	23,726	6,488	672.2	2,011.8	173.2
1965....	I	23,825	6,769	679.4	2,003.6	174.6
	II	24,269	6,928	656.7	2,062.1	173.5
	III	24,210	7,252	672.7	2,062.9	174.8
	IV	24,498	7,247	697.7	2,064.1	175.5
1966....	I	25,612	7,578	680.8	2,199.0	182.4
	II	26,384	7,823	655.2	2,238.0	189.5
	III	27,402	8,231	642.9	2,378.7	199.1
	IV	27,993	7,945	647.0	2,589.4	209.6

TABLE 10

NOMINAL RATES OF CHANGE

Year	Quarter	$\dot{Y}$	$\dot{M}$	$\dot{R}$	$\dot{i}m$
1953.......	I				
	II	7.2	4.2	−2.4	7.2
	III	3.5	3.6	−2.8	10.8
	IV	3.1	.4	−18.1	7.3
1954.......	I	4.5	−.4	−21.7	−4.3
	II	−.7	−.3	−3.5	−14.5
	III	−1.5	1.9	20.5	−9.2
	IV	1.7	2.3	18.7	4.5
1955.......	I	1.0	1.4	10.0	7.3
	II	4.7	2.9	13.4	4.3
	III	9.3	3.9	14.9	8.4
	IV	2.2	3.6	11.0	5.5
1956.......	I	−.9	4.2	5.0	3.9
	II	1.3	5.7	1.1	12.1
	III	5.3	5.2	.2	12.9
	IV	7.0	3.9	−8.1	10.7
1957.......	I	5.0	2.0	−24.4	11.8
	II	1.7	−.8	−28.0	2.9
	III	−.3	.6	−6.8	−12.3
	IV	.4	1.8	15.9	−14.9
1958.......	I	0	1.6	14.5	−10.7
	II	2.0	3.3	15.4	−2.9
	III	.4	4.5	18.7	1.9
	IV	1.3	3.4	13.0	2.1
1959.......	I	4.3	3.3	9.1	9.1
	II	5.7	3.9	8.9	8.7
	III	4.7	4.0	8.6	5.8
	IV	3.9	4.6	5.5	10.2
1960.......	I	5.0	4.0	−4.1	3.1
	II	3.5	4.0	9.8	1.6
	III	4.0	5.1	10.8	5.1
	IV	6.4	6.5	8.5	6.0
1961.......	I	6.1	7.6	2.1	9.3
	II	3.7	5.0	−7.8	8.9
	III	4.8	1.7	−12.1	7.4
	IV	4.2	1.2	−7.8	−1.1
1962.......	I	2.6	2.4	−6.7	−7.0
	II	.7	3.6	−3.1	−4.6
	III	1.6	4.6	10.4	.2
	IV	2.5	8.9	11.5	4.3
1963.......	I	3.2	11.2	6.5	7.6
	II	6.7	8.0	2.4	8.3
	III	4.4	5.2	−.8	9.2
	IV	3.1	3.6	−2.5	7.5

TABLE 10—*Continued*

1964.......	I	3.9	3.3	− 5.7	1.0
	II	4.2	3.4	− 5.0	− 2.5
	III	3.6	3.1	2.2	3.4
	IV	1.6	4.1	5.5	2.3
1965.......	I	2.2	4.1	− 1.0	− .5
	II	2.2	3.8	− 2.9	− .8
	III	2.4	4.6	2.7	4.0
	IV	3.5	4.1	3.4	5.4
1966.......	I	4.0	3.5	− .9	4.4
	II	4.8	4.1	− 3.2	6.5
	III	4.0	3.4	− 1.8	6.7
	IV				

TABLE 11

REAL RATES OF CHANGE

Year	Quarter	$\dot{Y}*$	$\dot{M}*$	$\dot{R}*$	$\dot{i}m*$	$\dot{X}$
1953....	I					
	II	3.9	2.0	−1.6	12.2	6.1
	III	1.8	.6	−1.5	13.0	4.5
	IV	2.8	−2.0	−16.4	6.0	4.1
1954....	I	2.4	−1.3	−20.3	−4.1	.9
	II	−1.7	−.6	−3.7	−12.0	−2.2
	III	−1.8	1.6	21.3	−9.5	.8
	IV	1.7	2.7	17.7	1.2	2.9
1955....	I	2.4	2.2	9.3	7.2	4.6
	II	4.4	3.4	14.0	5.8	3.0
	III	8.4	3.8	13.9	8.4	4.3
	IV	1.5	3.3	12.5	4.9	5.1
1956	I	−1.4	4.0	5.7	3.6	6.1
	II	.5	5.8	0	12.5	6.2
	III	3.4	4.7	.7	11.7	5.8
	IV	5.3	2.5	−10.6	8.6	4.6
1957....	I	3.6	1.0	−25.7	11.7	6.2
	II	1.0	−1.7	−26.8	3.9	3.6
	III	−.2	.3	−4.4	−9.7	−2.4
	IV	1.2	2.6	20.6	−10.2	−2.2
1958....	I	.7	2.4	19.3	−7.1	−1.5
	II	2.0	3.2	19.6	−2.6	−.2
	III	.1	3.8	20.0	3.8	2.9
	IV	.6	3.3	15.5	5.4	4.5
1959....	I	4.0	3.5	10.4	8.6	6.4
	II	4.9	3.4	8.0	7.2	6.6
	III	3.5	3.0	8.8	5.0	6.3
	IV	3.2	3.4	3.7	9.7	6.5
1960....	I	3.7	2.9	−3.4	3.9	5.6
	II	2.2	3.1	11.1	2.9	4.5
	III	4.7	4.7	12.5	5.9	4.5
	IV	5.4	5.4	9.4	6.3	4.6
1961....	I	3.5	5.9	1.1	8.3	4.6
	II	2.2	3.3	−9.6	7.7	5.0
	III	2.8	−.6	−12.1	7.3	4.3
	IV	2.5	−.9	−6.5	.1	2.7
1962....	I	1.8	−.3	−5.5	−4.9	1.3
	II	−.1	2.3	−2.0	−3.4	−.1
	III	1.3	5.2	11.2	−.6	−.7
	IV	.8	6.6	11.8	3.7	.9
1963....	I	1.0	7.6	5.1	7.2	3.6
	II	6.0	6.1	1.0	7.2	5.7
	III	3.9	5.0	−2.4	5.5	5.7
	IV	2.9	3.7	−4.5	5.2	4.4

TABLE 11—*Continued*

1964....	I	3.3	2.1	−5.9	3.0	3.6
	II	2.8	1.8	−3.8	−.6	3.4
	III	1.7	1.5	4.5	2.5	2.3
	IV	.2	1.8	5.7	2.9	.8
1965....	I	1.1	1.8	1.1	1.2	−.5
	II	.8	2.4	−3.4	1.5	.3
	III	.5	3.2	2.4	.1	.5
	IV	2.9	2.4	3.7	3.3	1.9
1966....	I	3.8	2.3	−2.4	4.1	4.0
	II	3.5	3.2	−3.8	4.0	5.0
	III	3.0	2.4	−1.9	7.6	5.1
	IV					

TABLE 12
RATIOS AND RATES OF CHANGE

Year	Quarter	D/C	$(D/\dot{C})$	D/R	$(D/\dot{R})$
1954.......	I	2.275		21.8	
	II	2.307	1.3	20.6	−2.1
	III	2.335	2.3	20.9	6.6
	IV	2.414	2.6	23.4	−.2
1955.......	I	2.460	2.4	20.8	−4.6
	II	2.532	2.6	21.3	2.8
	III	2.587	2.1	22.0	2.1
	IV	2.639	2.3	22.2	.5
1956.......	I	2.707	2.8	22.2	1.3
	II	2.789	2.9	22.8	.9
	III	2.864	1.7	22.6	−2.0
	IV	2.887	.2	21.9	−1.6
1957.......	I	2.877	−.6	21.9	−3.2
	II	2.854	−1.3	20.5	−7.3
	III	2.800	−.2	18.8	−5.0
	IV	2.843	1.7	18.5	−1.9
1958.......	I	2.897	1.9	18.1	−1.1
	II	2.953	2.3	18.1	1.1
	III	3.030	2.7	18.5	4.1
	IV	3.117	.7	19.6	−.8
1959.......	I	3.072	0	18.2	−2.8
	II	3.116	.4	18.5	−.8
	III	3.095	−.4	17.9	−1.6
	IV	3.089	.9	17.9	−.3
1960.......	I	3.151	.6	17.8	−2.8
	II	3.125	−.2	16.9	−1.4
	III	3.139	.7	17.3	−.6
	IV	3.170	1.1	16.7	−1.2
1961.......	I	3.211	1.4	16.9	3.5
	II	3.260	−.3	17.9	−1.8
	III	3.194	−2.0	16.3	−4.3
	IV	3.134	−2.8	16.4	−3.4
1962.......	I	3.017	−2.2	15.2	−3.4
	II	2.997	0	15.3	.7
	III	3.016	2.5	15.4	0
	IV	3.148	7.0	15.3	2.9
1963.......	I	3.453	7.8	16.3	4.2
	II	3.659	6.1	16.6	1.2
	III	3.889	3.4	16.7	0
	IV	3.913	−.1	16.6	−2.7

TABLE 12—*Continued*

1964.......	I	3.878	−1.4	15.8	−.9
	II	3.807	−1.0	16.3	1.0
	III	3.799	−.1	16.1	−.3
	IV	3.797	−.1	16.2	3.7
1965.......	I	3.790	.5	17.3	3.0
	II	3.838	1.3	17.2	2.3
	III	3.890	1.8	18.1	5.7
	IV	3.975	.6	19.2	1.1
1966.......	I	3.934	−.1	18.5	−1.0
	II	3.965	.4	18.8	3.2
	III	3.968	−.1	19.7	1.1
	IV	3.955		19.2	

References

Adelman, F., and Adelman, I., "The Dynamic Properties of the Klein-Goldberger Model," *Econometrica* 27 (1956). Reprinted in *Readings in Business Cycles*. Homewood, Ill.: Richard D. Irwin, 1965.

Allen, C. G., *Japan's Economic Recovery*. New York: Oxford Univ. Press, 1958.

———. *Japan's Economic Expansion*. New York: Oxford Univ. Press, 1965.

Allen, R. G. D. *Mathematical Analysis for Economists*. London: Macmillan & Co., 1938.

———. *Mathematical Economics*. London: Macmillan & Co., 1956.

Bank of Japan. *The Bank of Japan Law and By-Laws*. October 1952.

———. *Foreign Exchange Statistics Monthly*. (JE)*

———. *Economic Statistics of Japan, Annual*. (JE)

———. *Economic Statistics Monthly*. (JE)

———. *Monthly Economic Review*.

———. *Outline of the Financial System in Japan*. 2d rev. ed. January 1957.

Baumol, William. *Economic Dynamics*, 2d ed. New York: Macmillan Co., 1959.

Cagan, P. *Determinants and Effects of Changes in the Stock of Money, 1875–1960*. New York: National Bureau of Economic Research, 1963.

———. "The Economics of Hyperinflation." In *Studies in the Quantity Theory of Money*, ed. Milton Friedman. Chicago: Univ. of Chicago Press, 1956.

Dewald, W., and Johnson, H. "An Objective Analysis of the Objectives of American Monetary Policy 1952–61." In *Banking and Monetary Studies*, ed. Deane Carson. Homewood, Ill.: Richard D. Irwin,1963.

Economic Counsel Board. *Economic Survey of Japan*. 1953–54.

---

* Many official publications of the Japanese government are in bilingual form in Japanese and English. For such publications the English title only is given, with the symbol (JE) at the end of the entry, indicating that the given publication is in both Japanese and English.

Economic Planning Agency. *Economic Survey of Japan.* 1956, 1957, 1958, 1959, 1960, 1961, 1962, 1963, 1964.

———. *New Long-Range Economic Plan of Japan* (FY 1953–FY 1962).

———. *New Long-Range Economic Plan of Japan (1961–70)—Doubling National Income Plan. Japan Times,* Tokyo, 1961.

———. *Medium Term Economic Plan,* 1964–68. June 1965.

Economic Planning Board. *Economic Survey of Japan,* 1954–55 and 1955–56.

Economic Stabilization Board. *Economic Survey of Japan,* 1951–52. July 1952.

Federal Reserve System, Board of Governors. *Federal Reserve Bulletin.* March 1965.

Friedman, Milton. "The Demand for Money." *Journal of Political Economy* 57 (1959): 327–51.

———, ed. *Studies in the Quantity Theory of Money.* Chicago: Univ. of Chicago Press, 1956.

———, and Schwartz, A. *A Monetary History of the United States.* National Bureau of Economic Research, 1964.

Frisch, R. "Propagation Problems and Impulse Problems in Dynamic Economics." In *Economic Essays in Honor of Gustav Cassel.* London, 1933. Reprinted in *Readings in Business Cycles.* Homewood, Ill.: Richard D. Irwin, 1965.

Goto, Yonosuke. "Keiki Dōkō to Junkan Kyokumen no Rikai no tame ni" (Understanding the Tendency of Economic Activity and the Business Cycle). In *Kinyū Zaisei Jijō,* vol. 8 (February 25, March 4, 1957).

International Monetary Fund. *International Financial Statistics.* Monthly.

Johnson, J. *Econometric Methods.* New York: McGraw-Hill Co., 1963.

Kareken, John, and Solow, Robert M. "Lags in Monetary Policy." *Stabilization Policies* (A Series of Research Studies Prepared for the Commission on Money and Credit). Englewood Cliffs, N.J.: Prentice-Hall, 1963.

Landberg, Eric. *Studies in the Theory of Economic Expansion.* London, 1937.

Metzler, Lloyd A. "The Nature and Stability of Inventory Cycles." *Review of Economic Statistics* vol. 23 (1941). Reprinted in *Readings in Business Cycles.* Homewood, Ill.: Richard D. Irwin, 1965.

———. "Three Lags in a Circular Flow of Income," *Income, Employment, and Public Policy: Essays in Honor of Alvin Hansen.* New York: W. H. Norton Co., 1948.

Modigliani, Franco. "Liquidity Preferences and the Theory of Interest and Money." *Econometrica* 12 (1944): 45–88. Reprinted in American Economic Association, *Readings in Monetary Theory*. Homewood, Ill.: Richard D. Irwin, 1951.

————. "The Monetary Mechanism and Its Interaction with Real Phenomena." *Review of Economics and Statistics* 45 (1963): 79–107.

Patrick, Hugh T. *Monetary Policy and Central Banking in Contemporary Japan*. Bombay: University of Bombay Press, 1962.

Polak, J. J. "Monetary Analysis of Income Formation and Payments Problems." International Monetary Fund, *Staff Papers* vol. 6, no. 1 (1957).

————. "Monetary Analysis of Income and Imports and Its Statistical Application." International Monetary Fund, *Staff Papers* vol. 7, no. 3 (1960).

Robertson, D. H. "Some Notes on Mr. Keynes' General Theory of Employment." *Quarterly Journal of Economics* 51 (1936): 168–91.

Samuelson, P. "Interactions between Multiplier Analysis and Principle of Acceleration." *Review of Economic Statistics* 21 (1939). Reprinted in *Readings in Business Cycle Theory*. American Economic Association, 1944.

Shimomura, Osamu. "Tomen no Keizai Kyokumen o Tsuranuku Kihon Dōkō." (The Fundamental Tendencies of the Immediate Economic Situation), *Kinyū Zaisei Jijō*, vol. 8 (February 11 and 18, 1957).

Shinjo, Hiroshi. *History of the Yen*. Kobe, Japan: Research Institute, Kobe University, 1962.

Shinohara, Miyoshi. *Growth and Cycles in the Japanese Economy*. Tokyo: Kenkyusha Printing Co., 1962.

IV

Supply and Demand for Money in Canada

GEORGE MACESICH

Supply and Demand for Money in Canada

1. Introduction

W E have it on good authority that Canada was perhaps the first country to commit itself to a firmly Keynesian policy.[1] To judge from the accumulating evidence, Canada may well have opted prematurely for Keynesian policy if that policy is interpreted as assigning a secondary role to money and monetary policy.[2] The evidence casts doubt on

I am indebted to the Graduate Research Council, Florida State University for financial assistance which partly made this study possible. To the Computing Center and its Director, Dr. E. P. Miles, goes thanks for making available machine time which made many of the computations possible. Professors Milton Friedman, David Meiselman, Phillip Cagan, Harry G. Johnson, and Mrs. Anna J. Schwartz have been particularly helpful at several stages of the study and I am thankful to them for it. I would like to express my appreciation also to my colleagues Professors Marshall R. Colberg, William P. Dillingham, A. G. Holtmann, W. E. Laird, Jr., Warren F. Mazek, Charles E. Rockwood, and Irvin Sobel, who have made valuable comments on various aspects of the study. Miss Mary Louise White, Miss Wynelle Wilson, Dr. Jan Duggar, Dr. F. A. Close, Mr. C. A. Haulman, Mr. Owen B. Murphy, Mr. R. E. Burney, and Dr. Frank Falero have also given valuable assistance, as have Mrs. Gennelle P. Jordan, Mrs. Eddine R. Kessler, and Mrs. Elizabeth B. Hunt, and my thanks to them.

I should like to make acknowledgments to the editors of the *Canadian Journal of Economics and Political Science* and the *Southern Economic Journal* for permission to reproduce material previously published in their pages. I have also made some of the results of these earlier studies available upon request to members of the staff of the Royal Commission on Banking and Finance, e.g., H. G. Johnson and John W. L. Winder, *Lags in the Effects of Monetary Policy in Canada* (Ottawa: the Queen's Printer, Mimeo, 1962). The present study, however, incorporates substantial amounts of additional material not hitherto published. In addition, the study updates previously published material and thus provides a check of the consistency of earlier results.

1. John Kenneth Galbraith, "Came the Revolution" [Review of J. M. Keynes, *The General Theory of Employment, Interest, and Money* (New York: Harcourt Brace and World. Paperback edition)] *New York Times Book Review*, May 16, 1965, p. 34.

2. What these results indicate is that a simple version of the quantity-theory approach to income changes is more useful than a simple version of the

the empirical assertions that the stock of money does not matter and that income velocity behaves in an erratic and unpredictable manner. Such assertions contributed in no small measure to the subordination of the role of money in economic analysis in the post-Depression years.

The purpose of this study is to examine in detail the supply and demand for money in Canada since 1926. Section 2 discusses the money supply against the Canadian cyclical background. Section 3 examines more intensively the supply of money in business cycles. Section 4 discusses the composition of the money stock and the relative demand for currency and deposits. Section 5 examines the demand for money. Section 6 presents the conclusions. An appendix contains the Canadian

---

income- expenditure theory. The results, however, are not as strikingly one-sided in favor of the quantity theory as earlier studies indicated. Since the Canadian tests are based on comparatively simple versions of the two theories the results are, like all scientific judgments, subject to later modifications as additional data and other ways of organizing these data become available.

George Macesich, "The Quantity Theory and the Income Expenditure Theory in an Open Economy: Canada 1926–1958," *Canadian Journal of Economics and Political Science* (August 1964), pp. 368–90; C. L. Barber, "The Quantity Theory and the Income Expenditure Theory in an Open Economy, 1926–1958: A Comment," and George Macesich, "Empirical Testing and the Income Expenditure Theory," *Canadian Jour. of Econ. and Pol. Sci.* (1966); Macesich, "The Quantity Theory and the Income Expenditure Theory in an Open Economy Revisited," *Canadian Jour. of Econ.* (1969); Macesich, *Economic Stability: A Comparative Analysis* (forthcoming); Macesich, *Money and the Canadian Economy* (Belgrade: National Bank of Yugoslavia, 1967); George Macesich and Frank Falero, Jr., "Permanent Income Hypothesis, Interest Rates, and Demand for Money," *Weltwirtshaftliches Archiv* (1969). See also F. A. Close, "A Study of the Comparative Stability of the Investment Multiplier and Monetary Velocity for Twenty-Two Countries" (Unpublished Ph.D. diss., Florida State Univ., June 1968); Milton Friedman and David Meiselman, "The Relative Stability of Monetary Velocity and the Investment Multiplier in the United States, 1897–1958" in *Stabilization Policies* (Englewood Cliffs, N.J.: Prentice Hall for the Commission on Money and Credit, 1963), pp. 185–268; D. H. Hester, "Keynes and the Quantity Theory: A Comment on the Friedman-Meiselman CMC Paper," "Reply to Donald Hester," and Hester's "Rejoinder," *Review of Economics and Statistics* (November 1964); Albert Ando and Franco Modigliani, "The Relative Stability of Monetary Velocity and the Investment Multiplier"; Michael DePrano and Thomas Mayer, "Tests of the Relative Importance of Autonomous Expenditures and Money"; Milton Friedman and David Meiselman, "Reply to Ando and Modigliani and to DePrano and Mayer"; and rejoinders by Ando and Modigliani and DePrano and Mayer, *American Economic Review* (September 1965); George Macesich and F. A. Close, "Monetary Velocity and Investment Multiplier Stability Relativity for Norway and Sweden," *Statsøkonomisk Tidskrift* (1969); Macesich and Close, "Comparative Stability of Monetary Velocity and Investment Multiplier for Austria and Yugoslavia," *Florida State University Slavic Papers*, 1969.

money supply series for the period 1868–1958, constructed on the basis of monthly reports by chartered banks plus other material.

2. The Canadian Cyclical Background

Canada shared in the general disenchantment with monetary policy as a principal instrument for stabilizing economic activity which came with the great Depression. This disenchantment fostered the belief that money does not matter except possibly in influencing interest rates. From the late 1930s to the very early 1950s Canada apparently pursued a monetary policy based on this belief. Both the stock of money and prices continued to rise, creating in their wake severe inflationary and balance-of-payments problems. It was only after firmer control over the stock of money was reinstituted that price stability followed. Such stability during the closing years of this study apparently put an end to the critical nature of Canada's recurring balance of payments crisis.

Under the gold standard and fixed exchange rates a small country has little room to pursue an independent monetary policy. Its stock of money must be whatever is required to maintain external balance. This describes Canada in the period between 1926, the year it returned to the gold standard, and the early part of 1929, the year the Department of Finance informally terminated the unrestricted convertibility of Dominion notes, a fact recognized formally in 1931.

The upswing in economic activity that occurred in the period between the trough in August 1924 and the peak in April 1929 began to lose momentum as early as 1927 with the appearance of a balance-of-payments deficit and subsequent outflow of gold. Preservation of external balance under the usual gold-standard rules of the game required an internal contraction in Canada, but an internal contraction did not occur at this time. This meant that the required adjustment to the deficit had to occur in another form. In Canada the deficit was met by gold outflows.[3]

Continued expansion of the money stock is traced to the expansion of notes and deposits by chartered banks. The failure on the part of these banks to contract their operations and so preserve external balance was the result of the operation of the Finance Act.[4] Under its provision chartered banks were able to replenish their reserves by pledging securities with the minister of finance and receiving in exchange Dominion notes convertible into gold. The gold drain was, in

3. R. Craig McIvor, *Canadian Monetary, Banking, and Fiscal Development*, Toronto: Macmillan Company of Canada, 1958), p. 123.

4. *Ibid.*

effect, transferred from the banks to the government. Following a heavy gold drain at the end of 1928 the Department of Finance ceased to convert Dominion notes into gold in early 1929, and Canada departed de facto from the gold standard rather than undertake the adjustments required by that standard.

Money, prices, and income contracted sharply during the period from 1930 to 1933. The exchange rate, however, remained buoyant. A combination of factors explains the failure of the Canadian dollar to depreciate vis-à-vis the American dollar and British pound following the country's de facto departure from the gold standard. In the first place, Canada gave the appearance that it would continue to follow the rules for the preservation of fixed exchange rates and the maintenance of external balance, even though it was no longer on the gold standard. One effect of such efforts was to maintain the confidence of foreigners in the Canadian economy, thereby avoiding a speculative outflow of capital. In the second place, a net inflow of capital occurred at this time. In the third place, the protective tariff was raised so that the demand for foreign exchanges was lessened.[5] These factors eased but did not eliminate Canadian difficulties.

By 1931 the external situation as reflected in a deficit in the Canadian balance of payments took a turn for the worse. In order to keep the exchange rate fixed, a further contraction of money, prices, and income was necessary. Although Canada continued to contract, and the chartered banks lost gold and external assets in attempting to support the dollar, these efforts proved inadequate. Rather than continue the internal contraction required to preserve external balance, Canada departed formally from the gold standard in October 1931, and the exchange rate depreciated significantly in terms of the United States dollar. That the exchange rate depreciation alone failed to eliminate Canadian difficulties is indicated by the decline in economic activity which continued until March 1933, when a trough was reached. Over this period the stock of money declined by about 8 per cent and prices by approximately 10 per cent.

The one particularly bright spot in Canadian experience is that, contrary to the experience of some other countries, such as the United States, the Canadian banking system did not collapse. The chartered banks continued to contract their operations although the government attempted in November 1932 to have them do otherwise by forcing

5. For a detailed analysis of this period see F. A. Knox, *Dominion Monetary Policy, 1929–34* (Ottawa: The King's Printer, 1939); and McIvor, *Canadian Monetary Development.*

them to borrow $35 million in Dominion notes at a cost of 3 per cent, under the provision of the Finance Act.[6] The measure did not achieve the desired results because the banks offset the effects of these transactions on the stock of money by reducing their indebtedness to the government. The effects of the measure on the stock of money appear to have been negligible.

However, within a month of the attempts by the government to force chartered banks to expand, the premium on United States funds increased from 11 per cent to 19 per cent, reflecting a further depreciation of the Canadian dollar. The depreciation may be attributed in part to the uncertainty generated by the government's expansionary policy that replaced the previous policy of contraction. By such a reversal of policy the government, in effect, promoted expectations of inflation and thus further exchange losses, thereby confirming public suspicion of its inability to maintain fixed exchange rates and to observe its rules of the game.

The year 1934 brought an improvement in Canadian economic affairs. As a result of the depreciation, exports, which had started to recover in 1933, advanced markedly in 1934.[7]

Following the World Economic Conference, the government in 1934 attempted once more to increase the stock of money by expanding bank cash by some $53 million through the issue of Dominion notes, but this time without gold backing.[8] The government's justification for this measure was that the conference had changed the rules of the gold-standard game. Canada, according to this view, was safe in expanding without worrying about exchange rate depreciation such as had occurred in 1932.

The declaration of war in September 1939 found the Canadian economy with much unused capacity. Employment was still below its 1929 peak and over 11 per cent of the labor force was unemployed. With the increased tempo of government expenditures, the gross national product during the first full year of the war increased nearly 20 per cent in terms of current prices. At the very outset the government adopted an expansionist monetary policy and the stock of money

6. McIvor, *Canadian Monetary Development*, p. 133.

7. *National Accounts Income and Expenditure*, p. 19.

8. McIvor, *Canadian Monetary Development*, p. 134. For a discussion and analysis of events leading to the establishment of the Bank of Canada during this period see, for example, A. F. W. Plumptre, *Central Banking in the British Dominions* (Toronto: Univ. of Toronto Press, 1940), and E. P. Neufeld, *Bank of Canada Operations, 1935–54* (Toronto: Univ. of Toronto Press, 1955).

increased. The government's justification was that in view of the existing conditions of unused capacity in the country, such a policy could be
"continued" without fear of inflation.[9]

Power to control foreign exchange and thereby foreign trade for war
purposes was vested in the government's Foreign Exchange Control
Board in September 1939. It marked the first time that government
restriction had been placed on foreign exchange transactions by private
Canadian citizens. The stated objective was to maintain exchange
stability, conserve American dollars for the war effort, and prevent
capital outflows.[10] When the United Kingdom imposed exchange
control in September 1939, in order to protect its dollar reserves and
exchange rate, the multilateral exchange system that had existed in
the prewar period broke down. Canada could no longer, as it had done
in the 1930s, convert sterling earned from a recurring net credit with the
United Kingdom into dollars in order to meet the recurring deficit
with the United States.

These measures, together with increased exports to the United States
and attempts to increase American investments in Canada, did not
prevent a serious deterioration in the country's dollar reserves in 1941.
Following the Hyde Park Agreement in April 1941 and the integration
of the Canadian and American economies for war production, a rapid
expansion of Canadian reserves of dollars and gold occurred. By the
end of 1945 Canadian holdings of American dollars and gold rose to
$1.5 million.[11]

The end of the war brought no end to the expansion in the Canadian
money stock. Although it was not achieved during this period, Canada
attached importance to the maintenance of internal balance. It thereby
rendered inoperative adjustments in the general level of prices and
incomes for the sake of external balance, to which apparently Canada
attached less importance. Thus, external balance could be preserved
either by countering pressure on the balance of payments by changes in
holdings of gold and other foreign exchange, by direct controls, or by
changes in exchange rates. Canadian fixed exchange rate policy excluded adjustments via the latter.

9. McIvor, *Canadian Monetary Development*, p. 182; and R. Craig McIvor,
"Canadian War-Time Fiscal Policy, 1939–45" *Canadian Jour. of Econ. and Pol.
Sci.* (February 1948), pp. 62–93.

10. Louis Rasminsky, "Foreign Exchange Control in Canada: Purposes and
Methods," J. F. Parkinson, ed., *Canadian War Economics* (Toronto: Univ. of
Toronto Press, 1941), pp. 1–16.

11. McIvor, *Canadian Monetary Development*, p. 171.

By the end of 1947, Canadian gold and dollar reserves were almost depleted, and a serious balance-of-payments crisis occurred. Given the commitment for maintenance of internal balance and fixed exchange rates, measures to cope with the crisis emphasized restrictions on American dollar expenditures by Canadians.

The 1949 devaluation of the Canadian dollar was considered by many people abroad to be unjustified, even though in 1950 the current account deficit in the balance of payments amounted to approximately 329 million dollars.[12] The effect was that the outbreak of war in Korea in 1950 coincided with a capital inflow in anticipation of a revaluation of the Canadian dollar, so that by the third quarter of that year the country's foreign exchange reserves amounted to over 500 million dollars. These pressures on the economy were eased when the Canadian dollar was freed to find its own level in October 1950.[13]

The reactivation of monetary policy as a principal tool for dealing with inflation also took place at this time. Hitherto, monetary policy had been judged primarily in terms of its consequences for debt management. Between the end of the war in 1945 and the reactivation of monetary policy in 1950, the stock of money increased by 40 per cent. Over the period 1954–56 the Canadian economy enjoyed general price level stability, although significant changes occurred in the general level of economic activity.

By late 1953 the economy began to feel the recessionary influences current in the United States. Although a decline in economic activity occurred in 1954, it was relatively mild, owing to the rising level of activity in Europe which sustained the demand for Canadian exports in the face of an easing American demand for Canadian products. The Bank of Canada, which had been pursuing a tight monetary policy until the autumn of 1953, became a net purchaser of securities with a view to easing the slowdown.

By the end of 1955 the slack in the economy had been absorbed. In order to preserve internal balance, and counter the effects of earlier

---

12. *Ibid.*, p. 219.

13. For a discussion of the "free" Canadian exchange rate see Harry C. Eastman, "Aspects of Speculation in the Canadian Market for Foreign Exchange," *Canadian Jour. Econ. and Pol. Sci.* (August 1958), pp. 355–73; Harry C. Eastman and Stefan Stykolt, "Exchange Stabilization in Canada, 1950–54, *Canadian Jour. Econ. and Pol. Sci.* (May 1956), pp. 221–33; and Paul Wonnacott, "Exchange Stabilization in Canada, 1950–54: A Comment," and Harry C. Eastman and Stefan Stykolt, "Exchange Stabilization Again," *Canadian Jour. Econ. and Pol. Sci.* (May 1958), pp. 262–66.

increases in the stock of money, the Bank of Canada began to pursue a policy of monetary restraint at the end of 1955. Monetary restraint affected the ability of chartered banks to lend, and by the end of 1956 borrowers entirely dependent on this source of credit "registered complaints" regarding the cost and availability of credit. Following the peak in economic activity reached in April 1957, the Canadian economy turned down and reached a trough in April 1958.

Relatively high unemployment rates (6 to 7 per cent) and the unsatisfactory performance of the Canadian economy brought criticism of the monetary and fiscal authorities, who were accused of failing to pursue sufficiently expansive policies. The Royal Commission on Banking and Finance, for example, regards this failure as probably the major error of postwar economy policy.[14] According to the commission's appraisal, a more expansive monetary and credit policy would have eased Canada's difficulties. The commission also argued that the country's flexible exchange rate system employed until 1962 facilitated the effectiveness of monetary policy.

The governor of the Bank of Canada, Mr. Coyne, defended existing policies in the bank's annual report for 1960, arguing in effect that there was little that monetary policy could do to ease the country's economic problems.[15] By 1961, disagreement over monetary policy between the Canadian government and Mr. Coyne reached a climax. On July 13, 1961, the government asked for Mr. Coyne's resignation. A bill to dismiss Coyne was submitted to Parliament, who voted it down. Though he stated that he considered himself exonerated, Mr. Coyne resigned.

The new governor, Mr. Rasminsky, issued a statement to the effect that in the event of conflict over monetary policy between the bank and the government, the government had the duty to direct the bank as to which policy it should follow.[16] The government, through the minister of finance, issued a statement concurring with the views expressed by the new governor.[17]

---

14. *Report of the Royal Commission on Banking and Finance*, 1964 (Ottawa: Queen's Printer, 1964); and Herbert Stein, "Report of the Royal Commission on Banking and Finance, 1964: A Review Article," *Journal of Political Economy* (June 1966), pp. 265–73. See also Economic Council of Canada, *Conference on Stabilization Policies* (Ottawa: Queen's Printer, 1966).

15. Bank of Canada, *Annual Report*, 1960, p. 22.

16. Bank of Canada, *Annual Report*, 1961, pp. 3–4.

17. *Ibid.*, p. 5.

In the second quarter of 1961 economic activity began to spurt upwards, and credit conditions eased. Chartered bank reserves increased significantly during 1962 and attained levels higher than for any year in the preceding eleven-year period. By June a large decline in the bank's holdings of government securities occurred. The decline was more than offset by the bank's increase in foreign asset holdings, which was deemed necessary in order to maintain the foreign exchange rate value of the country's currency. The increase in foreign asset holdings was the result of international credits extended to Canada.[18]

In May 1962, Canada abandoned the system of flexible exchange rates in force since 1950 and returned to a fixed exchange rate. In June it also abandoned the floating bank rate whereby the rate for purchase and resale agreements in the money market was set at 0.25 per cent above either the average weekly tender rate on three-month treasury bills, or the bank rate, whichever was lower. By November 1962 the bank rate had been adjusted downward to 4 per cent.

Expansion in economic activity continued during 1963–65. The Bank of Canada directed its operations toward "encouraging credit conditions and an external financial position which would help to sustain and strengthen the expansion of the Canadian economy."[19] A review of the period also indicates that open-market operations were the principal instrument used by the bank to achieve its ends. On occasion "moral suasion" was used to restrict given types of credit. Experiments with a floating bank rate ended in 1962. The bank did not, however, exercise the authority granted to it in 1954 to change reserve requirements of chartered banks.

3. THE SUPPLY OF MONEY AND BUSINESS CYCLES

In general, Canadian cyclical experience suggests that money has played an important role. Consider now the behavior of the rate of change in the money stock as a lead indicator of the Canadian economy in the period 1867–1965. Evidence reported by Milton Friedman and others for the United States shows that changes in the rate of change in the stock of money lead changes in economic activity.[20]

18. For details of these transactions see Bank of Canada, *Annual Report*, 1962, p. 8.

19. Bank of Canada, *Annual Report*, 1963, p. 3.

20. Milton Friedman, "The Supply of Money and Changes in Prices and Output," U.S. Congress, Joint Committee, *The Relationship of Prices to Economic Stability and Growth*, Compendium (85th Congress, 2d Sess., 1958), p. 249. Milton Friedman and Anna J. Schwartz, "Money and Business Cycles," *Review of*

A. COMPOSITION OF THE MONEY SUPPLY

The major components of Canada's money supply over the period of this study are: (1) notes of chartered banks, Dominion notes, and Bank of Canada notes; (2) deposits by the public in chartered banks, deposits by chartered banks with the minister of finance, central gold reserve, and Bank of Canada, and deposits of the Dominion government with chartered banks and Bank of Canada; and (3) subsidiary coin in public hands and chartered banks. Since in Canada foreign currencies do not constitute an important form in which the Canadian public stores liquidity and are not used to any great extent in settling domestic transactions, consideration is given only to currency and bank deposits payable in Canadian currency.

At this point it will be helpful to trace briefly the role of currency and the developments by which bank notes of chartered banks become the chief circulating medium in the period preceding the establishment of the Bank of Canada in 1935.[21] Under the Bank Act in 1870 (later consolidated with the general Bank Act of 1871), the note issue of a bank was not to exceed its paid-up capital, no bank notes were to be issued under $4 in value (later changed to $5 and multiples thereof), and, while the banks were allowed to use their own discretion regarding the amount of their cash reserves, it was stipulated that at least one-third (later increased to 40 per cent) of such cash reserves as they chose to carry should consist of Dominion notes. In the revision of 1880, a note holder was definitely recognized as a preferred creditor. The Bank Act of 1890 provided for the Bank Note Circulation Redemption Fund, made up by each bank's depositing with the minister of finance an amount equal to 5 per cent of its note circulation. As a result of the operation of this fund and of making notes a prior lien against the assets of failed banks, no bank-note holder in Canada has suffered a loss since 1881.

In 1908, after the financial crisis of 1907, provision was made for the banks to issue, during the crop-moving season (October to January, inclusive—later extended to September to February, inclusive), an

---

Economics and Statistics, Supplement (February. 1963), pp. 32–64. See also K. A. J. Hay, "Money and Cycles in Post-Confederation Canada," *Jour. Pol. Economy* (June 1967), pp. 263–73; and George Macesich, "The Rate of Change in the Money Supply as a Leading Canadian Indicator," *Canadian Jour. Econ. and Pol. Sci.* (August 1962), pp. 424–30.

21. *Canada Year Book, 1941* (Ottawa: Dominion Bureau of Statistics, 1941), pp. 809–10.

excess circulation up to 15 per cent of their combined capital, such an excess to be taxed at a rate not exceeding 5 per cent per annum. The revision of the Bank Act in 1913 provided for the establishment of central gold reserves in which banks might deposit gold or Dominion notes and issue additional notes of their own. The Invoice Act of 1914 gave the minister of finance authority to issue Dominion notes to the banks against approved securities deposited with him. Originally passed as a war measure, this was made a permanent feature of the system by the Finance Act of 1923 and provided the banks with the means of further expanding their note issue by depositing these Dominion notes, so obtained, in the central gold reserve. Although the chief circulating medium in the hands of the public, bank notes of chartered banks were a fiduciary issue; they were not legal tender but were convertible into Dominion notes which were legal tender.

The provisions regarding bank notes were materially changed with the establishment of the Bank of Canada under the Bank Act of 1934. Authority for both seasonal expansion and additional issue secured by deposit in the central gold reserves was then terminated. Under the Bank Act of 1934 chartered banks were required to reduce the issue of their own bank notes gradually during the years 1935–45 to an amount not in excess of 25 per cent of their paid-up capital on March 11, 1935. Bank of Canada notes then replaced chartered bank notes as the issue of the latter was reduced.

Further restrictions introduced by the 1944 revisions of the Bank Act cancelled the right of chartered banks to issue or reissue notes after January 1, 1945, and in January 1950 the chartered banks' liability for such of their notes issued for circulation in Canada as then remained outstanding was transferred to the Bank of Canada in return for payment of a like sum to the Bank of Canada. Some of these banks with foreign branches continued to maintain a small issue of foreign currency notes, but the costs, including taxes, have made it an unprofitable operation. The Bank Act now requires that all note-issuing privileges of the banks shall end and also provides methods of retiring the outstanding foreign note circulation.

Prior to the Bank of Canada's taking over the legal tender note issue when it opened on March 11, 1935, Dominion notes had been issued under the authority by three statutes: [22] (1) under the Dominion Notes Act of 1934, which required a gold reserve of 25 per cent to be held against the first $120 million of notes issued and full gold coverage

22. *Canada Year Book, 1938* (Ottawa: Dominion Bureau of Statistics, 1938), p. 912.

against any issue in excess of $120 million; (2) under the Finance Act of 1927 which authorized the minister of finance to advance to any chartered bank unlimited Dominion notes on the pledge of approved securities deposited with the minister. These advances bore interest and no gold coverage on them was required to be held in Dominion notes; (3) under the Statutes of 1915, which authorized the government to issue Dominion notes to the amount of $26 million without gold coverage but partly covered by the deposit of $16 million of railway securities guaranteed by the Dominion government.

The Dominion note issue was, therefore, partly gold-backed and partly fiduciary. Dominion notes were legal tender, and redeemable in gold when Canada was on the gold standard.

Dominion notes were of two types, those for general circulation, and "special" notes. Special notes, which were mainly of $5 and $50 denominations, were used only by banks for inter-bank transactions and clearings, for cash reserves, or for deposits in the central gold reserves. Dominion notes for the purpose of general circulation were of denominations of 25 cents, $1, $2, $4, $5, $50, $500, and $1,000, although for many years no $4 or $50 notes had been issued. Since the minimum denomination for chartered bank notes was set at $5, Dominion notes of lower denominations were largely in circulation among the general public. However, Dominion notes could also be included in the reserves of the banks. Further it was provided that at least 40 per cent of the banks' reserves were to consist of Dominion notes.

When the Bank of Canada commenced operations it assumed liability for Dominion notes outstanding which had been in public circulation. Deposits of chartered banks at the Bank of Canada completed the replacement of Dominion notes as cash reserves.

Canadian minor coin circulation includes silver coins in denominations of one dollar, 50 cents, 25 cents, and 10 cents; pure nickel 5-cent coins; and bronze 1-cent coins.[23]

In Canada checks are drawn against "deposits payable after notice or fixed day in Canada" as well as "deposits payable on demand in Canada." For purposes of this study the two types of deposits are considered simultaneously under "total deposits with public." There are three distinct types of saving banks in Canada in addition to the savings departments of the chartered banks and of trust and loan companies: (1) Post Office Savings Bank, in which deposits are a direct

23. *Canada Year Book, 1954* (Ottawa: Dominion Bureau of Statistics, 1954), p. 1130.

obligation of the government of Canada; (2) provincial government savings institutions in Newfoundland, Ontario, and Alberta, where the depositor becomes a direct creditor of the province; and (3) savings banks in the province of Quebec. The estimates of deposits in this study include only those with chartered banks. The omission of the other institutions, although unfortunate, does not subtract greatly from the accuracy of the overall picture, since deposits in these other institutions are comparatively small.[24] For the period 1959–65, money supply data are obtained from *Bank of Canada's Statistical Summary* for relevant months and years.

B. THEORETICAL FRAMEWORK

The quantity theory of money is the theoretical framework underlying the "leading monetary indicator approach."[25] Its theoretical argument is that the stock of money is an important determinant of economic activity. According to this view individual nonbank holders of money cannot change its nominal quantity but they can in the aggregate change the real value of their cash balances. Thus, holders of money may decide that they are holding excessive cash balances which they may individually attempt to reduce by an increase in their rate of spending. In the aggregate, however, they cannot do so, for the money disposed of by one holder will be acquired by another so that the nominal stock of money will remain unchanged. The attempts of holders of money to reduce their nominal cash balances will raise the flow of expenditures, thus raising money income and prices. In the process they will reduce their real cash balances to the desired level. The converse reaction takes place when holders decide to increase their real cash balances. Thus, on this view we should expect to find that if the nonbank public's demand for real money is constant, a decline in the rate of growth in the stock of money will tend to discourage aggregate spending. Conversely, a rise in rate of growth in the stock of money, given the demand by the nonbank public for real money, will tend to encourage additional spending.

24. *Canada Year Book, 1955* (Ottawa: Dominion Bureau of Statistics, 1955), p. 1208 ff.

25. For a detailed discussion of the sophisticated quantity theory that underlies the "leading monetary indicator" see Beryl W. Sprinkel, "Monetary Growth as a Cyclical Indicator," *Journal of Finance* (September 1959), pp. 333–46; and Milton Friedman, "Demand for Money: Some Theoretical and Empirical Results," *Jour. Pol. Economy* (August 1959), pp. 327–51; as well as Friedman's essay in Milton Friedman, ed., *Studies in the Quantity Theory of Money* (Chicago: Univ. of Chicago Press, 1956).

C. CANADIAN EXPERIENCE

The rate of increase of the Canadian money stock satisfies the National Bureau of Economic Research's criteria for a leading indicator.[26] This bureau considers a series as an "acceptable indicator of revivals if its specific cycle troughs led the corresponding reference troughs at two-thirds or more of the reference troughs it covered; or if it was roughly coincident (turning within three months of the reference trough) at two-thirds or more of the trough" (the bureau's two-thirds rule).[27] Series selected by the national bureau on the basis of the "two-thirds rule" were further secured by spelling out the five general criteria in eleven characteristics.[28] A detailed discussion of these eleven characteristics is readily available, so they need not be repeated here. The important issue for purposes of this paper is that the "leading" and "lagging" indicators were not selected in the process of testing the implications of any theoretical framework.[29] Our confidence in the behavior of these indicators is reduced because the empirical regularities cannot "explain" themselves or their past performance, and so there is reduced confidence that the empirical patterns will repeat themselves in the future. Note that this does not mean that we cannot rationalize the performance of individual indicators. It does mean that their behavior has generally not been rationalized or tested within a comprehensive framework. A "leading" money indicator would possess a powerful attraction as an integral part of a more comprehensive theoretical framework such as the quantity theory of money which implies that changes in the rate of increase of the stock of money affect spending in a predictable manner.

Tables 1 and 2 present, from 1967 to 1965 and from 1868 through 1908, the specific cycles in the monthly rate of change in the Canadian stock of money and its relation to Canadian cycles. The specific cycles are dated according to national bureau criteria. These criteria include dating on the cycle by at least three judges. Five people (including Milton Friedman and Anna J. Schwartz for the period 1924–58) assisted me in dating the cycles. It is obvious from an examination of the evidence that the Canadian indicator falls short of satisfying criteria

26. Geoffrey H. Moore, *Statistical Indicators of the Cyclical Revivals and Recessions*, Occasional Paper Number 31 (New York: National Bureau of Economic Research, 1950), p. 20.

27. *Ibid.*, p. 21.

28. For a discussion of these eleven characteristics, *ibid.*, pp. 21–22.

29. See Sprinkel, "Monetary Growth."

set out by the national bureau for an "ideal" statistical indicator. It leads the cyclical revival center by variable amounts; it does not sweep smoothly up or down; its cyclical movements are not always pronounced

By way of contrast, the indicator does seem to approximate closely the last "ideal" criterion that it be "so related to general business activity as to establish . . . confidence . . . that its future behavior in regard to business cycles will be like its past behavior." Moreover, the indicator also satisfies the "two-thirds rule" for acceptable indicators. Table 1 indicates that between 1867 and 1900, the peak in the rate of change of the money stock preceded the peaks in general business activity by an average of almost 7 months at peaks and almost 8 months at troughs. For the postwar period and six complete reference cycles between 1924 and 1964, peaks in money precede peaks in general business by an average lead of 15.5 months at peaks and about 7 months at troughs. These results are consistent in direction and of roughly the same order of magnitude with the 15-month leads at peaks and 12-month leads at troughs, for reference cycles since 1907, found for the United States by Milton Friedman.[30]

Evidence presented in Table 2 indicates that peaks and troughs occurring in my monthly series are clearly approximated by Chambers's quarterly money series. Indeed, the turning points in both monthly and quarterly money series precede in almost every instance their counterpart cyclical reference dates. One exception is August 1874 when, according to Chambers, special circumstances were present—namely, the transfer of Canadian bank deposits following the New York financial panic.

In the post–World War I period there are several extra cycles in the Canadian money series. One covers 1925 to 1926. There is some uncertainty connected with the dating in Canada of a reference cycle in 1926–27.[31] The occurrence of an extra cycle in the money series in 1925–26 preceded the observed slowing-down of economic activity in 1926–27.[32]

Another extra cycle occurs in 1930 and 1931. This is consistent with

30. Milton Friedman, *A Program for Monetary Stability* (New York: Fordham Univ. Press, 1960), p. 87; and U.S. Congress, Joint Economic Committee, *Hearings: Employment, Growth, and Price Levels*, part 4 (86th Congress, 1st Sess.); "Friedman on the Lag Effect of Monetary Policy," *Jour. Pol. Economy* (December 1960), pp. 617–21.

31. Edward J. Chambers, "Canadian Business Cycles since 1919: A Progress Report," *Canadian Jour. Econ. and Pol. Sci.* (May 1958), p. 172.

32. *Ibid.*, p. 180.

TABLE 1

LEADS AND LAGS BETWEEN PEAKS AND TROUGHS OF RATE OF CHANGE OF MONEY STOCK AND CANADIAN BUSINESS CYCLE PEAKS AND TROUGHS
1867 TO 1965
(Monthly Data)

	Specific Cycle Date Change in Rate of Money Series	Business Cycle Reference Date	Lead (−) or Lag (+) of Canadian Reference Date	
			P	T
P.....	12/68			
T.....	5/69			
P.....	6/70			
T.....	9/71			
P.....	5/74	10/73	+7	
T.....	5/75			
P.....	4/76			
T.....	5/79	5/79	0	
P.....	12/81	7/82	−7	
T.....	9/84	3/85		−6
P.....	11/86	2/87	−3	
T.....	9/87	2/88		−5
P.....	6/88	7/90	−25	
T.....	9/89	3/91		−18
P.....	12/92	2/93	−2	
T.....	9/93	3/94		−6
P.....	4/94	8/95	−16	
T.....	4/96	8/96		−4
P.....	1/99			
T.....	4/00			
P.....	1/06			
T.....	9/07			
P.....	1/13			
T.....	...			
P.....	7/20	6/20	+1	
T.....	10/22	9/21		+11
P.....	9/25			
T.....	11/26			
P.....	12/27	4/29	−16	
T.....	5/30	...		
P.....	5/31	...		
T.....	11/31	3/33		−16
P.....	9/35	7/37	−22	
T.....	10/37	10/38		−12
P.....	5/42	...		
T.....	2/47	...		
P.....	10/48	10/48	0	
T.....	1/51	9/49		+16
P.....	12/51	5/53	−17	
T.....	10/53	6/54		−8
P.....	12/54	4/54*	−28	
T.....	3/57	4/58*		−13
P.....	8/58	3/60	−19	
T.....	3/60**	4/61		−13
P.....	6/63**	3/64	−9	

SOURCE: Material reference dates are from the studies of Edward J. Chambers, "Late Nineteenth Century Business Cycles in Canada," *Canadian Journal of Economics and Political Science* (1964), pp. 391–412, and "Canadian Business Cycles since 1919: A progress Report," *Canadian Jour. Econ. and Pol. Sci.* (1958), p. 181. See also *Canadian Statistical Review*, January 1963 and January 1965; and *Bank of Canada: Annual Report of the Governor to the Minister of Finance*, 1959–65.

* I am indebted to D. J. Daly for these tentative reference dates.

** These reference dates are very tentative.

TABLE 2

TURNING POINTS IN RATE OF CHANGE IN THE
CANADIAN MONEY STOCK, 1868–1908

	Monthly: Macesich	Quarterly: Chambers
P........	12/68	11/68
T........	5/69	5/69
P........	6/70	5/70
T........	9/71	8/71
P........	5/74	8/74
T........	5/75	5/75
P........	4/76	5/76
T........	5/79	5/79
P........	12/81	11/81
T........	9/84	8/84
P........	11/86	11/86
T........	9/87	11/87
P........	6/88	8/88
T........	9/89	8/89
P........	12/92	11/92
T........	9/93	8/93
P........	4/94	5/94
T........	4/96	2/96
P........	1/99	2/99
T........	4/00	2/00
P........	1/06	2/06
T........	9/07	11/07

SOURCE: Chambers's quarterly dates from personal correspondence with me dated November 5, 1962.

American experience where a similar but less obvious movement occurs.
It may be that but for the departure of Canada and Great Britain from
the gold standard in the fall of 1931, the 1930 trough would have
corresponded to a reference trough in the summer of 1931. This was
cut short because of the departure from the gold standard.

The other extra cycle occurs during the war period. Although these
data are difficult to read when plotted because of the extraordinary
gyrations, some of these of approximately 7 to 9 months, like corresponding movements in American figures, are associated with the bond
drives; others, perhaps, with inadequate seasonal adjustment. Thus in
the case of government bond drives, the estimates exclude government
cash balances. During a war-bond campaign, deposits were transferred
from public to government accounts. When the government paid them
out again they came back into the hands of the public and account for
the sharp gyrations in the figures.[33]

33. For a discussion of Canadian war finance see McIvor, *Canadian Monetary
Development*.

Although the "leading monetary indicator" roughly satisfies the national bureau's criteria for an adequate indicator, taken by itself its usefulness for accurately predicting turning points is very limited. The lead in months at peaks for the several reference cycles ranges from 0 to 28 months. At the trough the lead of the indicator ranges from 4 to 18 months. The evidence, however, is consistent with American results where similar difficulties occur in attempting to use this indicator alone to predict turning points in economic activity.[34]

If we restrict ourselves to the post–World War II period when quarterly data on variables other than money are available, lagged relations and relation between first differences may be tried. The evidence is that money is more highly correlated with consumption from one to four quarters later than with consumption in an earlier or later quarter. Autonomous expenditures are more highly correlated with consumption one quarter later than in the same or any later quarter. When first differences are considered, money is more highly correlated with consumption one or two quarters later than in the same quarter. One implication of these results is to weaken the contention that changes in autonomous expenditures bring about changes in money as well as total income. Of course this does not mean that money causes induced expenditures just because it precedes them. It may be that both variables are responding to a third variable which influences one variable before another. This third variable conjecture can be raised about any theory. If indeed an alternative theory is being posed, evidence in its support should be presented.[35]

34. It is partly on the basis of such evidence for the United States that Milton Friedman and others have argued against the use of discretionary monetary policies and for the pursuit of policies which would require that the money supply increase at a constant rate. The basic problem is that the effects of actions taken by the monetary authority will be felt at some highly variable future date. One consequence of this imperfect knowledge is that discretionary monetary policy may contribute to economic instability.

35. Hay, "Money and Cycles," for example, argues that in Canada money is passive in the upswing of the cycle but an active agent in promulgating recessions in the country and that this is in keeping with Douglass North's suggestion, in *Economic Growth of the United States, 1790–1860* (Englewood Cliffs, N.J.: Prentice Hall, 1961), that money has had a role in curtailing long upswings in American growth. This may be a surface manifestation of even more fundamental forces which appear to a considerable extent to be monetary in nature. I have argued elsewhere that defunct ideas, including the real bills doctrine and the specie standard with its fixed exchange rates, operating through the monetary mechanism have made significant contributions to the economic stagnation in the post-Civil War American South. See George Macesich, *Commercial Banking and Regional*

These results tend also to provide an independent check on the observation that the timing and duration of Canadian and American reference cycles have been very similar, especially since the 1920s.[36] The behavior of the rate of change of the Canadian money stock and its relation to reference cycles has been similar to American experience, thereby reinforcing the observation of similarity of timing and duration of reference cycles in the two countries.

4. THE RELATIVE DEMAND FOR CURRENCY AND DEPOSITS

It has been argued that as a country develops and its people become familiar with banking institutions they will tend to hold a larger fraction of their total money in the form of bank deposits, so that the fraction of the money supply held in the form of currency will decline. Short-run variations in the currency-money ratio, on the other hand, have been primarily attributed to variations in the seasonal demand for currency. Thus, during holiday periods the public will temporarily convert some bank deposits into currency.

More recently Phillip Cagan has demonstrated that for the United States the demand for currency is also influenced by the percentage of income that is taxed because accepting payments in cash and subsequently holding cash facilitates tax evasion, especially income taxes.[37] Other factors that he considers important in determining the public's currency-money ratio are expected per-capita income and expected returns on bank deposits.

Development in the United States, 1950–60 (Tallahassee: Florida State Univ., 1965), and "A Monetary Hypothesis and Southern Development," *Rivista Internazionale di Scienze Economiche e Commerciali*, (1966), pp. 128–47. I have also argued that the problems of the turbulent 1830s and early 1840s in the American economy in no small part derive from capital flows and the operation of the epcie-flow mechanism under fixed exchange rates. Macesich, "Sources of Monetary Disturbance in the United States, 1834–45," *Journal of Economic History* (1960), pp. 407–34. See also Clark Warburton, "Variations in Economic Growth and Banking Development in the U.S. from 1835 to 1885," *Jour. Econ. Hist.* (September 1958), pp. 283–97; Milton Friedman and Anna J. Schwartz, *A Monetary History of the United States, 1867–1960* (Princeton Univ. Press, 1963); Phillip Cagan, *Determinants and Effects of Changes in the Stock of Money, 1875–1960* (New York: National Bureau of Economic Research, 1965), "The First Fifty Years of the National Banking System: An Historical Appraisal," Deane Carson, ed., *Banking and Monetary Studies* (Homewood, Ill.: Richard D. Irwin, 1963).

36. Chambers, *Canadian Business Cycles*, p. 186.

37. Phillip Cagan, *The Demand for Currency Relative to Total Money Supply*, Occasional Paper 62 (New York: National Bureau of Economic Research, 1958), and *Determinants of Changes in Stock of Money*.

One purpose of this section is to test and elaborate on Cagan's hypotheses in Canada over the period 1924–64. Evidence is also presented on an important determinant of the Canadian money supply. Canada's experience provides almost an ideal test for these hypotheses, for at least two reasons. First, Canada has a concentrated banking system whose development has been very different from that in the United States. For example, the development of banking in Canada has not been punctuated by the serious banking failures that occurred in the United States, which shook public confidence in bank deposits. Second, Canada instituted an income tax in 1917 and a withholding tax during World War II. On this score its experience has been similar to that of the United States. Section A discusses the hypotheses. Section B presents the statistical analysis and discusses a number of implications of the test results.

A. HYPOTHESES

The demand for currency by the public can be cast into familiar demand theory. Accordingly, the factors influencing the demand for currency can be divided into price (or cost) and income variables. The cost of holding a given ratio of currency reflects the comparative advantages of holding currency and deposits. These advantages may in turn be functions of such variables as expected real income per capita, volume of retail trade, the volume of travel per capita, the degree of urbanization, and the rate of tax on transactions. Cagan has argued that many of these variables have negligible influence on the currency ratio, in both the short run and the long run, and that still other variables may be collapsed into single variables, thereby reducing the complexity of the problem. Following Cagan, I shall restrict the analysis to the three independent variables, the cost of holding currency, expected real per capita income, and the percentage of income taxed.

On the basis of Cagan's results we should expect to observe that a rise in the cost of holding currency will, other things equal, lead to a substitution of deposits for currency. The cost of holding currency may be expressed as the interest foregone in not holding deposits. Interest paid on deposits, however, is the gross return, from which should be subtracted expected losses on deposits arising out of bank failures in order to arrive at the "expected net rate of return" on deposits. In Canada, losses from bank failures have been so negligible that I have taken the gross return as identical with the "expected net rate of return" on deposits.

Since money is not taken to be an inferior good, we should expect to observe that, other things equal, the quantity of real money demanded will rise as per capita real income rises. Money, however, is principally composed of the sum of currency and bank deposits, and what may be true for the total stock of money may not be true for its individual components. Convenience provided by bank deposits means that, other things equal, the services of a dollar of bank deposits are preferred to those of a dollar of currency. As Cagan points out, we should expect to observe that the currency-money ratio will tend to decline as real per capita income rises. This "does not mean that, for a given level of income, deposits are to be preferred to currency no matter how large a fraction of money balances is already held as deposits; if this were so, no currency would be held at all, since some deposits pay interest and currency pays none."[38] Accordingly, what is required to prevent such a development is that beyond a certain size of the total money balance, an extra dollar of deposits is preferable to an extra dollar of currency. In other words, the income elasticity of deposits is greater than that of currency.

The income variable I have selected is "expected (or permanent) real per capita disposable income." I selected expected or permanent rather than current income because many researchers have found it to have superior explanatory power in a wide range of demand phenomena. The measure of permanent or expected real per capita income is estimated on an average of past levels of personal disposable income weighted by an exponential curve deflated by "expected" or "permanent" prices, which are estimated by the same technique as expected or permanent income, and divided by the population.[39] Since income and price data start in 1926, only those estimates of permanent income and prices from 1935 are based on averages of ten years' experience, which are required by Friedman's weights which I have used. Years before 1935 are based on the observed data for 1926 and 1927, and the permanent magnitudes for 1926 are taken to be equal to the observed values. Thus, the permanent magnitudes, and so "expected real per capita disposable income" before 1935, are progressively less accurate as one approaches 1926.

Using currency helps to conceal, albeit illegally, taxable transactions. A tax on income thereby encourages the use of currency and discourages the use of deposits because the use of checks makes it easier to record

38. Cagan, *Demand for Currency*, p. 4.

39. For the method employed see Friedman, "Demand for Money," pp. 327–51 (also published by the National Bureau of Economic Research as Occasional Paper 68).

transactions while the use of currency makes it difficult. We should expect to observe that as income taxes rise so too will the incentive increase to evade the tax by use of currency. The currency-money ratio, other things equal, will thereby rise accordingly.

The series I have selected to represent the "rate of tax on income" is the percentage of total personal income collected for income taxes. Implicit in the use of this series is the assumption that the amount of tax evasion depends directly on the records. Such a measure is not ideal because it is an average rate and not a marginal, and it excludes evaded taxes. Nevertheless, the series does serve as a useful approximation to the "rate of tax on income."

B. STATISTICAL ANALYSIS AND SOME IMPLICATIONS OF THE RESULTS

1. Statistical analysis. Chart 1 presents the series used in the statistical analysis for the period 1924–58. The "expected net rate of return on deposits" and "expected per capita disposable income" are inverted because of their inverse relationship to the currency ratio. The percentage of personal income taxed is not inverted, owing to its positive relationship to the currency ratio. Actual and estimated currency ratio is also plotted in the figure.

The behavior of the actual currency ratio over the period 1924–58 indicates a gradual rise from about 1926 to about 1940. Thereafter, the ratio rises rapidly during the war, reaching a peak in 1944, and then declines until 1950 and the outbreak of the Korean conflict. A postwar peak in the ratio is reached in 1952, followed by an unsteady decline to the end of 1958.

Inspection of figure 1 suggests that all three variables are important determinants of the currency ratio. "Expected net rate of return on deposits" is the one variable that is available for the entire period 1924–58. Although the correlation between the logarithms of the rate of return on deposits and the currency ratio shows that the return on deposits "explains" approximately 37 per cent of the variation in the currency ratio since 1924, only the "percentage of income taxes" appears able to explain the rapid rise in the currency ratio since 1940. Other factors, such as the volume of travel and size of the armed forces, may also be important, but I have not treated them.[40] To the extent that these other factors are important, their effect appears to have

40. See the very interesting discussion in Stephen L. McDonald, "Some Factors Affecting the Increased Relative Use of Currency since 1939," *Journal of Finance* (September 1959), pp. 313–27; and the discussion of McDonald's results by Cagan, *Demand for Currency*, p. 17, note 31.

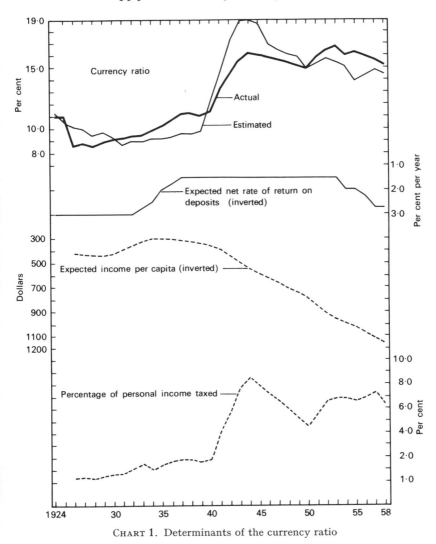

CHART 1. Determinants of the currency ratio

reinforced the influence of the income-tax variable on the behavior of
the currency ratio in the post-1940 period.

We may now cast the three variables into a multiple regression
analysis for the period 1926–58 and 1935–58. The two periods, 1926–58
and 1935–58, are selected because of the availability of data. The
"expected income variable" is accurate only for the period 1935–58.
The estimated currency ratio, 1924–58, plotted in chart 1 is derived
from the results obtained for the period 1935–58.

For the period 1926–58, multiple regression analysis with the currency ratio and three independent variables in logarithmic form gives the following regression equation:

$$\log C/M = -.846 + .298 \log Z_1 + .070 \log Z_2 - .100 \log Z_3.$$
$$\qquad\qquad (.067) \qquad\quad (.080) \qquad\qquad (.104)$$

where Z_1 = percentage of personal income taxed, Z_2 = expected income per capita, and Z_3 = expected net rate of return on deposits. The multiple regression equation explains 85 per cent of the variation in the currency ratio. The signs of Z_1 and Z_3 are the expected ones, but the sign of the income variable was expected to be negative. Since the income variable is not accurate for the years before 1935 the results are inconclusive for the period 1926–58.

All variables in the following regression for the period 1935–58, when the income variable is accurate, are consistent with my hypotheses. The multiple regression function accounts for 94 per cent of the variation in the currency ratio in the period 1935–58.

$$\log C/M = -.284 + .551 \log Z_1 - .099 \log Z_2 - .222 \log Z_3.$$
$$\qquad\qquad (.048) \qquad\quad (.054) \qquad\qquad (.080)$$

For the period from the fourth quarter 1958 through the fourth quarter 1964 the hypotheses are not as strongly supported by the data. The multiple regression equation is:

$$\log C/M = -.898 + .023 \log Z_1 - .520 \log Z_2 + .084 \log Z_3.$$
$$\qquad\qquad (.049) \qquad\quad (.158) \qquad\qquad (.075)$$

The R^2 is .81.

2. *Implications of the statistical results.* The results for Canada are consistent with Cagan's findings for the United States. Thus the income-tax variable is positively related to the currency ratio, so that a higher tax rate brings currency into greater use; expected real disposable income per capita is negatively related, indicating that deposits are a superior good to currency and are held in great proportion as expected real per capita disposable income rises; interest payments are also negatively related, indicating a shift to deposits when these payments rise. The percentage changes in the currency ratio corresponding to a 1 per cent increase in each of the independent variables are approximately $+.55$, $-.10$, and .22 per cent respectively for the period 1935–58. Confidence in this conclusion, however, is reduced when the quarterly analysis is taken into account for the period 1958–64.

To judge from the results summarized in this paper the rise in income tax rates in Canada—at least for the longer period—has resulted in a rise in the use of currency. The income-tax variable is a much more important determinant of the currency ratio in Canada than it is in the United States. This is not surprising since, compared with the United States, the structure of the Canadian economy, especially with the relative importance of agriculture, seems to present greater relative "opportunities" for unreported income and so greater opportunity for tax evasion through the use of currency. This does not mean that farmers are less honest than other citizens. It does suggest that they take no less "advantage" of their tax-saving opportunities than others.

If we take into account the longer-term evidence, the Canadian chartered banks have been indirect "victims" of the income tax. In effect, the income tax has been a drain on their reserves. (Other things equal, this also decreases the stock of money.) The other two factors work in the favor of chartered banks by expanding their deposit liabilities and thus the stock of money. These results suggest that one way to offset the indirect effects of the income tax on the chartered banks is to raise the interest rate paid on their deposits. These results also suggest that some effects of income taxes on the economy are more pervasive than is usually believed.

5. DEMAND FOR MONEY

There is general agreement that recent monetary research has cast up three substantive issues in regard to demand for money.[41] One issue is

41. M. Bronfenbrenner and T. Mayer, "Liquidity Functions in the American Economy" *Econometrica*, 28, no. 4 (October 1960), pp. 819–34.

Karl Brunner and Allan H. Meltzer, "Predicting Velocity: Implications for Theory and Policy," *Jour. Finance*, 18 (May 1963), pp. 319–54; "Some Further Evidence on the Supply and Demand Functions for Money," *ibid.*, 19 (May 1964), pp. 240–83.

G. C. Chow, "On the Long-Run and Short-Run Demand for Money," *Jour. Pol. Econ.*, 74 (April 1966), pp. 111–31.

Milton Friedman, "The Quantity Theory of Money, A Restatement," in Milton Friedman, ed., *Studies in the Quantity Theory of Money* (Chicago: University of Chicago Press, 1956); "The Demand for Money—Some Theoretical and Empirical Results," in *ibid.*; "Interest Rates and the Demand for Money," *Journal of Law and Economics*, 9 (October 1966), pp. 71–85; "'Windfalls,' the 'Horigon,' and Related Concepts in the Permanent Income Hypothesis" in Carl F. Christ *et. al.*, *Measurements in Economics, Studies in Mathematical Economics and Econometrics in Memory of Yehuda Grunfeld* (Stanford University Press, 1963).

Milton Friedman and Anna J. Schwartz, *A Monetary History of the United States, 1867–1957* (Princeton, N.J.: Princeton Univ. Press, for the National Bureau of Economic Research, 1963).

the budget constraint imposed on the demand for money and whether the appropriate constraint is income or wealth. Another issue is the role of interest rates and price changes as arguments in the demand for money. A third issue is the appropriate definition of cash balances and whether a more stable demand-for-money function is obtained. The purpose of this section is to examine Canadian postwar experience against the background of these three issues. I will also compare several results presented in this section with those presented in my earlier study for the period 1926–58 in Canada.

A. DETERMINANTS OF THE DEMAND FUNCTION OF MONEY

Friedman (1956, 1959, 1966) has recast the demand function for money so that it is formally identical with general considerations of the demand for any commodity or service. Substantive differences between the analyses of the demand for money and of that for other commodities or services are (1) the necessity of taking account of intertemporal rates of substitution among forms in which total wealth may

H. R. Heller, "The Demand for Money—The Evidence from the Short-Run Data," *Quarterly Journal of Economics*, 79 (May 1965), pp. 291–303.

George Horwich (ed.), *Monetary Process and Policy: A Symposium:* (Homewood, Ill.: Richard D. Irwin, 1967).

H. G. Johnson, "Monetary Theory and Policy," *Amer. Econ. Rev.*, 52 (June 1962), pp. 335–84.

David Laidler, "Some Evidence on the Demand for Money," *Jour. Pol. Econ.*, 76 (February 1966), pp. 55–58; "Rate of Interest and the Demand for Money—Some Empirical Evidence," *Jour. Pol. Econ.*, 74 (December 1966), pp. 543–55.

Henry A. Latané, "Income Velocity and Interest Rates: A Pragmatic Approach," *Rev. Econ. Statis.*, 42 (November 1960), pp. 445–49.

George Macesich, "Determinants of Monetary Velocity in Canada, 1926–58," *Canadian Jour. Econ. and Pol. Sci.*, 28, no. 2 (May 1962), pp. 245–54 (see also Harry G. Johnson and John W. L. Winder, "Lags in the Effects of Monetary Policy in Canada," working paper prepared for the Royal Commission on Banking and Finance, November 1962, especially Chapter 8, "The Demand for Money in Canada"); "Permanent Income Hypothesis," *Finansija* (September–October 1964), pp. 230–40.

Allan H. Meltzer, "The Demand for Money: The Evidence from the Time Series," *Jour. Pol. Econ.*, 71 (June 1963), pp. 219–46.

Boris Pesek and Thomas R. Saving, *Money, Wealth, and Economic Theory* (New York: Macmillan Co., 1967).

Richard T. Selden, "Monetary Velocity in the United States," in Milton Friedman, ed., *Studies in Quantity Theory of Money*.

R. Teigen, "Demand and Supply Functions for Money in the United States," *Econometrica*, 32, no. 4 (October 1964), pp. 477–509.

James Tobin, "The Monetary Interpretation of History," *Amer. Econ. Rev.*, 55 (June 1965), pp. 464–85.

be held, and the tastes and preferences of wealth-owning units, and (2) casting the budget constraint in terms of wealth.

Selden (1956) in his study defines the demand for money as a function relating the Cambridge k to the cost of holding money and other variables. Velocity is, of course, the reciprocal of k and thus velocity changes may reflect, among other variables, changes in the cost of holding money. Chow (1966) argues that the correct arguments in the demand function for money are permanent income and interest rates. Meltzer (1963), on the other hand, argues that wealth rather than income is the proper constraint.

Although Friedman's (1956) theoretical discussion of the demand for money supports the inclusion of interest rates and per capita permanent income as arguments, he has concluded that his empirical findings (Friedman 1959, 1966) do not indicate that they play an important role. He was unable to find a close connection between, for example, changes in velocity from cycle to cycle and several interest rates. On the other hand, he also reports that corporate bond yields are correlated with the real stock of money and velocity in the expected direction, though income is consistently a more important factor than interest rates in explaining velocity changes.

Meltzer (1963) reports, however, that both the demand for money and velocity depend significantly on interest rates. According to Meltzer, Friedman's finding that interest rates play a minor role in the demand function for money flow from the procedure Friedman employs.

If American experience is any guide, we should expect to observe in Canada that income and interest rates are important arguments in the demand function for money or in its rate of turnover velocity. Empirically we should find when estimating a demand function for real money a positive income coefficient and a negative interest-rate coefficient. The implication of one version of the quantity theory may be that the income elasticity is close to unity, and that the interest elasticity is close to zero, thus yielding an income velocity close to unity. But these are empirical matters discussed below.

B. CANADIAN EXPERIENCE

Since current literature in monetary theory does in fact contain a considerable amount of discussion about velocity as a convenient concept for understanding the demand for money, I shall begin by examining several hypotheses regarding its behavior against Canadian experience.

1. The cost of holding money. Selden (1956) tested the hypothesis that the cost of holding money is the chief determinant of velocity's behavior by examining the relations between each of three long-term yield series and each of two annual velocity series. If the cost of holding money is the chief determinant of velocity we should expect to find a close positive relation between velocity and the cost of holding money. He finds, however, little evidence to support this hypothesis in the United States.

In an earlier study, I reported that a significant correlation coefficient exists between government bond yield unadjusted for the yield on money and income velocity as well as deposit turnover for the period 1926–58 in Canada (Macesich 1962). These results are consistent with those presented in table 3 for quarterly data in the period 1958–64. When the government bond series is adjusted, as Selden suggests, to take into account the yield on money, there is a slight decline in the performance of the hypothesis that the cost of holding money is the chief determinant of velocity behavior. It is interesting to note that treasury-bill yields do not perform as well as the longer-term yields. This is in contrast to the results reported in my earlier study when they performed almost as well as the longer-term yields.

If we consider, as does Selden, only price-level changes as indicators to the cost of holding money, the results presented in table 3 do not strongly support the hypothesis that price-level changes are an important determinant of velocity behavior. This is true whether the price level used is that of wholesale prices or the implicit price deflator in consumer expenditures. Moreover, no appreciable change is obtained in the relation if the "yield on money" is deducted from these two series. These results are consistent with those that I reported earlier (Macesich 1962).

Thus far I have treated the various measures of the cost of holding money as alternatives. The results, though mixed, indicate that government bond yield, whether or not adjusted for the yield on money, is a statistically significant determinant of velocity behavior in Canada but not one that explains much of the variation in velocity. Since the long-term yield series used in these tests is not comparable to those used by Selden for similar tests in the United States, the results, though certainly suggestive, are not necessarily inconsistent with United States monetary behavior. Indeed, in my earlier study (1962) the one comparable yield series available for Canada, ten industrial-bond yields, tends to support Selden's conclusion that the relation between interest rates and velocity behavior is not close. Furthermore, when the yield

TABLE 3

SIMPLE CORRELATION COEFFICIENTS BETWEEN INCOME VELOCITY (Y_1),
DEPOSIT TURNOVER (Y_2), COST OF HOLDING MONEY, COST OF MONEY
SUBSTITUTES, AND INCOME PER CAPITA, 1958-IV—1964-IV
(Quarterly Figures)

	Income Velocity (Y_1)	Deposit Turnover (Y_2)
Cost of holding money		
Government bond yields....................	.43*	.21
Treasury bill yields.........................	.09	−.07
Rate of change of wholesale prices............	−.01	−.19
Rate of change of implied price deflator for consumer expenditures.................	.22	.11
Government bond yields minus yield on money...	.42*	.18
Treasury bill yields minus yield on money.......	.09	.07
Rate of change of wholesale prices minus yield on money............................	−.31	−.79†
Rate of change of implied price deflator for consumer expenditures minus yield on money................................	−.04	−.65†
Income per capita		
Per capita disposable income.................	.39*	.96†

Data for the remaining variables are obtained by derivation and appropriate issue of the *Canadian Statistical Review.*

* Significant at .05 level.

† Significant at .01 level.

SOURCES:
Y_1—Monthly issues of the *Canadian Statistical Review.* The numerator for the estimate of income velocity is personal disposable income. The money supply in the denominator is the standard Bank of Canada definition and includes the public's notice deposits in chartered banks.

Y_2—Monthly issues of the *Canadian Statistical Review.*
Government bond yield—For the period 1958-IV through 1961-IV, maturity dates used were 6/74–76 and for period 1962–64 maturity dates used were 10/79; all yields were $3\frac{1}{4}$ per cent. Data are from monthly issues of *Canadian Statistical Review.*
Treasury bill yield—Ibid.

series are adjusted to take into account the yield on money, the correlation coefficients decline, which is consistent with Selden's findings.

If we adopt the approach that the various measures of the cost of holding money are not alternatives but joint determinants of velocity, the results tend to confirm the above conclusions. I have included the several variables indicating the cost of holding money in a multiple regression analysis. The regression covers the period 1958–64, first taking income velocity (Y_1) as the dependent variable and government bond yields (X_1), treasury bill rates (X_2), and the rate of change in prices (X_5 for wholesale prices and X_6 for implicit price deflator in consumer expenditures) as independent variables. The independent variables are adjusted by subtracting from each of them the yield on money. The entire analysis is repeated by substituting deposit turnover (Y_2) as the dependent variable. These analyses yielded the regression equations presented in table 4. All of the regressions presented in the table used von Neumann's ratio to test for the presence of autocorrelation.

TABLE 4

RESULTS OF MULTIPLE REGRESSION ANALYSIS FOR INCOME VELOCITY
(Y_1) AND DEPOSIT TURNOVER, 1958-IV—1964-III
(Quarterly Figures)

DEPENDENT VARIABLE	CONSTANT TERM	REGRESSION COEFFICIENTS AND STANDARD ERROR					R^2	VON NEUMANN RATIO
	a	X_1	X_2	X_5	X_6	X_7		
Y_1	.747	.242 (.142)	−.242 (.037)	−2.522 (3.734)	.220 (3.740)		.215	2.224
Y_2	12.662	−2.688 (3.936)	−.382 (1.015)	−436.797 (103.177)	−179.990 (103.353)		.697	.522*
Y_1	−.256	.266 (.136)	−.011 (.035)	4.129 (5.194)	3.785 (4.098)	.001 (.001)	.324	2.516
Y_2	−52.373	−1.129 (1.947)	.259 (.506)	−5.214 (74.249)	51.350 (58.581)	.060† (.008)	.930	2.484

Y_1 = Income velocity.
Y_2 = Deposit turnover.
X_1 = Government bond yields minus yield on money.
X_2 = Treasury bill yields minus yield on money.
X_5 = Rate of change of wholesale prices minus yield on money.
X_6 = Rate of change in implied price deflator for consumer expenditures minus yield on money.
X_7 = Per capita disposable income.
R^2 = Coefficient of determination.

* Significant autocorrelation.

† t value significant at .05 level.

As judged by a t test the best performer is per capita disposable income and then only in the equation where the dependent variable is deposit turnover (Y_2). On balance, however, the results of the multiple regression analysis show essentially that none of the variables is significant. The results do not indicate that the various measures of the cost of holding money are joint determinants of velocity behavior in Canada. These results are also consistent with those I reported in 1962.

2. Real income per capita. Let us test the other variable, real income per capita. A strong and consistent relation does not appear to exist between real per capita disposable income and velocity. Indeed a positive relation exists for the period as a whole rather than the negative relation we would expect to find if real per capita disposable income is a determinant of velocity behavior. For the periods 1934–58 which I examine here, the positive relation is even stronger. Furthermore, using real per capita disposable income as an additional independent variable (X_7) in the multiple regression analysis changes little. The evidence in table 4 does not alter the results of the simple correlation analysis. The hypothesis may therefore be rejected as inconsistent with Canadian experience for the periods 1934–58 and 1958–64.

3. Permanent income hypothesis. Friedman (1959) had presented a novel hypothesis to explain observed velocity and the demand for money. It derives from his permanent income hypothesis and, like it, concentrates on the meaning attached to "income" and "prices." According to Friedman's hypothesis the demand for money is a function of money holdings adapted to permanent incomes and of permanent prices, rather than measured income and prices. When computed with permanent rather than measured income in the numerator, velocity tends to remain stable within each business cycle. Since measured income is above permanent income at cyclical peaks and below permanent income at cyclical troughs, the positive conformity of measured velocity to cyclical changes in income is taken to reflect corresponding cyclical differences between measured and permanent income.

If this application of the permanent income hypothesis can rationalize the observed secular and cyclical behavior of income velocity in the United States in terms of a movement along a stable demand curve for money, it may mean that income velocity does not behave unpredictably but that changes in measured velocity instead reflect movements along a stable demand function for money resulting from changes in variables entering the function. Applications of this hypothesis to United States data reported by Friedman (1959), Chow (1966), Meltzer (1963), Meltzer-Brunner (1963), Laidler (1966), and others show that most of the variation in measured velocity is indeed consistent with stable demand functions.

Consider now Canadian experience in the light of the Friedman analysis.[42] The demand for money is treated explicitly as a function of

42. Test data are quarterly and are obtained from Bureau of Dominion Statistics, *Canadian Statistical Review*, for appropriate time periods, and George Macesich and Frank Falero, Jr., "Permanent Income Hypothesis, Interest Rates, and the Demand for Money."

permanent income and interest rates. The demand equation for money balances used in the tests is $M = f(Y,r)$ where M is the demand for money, Y is permanent income and r is the rate of interest.

Let:

$y_{(i)}$ = Measured nominal income;
$p_{(j)}$ = Measured price level;
$Y_{(i)}$ = Permanent nominal income;
$P_{(j)}$ = Permanent price level;
$M_{(q)}$ = Money supply;
N = Population;
$r_{(m)}$ = Interest rate;

subscript $(i) = 1, 2, 3$, where 1 = gross national product, 2 = national income, and 3 = personal disposable income;

subscript $(j) = 1, 2, 3$, where 1 = consumer price index, 2 = wholesale price index, and 3 = implicit consumer expenditure deflator;

subscript $(q) = 1, 2$, where 1 = the money supply excluding time deposits and 2 = the money supply including time deposits;

subscript $(m) = 1, 2, 3$, where 1 = long-term government bond yield, 2 = short-term treasury yield, 3 = long-term industrial bond rate.

$$V_{(O)} = \frac{y_{(i)}}{M_{(q)}} = \frac{y_{(i)}/p_{(j)}}{M_{(q)}/p_{(j)}} = \text{observed velocity,}$$

$$V_{(P)} = \frac{Y_{(i)}}{M_{(q)}} = \frac{Y_{(i)}}{M_{(q)}}\frac{P_{(j)}}{P_{(j)}} = \frac{Y_{(i)}/P_{(j)}}{M_{(q)}/P_{(j)}} = \text{permanent velocity.}$$

Canadian experience is examined by the following procedure. The data are quarterly for the period 1948–65. First, and for purposes of simplicity, Friedman's form of the demand function for money is employed. Thus,

$$\frac{M_{(q)}}{NP_{(j)}} = F\left(\frac{Y_{(i)}}{NP_{(j)}}\right).$$

The relationship fitted is

$$\frac{M_{(q)}}{NP_{(j)}} = \gamma\left(\frac{Y_{(i)}}{NP_{(j)}}\right)^{\delta}.$$

Second, the fitted relationship is used to compute velocity.

$$V_{(P)} = \frac{Y_{(i)}}{M_{(q)}P_{(j)}} = \frac{1}{\gamma}\left(\frac{Y_{(i)}}{NP_{(j)}}\right)^{1-\delta}.$$

By definition,

$$V = \frac{y_{(i)}}{M_{(q)}} = \frac{y_{(i)}}{Y_{(i)}} \cdot \frac{y_{(i)}}{M_{(q)}} = \frac{y_{(i)}}{Y_{(i)}} \cdot V_{(P)},$$

and

$$V_{(c)} = \frac{y_{(i)}}{Y_{(i)}} \frac{1}{\gamma} \left(\frac{Y_{(i)}}{NP_{(j)}}\right)^{1-\delta},$$

where $V_{(c)}$ is computed velocity. Velocity is computed in two forms: $V_{(c)}$, or computed velocity, is estimated using the functional relationship presented above; $V_{(o)}$, or observed velocity, is computed by dividing each estimate of real nominal income by each estimate of real nominal money supply. Third, a simple correlation coefficient is computed between computed and observed velocity. Fourth, the residual between computed and observed velocity is correlated with selected interest rates in order to ascertain their significance as explanatory variables for the behavior of this residual. Fifth, the demand for money is treated explicitly as a function of permanent income and interest rates in an effort to see if this formulation yields significant results. Sixth, I do not regard the series of tests as "definitive." More refined statistical procedures may very well be desirable as a sequence to the tests and results summarized in this paper.

Table 5 presents the results of fitting a demand for money equation to Canadian data. Table 6 presents the simple correlation coefficient between observed and computed velocity.

Tables 7 and 8 present the simple correlation coefficient between the residual element in observed velocity (after computed velocity has been removed) and the three selected interest rates and the multiple correlation coefficients between the residual element and all three interest rates.

The regression equations are cast into logarithmic form to facilitate estimation of income and interest elasticities in order to test the unit income elasticity hypothesis and the interest elasticity hypothesis. The several combinations estimated are summarized in tables 9 and 10. The statistical analysis yields the following best results in terms of the R^2, the coefficient of multiple determination. In table 9 equations (2) and (5) are roughly consistent with the hypothesis of unit income elasticity. They are also consistent with the American results reported by Meltzer (1963), Chow (1966), and Laidler (1966). The interest rate elasticities also appear to be consistent with those reported by Laidler (1966) for the United States. He reports that the range for the United

TABLE 5

Fitting of Demand for Money Equation to Canadian Quarterly Data, 1948 through 1965

Form of the Equation $Z = X\gamma\delta u$*

Variable Z	Value of γ	Variable X	Value of δ (Std. Error)	R^2
M_1/NP_1	.967	Y_1/NP_1	.377 (.064)	.356
M_1/NP_1	.183	Y_2/NP_1	.525 (.075)	.445
M_1/NP_1	.127	Y_3/NP_1	.462 (.063)	.465
M_1/NP_2	.236	Y_1/NP_2	.544 (.046)	.696
M_1/NP_2	.366	Y_2/NP_2	.663 (.050)	.742
M_1/NP_2	.252	Y_3/NP_2	.600 (.042)	.769
M_1/NP_3	.130	Y_1/NP_3	.430 (.038)	.675
M_1/NP_3	.188	Y_2/NP_3	.529 (.044)	.699
M_1/NP_3	.144	Y_3/NP_3	.485 (.039)	.717

M_1 = Money supply excluding time (notice) deposits.
N = Population.
P_1 = Permanent consumer price index.
P_2 = Permanent wholesale price index.
P_3 = Implicit consumer expenditure deflator.
Y_1 = Permanent GNP in nominal terms.
Y_2 = Permanent national income in nominal terms.
Y_3 = Permanent personal disposable income in nominal terms.
* All parameters are significant at or above the .005 level.

TABLE 6

Simple Correlation Coefficients between Computed and Observed Velocity, Canada

	V_{o1}	V_{o2}	V_{o3}
V_{c1} ··········	.717	.574	.698
V_{c2} ··········	.729	.596	.739
V_{c3} ··········	.840	.742	.824

Note:
   Subscripts for V_o: 1 refers to Y_1, 2 to Y_2, 3 to Y_3.
   Subscripts for V_c: 1 refers to P_1, 2 to P_2, 3 to P_3.

TABLE 7

SIMPLE CORRELATION COEFFICIENTS BETWEEN SELECTED
INTEREST RATES AND RESIDUAL ELEMENT IN VELOCITY, CANADA

Residual Element of Velocity	Long-Term Government Bond Rate	Short-Term Treasury Yield	Industrial Bond Yield
$r_{1,1}$	.106	−.035	−.177
$r_{1,2}$	.195	.062	−.081
$r_{1,3}$	.312	.162	−.042
$r_{2,1}$	.119	−.025	−.145
$r_{2,2}$	.153	−.025	−.113
$r_{2,3}$	.245	.103	−.020
$r_{3,1}$	.004	−.127	−.278
$r_{3,2}$	−.055	−.159	−.352
$r_{3,3}$	.106	.017	−.165

$r_{i,j}$ is the residual element in velocity where i is the measure of income, $1 = Y_{(1)}$, $2 = Y_{(2)}$, $3 = Y_{(3)}$ and j is the measure of prices, $1 = P_{(1)}$, $2 = P_{(2)}$, $3 = P_{(3)}$.

States is −.15 to −.20 and that the relevant rate is a short one. In Canada both the long-term and the short-term rates appear to be important.

When notice on time deposits is included in the money supply as in the equations in table 10, the R^2's are increased. The best results in terms of the R^2's are yielded by equations (5) and (6) in table 10. The performance of the long-term interest rate variable is mixed. The short-term rate, on the other hand, performs in the expected direction yielding a negative sign. The results are consistent with Meltzer's report (1963) that inclusion of time deposits tends to submerge interest rate

TABLE 8

MULTIPLE CORRELATION COEFFICIENTS
FOR ALL THREE INTEREST RATES
AND THE RESIDUAL VELOCITY ELEMENT,
CANADA, 1950–65

Residual Element in Velocity*	All Interest Rates
$r_{1,1}$	.474
$r_{1,2}$	.463
$r_{1,3}$	.514
$r_{2,1}$	.459
$r_{2,2}$	.430
$r_{2,3}$	.466
$r_{3,1}$	.433
$r_{3,2}$	.390
$r_{3,3}$	.361

* See table 7 for definition.

TABLE 9

The Demand for Money as a Function of Income and Interest Rates, Canada, 1950–65

$\ln M_1/N_{pj} = a + b \ln Y_t/N_{pj} + c \ln r_1 + d \ln r_2 + \ln r_3$	R^2
(1) $\ln M_1/N_{p1} = -2.194 + .973 \ln Y_1/N_{p1} - .077 \ln r_1 - .277 \ln r_2 + .167 \ln r_3$	.589
(Std. Error) (.141) (.066) (.035) (.044)	
Add'l. Expl. .2803 .0094 .2053 .0936	
(2) $\ln M_1/N_{p1} = -3.275 + 1.224 \ln Y_2/N_{p1} - .114 \ln r_1 - .251 \ln r_2 + .144 \ln r_3$	.654
(Std. Error) (.149) (.061) (.029) (.039)	
Add'l. Expl. .3668 .0201 .2053 .0620	
(3) $\ln M_1/N_{p1} = -2.453 + 1.051 \ln Y_3/N_{p1} - .186 \ln r_1 - .227 \ln r_2 + .142 \ln r_3$	.598
(Std. Error) (.150) (.072) (.031) (.042)	
Add'l. Expl. .2968 .0459 .2053 .0476	
(4) $\ln M_1/N_{p2} = -1.483 + .860 \ln Y_1/N_{p2} - .047 \ln r_1 - .249 \ln r_2 + .146 \ln r_3$	.561
(Std. Error) (.104) (.067) (.036) (.045)	
Add'l. Expl. .111 .004 .369 .078	
(5) $\ln M_1/N_{p2} = -2.141 + 1.022 \ln Y_2/N_{p2} - .085 \ln r_1 - .233 \ln r_2 + .136 \ln r_3$	.606
(Std. Error) (.113) (.064) (.033) (.042)	
Add'l. Expl. .1328 .0118 .4024 .0592	
(6) $\ln M_1/N_{p2} = -1.614 + .910 \ln Y_3/N_{p2} - .143 \ln r_1 - .207 \ln r_2 + .127 \ln r_3$	.560
(Std. Error) (.111) (.072) (.033) (.044)	
Add'l. Expl. .126 .030 .367 .038	
(7) $\ln M_1/N_{p3} = -1.756 + .898 \ln Y_1/N_{p3} - .072 \ln r_1 - .260 \ln r_2 + .159 \ln r_3$	.517
(Std. Error) (.127) (.063) (.038) (.044)	
Add'l. Expl. .3266 .0107 .0829 .0971	
(8) $\ln M_1/N_{p3} = -2.243 + 1.041 \ln Y_2/N_{p3} - .084 \ln r_1 - .235 \ln r_2 + .136 \ln r_3$	.575
(Std. Error) (.129) (.059) (.033) (.040)	
Add'l. Expl. .4082 .0143 .0829 .0698	
(9) $\ln M_1/N_{p3} = -2.611 + 1.079 \ln Y_3/N_{p3} - .188 \ln r_1 - .234 \ln r_2 + .145 \ln r_3$	.522
(Std. Error) (.151) (.067) (.035) (.043)	
Add'l. Expl. .3237 .0629 .0829 .0526	

M_1 = Money supply excluding time (notice) deposits.
Y_t/N_{pj} = Permanent per capita income.
r_1 = Long-term government bond yield.
r_2 = Short-term treasury yield.
r_3 = Long-term industrial bond rate.
* Not significant at .005 level.

effects. The results also appear to be roughly consistent with the unit income elasticity hypothesis. In all four equations the income coefficient estimates are within one standard deviation of 1 (Macesich and Falero, 1969). Moreover, a higher R^2 is obtained, as in equation (6) in table 10, when personal disposable income is used to compute permanent nominal income. This is consistent with results reported elsewhere (Chow 1966; Macesich and Falero 1969) that the results may be sensitive to measurement procedures, which is often the case in econometric work.

Tests of first differences confirm the results obtained with level values.

TABLE 10

The Demand for Money as a Function of Income and Interest
Rates, Canada, 1950–65

$\ln M_2/N_{pj} = a + b \ln Y_j/N_{pj} + c \ln r_1 + d \ln r_2 + h \ln r_3$	R^2
(1) $\ln M_2/N_{p1} = -.558 + .913 \ln Y_1/N_{p1} + .044 \ln r_1 - .188 \ln r_2 + .137 \ln r_3$	.750
(Std. Error) (.089) (.042) (.022) (.027)	
Add'l. Expl. .437 .005 .171 .137	
(2) $\ln M_2/N_{p1} = -1.194 + 1.081 \ln Y_2/N_{p1} + .019 \ln r_1^* - .157 \ln r_2 + .112 \ln r_3$	.778
(Std. Error) (.096) (.040) (.019) (.025)	
Add'l. Expl. .503 .0009 .186 .088	
(3) $\ln M_2/N_{p1} = -1.222 + 1.059 \ln Y_3/N_{p1} - .076 \ln r_1 - .148 \ln r_2 + .116 \ln r_3$	.829
(Std. Error) (.079) (.038) (.016) (.022)	
Add'l. Expl. .534 .012 .216 .068	
(4) $\ln M_2/N_{p2} = -.300 + .876 \ln Y_1/N_{p2} + .061 \ln r_1 - .172 \ln r_2 + .123 \ln r_3$	.886
(Std. Error) (.065) (.042) (.023) (.028)	
Add'l. Expl. .770 .004 .055 .056	
(5) $\ln M_2/N_{p2} = -.773 + 1.007 \ln Y_2/N_{p2} + .030 \ln r_1 - .150 \ln r_2 + .109 \ln r_3$	.893
(Std. Error) (.072) (.041) (.021) (.027)	
Add'l. Expl. .795 .001 .056 .041	
(6) $\ln M_2/N_{p2} = -.695 + .969 \ln Y_3/N_{p2} - .052 \ln r_1 - .137 \ln r_2 + .109 \ln r_3$	.918
(Std. Error) (.059) (.038) (.018) (.023)	
Add'l. Expl. .823 .003 .064 .028	
(7) $\ln M_2/N_{p3} = .786 + .684 \ln Y_1/N_{p3} + .058 \ln r_1 - .135 \ln r_2 + .111 \ln r_3$	.801
(Std. Error) (.069) (.035) (.021) (.024)	
Add'l. Expl. .657 .009 .036 .100	
(8) $\ln M_2/N_{p3} = .693 + .743 \ln Y_2/N_{p3} + .053 \ln r_1 - .108 \ln r_2 + .091 \ln r_3$	.802
(Std. Error) (.075) (.035) (.019) (.023)	
Add'l. Expl. .692 .008 .032 .070	
(9) $\ln M_2/N_{p3} = -.030 + .851 \ln Y_3/N_{p3} - .035 \ln r_1 - .120 \ln r_2 + .102 \ln r_3$	.829
(Std. Error) (.077) (.034) (.018) (.022)	
Add'l. Expl. .696 .003 .069 .061	

M_2 = Money supply including time (notice) deposits.
All the other variables are the same as in table 9.

* Not significant at .005 level.

The R^2's, for example, range from .978 to .122. The use of first differences, however, may introduce additional complications such as, for example, the issue that adjustments in money holdings may take longer than the change covered.[43]

Caution is urged, however, in interpreting the results presented in tables 9 and 10. The evidence, though mixed, suggests the existence of multicollinearity in the set of independent variables. While the simple correlation coefficients are high (e.g., .85, .83, and −.15) relative to the coefficient of multiple correlation, they are nonetheless generally

43. Phillip Cagan has made this observation. See also Macesich and Falero, "Permanent Income Hypothesis."

lower than the coefficients of multiple correlation in tables 9 and 10.[44]

In the theory of money, students until recently have taken the view of velocity as a mechanically determined or arbitrary number. The approach I have used, one that is also suggested in the works of Friedman, Selden, Meltzer, and others, is to view velocity in terms of orthodox demand analysis. I have classified the determinants of velocity in terms of traditional demand analysis.

The analysis has been restricted to an examination of the consistency with Canadian experience of several hypotheses which purport to explain the behavior of velocity. If we keep in mind the limitations of correlation analysis of time series, the results are suggestive. Permanent magnitudes appear to be important determinants of velocity behavior. Another variable that has been a significant determinant of velocity behavior in Canada is the cost of holding money as indicated by yields on government bonds. The strongest relation, however, appears to exist when the demand for money is treated explicitly as a function of permanent income and interest rates.

The evidence is consistent with the hypothesis that the elasticity of demand for money with respect to permanent income is close to unity. In addition, the elasticity of demand for money with respect to interest rates appears to be small enough to place important limits on movements in velocity attributable to induced changes in saving and investing behavior. These results are consistent, for example, with those reported for the United States by Friedman, Meltzer-Brunner, Laidler, and Chow.

6. Conclusion

Canada is a relatively small country heavily dependent on foreign trade in spite of a high rate of labor-force growth and capital inflow. Although the importance to the country of the external sector as a percentage of total expenditure declined during the period under review, reflecting the growth of the Canadian economy both as a market and domestic source of supply, foreign trade remains important. In 1928, for example, exports of goods and services accounted for 29 per cent of total expenditures, and imports for 30 per cent. In 1956 exports accounted for 21 per cent and imports for 26 per cent of total expenditures. The Canadian economy still remains sensitive in the 1960s to external disturbances.[45] In contrast, American exports of goods and

44. D. E. Farrar and R. R. Glauber, "Multicollinearity in Regression Analysis: The Problem Revisited," *Review of Economics and Statistics* (1967), pp. 98–99.

45. Don J. Daly, "Is the Business Cycle Obsolete?" (manuscript, 1967).

services in recent years constituted only about 5 per cent of the gross national product.

The fact that these two countries differ so radically in terms of their dependence on external trade renders all the more important the similarity of the various test results presented here. It underscores the generality of our theoretical apparatus. In particular it suggests that money matters even in a small country with a different socioeconomic environment.

Monetary policy as a major branch of economic policy has undergone a remarkable revival in the postwar period, both in Canada and elsewhere. The evidence and analysis presented in this study suggest that this is the way it should be. This does not mean, however, that the importance of fiscal policy is diminished. Indeed, the evidence underscores its importance.

In pre-Keynesian times monetary policy was the principal instrument of aggregate economic policy. Its principal objective was price stability. Fiscal policy as an alternative instrument is considered as largely a byproduct of the Keynesian revolution which emphasized internal economic stability or full employment. Thanks to the war debt and its size, debt management is now also considered an important instrument for effecting economic stability. Increased concern for economic growth in the postwar period has forced its recognition as a third objective. Concern over balance-of-payments problems in many countries has prompted the recognition of still another objective—external balance.

It should be readily apparent that such a manifold of objectives may be, at times, in conflict with each other. Equally apparent is the issue regarding the effectiveness of the several instruments now recognized as available for achieving the various objectives. In many countries since the early 1950s monetary policy has increasingly assumed the responsibility for short-run stabilization. Its use for such a purpose is justified on the basis of its "flexibility," which usually means that it can be changed quickly.[46] The important question, however, is whether or not monetary authorities are able in their conduct of monetary policy to eliminate the lags which exist between correctly appraising an existing situation, then taking appropriate action, and finally having such action reliably and quickly influence the economy in the desired direction.

46. Harry G. Johnson, "Monetary Theory and Policy," *Amer. Econ. Rev.* (June 1962), p. 368, *Canada in a Changing Economy* (Toronto: Univ. of Toronto Press, 1962), *Money, Trade, and Economic Growth* (London: George Allen and Unwin, 1962).

Canadian experience appears to support the results presented by others for the United States on the variability and lag in the effect of monetary policy. This underscores the difficulty in executing appropriate monetary policy.

The foregoing evidence also sheds light on an important dispute in monetary theory and policy. This dispute arises over the effects of changes in the stock of money on the economy. One side argues that such changes are important sources of instability in the economy, and the other holds that control over changes in the money stock will do little to promote economic stability.[47] If central bank action on the stock of money influences the economy only after long and variable lags, the dispute loses much of its substance.

Prior to the 1930s theoretical and empirical research in monetary theory focused on the institutional determinants of velocity or the demand for money. Since that time considerable attention has been given to the relation between velocity, or its alternative formulation the demand for money, and interest rates. The possible existence of the Keynesian liquidity-trap and the consequent ineffectiveness of monetary policy probably motivated much of this research. In themselves many of the studies left much to be desired. The consistency of their results against Canadian experience is discussed in this study.

To judge from Canadian results the demand for cash balances does in fact depend partly on interest rates. A promising explanation seems also to be contained in the permanent income hypothesis discussed by Milton Friedman, which would also include interests rates as a determinant. Indeed, such a relation appears to explain much of velocity behavior in Canada.

Our results have important implications bearing on an old but enduring controversy in the field of money. Is it more useful to cast monetary theory in terms of the demand for and supply of money, as in the equation of exchange of velocity approach, or in terms of the influence of money on expenditure and income, as in the income expenditures approach? It would seem that, on balance, monetary theory cast into the demand for and supply of money is the more useful approach.

When the supply of money is taken into account the results suggest that an economic explanation of its determinants is preferable to the typical but mechanical explanation that the supply of money is

47. Phillip Cagan, "A Commentary of Some Current Issues in the Theory of Monetary Policy," in *Patterns of Market Behavior*, Michael J. Brennan, ed. (Providence: Brown Univ. Press, 1965), p. 39.

determined directly by the monetary authority. An economic interpretation is more in keeping with developments in the demand side, treating the various ratios as behavior relationships reflecting asset choices rather than exogenous variables.[48]

Particularly suggestive is the work by Phillip Cagan in his study of the demand for currency relative to the total money supply. Cagan demonstrates that for the United States the demand for currency is influenced partly by the percentage of income that is taxed. Apparently accepting payments in cash and subsequently holding cash balances is a method for evading payment of income taxes. Other factors that he considers important in determining the public's currency-money ratio are expected per capita income and expected returns on bank deposits.[49]

Canadian results for the period 1926–58 are consistent with those presented by Cagan for the United States. Indeed, the indirect "victims" of the income tax in Canada are Canadian chartered banks. For all practical purposes the income tax is a drain on their reserves. Other things equal, the effect is also to decrease the stock of money. Expected per capita income and expected returns on deposits in Canada have operated in favor of chartered banks by expanding their deposit liabilities and thus the stock of money.

48. See, for example, discussion of the "liquidity preference" of member banks in George Macesich, *Commercial Banking and Regional Development*, and the material cited elsewhere on the currency-to-money ratio.

49. In addition to Cagan and Macesich for developments in supply theory see Karl Brunner, "A Schema for the Supply Theory of Money," *International Economic Review*, January 1961; Allan H. Meltzer, "The Behavior of the French Money Supply, 1938–54," *Jour. Pol. Economy*, June 1959; Karl Brunner and Allan Meltzer, "The Place of Financial Intermediaries in the Transmission of Monetary Policy," *Amer. Econ. Rev.*, May 1963.

APPENDIX

SEASONALLY ADJUSTED MONEY SUPPLY IN PUBLIC HANDS MONTHLY, JANUARY 1868–JUNE 1923 AND JANUARY 1924–DECEMBER 1958

The statistical information presented on the money supply in public hands for the period January 1868 through 1929 is compiled from C. A. Curtis's *Statistical Contributions to Canadian Economic History* (Toronto: Macmillan Company of Canada, 1931). Curtis compiled his estimates from the monthly supplement to the *Canada Gazette*. The money supply figures from 1930 through 1958 are constructed from information contained in monthly "Returns of Chartered Banks of Canada" and presented in the monthly supplement to the *Canada Gazette*. The information contained in these two sources is supplemented by data on money supply components contained in *Minutes and Proceedings and Evidence respecting Bank of Canada*, Session 1939, House of Commons; Bank of Canada Research Memorandum *General Public Holdings of Certain Liquid Assets* (Ottawa: Bank of Canada, 1953); "Monthly Statement of Assets and Liabilities: Bank of Canada"; *Canada Year Book* for the years 1938, 1941, 1954, and 1955 (Ottawa: Dominion Bureau of Statistics, 1938, 1941, 1954, and 1955).

TABLE 11

SEASONALLY ADJUSTED CANADIAN MONEY SUPPLY, MONTHLY 1868–JUNE 1923
(Thousands of Dollars)

Year	Jan.	Feb.	Mar.	Apr.	May	June
1868	45,208	45,556	47,003	48,269	48,673	48,627
1869	50,867	51,695	53,548	56,033	57,293	57,617
1870	62,350	63,211	64,503	67,069	68,355	68,958
1871	73,347	73,738	73,662	75,647	75,839	76,216
1872	73,974	75,448	75,747	78,403	78,263	78,789
1873	80,804	81,689	81,623	83,562	83,252	83,596
1874	86,062	87,224	88,229	90,321	90,617	90,860
1875	88,277	87,931	88,022	88,262	87,534	86,907
1876	82,223	82,603	83,034	84,226	84,085	84,064
1877	85,088	85,302	85,923	87,690	85,898	85,516
1878	84,598	84,263	85,642	86,435	85,130	85,313
1879	84,428	83,958	85,414	86,412	86,567	86,758
1880	90,013	90,818	93,396	96,556	97,694	89,479
1881	104,673	106,346	109,199	112,168	113,547	113,737
1882	122,440	124,293	126,442	128,504	129,539	129,606
1883	133,500	133,288	133,589	134,630	133,880	133,108
1884	130,544	129,442	129,242	130,316	128,918	127,874
1885	126,215	126,611	127,350	129,117	129,352	128,994
1886	131,636	132,288	133,629	135,681	136,343	133,376
1887	137,099	138,154	139,900	141,945	141,382	138,567
1888	143,340	144,994	146,241	147,987	148,028	148,134
1889	154,410	155,539	156,810	158,379	158,993	158,685
1890	160,178	160,972	163,041	165,181	165,083	164,719
1891	171,196	172,410	174,580	177,285	177,693	178,045
1892	186,960	187,361	191,039	194,167	195,987	196,648
1893	202,661	201,861	204,308	205,905	206,235	206,156
1894	206,237	206,140	207,659	209,233	210,136	210,108
1895	212,955	214,195	215,855	217,721	218,786	217,098
1896	218,186	219,707	220,859	223,775	224,666	223,449
1897	230,570	233,553	236,365	241,033	242,922	243,067
1898	256,749	260,485	264,080	267,845	270,824	271,628
1899	287,305	291,206	296,132	300,176	303,795	304,259
1900	317,527	321,211	325,341	329,058	331,356	330,717
1901	351,295	355,746	360,051	363,796	367,649	368,558
1902	389,235	393,862	398,061	402,282	405,351	406,374
1903	425,655	430,757	435,610	441,251	442,687	443,121
1904	465,198	470,488	475,572	481,868	484,445	485,234
1905	512,549	518,594	524,663	532,701	537,915	538,898
1906	573,860	582,864	591,101	601,934	608,915	610,901
1907	638,625	644,300	647,829	652,169	650,792	644,827
1908	637,471	640,966	644,408	649,115	646,945	649,421
1909	694,737	706,454	719,133	734,357	747,217	753,444
1910	811,462	821,332	833,959	849,398	855,818	855,689
1911	903,281	911,565	921,767	933,631	939,557	940,192
1912	1,013,077	1,020,882	1,027,995	1,039,350	1,046,915	1,045,173
1913	1,072,566	1,075,333	1,078,417	1,083,478	1,084,648	1,076,141
1914	1,081,108	1,086,862	1,094,763	1,098,127	1,100,225	1,091,836
1915	1,110,445	1,111,034	1,120,649	1,133,723	1,144,601	1,149,631
1916	1,217,986	1,232,455	1,256,354	1,282,512	1,298,971	1,311,524
1917	1,410,918	1,430,217	1,453,414	1,483,152	1,511,088	1,527,072
1918	1,607,341	1,629,614	1,659,644	1,711,779	1,707,812	1,724,612
1919	1,797,535	1,828,706	1,878,471	1,928,460	1,886,029	1,894,493
1920	1,989,909	1,998,311	2,031,797	2,059,941	2,035,307	2,021,197
1921	2,017,336	2,001,784	2,002,795	2,000,163	1,990,628	1,971,615
1922	1,856,434	1,839,200	1,830,650	1,824,687	1,825,500	1,822,026
1923	1,794,888	1,796,211	1,803,946	1,794,874	1,815,045	1,820,662

TABLE 11—*Continued*

July	Aug.	Sept.	Oct.	Nov.	Dec.
48,719	49,372	49,121	49,158	49,664	40,598
57,007	57,411	56,131	56,861	57,888	60,773
69,333	69,929	70,070	71,400	72,713	75,664
76,647	76,300	76,444	75,571	75,195	76,728
79,100	79,313	79,208	78,295	78,760	80,927
83,070	83,596	84,080	83,635	84,784	84,784
89,829	89,632	89,045	88,116	88,562	87,166
84,941	83,221	82,418	81,907	81,383	82,231
84,341	84,197	84,760	84,937	84,272	84,426
85,621	84,950	84,592	84,335	83,609	83,313
84,770	84,402	83,925	83,995	83,104	84,117
86,592	86,711	86,640	86,907	87,736	89,650
98,588	99,471	100,337	101,085	101,991	103,851
114,228	115,429	116,800	117,971	118,239	120,941
129,269	130,249	131,205	131,102	130,900	132,199
131,638	131,826	132,011	131,008	130,769	130,407
126,734	126,461	126,255	125,519	125,542	125,244
128,559	128,903	128,938	128,821	129,739	129,904
135,109	135,223	135,105	134,728	135,339	136,232
140,573	140,498	140,639	138,320	140,897	142,198
147,913	148,758	149,686	148,919	152,358	154,729
157,471	157,608	157,921	158,424	158,993	160,657
164,142	164,460	165,386	166,600	168,181	169,461
178,120	179,163	180,599	182,123	183,599	185,418
196,438	197,534	198,389	199,314	199,995	202,029
204,550	204,205	204,412	205,021	204,813	206,136
208,854	208,964	209,611	210,541	210,512	212,148
215,592	215,461	215,201	215,429	215,726	216,756
222,222	222,341	222,867	224,110	225,723	227,276
243,029	244,194	254,442	247,736	250,245	253,138
271,333	273,445	274,869	277,426	280,227	284,014
303,112	304,662	305,927	308,213	311,236	314,701
330,699	332,161	334,931	338,221	343,392	347,370
369,361	371,490	374,863	377,954	382,291	385,343
406,562	408,791	411,943	415,548	418,684	421,436
442,971	444,495	448,778	451,836	455,666	459,459
485,243	487,434	493,369	497,350	501,930	506,667
541,469	545,716	551,146	556,330	560,706	567,644
611,756	616,318	619,093	622,279	627,960	635,012
636,501	634,569	634,271	633,990	635,251	637,076
648,757	651,439	659,500	666,967	674,611	684,077
754,867	759,429	771,377	782,017	791,033	802,835
853,632	857,289	867,675	876,043	884,548	895,056
939,086	945,762	958,762	969,864	988,540	1,002,418
1,041,296	1,045,026	1,054,589	1,060,878	1,072,092	1,072,469
1,066,879	1,066,682	1,071,301	1,074,034	1,078,700	1,078,593
1,084,609	1,088,025	1,094,275	1,099,937	1,105,026	1,107,692
1,150,987	1,153,979	1,165 299	1,178,184	1,191,775	1,200,960
1,313,039	1,323,491	1,346,432	1,356,701	1,368,352	1,387,166
1,510,057	1,530,831	1,547,783	1,554,207	1,558,880	1,584,155
1,697,145	1,702,167	1,714,158	1,731,240	1,746,801	1,779,941
1,883,986	1,891,882	1,914,330	1,931,794	1,949,966	1,977,887
2,007,766	2,012,534	2,016,045	2,018,789	2,017,055	2,021,261
1,936,738	1,922,858	1,911,610	1,904,491	1,884,732	1,871,762
1,797,821	1,798,360	1,801,724	1,809,625	1,799,695	1,801,118

TABLE 12

Money Supply in Canada, Seasonally Adjusted

(In Millions of Dollars)

Year	Jan.	Feb.	Mar.	Apr.	May	June	July	Aug.	Sept.	Oct.	Nov.	Dec.
1924	1,772	1,778	1,771	1,798	1,810	1,821	1,800	1,805	1,792	1,791	1,823	1,827
1925	1,836	1,843	1,849	1,848	1,861	1,858	1,877	1,889	1,915	1,926	1,915	1,932
1926	1,936	1,953	1,972	1,961	1,988	1,985	1,998	2,006	2,011	2,023	2,033	2,022
1927	2,029	2,025	2,033	2,046	1,880	2,076	2,066	2,080	2,083	2,100	2,132	2,166
1928	2,179	2,199	2,219	2,225	2,287	2,276	2,254	2,241	2,235	2,255	2,258	2,252
1929	2,275	2,268	2,265	2,254	2,248	2,246	2,233	2,230	2,230	2,227	2,217	2,194
1930	2,179	2,162	2,144	2,126	2,104	2,097	2,103	2,103	2,095	2,093	2,105	2,112
1931	2,105	2,106	2,111	2,121	2,133	2,124	2,114	2,110	2,103	2,080	2,032	2,088
1932	2,008	1,999	1,986	1,976	1,961	1,947	1,941	1,924	1,917	1,923	1,926	1,938
1933	1,952	1,956	1,961	1,947	1,982	1,986	1,972	1,962	1,951	1,937	1,936	1,940
1934	1,941	1,945	1,947	1,947	1,952	1,957	1,970	1,993	2,000	2,016	2,044	2,050
1935	2,058	2,066	2,076	2,087	2,092	2,098	2,109	2,123	2,157	2,178	2,181	2,187
1936	2,188	2,193	2,206	2,220	2,226	2,232	2,246	2,252	2,260	2,285	2,303	2,325
1937	2,351	2,373	2,388	2,393	2,400	2,408	2,412	2,410	2,390	2,364	2,362	2,370
1938	2,376	2,390	2,405	2,425	2,447	2,459	2,461	2,466	2,485	2,495	2,491	2,492
1939	2,506	2,529	2,535	2,528	2,531	2,548	2,556	2,578	2,631	2,683	2,708	2,729
1940	2,663	2,593	2,616	2,657	2,706	2,735	2,766	2,820	2,800	2,782	2,842	2,898
1941	2,961	3,010	3,037	3,119	3,007	2,841	2,872	2,896	2,949	3,075	3,204	3,287
1942	3,312	3,162	3,033	3,140	3,314	3,450	3,536	3,589	3,655	3,634	3,642	3,726
1943	3,791	3,922	4,037	4,003	3,968	3,999	4,066	4,160	4,204	4,237	4,293	4,380
1944	4,480	4,588	4,696	4,730	4,744	4,820	4,898	4,966	5,068	5,096	5,107	5,193
1945	5,262	5,342	5,413	5,375	5,378	5,492	5,586	5,676	5,797	5,813	5,778	5,826
1946	5,878	5,947	6,037	6,249	6,421	6,444	6,452	6,442	6,432	6,501	6,576	6,560
1947	6,539	6,502	6,496	6,579	6,653	6,661	6,665	6,658	6,650	6,679	6,742	6,814
1948	6,882	6,929	6,937	6,949	6,969	7,004	7,051	7,096	7,158	7,278	7,358	7,354
1949	7,340	7,374	7,462	7,496	7,498	7,524	7,544	7,586	7,639	7,657	7,669	7,713
1950	7,782	7,827	7,809	7,805	7,845	7,880	7,943	8,018	8,040	8,014	8,030	8,016
1951	8,001	8,016	8,012	8,039	8,055	8,049	8,030	8,026	8,072	8,168	8,222	8,318
1952	8,352	8,333	8,385	8,417	8,471	8,513	8,533	8,553	8,613	8,707	8,787	8,794
1953	8,840	8,898	8,947	8,984	8,968	8,966	8,999	9,028	8,980	8,913	8,905	8,937
1954	8,980	9,051	9,077	9,136	9,234	9,389	9,502	9,539	9,643	9,726	9,846	10,013
1955	10,138	10,211	10,324	10,431	10,490	10,574	10,624	10,637	10,694	10,723	10,667	10,634
1956	10,661	10,706	10,766	10,806	10,832	10,845	10,872	10,922	10,914	10,960	10,989	10,996
1957	11,011	11,012	10,989	10,977	11,029	11,033	11,008	11,031	11,091	11,111	11,174	11,243
1958	11,283	11,364	11,476	11,601	11,716	11,888	12,086	12,256	12,387	12,482	12,531	12,586

V

*International Differences in Liquid
Assets Portfolios*

MORRIS PERLMAN

International Differences in Liquid Assets Portfolios

T HERE are large differences among countries both in the holdings of liquid assets by the nonbanking sector of the economy and in the allocation among these assets. This study attempts to explain these differences with the use of the tools of monetary theory which have been developed over the last decade or so. In this period monetary theory has tended to move away from an "institutional" approach to a capital theory approach, concentrating more on the holding of money as an asset and less on its function as a medium of exchange;[1] this development increases its usefulness for the present study which by its nature has to deal with diverse institutional structures. The results of the study indicate that the differences among countries in liquid asset portfolios can be explained by the use of those variables entering into a capital theory model of the demand for assets and, what is more striking, that the actual coefficients of the explanatory variables are within a plausible range of those found in national time series studies.

Section 1 of this paper illustrates the magnitude of the differences among forty-seven countries in the holdings of liquid assets by the nonbanking sector of the economy and the allocation of these assets among alternative types. Section 2 presents the theoretical framework used to explain these differences. Sections 3 and 4 present the empirical findings, and Section 5 the summary and conclusions of the study.

1. DIFFERENCES AMONG THE COUNTRIES IN LIQUID ASSET HOLDINGS

The forty-seven countries included in this study represent all the major regions of the world except the communist bloc and Africa (the

This paper is a revised version of my "International Differences in Liquid Assets Portfolios" (unpublished doctoral dissertation, University of Chicago, 1966). I am greatly indebted to Professor Milton Friedman for his helpful suggestions and encouragement during the course of this study.

1. See for example Harry G. Johnson, "Monetary Theory and Policy," *American Economic Review*, vol. 52 (1962).

United Arab Republic is the only African country included, and is classified under "Asia" in the regional classification). The range of social, economic, and institutional characteristics covered by this sample of countries is very great; from a real per capita income of $50 a year in Burma to one of $2,200 a year in the United States; from an average rate of inflation of nearly 70 per cent per year in Korea (1948–56) to a zero rate of inflation in Portugal (1948–56); from a proportion of the population living in cities of over 20,000 people of 70 per cent New Zealand to one of only 8 per cent in Thailand. The number of financial institutions supplying the assets and their characteristics also vary greatly among the countries. In Burma there is approximately one bank office for every half a million people, in Australia one for every two thousand. Besides banks (commercial, savings, cooperatives, and many others) twenty-one countries have widespread post office savings systems and eleven countries have post office giro systems.[2] Table 1 presents the forty-seven countries classified into four regional groups, Europe, Asia, Latin America, and Others, with some of the economic and institutional characteristics of the groups.

Three liquid assets—currency, demand deposits, and time and savings deposits—held by the private nonbanking sector of the economy and the currency-deposits ratio are examined in this study. The quantities of the assets for each of the years 1952–61 were expressed in terms of the number of weeks of income held, and averaged over two five-year periods (1952–56, 1957–61).[3] Expressing the assets in terms of income serves two purposes: it converts the assets into real terms, and it allows an international comparison of quantities. The averaging tends to eliminate short-term cyclical distortions. In final form, the dependent variables are the average number of weeks of income held in the form of a particular asset. There are two observations for all but two countries and one observation for each of these.[4] All deposits except those

2. A post office giro system provides facilities for the transfer of accounts among individuals by use of "giro transfer" orders. These differ form checks only in that it is the payer, not the payee, who executes the transfer either with cash or from his giro account (only the payee needs to have an account). See for example John Hein, "A Note on the Giro Transfer System," *Journal of Finance*, vol. 19 (1959).

3. For the sources of the data see appendix B. For some countries data were not available for a full five-year period, so the averaging was done over the number of years for which data were available. Each observation is an average of at least two years.

4. Indonesia and El Salvador.

TABLE 1

Regional Classification of Countries and Some Group
Characteristics

	Europe	Others**	Asia	Latin America
	Austria	Australia	Burma	Argentina
	Belgium	Canada	Ceylon	Brazil
	Denmark	Ireland	India	Chile
	Finland	Israel	Indonesia	Colombia
	France	Japan	Korea	Costa Rica
	Germany	New Zealand	Malaya	Ecuador
	Greece	United Kingdom	Pakistan	El Salvador
	Italy	United States	Philippines	Guatemala
	Netherlands		Taiwan	Honduras
	Norway		Thailand	Mexico
	Portugal		Turkey	Nicaragua
	Spain		U.A.R.	Paraguay
	Sweden			Peru
				Venezuela
No. of countries........	13	8	12	14
Av.* per capita income (in dollars)..........	768.4	1154.7	109.0	218.8
Av.* Rate of inflation...	4%	5%	7%	10%
Av.* Urbanization......	.373	.531	.153	.242

* For a description of these variables and their derivation see section 4.

** Japan and Israel are included in this group because most of their economic and institutional characteristics are much more similar to those of the countries in this group than to the countries in the Asian group.

tied to a price index or an exchange rate[5] are included, whether held in commercial banks, savings banks, credit cooperatives, or post offices.

One of the problems in comparing differences among the countries in the holdings of deposits is the arbitrary nature of the distinction between demand, time, and savings deposits.[6] In the United States demand deposits are identical to checking deposits, but in many countries all deposits withdrawable on demand are included among

5. The reason for the exclusion of these deposits is that to the holder they are real assets, in terms of the domestic price level, either on a continuous basis for the index-tied deposits or with a lag for the others, depending on the lag between changes in the price level and changes in the exchange rate; as such they are basically different from all the other assets included in this study.

6. In the January 1960 issue of *International Financial Statistics*, the IMF defines deposit money—what I consider as demand deposits—as "deposits unrestrictedly exchangeable on demand into currency at par without penalty." However, in the following paragraph it has this qualification: "It is the way that deposits are regarded by the holders that ultimately determines the boundary between money and quasi money," and presumably the IMF includes among demand deposits what the compiler of the data thinks that the holder regards as money.

demand deposits, whereas in Canada some deposits which are trans-
ferable by check are included in time deposits. In the United States
time deposits are withdrawable on demand (in practice); in many
countries they have to be held for a specific period of time (usually
three months to a year) and can only be withdrawn either with prior
notice or not at all before the contracted time elapses. Because of the
above considerations the same name does not necessarily imply the
same asset and total deposits may be a more homogeneous concept for
the purpose of international comparisons than the subtotals of the
various kinds of deposits.

The four bar charts (1–4) show the distribution of the countries by
their holdings of individual assets and by their currency-deposits ratio.
Each period average is counted separately so that each country enters
twice, except for the two countries for which data for only one period
were available. The four regions are combined into two groups: (1) Asia
and Latin America, and (2) Europe and Others. The number of observations is measured on the vertical axis, and the quantity of the assets (in
weeks of income), or the currency-deposits ratio, on the horizontal axis.
The width of each bar is one-half a standard deviation. The vertical
line in the center of each chart passes through the mean of each group
(the means of the regions within each group are indicated by the lines
marked A, E, L, O). In each bar the number of observations from each
region is shown. The countries making up some of the extreme observations are also shown.

These charts clearly show the large differences among the countries
in liquid asset holdings and in the currency-deposits ratio. The range of
currency holdings is over twelve weeks of income, of deposits over fifty
weeks, and of currency plus deposits over fifty-two weeks. The highest
currency-deposits ratio is nearly thirty times the lowest.[7] The differ-

7. As can be seen from charts 2 and 4, the range is greatly affected by the first-
period observations of Greece in the Europe and Others group and Indonesia in
the Asia and Latin America group. There is some justification in excluding Greece
(1952–56) and Indonesia (1952–56) from the sample. Greece did not attain
political stability after World War II until 1950, with the intervening years
marked by great instability due to the civil war. Under such conditions the risk
associated with the holdings of deposits is very great and it may take some time
to restore confidence in this form of holding wealth. Some evidence for this is the
change of deposits between the first and second period—a change of over 200 per
cent. This is by far the largest change from period to period in the holdings of any
asset of any country in the sample. A similar argument applies to Indonesia and
Korea. For these reasons the first-period observations of Greece, Korea, and
Indonesia were excluded in the regression analysis of section 3.

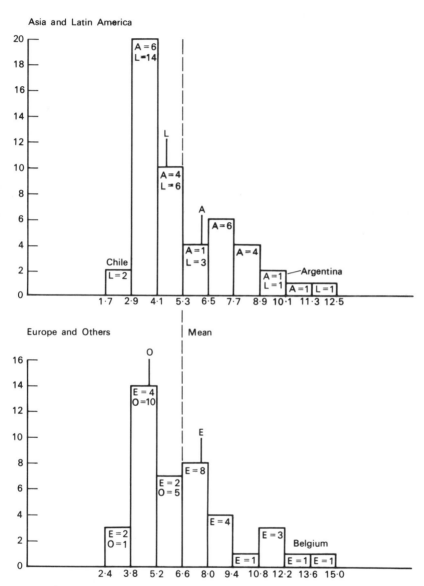

CHART 1. Distribution of countries by holdings of currency

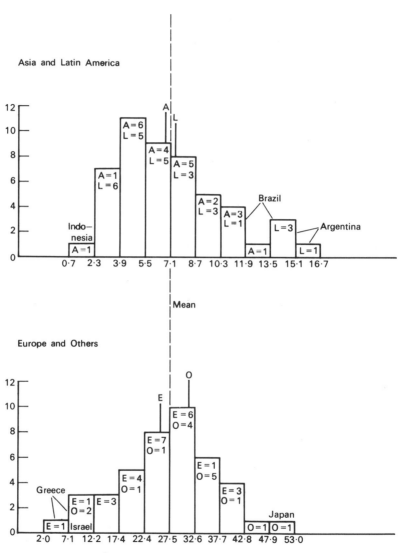

CHART 2. Distribution of countries by holdings of deposits

ences are both intraregional and interregional. Both charts 1 and 4 show a clear dichotomy between Asia and Latin America, and between Europe and Others in currency holdings, and in the currency-deposits ratio. This dichotomy is much more blurred in charts 2 and 3 and no definite regional pattern emerges.

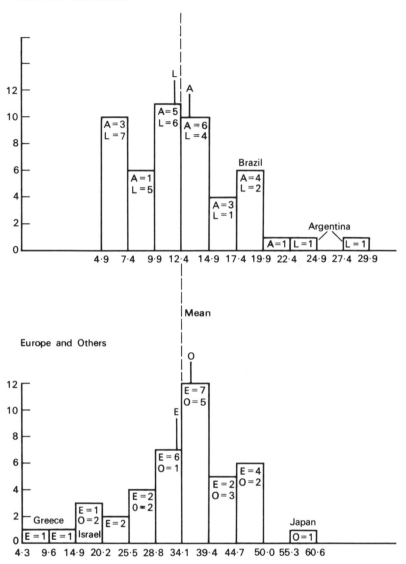

CHART 3. Distribution of countries by holdings of currency and deposits

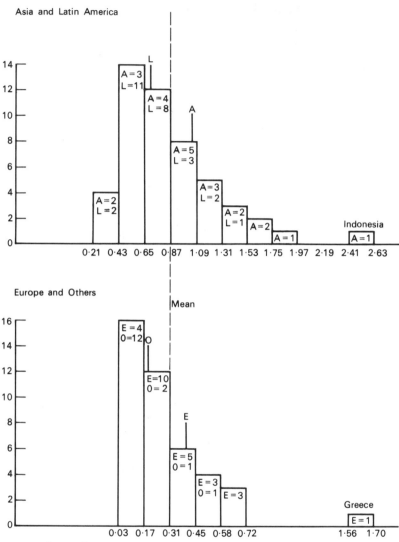

CHART 4. Distribution of countries by currency-deposits ratio

2. A THEORETICAL ANALYSIS OF THE DETERMINANTS OF LIQUID ASSET HOLDINGS

In a world of certainty in which the yields of nonhuman wealth were solely pecuniary, there would be no reason to distinguish among different assets in a portfolio. Each asset would be a perfect substitute for every other asset so the whole portfolio could be treated as a single asset. If the yield of each asset were both pecuniary and nonpecuniary (convenience, security, "liquidity," and other services), there would be a difference between assets producing different combinations of pecuniary and nonpecuniary returns or providing different types of services. As with other services treated in value theory, one would expect diminishing rates of substitution (convex indifference curves) among the services yielded by the assets.

By treating the "liquid" assets as capital goods yielding streams of services, and postulating that people hold these assets for the purpose of acquiring their services, one can describe a very general demand function for an asset,

$$Q_i = f(P_i, P_o, Y, k_i, u)$$

where Q_i is the quantity of the asset measured in real terms, P_i is the price of holding wealth in the form of the ith asset (this price, which would measure the alternative cost of acquiring the services yielded by the asset, would be the difference between the interest yield of this asset and the yield on real capital which does not yield any service stream); P_o is the price or prices of related goods and services, Y represents the budget constraint variables measured in real terms (the exact form these should take is left unspecified for the moment); k_i represents some index of the type and quantity of the services yielded by the asset, to convert the stock of the asset Q_i into the relevant quantity units—the flow of services; and u represents all those variables which may affect the demand for the asset via tastes and preferences, which for the most part will be assumed constant.

If more than one asset is included in Q_i, for example, currency as well as demand deposits, I treat Q_i as a composite good and therefore assume throughout the analysis that the relative prices of the assets within the composite do not change. P_i is now a weighted average of the prices of the assets included in Q_i, and the assumption of proportional price changes among the assets in Q_i is required so that changes in P_i should not result in any substitution among the assets in Q_i. The ratio of two assets (for example, the currency-deposit ratio), each of which has a demand function of the general form described above, will be a function of the variables which enter the individual demand functions; for example,

$$\frac{Q_i}{Q_j} = f(P_i, P_j, P_o, Y, k_i, k_j, u),$$

where P_o now represents the prices of goods and services related to the services yielded by either asset i or j.

Most earlier studies of the demand for assets have used a general function of the above form except that they have not included the set of variables which represents the type or quality of the services yielded by the assets,[8] a set of variables especially relevant to our immediate problem. As most of the earlier studies have used time series, or cross-section data, for subsections of a single country, they have been able to assume that the quality variables, k_i and k_j, are constant; so that changes in the quantity of the assets also measure changes in the quantity of the services of the assets. For the present study, which uses data for countries which vary widely, this assumption is not very appealing and it is pertinent to pay specific attention to variables which reflect differences in the type or quality of the assets. Hence the rest of this section will extend the demand model described above to incorporate specifically the effects of quality variables.

The quality of services yielded by an asset depends both on the specific services provided by the individual suppliers of the assets and on the general economic environment in which the service is used. A quality difference on the supply side would occur, for example, if banks in some countries allowed checks to be written on time deposits or waived the notice requirement on time deposits. An example of an environmental difference would be a difference in the acceptability of checks, which in turn might be the result of such factors as the legal structure of a country or the degree of urbanization. If urbanization involves a greater amount of transactions among strangers, it may lead to checks being less generally acceptable and thus decrease the services provided by a checking account. Another set of variables can be treated as affecting either the quality or the price of the services yielded by an asset. A reduction of the distance between an individual and a bank

---

8. One specific example of such a general function, and the one used as a starting point for this section, is Friedman's demand function for money,

$$\frac{M}{P} = f\left(r_b,\ r_e,\ \frac{1}{p}\frac{dp}{dt};\ w;\ \frac{Y}{P};\ u\right),$$

in M. Friedman, "The Quantity Theory of Money: A Restatement," in M. Friedman, ed., *Studies in the Quantity Theory of Money* (Chicago: Univ. of Chicago Press, 1956). In the above function, r_b and r_e are rates of interest on bonds and equities respectively, and $(1/p)(dp/dt)$ is the rate of change of prices. These are the price variables. w is the ratio of human to nonhuman income, which takes human wealth into account. Y/P is real income, the budget constraint variable. u stands for the quantifiable "objective" variables which may be expected to affect the tastes and preferences of individuals, and M/P is the real quantity of money demanded.

office can be viewed as either increasing the quality of a time deposit because it is now easier to use as a medium to exchange and thus yields more "liquidity" services, or as decreasing the price of the service stream yielded by the time deposit because transaction costs have been reduced.

Quality variables of the above kind should be distinguished from variables which reflect or produce changes in the tastes and preferences of individuals. For example, when individuals travel a great deal they may demand more money, not because money as such has changed in quality but because the individual has changed his behavior in the form of his increased desire or necessity to travel. It is the quality variables affecting the service stream of an asset that I want to incorporate into the demand model previously described.

The analysis will use the following symbols:

W = total nonhuman wealth in real terms,

Y_h = human income in real terms,

r_s = real rate of interest (the return to capital which has no service yield),

$Y = r_s W + Y_h$ = total real income,

$\overline{Y}$ = expenditures on all goods and services, other than liquidity services (defined as the services yielded by the assets considered in this study),

$A_i(i = 1, \ldots, n)$ = assets yielding liquidity services,

$Q_i(i = 1, \ldots, n)$ = the quantity of assets, measured in real terms, yielding liquidity services,

$r_i(i = 1, \ldots, n)$ = monetary yield per unit of A_i net of that part of the monetary yield that compensates for the expected rate of inflation,

$k_i(i = 1, \ldots, n)$ = service coefficient of $A_i \cdot k_i$ tells us what flow of services per unit time is yielded by a unit of A_i,

$S_i = k_i Q_i$ = flow of services yielded by Q_i per unit time,

P_i = price per unit of S_i.

On the assumption that the stocks are allocated to maximize the utility of the flows yielded by them, the relevant behavioral variables are the flow of goods and the flow of liquidity services.[9] To get the slope of the relevant price line we have to determine the price per unit of

9. "People have no direct preferences for assets, but only for things consumed." H. Makower and J. Marschak, "Assets, Prices, and Monetary Theory," in G. Stigler and K. E. Boulding, eds., *Readings in Price Theory* (London, 1960), p. 286.

liquidity services. The alternative opportunity cost of holding a unit of wealth in the form of A_i is $(r_s - r_i)\$1$, the difference between the real rate of interest and the rate of return on A_i. However, one unit of A_i yields k_i units of S_i. Therefore P_i, the price per unit of S_i, is $[(r_s - r_i)/k_i]\$1$. The price per unit of other goods is considered to be $\$1$; they are measured in units of income. The utility function to be maximized is $U(S_i \cdots S_n, \overline{Y})$ subject to the constraint $\sum P_i S_i + \overline{Y} = Y$. Following usual procedures the equilibrium conditions are:

$$U_1 - \lambda \frac{r_s - r_1}{k_1} = 0$$

$$\vdots$$

$$U_n - \lambda \frac{r_s - r_n}{k_n} = 0$$

$$U_{\overline{Y}} - \lambda = 0$$

From the above we can determine the optimum allocation of income among the different types of liquidity services and goods. However, the observable variables are not the services but the assets which yield the services. Therefore we must examine the effect of changes in the independent variables in the model, r_s, r_i, k_i, Y, on the observable dependent variables, $Q_i, i = 1, \ldots$, the stocks, as they operate via the relevant unobservable variables, the flows.

Three cases will be examined: a change in income, a change in r_i, the monetary yield of A_i, and a change in k_i, the service coefficient of A_i.[10] I want to examine the effect of the above changes on the total stock of liquid assets $(\sum Q_i)$ and on the allocation among different assets (Q_i/Q_j). Because of the proportional relationship between the stocks of the assets and the flows of services $(S_i = k_i Q_i)$, any change in Q_i will be proportional to a change in S_i for given k_i. Therefore, when the change in price is due to a change in either the monetary yield of the asset or a change in the real rate of interest, income and price elasticities will be the same for the stocks and for the flows.

If neither goods nor liquidity services are inferior, an increase in income will increase the quantity demanded both of goods and of liquidity services. What happens to the ratio Q_i/Q_j depends on the income elasticities of the liquidity services:

$$d\left(\frac{Q_i}{Q_j}\right) \gtrless 0 \quad \text{as} \quad \eta_{S_i Y} \gtrless \eta_{S_j Y} \quad \text{or} \quad \eta_{Q_i Y} \gtrless \eta_{Q_j Y}.$$

10. For example, an improvement in the services offered by banks to deposit holders, an increase in the general acceptability of checks, etc.

A change in r_i changes the relative price of liquidity services and other services and the relative price of S_i and S_j. Therefore, both $\sum Q_i$ and Q_i/Q_j will change. The magnitude of these changes will depend on the price elasticities of the various services or assets. Here again, as in the previous case, the elasticities of the assets will be the same as the elasticities of the services.

A change in k_i is more complicated because it involves a change in both relative prices and the quantity of services yielded by the stock of assets. An increase in k_i, implying a fall in the price of S_i which is $[(r_s - r_i)/k_i]\$1$, changes the relative price of liquidity services and other services and of S_i and other liquidity services. The effect of this change on the demand for S_i will depend on $\eta_{S_i P_i}$, the price elasticity of demand for S_i, because $\eta_{S_i k_i} = -\eta_{S_i P_i}$, the elasticity of demand for liquidity services with respect to changes in k, is equal in absolute value but opposite in sign to the price elasticity. However, we want to see what will be the effect of a change in k_i on Q_i, that is, $\eta_{Q_i k_i}$, the elasticity of demand for the asset with respect to a change in quality. Because of the proportional relationship between the stocks of assets and the flows of services ($S_i = k_i Q_i$), $\eta_{Q_i k_i} = \eta_{S_i k_i} - 1.$[11]

However, as the previous discussion has shown,

$$\eta_{S_i k_i} = -\eta_{S_i P_i}$$

and

$$\eta_{S_i P_i} = \eta_{Q_i P_i}.$$

Hence

$$\eta_{Q_i k_i} = -\eta_{Q_i P_i} - 1.$$

From this we see that the effect of a change in k_i on Q_i will depend on the price elasticity of demand for A_i. If it is greater than unity in absolute terms an increase in k_i will increase the demand for the asset.

11.
$$S_i = k_i Q_i,$$

$$\frac{dS_i}{dk_i} = k_i \frac{dQ_i}{dk_i} + Q_i,$$

$$\frac{dQ_i}{dk_i} = \frac{dS_i}{dk_i} \frac{1}{k_i} - \frac{Q_i}{k_i},$$

$$\frac{dQ_i}{dk_i} \frac{k_i}{Q_i} = \frac{dS_i}{dk_i} \frac{1}{Q_i} - 1$$

$$= \frac{dS_i}{dk_i} \frac{k_i}{S_i} - 1 \quad \therefore \quad \eta_{Q_i k_i} = \eta_{S_i k_i} - 1.$$

If it is less than unity, an increase in k_i will decrease the demand for the asset. To see what will happen to the ratio Q_i/Q_j when k_i increases, we can look at

$$\eta_{(Q_i/Q_j)k_i}, \quad \text{which is equal to} \quad \eta_{Q_i k_i} - \eta_{Q_j k_i}.$$

But from the above discussion,

$$\eta_{Q_i k_i} = -\eta_{Q_i P_i} - 1 \quad \text{and} \quad \eta_{Q_j k_i} = -\eta_{Q_j P_i}.$$

Therefore,

$$\eta_{(Q_i/Q_j)k_i} = -\eta_{Q_i P_i} - 1 + \eta_{Q_j P_i},$$

and

$$\eta_{(Q_i/Q_j)k_i} \gtrless 0 \quad \text{as} \quad (\eta_{Q_j P_i} - \eta_{Q_i P_i}) \gtrless 1.$$

The three basic assumptions underlying the above argument are:

a. Changes in quality can be considered as changing the stream of services yielded by an asset and thus changing the unit price of the services which are the ultimate "quantity" variables in the demand functions for liquid assets.
b. People react in the same way to a change in the number of units given a fixed money price as to a change in the "money" price per unit.
c. Changes in quality do not change the price elasticity of an asset.[12]

Although a change in quality is considered as actually changing the quantity of services yielded by an asset, some changes may be conceived of as affecting the price of the service rather than its quantity. In this case the effect would be the same as a change in r_i, a straightforward change in the price of the service. However, we can see that these two ways of looking at the effect of a particular variable, for example the average distance from a bank office, do not necessarily yield identical predictions under all circumstances. Let A_1 and A_2 be currency and time deposits respectively and assume that they are substitutes. If a decrease in the average distance from a bank office is considered as a decrease in the price of time deposits, one would predict that the quantity of time deposits demanded would increase, the quantity of currency demanded would decrease, and thus the currency-time deposit ratio would fall, whatever the magnitudes of the various

---

12. This is probably the assumption that is most easily violated, because some changes in quality, especially those induced from the supply side, increase the similarity of two assets (e.g., time and demand deposits) and thus increase the elasticity of demand for each with respect to price.

price elasticities. The sum of currency and time deposits $(A_1 + A_2)$ would rise if[13]

$$\frac{A_1}{A_2} > \frac{|\eta_{A_2 P_2}|}{|\eta_{A_1 P_2}|}.$$

If the decrease in the average distance from a bank office is considered as an increase in the service yield of time deposits, one would predict that the demand for currency would decrease, the quantity of time deposits demanded would increase if $|\eta_{A_2 P_2}| > 1$, but would decrease if $|\eta_{A_2 P_2}| < 1$; in the former cases, A_1/A_2 would fall, in the latter case A_1/A_2 would fall only if $\eta_{A_2 P_2} + 1 < \eta_{A_1 P_2}$,[14] and the sum $A_1 + A_2$ would rise only if[15]

$$\frac{A_1}{A_2} < \frac{-(\eta_{A_2 P_2} + 1)}{\eta_{A_1 P_2}}.$$

13. Let

$$\beta = \frac{A_1}{A_1 + A_2}; \frac{\beta}{1 - \beta} = \frac{A_1}{A_2};$$

$$\eta_{(A_1 + A_2) P_2} = \eta_{A_1 P_2}\beta + \eta_{A_2 P_2}(1 - \beta).$$

If A_1 and A_2 are substitutes,

$$\eta_{A_1 P_2} > 0,$$

$$\eta_{(A_1 + A_2) P_2} \underset{<}{\overset{>}{\gtrless}} 0 \quad \text{as} \quad \frac{\beta}{1 - \beta} \underset{<}{\overset{>}{\gtrless}} \frac{|\eta_{A_2 P_2}|}{|\eta_{A_1 P_2}|}$$

or as

$$\frac{A_1}{A_2} \underset{<}{\overset{>}{\gtrless}} \frac{|\eta_{A_2 P_2}|}{|\eta_{A_1 P_2}|}.$$

14.

$$\eta_{(A_1/A_2) k_2} = \eta_{A_1 k_2} - \eta_{A_2 k_2}$$

$$= -\eta_{A_1 P_2} - (-\eta_{A_2 P_2} - 1)$$

$$= \eta_{A_2 P_2} - \eta_{A_1 P_2} + 1$$

$$\eta_{(A_1/A_2) k_2} \underset{<}{\overset{>}{\gtrless}} 0 \quad \text{as} \quad \eta_{A_2 P_2} + 1 \underset{<}{\overset{>}{\gtrless}} \eta_{A_1 P_2}.$$

15. Let

$$\beta = \frac{A_1}{A_1 + A_2}; \frac{\beta}{1 - \beta} = \frac{A_1}{A_2};$$

$$\eta_{(A_1 + A_2) k_2} = \eta_{A_1 k_2}\beta + \eta_{A_2 k_2}(1 - \beta)$$

$$= -\eta_{A_1 P_2}\beta + (-\eta_{A_2 P_2} - 1)(1 - \beta).$$

$$\eta_{(A_1 + A_2) k_2} \underset{>}{\overset{<}{\lessgtr}} 0 \quad \text{as} \quad \frac{\beta}{1 - \beta} \underset{>}{\overset{<}{\lessgtr}} \frac{-(\eta_{A_2 P_2} + 1)}{\eta_{A_1 P_2}};$$

that is, as

$$\frac{A_1}{A_2} \underset{>}{\overset{<}{\lessgtr}} \frac{-(\eta_{A_2 P_2} + 1)}{\eta_{A_1 P_2}}.$$

If we drop the assumption of perfect certainty the holding of any asset involves some risk, and another reason for distinguishing among different assets in a portfolio is introduced. Different assets may have different types or degrees of risk associated with them. For example, the holding of currency involves the risk of theft; the holding of deposits, the risk of a bank failure; and the holding of any fixed coupon rate asset, the risk of a change in the interest rates which would affect its capital value. To incorporate the risk factor into the model of the demand for assets we must introduce some variable(s) that would serve as a proxy for the kind and degree of risk that may affect the holdings of the assets, for example the variance of interest rates.[16]

In summary, my model of the demand for any asset(s) is

$$Q_i = f(P_i, P_o, Y, K, R, u)$$

where Q_i, P_i, P_o, Y, and u are as defined in the first part of this section, K represents the group of variables which characterize the "quality" of the services yielded by the assets, and R represents the risk variables.

3. STATISTICAL ANALYSIS OF ASSET HOLDINGS

A. THE BUDGET CONSTRAINT AND PRICE VARIABLES

In this section[17] I attempt to explain the international differences in the holdings of liquid assets with the use of the budget constraint and own price variables only. It is found that these variables explain a large proportion of the observed differences. Per capita real income in dollars, adjusted for distortions introduced by fixed exchange rate systems, is used as the budget constraint variable. Two variables are used to represent the alternative opportunity cost of holding wealth in the form of the assets studied here: the rate of interest on long-term government bonds, which is available for only twenty-two countries, and the expected rate of inflation, which is approximated by the slope of the logarithmic trend fitted to the cost-of-living index.[18] As it is likely that most interest rates are closely related, the use of the govern-

16. Even though none of the assets studied here is a fixed coupon–rate asset, a change in interest rates may affect them via the substitution from or into fixed coupon–rate assets. See J. Tobin, "Liquidity Preference as Behavior towards Risk," *Review of Economic Studies* (February 1958).

17. For the sources and detailed description of the data, see Appendix B. The data are presented in Appendix C.

18. For the first period average (1952–56) the trend line was fitted to the years 1948–56. For the second period average (1957–61) the trend was fitted to the years 1952–61.

ment bond rate as a measure of the alternative opportunity cost of holding liquid assets raises a problem for those assets that have a pecuniary yield. A "high" bond yield may also imply a "high" yield on deposits and vice versa. Thus, two countries may have different bond yields and yet the alternative opportunity cost of holding liquid assets may be the same in both. However, as this is the only interest rate available for a large number of countries it is the only available measure that might indicate the alternative opportunity cost of at least some of the assets. To examine the effects of the rate of interest on liquid assets holdings a subsample of the twenty-two countries for which it is available is also analyzed. The three assets used as dependent variables are: currency (C), deposits (D), and the total of currency and deposits (CD).

TABLE 2

REGRESSION EXPLANATIONS OF ASSET HOLDINGS USING ONLY INCOME
AND OWN-PRICE VARIABLES

	Constant	log Y	$\dot{P}$	r	R^2	Standard Error of Estimate
Main Sample						
log C........	.751	.011	−.729		.09	.176
		(.042)	(.254)			
log D	−.279	.571	−.932		.61	.222
		(.053)	(.321)			
log CD......	.337	.396	−.923		.53	.188
		(.045)	(.272)			
Small Sample						
log C........	.956	−.048		−3.504	.11	.170
		(.052)		(1.74)		
log D........	.084	.500		−3.07	.71	.164
		(.053)		(1.77)		
log CD......	.678	.340		−3.567	.64	.135
		(.044)		(1.46)		

NOTE: The main sample consists of 46 countries with 89 observations; it excludes the first period observations of Greece, Indonesia and Korea (see footnote 7). The small sample consists of 22 countries with 42 observations. The major difference between the two samples is the proportion of observations of Latin American countries included. The proportion of observations from the four regions in the two samples is as follows:

	Europe	*Asia*	*Latin America*	*Others*
Main sample	.28	.24	.30	.18
Subsample	.38	.24	.10	.29

Table 2 presents the three regressions for the two samples, using only real income (Y) and one of the two price variables, $\dot{P}$, the expected rate of inflation, in the main sample, and r, the rate of interest, in the small sample. The logarithmic forms of the functions are used throughout. The standard errors are given in the parentheses.

The regressions presented in table 2 clearly show the importance of income and the price variables in explaining the differences in the holdings of deposits and currency plus deposits. They are significant[19] in all the regressions and explain a major part of the total variation in the holdings of these assets.

What is more striking, however, is the similarity between the price and income elasticities indicated by these results and those obtained in time series studies for the United States, which have been in the range of 1.2 to 1.7 for income elasticities and $-.3$ to $-.7$ for interest rate elasticities. As the assets are measured in terms of income and as $\eta_{XY} = \eta_{(X/Y),Y} + 1$, a zero log coefficient of income implies an income elasticity of demand of unity. (If the coefficient is significantly different from -1, the income elasticity is significantly different from zero.) Thus, the income elasticities of demand are 1.6 and 1.4 for deposits and for the total of currency and deposits respectively in the main sample, and 1.5 and 1.3 in the subsample. The interest elasticities in the subsample are $-.33$ and $-.39$ for deposits and currency plus deposits respectively.[20] In the currency equations even though the price variable is significant, the R^2 is very low and the income and price variables explain very little of the differences in currency holdings.

B. OTHER DETERMINANTS OF LIQUID ASSET HOLDINGS

The other set of variables that may affect liquid asset holdings are the risk variables and the quality variables, variables which are used to distinguish among different types of services yielded by the same asset in different countries because of institutional and environmental differences. Two variables are used to examine the effects of environmental differences: urbanization (U) and the per cent of agriculture in gross national product (Ag).

With respect to urbanization, Cagan in his study of the currency ratio in the United States has mentioned two opposing effects of urbanization on the currency ratio.[21] It "causes people to trade where they are not known which could reduce the use of checks," and it may

19. The 5 per cent level is used throughout when discussing significance levels.

20. The interest rate is measured in $100r$ per cent and the mean value of the interest rate for the sample is .047. The elasticity at the mean is therefore .047 times the coefficient times 2.3 because the dependent variables are in logarithms to the base 10.

21. Phillip Cagan, "The Demand for Currency Relative to the Total Money Supply," *Journal of Political Economy*, 66 (1958): 309ff.

make people more familiar with the use of checks and thus it "encourages the banking habit."

With respect to the ratio of agricultural production to GNP the following argument applies. As one of the functions of money is to bridge the gap between income receipts and expenditures, the length of the pay period may be an important variable in the allocation of assets among cash and interest-yielding assets.[22] Specifically, the longer the pay period, the lower the ratio of cash to income and the lower the currency deposits ratio. It is probably true that the pay period is longer in the agricultural sector than in the commercial or industrial sectors of an economy. Therefore one would expect that the larger the proportion of agriculture in GNP, the longer the pay period and therefore the lower the ratio of cash held to income. In the underdeveloped countries the proportion of agriculture in gross national product and the level of urbanization are so highly correlated that no effort is made to distinguish the two and only the urbanization variable is used. For the developed countries an attempt is made to separate the effects of the two variables by combining a dummy variable for development with the agricultural variable.[23]

The structure of the financial institutions in a country, the number of institutions or offices supplying deposit services, and the type of services supplied may affect the price or the quality of the services yielded by the assets. No reliable data are available for the number of bank offices for the countries examined here.[24] One financial institution that might have important implications for the allocation of assets between currency and demand deposits is the giro post office system. The three major advantages of using checks rather than currency are that the use of checks avoids the risk involved in transmitting payments, the risks of loss or theft; checks provide a record and evidence of payment; and checks allow the transmission of payment without requiring the presence of both parties to the transaction. The existence of a widespread giro system makes it possible for currency to yield many of the

22. See Harry G. Johnson, "Notes on the Theory of Transactions Demand for Cash," *Indian Journal of Economics*, vol. 44 (1963).

23. Any country with a per capita income of over $300 was considered as developed. The construction of this variable makes it partially a development variable.

24. The data for most countries on the number of bank offices are extremely poor. Some give the number of banks without specifying the number of branches; some figures include savings banks, others do not; some countries have post office savings systems so that the number of post offices is relevant, but it is seldom reported.

services provided by checking deposits. It allows payment of currency into the account of the payee and thus makes the transmission of currency via the giro system safer and eliminates the need of having the payee present during the transaction. It also records the transaction. For these reasons a dummy variable for the existence of a post office giro system (G) is included.

To take into account any institutional or other differences for which no specific variable is included, four regional dummies are also included in the regressions.

When the above variables are included as explanatory variables the regressions for deposits and for currency plus deposits for the main sample are:

$$\log D = 1.389 - .407DA - .472DL + .052 \log Y - .615\dot{P}$$
$$\quad\quad (.089) \quad\quad (.070) \quad\quad (.107) \quad\quad\quad (.305)$$
$$+ .256 \log U,$$
$$(.144)$$

$$R^2 = .64, \quad \text{Std. error} = .21;$$

$$\log CD = 1.457 - .325DA - .006DL + .007 \log Y - .513\dot{P}$$
$$\quad\quad\quad (.074) \quad\quad (.061) \quad\quad (.089) \quad\quad\quad (.252)$$
$$- .078 \log Ag,$$
$$(.073)$$

$$R^2 = .72, \quad \text{Std. error} = .15.$$

DA and DL are the regional dummies for Asia and Latin America respectively.

The most striking aspect of these two regressions, which can be seen by comparing them with those in table 2, is what happens to the income variable when the regional dummies are included.[25] In both the regressions income becomes insignificant (when tested against zero). When the regional dummies are left out income has a positive significant coefficient in both regressions but the R^2's are lower and the standard errors of estimate are greater.[26] Similar results are found in the interest rate subsample. The above results raise the question of whether the significance of income when the regional dummies are excluded is due to its correlation with some unspecified characteristics of the regions or whether the insignificance of income when the dummies are included

25. That this is due to the regional dummies and not to the other variables that are included was seen from the regressions which included the other variables but excluded the regional dummies.

26. For deposits alone $R^2 = .64$ (standard error $= .21$). For currency plus deposits $R^2 = .58$ (standard error $= .18$).

is due to the dummies' picking up both the income effects and some other regional effect. This is especially likely to happen when the interregional variations of a particular variable, or worse, a set of variables, are greater than the intraregional variations.[27]

When the observations for deposits and for currency plus deposits were plotted against income, it was found that there is a very marked positive relationship between them and income, except for five countries whose ten observations have a positive relationship with income but seem to lie above the rest of the observations. The five countries are Japan, Ireland, Portugal, Italy, and Spain. Their average holdings of deposits over the two periods are 36.3 weeks of income, their average holdings of currency plus deposits are 43.8 weeks of income, and their average per capita income is $409. (The income range covered by these ten observations is $226–$662.) It is therefore possible that when the dummies for Asia and Latin America are introduced into the regressions, they pick up much of the income effect in the low-income countries, and the presence of the above five countries distorts the income effect on the remaining observations. Two tests were made to see whether this is the case. A dummy variable for the five countries was included as an independent variable, and a sample excluding the five countries was analyzed. It was found that the coefficients of income and most of the other variables in the regressions were nearly identical in the case where all the observations were used with a dummy for the five countries and in the case where the five countries were excluded. In both cases the regional dummies as a group became unimportant and did not affect the coefficients of the income variable and the other variables as significantly as in the regressions presented above.

Table 3 shows the first three steps of a stepwise regression program using deposits as the dependent variable. Case A is the whole sample without a dummy for the five countries discussed above. Case B is the whole sample including a dummy for the five countries (DM), and case C is the sample that excludes the five countries, so that it contains only seventy-nine observations while the other two have eighty-nine. Three points are worth noting in table 3. First, when one compares cases B and C (step 2 of B with step 1 of C, and step 3 of B with step 2 of C) one can see that except for the presence of DM in case B, the coefficients, the standard errors, and the standard errors of estimate of the regressions are nearly identical. Second, in case A the effects of DA on

27. In my sample this is true for both the income variable and the price variable (in the main sample) with Asia and Latin America consisting of the low income, high price countries.

TABLE 3

Test for the Use of *DM* in the Whole Sample

	Constant	log Y	DL	DA	DM	R^2	Standard Error
Case A							
Step 1........	−.380	.590 (.055)				.567	.232
Step 2........	−.080	.502 (.051)	−.265 (.049)			.677	.200
Step 3........	.917	.172 (.085)	−.509 (.069)	−.417 (.090)		.740	.180
Case B Step 1 (Same as CaseA)							
Step 2........	−.383	.570 (.043)			.462 (.060)	.74	.180
Step 3........	−.156	.507 (.040)	−.199 (.040)		.399	.80	.159
Case C							
Step 1........	−.395	.575 (.045)				.68	.187
Step 2........	−.168	.511 (.042)	−.198 (.041)			.75	.165

both log Y, DL, and the constant term are very pronounced; and third, the R^2 and the standard errors of estimate after step 3 in case A and after step 2 in case B are identical.[28] The same pattern occurs when currency plus deposits is used as a dependent variable. This evidence supports the hypothesis that DA, especially when combined with DL, mainly represents the income effect, which is more significant and enlightening in explaining the dependent variables when used directly, rather than by proxy via the dummies, once the five countries previously discussed are excluded or treated separately via a dummy.

The question remains whether there is any justification for using a dummy for the five countries because they seem to be different. I think, however, that this dummy is no different from the regional dummies. In both cases the use of the dummy signifies ignorance about some variable(s) which affects the holdings of assets. This is true whether one calls this ignorance Asia, Latin America, or "the five countries that are

28. In both case B and case C, DA and the other regional dummies are not significant throughout the regressions.

different." In many ways this dummy is more useful than some of the regional dummies; it seems to represent some unknown effect not revealed by the specified continuous variables, while the other dummies, especially Asia, seem to pick up some of the effects of known and specified variables and therefore do not reveal anything new, but rather becloud what is already known.

Similar results to those presented above are found for the interest rate subsample. They are presented in Appendix A. When the dummy variable for the five countries (DM) is included as an independent variable the three regressions for currency, deposits, and the total of currency plus deposits as dependent variables for the main sample are:

$$\log C = 1.11 + .256DE + .107DA - .079G - .204 \log Y$$
$$(.051) \qquad (.055) \qquad (.060) \quad (.086)$$
$$- .601\dot{P} - .209 \log Ag,$$
$$(.244) \quad (.076)$$

$$R^2 = .39, \quad \text{Std. error} = .15;$$

$$\log D = .491 + .419DM - .126DL + .065G + .258 \log Y$$
$$(.054) \qquad (.044) \qquad (.048) \quad (.096)$$
$$+ .163 \log U - .165 \log Ag - .696\dot{P},$$
$$(.125) \qquad (.080) \qquad (.281)$$

$$R^2 = .83, \quad \text{Std. error} = .15.$$

(Using only DM and the four continuous variables: $R^2 = .80$; Std. error $= .16$)

$$\log CD = .820 + .333DM - .134DL + .057G + .16 \log Y$$
$$(.045) \qquad (.037) \qquad (.040) \quad (.06)$$
$$- .17 \log Ag - .591\dot{P},$$
$$(.06) \qquad (.220)$$

$$R^2 = .80, \quad \text{Std. error} = .13.$$

(Using only DM and the three continuous variables: $R^2 = .76$; Std. error $= .14$)

When these regressions for deposits and for currency plus deposits are compared with those presented earlier which excluded DM, we can see that not only is the standard error of estimate reduced significantly when DM is included; but, what is more significant, when DM is included as the only "regional" dummy, the R^2's are greater and the standard errors are lower than those of the earlier regressions which excluded DM but included the other dummies.

In all the regressions the income and price variables are significant. Currency is the only asset with an income elasticity of less than one (the income coefficient is significantly different from -1). Deposits and currency plus deposits have income elasticities that are greater than one.[29] The proportion of agriculture in GNP is significant in all the regressions; the higher is the degree of agriculture, the lower are the holdings of all liquid assets. Europe and Asia still stand out with respect to their currency holdings; not only are DE and DA significant in the regression for currency but the use of *only* these two dummies results in an R^2 of .32 as compared with .39 when the other variables are also included. The dummy for Latin America is the only significant regional dummy (not counting DM) in the regressions for deposits and currency plus deposits.

For the interest rate subsample the explanatory variables used are the same as those for the main sample, except that the interest rate is used as the price variable,[30] and a "risk" variable, PV, the mean squared deviations around the logarithmic trend line of prices, is also included.[31] This variable is used as a measure of the unexpected changes in the price level and thus as a possible proxy for economic instability. One would expect that the proportion of total wealth held in the form of some or all liquid assets would be positively related to the uncertainty about general economic conditions, because one of the services yielded by liquid assets is that of insurance against the unexpected.[32] The three regressions for currency, deposits, and currency plus deposits are:

$$\log C = 1.521 + .266DM + .244G - .295 \log Y$$
$$(.050) \qquad (.042) \quad (.085)$$
$$- .171 \log Ag - 3.501r + 161PV,$$
$$(.085) \qquad (1.15) \qquad (94)$$
$$R^2 = .66, \qquad \text{Std. Error} = .105;$$

$$\log D = .60 + .363DM + .315 \log Y$$
$$(.040) \qquad (.070)$$
$$+ .315 \log U - 3.145r - 131PV,$$
$$(.125) \qquad (.99) \qquad (79)$$
$$R^2 = .92, \qquad \text{Std. Error} = .087;$$

29. If DM is excluded from the regressions, i.e., the first set of regressions is used, the elasticities of deposits and currency plus deposits are around unity.

30. The expected rate of inflation is too closely correlated with the interest rate (which presumably incorporates it) to separate out their two effects, and is not included in these regressions.

31. An attempt was made to use interest rate variation as a measure of the risk of interest rate changes as an explanatory variable, but it had no effect on the asset holdings.

32. See Milton Friedman and Anna J. Schwartz, *A Monetary History of the United States, 1867–1960* (Princeton: Princeton Univ. Press, 1963).

$$\log CD = 1.299 + .321DM + .099G + .150 \log Y$$
$$\qquad\quad (.031) \qquad (.027) \quad (.055)$$
$$\qquad\qquad\qquad + .307 \log U - 3.776r - 62PV,$$
$$\qquad\qquad\qquad\quad (.092) \qquad\qquad (.709) \quad (58)$$
$$R^2 = .92, \qquad\qquad\qquad \text{Std. Error} = .065.$$

As is true with the main sample, the inclusion of DM (or the exclusion of the countries represented by DM—in this subsample Portugal, Ireland, and Italy) makes a significant difference in the regressions. When DM is not included in the regressions, the use of all the continuous variables and the dummies for Asia and Latin America results in a lower R^2 and a higher standard error of estimate for deposits and nearly the same R^2 and standard error for currency plus deposits.[33]

Currency again stands out both because of its relatively low R^2, its high standard error of estimate, and because of the importance of the two dummy variables. Without them the R^2 falls to .48 and the standard error rises to .13.

The results shown by the three regressions presented above are very similar to those obtained in the last section when the whole sample was used. In both cases all the assets show positive income elasticities, with only currency having an elasticity of less than one. In both cases the coefficient of $\log Y$ in the currency equation is significantly different from -1. In both cases all the assets show negative price elasticities, whether measured in terms of an expected rate of change of prices or the rate of interest, with currency having the lowest price elasticity of all the assets.[34] In both cases either $\log Ag$ is significant with a negative coefficient or $\log U$ is significant with a positive coefficient for all the assets. The multicollinearity between $\log Ag$ and $\log U$ makes it very difficult to separate out their two effects. However, both represent some aspect of the difference between an urban and a rural environment, and in both the whole sample and the subsample such a difference clearly appears with respect to all the assets, whether expressed by $\log Ag$ or $\log U$.

33. When DM is excluded the only significant variables are the dummies for Asia and Latin America and $\log Ag$, which by its construction is partially a dummy for development and has a positive coefficient for both deposits and currency plus deposits (which is opposite to that found in the regressions of the main sample).

34. In the interest rate subsample the price elasticity of deposits is probably understated relative to that of currency. Because most interest rates move in the same direction, a specific change in the government bond yield implies a smaller change in the price of deposits, which yield some interest, than in the price of currency, which yields no interest.

The major difference between the whole sample and the subsample is the significance in the former of DL in the regression of deposits and currency plus deposits, and DA in the regression of currency.[35] The negative coefficients of the dummy for Latin America in the whole sample might represent an additional price effect on the assets not picked up by our measure of expected inflation. In the whole sample 30 per cent of the observations are from Latin America. If the price effect of the expected rate of inflation on the assets is underestimated either because of certain extreme observations, for example those of Brazil and Argentina, or because price expectations are affected by what has occurred over a longer period of time than that covered in constructing P, DL might be showing the additional effect of inflation not picked up by $\dot{P}$.[36] The positive coefficient of G in the interest rate subsample can be interpreted either as showing the effect of a giro post office system on currency holdings, as is argued in the next section on the currency deposits ratio, or as showing some other unspecified European effect. PV, although not significant in any of the regressions, has the correct sign in the currency equation but not in the others. If PV does actually represent some measure of economic instability, one would expect that all liquid assets would be positively related to PV.

The results presented in the last section indicate that both the income and the price variables are important determinants of the demand for liquid assets. All the assets have significant positive income elasticities and negative price variable elasticities. If for the moment we exclude the dummy variables, the only other significant determinant of liquid asset holdings is the degree of urbanization. The demand for all liquid assets is greater in urban than in rural areas. There are significant differences among the assets, the most striking being the difference of the income effect on currency and on deposits. Only currency has an income elasticity of less than unity. Using the estimating equations for the interest rate subsample, the estimated income elasticity of currency plus deposits is 1.15 and the price elasticity (using the rate of

35. The positive coefficient of DE and negative coefficient of G in the currency equation of the whole sample do not imply a different result from the positive coefficients of DM and G in the subsample. Except for Greece all the European countries have either a giro system or belong to the DM group and the combinations of G and DE in the whole sample and G and DM in the subsample are very similar.

36. Most of Latin America has a longer history of inflation than other countries and therefore the behavioral adjustment to inflation may be more complete than in other countries. See Phillip Cagan, "The Monetary Dynamics of Hyperinflation" in Friedman, ed., *Studies in Quantity Theory*, p. 63.

interest as the price variable) is $-.42.$[37] For the whole sample the estimated income elasticity is 1.16.

The five countries represented by *DM*—Japan, Portugal, Spain, Italy, and Ireland—remain a puzzle. What do these countries have in common that makes their demand for liquid assets so high relative to the rest of the world? It seems clear that it is not any characteristics of the structure of their financial institutions, because these differ greatly among the five countries. Spain and Portugal have very few financial institutions and the number of financial institution offices per capita in these two countries is lower than in any other European country with the possible exception of Greece. On the other hand, Italy and Japan have a complex conglomeration of financial institutions serving different sectors of the economy with a large number of offices per capita. The growth rate of real per capita income has also been very different in the five countries. Japan and Italy have had a very high rate of growth over the two periods—41 per cent and 28 per cent respectively; Portugal and Spain a moderate growth rate—18 per cent and 11 per cent respectively; and Ireland a very low rate of 6 per cent. It might of course be true that there is no common factor in the five countries that affects their demand for liquid assets but that different factors in the five countries lead to the same effect, a higher demand for liquid assets.[38]

4. EMPIRICAL ANALYSIS OF THE CURRENCY-DEPOSITS RATIO

In the preceding section we saw that the observed international differences in the holdings of liquid assets could be largely explained by the use of a few economic variables. In this section I want to explore whether the same variables that explain the allocation of wealth between liquid assets and other assets can also explain the allocation of liquid assets among different types. To answer this question the currency-deposits ratio is used as the dependent variable. The samples and the independent variables used in this section are the same as those used in the last section. The problems of the regional dummies discussed there are not as pronounced for the currency-deposits ratios. The dummies for Asia and Latin America have no effect on the regression results. Whether *DM* is included or not they leave the coefficients, the

37. See note 20.

38. After the work for this study was completed, I learned that Japanese banks require corporations to hold minimum balances when taking out loans and that these balances are held in the form of time deposits yielding interest payments. Thus a large fraction of time deposits in Japan is held by corporations. This may explain the large holdings of deposits in Japan.

standard errors, and the standard errors of estimate unchanged. However, the inclusion of DM, or the exclusion of the countries represented by DM, does reduce the standard error of estimate.

When income alone is used as an explanatory variable, the estimated regression for the main sample is

$$\log \frac{C}{D} = 1.05 - .56 \log Y,$$
$$(.05)$$

$$R^2 = .59, \qquad \text{Std. Error} = .21.$$

When DM is included:

$$\log \frac{C}{D} = .105 - .55 \log Y - .33 \, DM,$$
$$(.04) \qquad\qquad (.06)$$

$$R^2 = .60, \qquad \text{Std. Error} = .19.$$

When the five countries are excluded from the sample:

$$\log \frac{C}{D} = 1.06 - .55 \log Y,$$

$$R^2 = .66, \qquad \text{Std. Error} = .19.$$

When all the variables are used, the only significant variable in addition to $\log Y$ and DM is DO, the dummy for "Others." The estimated equation is

$$\log \frac{C}{D} = .503 - .322DM - .220DO$$
$$(.059) \qquad (.067)$$
$$- .082G - .345 \log Y - .155 \log U,$$
$$(.057) \qquad (.087) \qquad\qquad (.151)$$

$$R^2 = .73, \qquad \text{Std. Error} = .18.$$

As can be seen, the reduction in the standard error of estimate due to the addition of the other variable is very small; the use of $\log Y$ and DM alone results in nearly the same standard error of estimate. However, the coefficient of $\log Y$ is affected by the addition of DO and $\log U$.

For the interest rate subsample, the estimated equation using only $\log Y$ as the independent variable is

$$\log \frac{C}{D} = .971 - .542 \log Y,$$

$$R^2 = .66, \qquad \text{Std. Error} = .17.$$

When all the variables are included:

$$\log \frac{C}{D} = 1.104 - .119DM + .209G - .602 \log Y + .46PV - 2.48\dot{P},$$
$$\phantom{\log \frac{C}{D} = 1.104} (.065) \qquad (.055) \qquad (.055) \qquad\quad (15) \qquad (1.11)$$

$R^2 = .84,$ Std. Error $= .14.$

The one puzzling variable in the above regression is $\dot{P}$. In the analysis of the assets in the preceding section there is no indication that currency has a larger price elasticity than deposits. In fact, when the rate of interest is used as the price variable, currency has a smaller price elasticity. Therefore, it seems doubtful that the negative coefficient of $\dot{P}$ in this equation indicates any difference in price elasticities between currency and deposits. What may be indicated by the coefficient of $\dot{P}$ is that with a higher expected rate of inflation the interest yield on deposits is adjusted to some extent to the expected rate of inflation; and therefore the price effect of inflation is smaller for deposits than for currency, so that the currency deposits ratio is lower.

The two other continuous variables have the expected sign. If PV is actually some measure of economic uncertainty, currency, being a better "cushion against uncertainty" than any other asset, would become a relatively more desirable asset; and thus the currency-deposits ratio would be greater with the greater degree of uncertainty.

Two questions remain to be answered. First, as indicated in the analysis of both the assets and the currency-deposits ratio, why does currency have a lower income elasticity than deposits? Second, is the significance of G in the equations for currency and the currency-deposits ratio due to the institutional peculiarities of the giro post office system or some other unspecified characteristic of Europe? The answer to the latter question cannot be based solely on the significance of G in the regression equations, because the European countries that do not have a giro post office system belong to the DM group. Thus, all the G countries are also all the European countries not included in DM.

In his study of the currency-deposits ratio in the United States, Cagan discusses the relative income effect on currency and deposits.[39]

> The rise in real income per capita would reduce the relative demand for currency if it enhanced the appeal of making payment by check and having a bank account or in technical terms if the income elasticity were less than unity. This may at first seem strange, because we customarily associate such a phenomenon with 'necessities'. With

39. Phillip Cagan, *Determinants and Effects of Change in the Stock of Money, 1875–1960* (New York: National Bureau of Economic Research, 1965), p. 126.

high incomes people switch from them to more expensive items; similarly in their portfolios they might forego income to acquire lower yielding securities that offer nonpecuniary advantages such as liquidity. From this point of view we should not be surprised to find a shift to money balances from higher yielding assets when real income rises. But why a shift from currency to deposits? . . . A shift from currency to deposits cannot be described as providing an asset with greater convenience at the expense of a lower yield.

From this Cagan concludes:

> The way out is not to argue that the income elasticity of currency cannot be less than unity but to recognize that income growth is a proxy for a host of other developments which, on balance, may work to increase the demand for deposits relative to currency.[40]

Two points are worth noting in Cagan's discussion. First, the argument in the first sentence is only applicable to the currency–checking-deposits ratio. It is not clear that the fall in the currency-deposits ratio is due solely to the change in the currency–checking-deposits ratio. In fact the other types of deposits (time and savings) have a higher income elasticity than checking deposits.[41] Second, the question of why a shift into assets yielding liquidity should be from currency to deposits is relevant only if liquidity is a single type of service yielded by all liquid assets. If this were true all liquid assets would be perfect substitutes at some price ratio depending on their relative yields, of "liquidity"; and their income elasticities would be the same, irrespective of their monetary returns. However, if one assumes that "liquidity" is not a single service but stands for a variety of different types of services, then different assets which yield different types of liquidity services might very well have different income elasticities. Thus Cagan's statement, "A shift from currency to deposits cannot be described as providing an asset with greater convenience at the expense of a lower yield," is irrelevant to the question of different income elasticities. If deposits provide a service not provided by currency, or provided by currency to a lesser extent, a shift from currency to deposits might show a shift from a service whose income elasticity is less than unity to one whose income elasticity is greater than unity. All that is really required for income to have a negative effect on the currency-deposits ratio is that the income elasticity of currency be less than that of deposits, not necessarily less than unity.

40. *Ibid.*, p. 126.

41. This is also noted by Meltzer for the United States, in Allan H. Meltzer, "The Demand for Money: The Evidence from the Time Series," *Journal of Political Economy*, 71 (1963): 219–46.

Let us separate "liquidity" into two services: (a) a transaction service—the ability at any moment of time now and in the future to make an economic transaction;[42] and (b) an insurance service—the ability to meet unexpected events at any time in the future.[43] Both currency and deposits provide both of these services but not to the same extent. The amount of transaction services provided by a dollar of currency, a dollar of checking deposit and a dollar of time deposit is not the same. Currency allows for instantaneous transactions at any point of time; checking deposits allow this for some types of transactions and in some environmental settings (for example the general acceptability of checks); time deposits require a previous conversion into currency or checking deposits before they can provide the transaction service. All these assets also provide the insurance service as defined above.

If they provided the same amount of insurance service per dollar of assets, then there should be no differential income effect. The allocation among the assets would be determined by relative prices only, which would be determined by the relative yields of transactions services. However, all deposits provide greater insurance services than does currency because of the risks involved in holding currency from theft, loss, fire, and so on. If the insurance service has a greater income elasticity than the transactions services, then as income rises the ratio of currency to all deposits will fall because the demand for the insurance service rises relative to the demand for the transactions service. Therefore, the demand for assets yielding a greater amount of insurance services rises relative to the demand for assets yielding less insurance services but more transactions services. If assets were perfect substitutes with respect to insurance services, the allocation among different types of deposits would be determined by their relative prices and relative yields of transactions services.

Institutional factors affect the quantity of the various types of services yielded by the assets. For example, general acceptability of checks would make checking deposits and currency perfect substitutes with respect to the transactions services. Allowing checks to be written on time deposits and waiving the notice requirement would make checking and time deposits perfect substitutes with respect to the

42. We are interested not only in current transactions services; during a transactions period, liquid assets are a store of wealth which yields the service of the ability to make transactions in the future.

43. This discussion follows the theory presented in section 2 but allows for a liquid asset yielding more than a single liquidity service.

transactions service, and as they are already perfect substitutes with respect to the insurance service they would become perfect substitutes in demand.

This brings us to the question of the giro post office system. This is an institutional arrangement which changes the type of service yielded by currency. It allows currency to yield many of the services provided by checks; and, as currency still yields currency services, one would expect a higher currency-deposits ratio (and a greater holding of currency) when the giro service is provided. I would therefore argue that G does represent the giro post office system as an institution and not some other European effect, especially since there does not seem to be any other obvious general characteristic common to Europe which would increase the demand for currency in Europe relative to the rest of the world.

5. Summary and Conclusions

This study attempted to answer two questions: What determines the absolute amount of liquid assets held by the nonbanking sectors of the economy in various countries? And, what determines the allocation among liquid assets, specifically the currency-deposits ratio? There are at least two ways to evaluate the answers presented in the last two sections. One is by the statistical fit obtained in the regressions and the conformity of the empirical results with those that would be predicted from theoretical considerations. The other is by comparing the results obtained in this study, which has used international cross-section data, with those obtained in other studies of the demand for liquid assets, which have used national data, to determine whether the results obtained in this study are consistent with the others.

The results of this study are impressive on both counts, especially when one considers the wide range of social, cultural, and institutional characteristics represented by the group of forty-seven countries included in the study.

In the interest rate subsample 92 per cent of the variation in the total holdings of currency and deposits was "explained" by the variables used.[44] The three most important determinants of total liquid asset holdings are per capita real income, the rate of interest, and the degree of urbanization. What is more striking, however, is the similarity of the

44. This is a slight overestimate of the explanation achieved, because one of the variables used, DM, is basically an ignorance variable, not an explanatory variable in any real sense of the word.

estimated income and interest rate elasticities to those obtained in the time series studies for the United States.

In his study of the demand for money in the United States, Meltzer[45] made an exhaustive analysis for various time periods using various definitions of wealth and income. His estimates of income or wealth elasticities vary according to the particular specification of these variables. It is a moot question whether measured real income used in a cross-section study such as this is more comparable to measured income, permanent income, or wealth. Even though measured income may not be a very good proxy for permanent income or wealth in a time series study, it may be a good proxy for them in an international cross-section study.[46] However, for the purpose of this comparison we are interested in seeing whether the results obtained in this study are within a plausible range of previous findings rather than in pinpointing a particular value. Therefore a complete resolution of the question of income is not necessary.

When Meltzer uses per capita permanent income and the rate of interest as his independent variables and the total of currency, demand deposits, and time deposits as his dependent variable he gets an estimated income elasticity of 1.4 and interest rate elasticity of $-.37$.[47] For other definitions of real wealth and for various subperiods the income elasticities range from about 1.2 to 1.7 and the interest rate elasticities from about $-.30$ to $-.70$. The estimated income and interest rate elasticities of currency and deposits for the interest rate subsample used in this study are 1.15 and $-.42$ respectively.[48] These estimates are close to those obtained by Meltzer, especially when one considers that urbanization is included as an independent variable in my regression for currency and deposits, which, because of its correlation with income, reduces the income coefficient. (When urbanization is excluded, the income elasticity becomes about 1.35.) Conversely,

45. Meltzer, "Demand for Money."

46. It is much more plausible that a 10 per cent difference in measured income between two countries implies about a 10 per cent difference in permanent income or wealth than that a 10 per cent rise in measured income in a country from one year to another implies about a 10 per cent rise in permanent income or wealth.

47. Meltzer, "Demand for Money."

48. Even though currency plus deposits is a broader category than that used by Meltzer (he only includes time deposits in commercial banks in his M_2), I think they are comparable because in most countries the savings deposits that I include are basically time deposits in savings banks rather than commercial banks, which should be an irrelevant consideration.

Meltzer's income variable probably picks up some of the urbanization effects.

The determinants of the holdings of the individual assets, currency, and deposits taken separately, are less clear than those of the sum of currency and deposits. This is indicated both by the higher standard errors of estimate obtained in the regressions and by the very high standard error in the regression for the currency-deposits ratio. The reasons for this are not hard to find. Given that currency and deposits are substitutes to some extent, the variables that would be relevant in determining the allocation of the assets in the portfolio would be, first, relative prices and, second, those institutional, environmental, and other variables, the quality variables, that affect the substitutability among the assets.

Both Cagan and Macesich[49] in their studies of the currency-deposits ratio in the United States and Canada respectively, find that the interest yield of deposits and the tax rate are important determinants of the currency-deposits ratio. Because these two variables are unavailable for the sample of countries used in this study, they were not included among the independent variables. The number of bank offices per capita is probably a more important determinant of the allocation among the assets than of the total asset portfolio. Thus the high standard errors of estimate in the regressions for the individual assets and the currency-deposits ratio may be attributable to the omission of many variables that are relevant to the allocation among the assets in a portfolio of liquid assets but not as relevant to the allocation of wealth among liquid assets and other assets. This also indicates that the portfolio consisting of currency, demand deposits, and time and savings deposits is a behaviorally meaningful and therefore useful subset of all assets because the demand for this subset of assets is stable with respect to a few known variables, in the sense that it is less affected by institutional and other environmental factors than other subsets of assets.

49. Cagan, *Determinants and Effects of Change*; G. Macesich, "Demand for Currency and Taxation in Canada," *Southern Economic Journal*, 29 (1962): 33–38.

APPENDIX A

Table 4 presents the regressions for deposits when only income and the rate of interest are used as dependent variables. Case A is the whole sample when no dummy for Portugal, Ireland, and Italy is included; Case B is the same sample with a dummy (DM) for these three countries; and case C is the sample which excludes the six observations for the three countries.

TABLE 4

TEST FOR THE USE OF DM IN THE INTEREST RATE SAMPLE

Dependent Variable	Constant	log Y	r	DM	R^2	Standard Error
Case A						
log D.........	.084	.500 (.053)	−3.07 (1.77)		.71	.164
log CD.......	.678	.340 (.044)	−3.567 (1.457)		.64	.135
Case B						
log D.........	.025	.505 (.031)	−3.277 (1.05)	.356 (.043)	.91	.090
log CD.......	.623	.349 (.026)	−3.819 (.860)	.289 (.035)	.87	.080
Case C						
log D.........	.046	.507 (.034)	−3.088 (1.17)		.88	.103
log CD.......	.615	.351 (.028)	−3.705 (.964)		.85	.085

APPENDIX B
SOURCES AND ADJUSTMENTS OF DATA

Agriculture—Percentage of GNP

United Nations Statistical Office, *Yearbook of National Accounts Statistics,* 1957–63.

Bruce M. Russett et al., *World Handbook of Political and Social Indicators* (New Haven, 1964).

For three countries (Australia, Sweden, New Zealand) data for only one period were available. An estimate for the second period was made using the growth rate of the percentage of the labor force in agriculture given in Russett et al., *World Handbook.*

Banking and Financial Institutions

H. W. Auburn, ed., *Comparative Banking* (London, 1963).

B. H. Beckhart, *Banking Systems* (New York, 1956).

Bank of Japan Economic Research Department, *Money and Banking in Japan, 1964.*

International Monetary Fund, *International Financial Statistics,* 1962/63 Supplement.

R. S. Sayers, *Banking in Western Europe* (London, 1962).

J. S. G. Wilson, *French Banking Structure and Credit Policy* (London, 1957).

Currency outside Banking System

International Monetary Fund, *International Financial Statistics,* 1963/64 Supplement and other monthly issues.

For two countries adjustment had to be made to the currency data. As Belgium and Luxembourg have a currency union, the currency holdings of Belgium have to be reduced by the currency held in Luxembourg. This was done by assuming that the ratio of currency to income is the same in both countries, and estimating the relative holdings of currency by the relative incomes in the two countries.

All data for the Federation of Malaya exclude Singapore, North Borneo, and Brunei except for the currency outstanding which includes currency held in the above three. As no income data are available for these three, an adjustment by relative income as was done for Belgium and Luxembourg was not possible. The currency was allocated by relative population.

Deposits—Demand, Time, and Savings

Nearly all the data were obtained from the I.M.F. *International Financial Statistics*, 1963/64 Supplement and other monthly issues.

Additional data for the following countries had to be obtained:

Brazil. Deposits at federal and state savings banks are not included in the I.M.F. data. These were obtained from the bulletin of the Superintendecia da Modeda e do Credito, 1965.

United Kingdom. Many deposits in financial institutions other than commercial banks are not reported by the I.M.F. These were obtained from the Bank of England, *Quarterly Bulletin*, 1961, 1962, and 1963.

United States. Deposits at national savings banks and the post office savings system from M. Friedman and Anna J. Schwartz, *The Stock of Money in the United States, 1867–1960*, Appendix A. Deposits at savings and loan associations from the board of governors of the Federal Reserve, *Federal Reserve Bulletin*.

Exchange Rates

The modified exchange rate adjusted for purchasing power parity in United Nations, *Yearbook of National Account Statistics*, 1963, table 3B.

Income

National income data from United Nations, *Yearbook of National Account Statistics*, 1957–63.

Interest Rates

Long-term government bond yield from I.M.F., *International Financial Statistics*, 1963/64 Supplement.

Prices

Cost-of-living index (1958 = 100) in I.M.F., *International Financial Statistics*, 1963/64 Supplement.

Population

Mid-year population estimates from the United Nations, *Statistical Yearbook*, 1952–63.

Urbanization

Percentage of the population living in cities of over 20,000 people from Russett et al., *World Handbook*, p. 49.

APPENDIX C

TABLE 5

DATA FOR THE DEPENDENT VARIABLES, INCOME, AND THE EXPECTED RATE OF CHANGE OF PRICES

Country	C	D	CD	C/D	Y	$\dot{P}$
Argentina	12.5	16.4	28.9	.76	355.8	.182
	9.8	12.7	22.5	.78	366.4	.240
Austria	8.1	15.4	23.5	.53	524.7	.093
	8.1	21.0	29.1	.39	703.0	.018
Brazil	5.4	13.9	19.3	.58	117.5	.144
	4.8	13.6	18.4	.46	115.4	.212
Burma	7.8	5.1	12.9	1.53	50.2	−.015
	10.1	6.4	16.5	1.57	53.0	.010
Chile	2.2	3.8	6.0	.58	340.5	.310
	2.0	4.6	6.6	.43	352.8	.326
Colombia	3.8	8.2	12.0	.46	210.2	.062
	4.1	9.3	13.4	.44	229.5	.078
Ecuador	3.8	4.7	8.5	.81	141.5	.023
	3.7	5.2	8.9	.72	155.4	.005
El Salvador						
	4.9	7.1	12.0	.68	115.7	.014
Finland	3.4	23.1	26.5	.15	514.8	.031
	3.2	26.3	29.5	.12	568.3	.045
Greece	4.4	2.6	7.0	1.68	243.7	.088
	6.1	8.7	14.8	.70	298.2	.042
Guatemala	6.3	4.6	10.9	1.37	132.6	.027
	5.8	6.9	12.7	.84	143.9	.006
Honduras	3.5	3.9	7.4	.91	158.7	.037
	2.9	3.8	6.7	.76	165.8	.013
Indonesia	3.5	1.4	4.9	2.59	93.4	.162
Israel	5.5	9.7	15.2	.57	665.4	.148
	4.6	10.4	15.0	.44	869.5	.063
Japan	5.2	36.2	41.4	.14	250.6	.054
	4.9	52.1	57.0	.09	353.8	.023
Korea	3.6	2.3	5.9	1.54	88.6	.628
	3.8	4.2	8.0	.91	98.4	.188
Malaya	8.6	9.7	18.3	.89	187.0	.023
	8.6	10.2	18.8	.84	185.6	−.011
Mexico	3.6	6.1	9.7	.59	277.0	.075
	3.0	6.4	9.4	.47	323.3	.062
Nicaragua	3.2	2.9	6.1	1.09	194.0	.090
	2.9	2.9	5.8	1.00	186.1	.021
Paraguay	3.8	3.5	7.3	1.08	88.4	.412
	3.8	3.1	6.9	1.21	91.2	.167
Philippines	4.8	5.4	10.2	.89	97.6	−.007
	4.6	7.5	12.1	.62	108.9	.010
Spain	7.0	25.6	32.6	.28	293.5	.038
	7.4	28.9	36.3	.26	324.1	.061

TABLE 5—*Continued*

Country	C	D	CD	C/D	Y	Ṗ
Taiwan...............	3.0	4.2	7.2	.71	84.6	.146
	3.3	7.7	11.0	.43	91.3	.098
Thailand............	7.7	4.1	11.8	1.87	95.3	.061
	7.2	6.2	13.4	1.15	88.1	.035
Venezuela...........	4.2	7.5	11.7	.57	420.3	.017
	3.8	11.2	15.0	.34	509.4	.012
*Australia...........	4.5	32.1	36.6	.14	1287.5	.086
	4.0	30.8	34.8	.13	1319.8	.027
Belgium.............	14.1	21.2	35.3	.67	905.7	.015
	13.2	23.1	36.3	.57	986.3	.014
Canada..............	3.8	22.4	26.2	.17	1398.1	.024
	3.6	22.2	25.8	.16	1471.7	.014
Ceylon..............	4.1	11.4	15.5	.36	119.9	.011
	5.4	12.1	17.5	.44	118.6	.006
Costa Rica..........	4.7	6.4	11.1	.74	224.2	.033
	4.3	7.1	11.4	.61	232.7	.018
Denmark............	4.7	27.0	31.7	.17	1019.0	.040
	4.5	28.1	32.6	.16	1165.6	.026
Egypt...............	10.5	11.2	21.7	.94	117.5	.001
	8.8	11.0	19.8	.80	144.5	.002
France..............	10.9	16.7	27.6	.65	874.0	.066
	9.7	20.4	30.1	.48	1092.5	.041
Germany............	5.3	13.8	19.1	.39	809.2	.010
	5.0	19.3	24.3	.26	1147.1	.014
India...............	6.8	5.7	12.5	1.20	67.2	.003
	7.2	7.9	15.1	.92	66.8	.026
Ireland.............	6.3	42.7	49.0	.15	581.2	.042
	5.5	43.3	48.8	.13	616.1	.026
Italy...............	8.0	31.0	39.0	.26	517.0	.031
	7.9	39.1	47.0	.20	662.9	.020
Netherlands.........	9.0	27.5	36.1	.33	824.3	.040
	7.8	27.4	35.2	.28	999.5	.026
New Zealand........	4.6	34.7	39.3	.13	1581.9	.053
	3.9	32.1	36.0	.12	1587.7	.033
Norway.............	8.9	31.7	40.7	.28	1090.4	.056
	7.8	31.4	39.2	.25	1194.0	.027
Pakistan............	7.0	5.2	12.2	1.35	60.3	.016
	7.2	6.0	13.2	1.20	66.0	.025
Peru...............	4.0	9.1	13.1	.44	123.5	.079
	4.2	9.1	13.3	.46	132.1	.071
Portugal............	11.6	30.3	41.9	.39	226.3	.004
	11.6	33.3	44.9	.35	268.1	.014
Sweden.............	7.4	39.4	46.8	.19	1284.9	.047
	6.8	41.6	48.4	.16	1442.7	.031
Turkey.............	5.0	7.4	12.4	.68	196.7	.044
	4.8	7.5	12.3	.63	227.8	.111
United Kingdom......	5.9	34.7	40.6	.17	1040.4	.052
	5.5	27.5	33.0	.20	1194.4	.027
United States........	4.6	33.6	38.2	.14	2072.0	.019
	3.8	35.6	39.4	.11	2190.1	.014

NOTE: There are two observations for each country except Indonesia and El Salvador. The first observation for each variable is the first period average (1952–56), the second is the second period average (1957–61). For sources and adjustments see Appendix B.

* The following 22 countries are the ones included in the interest rate subsample.

VI

The Velocity of Money and the Rate of Inflation: Recent Experiences in South Korea and Brazil

COLIN D. CAMPBELL

The Velocity of Money and the Rate of Inflation: Recent Experiences in South Korea and Brazil

1. Introduction

MANY economists have stated that changes in the rate of inflation are one of the important factors affecting the velocity of money, causing it to rise if the rate of inflation accelerates and fall if the rate of inflation slows up.[1] When price changes are only a few per cent a year, they may have no discernible effect on the velocity of money. But, when the inflation is rapid and long continued, it is believed that changes in the rate of inflation will have a major effect on the velocity of money—and will be discernible.

When prices are expected to rise, holding cash balances becomes less attractive relative to holding other types of assets. And, if people want to hold smaller real cash balances, they can succeed in doing so only by bidding up prices faster than the rise in the money stock per unit of output—causing income velocity to rise. For example, if prices were rising 10 per cent a year, cash would be worth less at the end of the year, and it would have cost the individual 10 per cent to hold it for this length of time. In contrast, under the same conditions, goods would be worth 10 per cent more at the end of the year, and the

The author is indebted to Dr. Sang-soo Kwak, economist with the Bank of Korea, for assistance in gathering and interpreting the statistical data on South Korea. A sabbatical leave of absence from Dartmouth College made it possible to do much of the early work on South Korea at the Money and Banking Workshop of the University of Chicago. The author is indebted to Professors David Meiselman and Milton Friedman for many suggestions. The work on inflation in Brazil was supported by the Comparative Studies Center of Dartmouth College.

1. For recent statements, see Reuben A. Kessel and Armen A. Alchian, "Effects of Inflation," *Journal of Political Economy*, 70 (1962): 521–37, and Milton Friedman, "The Quantity Theory of Money—A Restatement," in M. Friedman, ed., *Studies in the Quantity Theory of Money* (Chicago: Univ. of Chicago Press, 1956). See also D. H. Robertson, *Money*, 6th ed. (New York: Pitman, 1948), pp. 117–19, and Lester V. Chandler, *An Introduction to Monetary Theory* (New York: Harper, 1940), pp. 34–40, 81–84.

individual would have lost nothing because of the inflation. As a result, when people realize that the cost of holding cash is increasing because the rate of inflation is rising, they will prefer to hold less cash relative to other assets.

Of course, the rate of inflation is only one of several factors affecting the velocity of money. For example, consider the enumeration of classes of variables that in Friedman's hypothesis[2] affect the ratio of money to income, the inverse of income velocity:

$$\frac{M}{Y} = f\left(r_b, r_e, \frac{1}{P}\frac{dP}{dt}, w, \frac{P}{Y}, u\right). \tag{1}$$

The other independent variables in addition to the expected rate of inflation are the market interest rates for bonds, the market interest rates on equities, the ratio of nonhuman to human wealth, the price level divided by money income, and tastes. This theory is derived from the view that money is a form of wealth which yields services of various kinds. Thus, as with other categories of wealth, changes in the demand for money depend on changes in total wealth and on changes in the desirability of money compared to other types of wealth. The principal factors that may cause such changes are shown in convenient and condensed form in this equation.

Although no one has successfully shown that in the United States the velocity of money has been significantly related to the rate of change of prices, it has been shown for other countries where the rate of inflation has been more rapid and continuous than in the United States. This was done by Cagan in his study of hyperinflation.[3] Cagan analyzed in detail short periods of hyperinflation—when the rate of inflation was at least 50 per cent per month in seven European countries after World War I and during World War II. He related velocity to a measure he called the *expected* rate of inflation rather than to the current measured rate of inflation, and the expected rate of inflation was estimated as a weighted average of past rates of change of prices. The technique that he developed for measuring expected inflation was an important contribution to the study of the velocity of money. In all of the cases examined by Cagan, the velocity of money and the expected rate of inflation typically moved upward together. The coefficients of determination ranged from .857 to .996.[4]

2. Friedman, "Quantity Theory," p. 11.

3. Phillip Cagan, "The Monetary Dynamics of Hyperinflation," in Friedman, ed., *Studies in the Quantity Theory*.

4. *Ibid.*, p. 43.

Also, Deaver analyzed the long inflation in Chile from 1879 to 1955 using the same techniques as Cagan.[5] In Chile, the rate of inflation tended to accelerate over the period. The average annual rate of inflation was about 2 per cent from 1879 to 1904, 7 per cent from 1904 to 1931, and 20 per cent from 1931 to 1955. From 1932 to 1955, income velocity rose 70 per cent, and for this period Deaver found an observable relationship between velocity and expected inflation. He examined several equations. One was a simple correlation relating annual data on real cash balances to the expected rate of inflation. The coefficient of determination was .621.[6] Another was a multiple correlation relating quarterly data on the real stock of money per capita to the expected rate of inflation and to current real income. The coefficient of determination was .852.[7]

My objective has been the same as that of Cagan and Deaver—to determine whether there was a relationship between changes in the expected rate of inflation and changes in velocity during recent periods of rapid inflation in South Korea and Brazil. The period studied in South Korea is from 1953 to mid-1961, and for Brazil, from 1948 through 1965. These two examples make an interesting comparison because the monthly rates of inflation averaged roughly the same, but moved *in opposite directions*! In South Korea the rate of inflation fell from over four per cent per month in 1953 to less than one per cent per month in 1960; in Brazil the rate of inflation rose from less than one per cent per month in 1948 to five per cent per month in 1964.

During the period from 1953 to 1961, South Korea was recovering from the extensive destruction caused by the Korean War. Seoul was rebuilt and the national government was moved back there in mid-1953, about the time the armistice agreement was signed. The Republic of Korea initiated the first of a series of programs to combat inflation in 1952. In an agreement with the United Nations command, they agreed to a wide variety of policies aimed at reducing the rate of inflation.[8] In February 1953, they enacted a monetary reform reducing the currency 100 to 1, and the unit of account was changed from won

5. John V. Deaver, "The Chilean Inflation and the Demand for Money," above.

6. *Ibid.*, p. 29.

7. *Ibid.*, p. 34, table 3.

8. "Agreement on Economic Coordination between the Unified Command and the Republic of Korea, Pusan, May 24, 1952," *United States Treaties and Other International Agreements*, III, part 3 (Washington, D.C., 1952), p. 4,426.

to hwan.[9] After South Korea joined the International Monetary Fund in 1955, staff members of the IMF consulted annually with the Korean government concerning measures to suppress inflation.

Syngman Rhee was president of the Republic of Korea during most of the period studied. He was first elected by the National Assembly in 1948, was reelected three times, and resigned in April 1960 following a student-led revolution. In May 1961, a military government led by General Chung-hee Park took control. In 1963, Park was elected president and in 1967 reelected. The period studied starts after the Korean War and ends at the beginning of the Park regime.

In Brazil, an industrial revolution that started earlier in the century continued with increased intensity from 1948 to 1965.[10] Though there were several changes in the political party in power, government policy continuously attempted to encourage economic development. Large increases in the volume of bank credit were made available to both government and private industry. By rapidly expanding its own activities, particularly in electric power and education, government expenditures regularly exceeded tax revenues, and the difference was made up by printing more money.

The rates of inflation in both South Korea and Brazil have exceeded those of most countries in the post–World War II period. In South Korea, prices increased four to five-fold from 1953 to 1961, and the average monthly rate of inflation was from 1.7 to 2 per cent, depending on the price index used. In Brazil, prices in 1965 were approximately seventy-nine times what they had been in 1948. The average monthly rate of inflation was 2 per cent, approximately the same as in South Korea. In countries with such rapid rates of inflation, economic analysis suggests that the velocity of money will be affected. In an earlier paper on Korea's economy by Tullock and myself, we suggested that the velocity of money in Korea may have varied with the rate of inflation in the period following World War II, but we did not test the hypothesis statistically.[11]

9. A monetary reform in June 1962 changed the unit of account back to won at a conversion ratio of 1 to 10.

10. Charles Wagley, "The Brazilian Revolution: Social Changes since 1930," in *Social Change in Latin America Today* (New York: Vintage, 1960), pp. 177–230.

11. Colin D. Campbell and Gordon Tullock, "Some Little-Understood Aspects of Korea's Monetary and Fiscal Systems," *American Economic Review*, 47 (1957): 340–41.

2. VELOCITY AND THE CURRENT RATE OF INFLATION

As already noted, the rates of inflation in South Korea and Brazil moved in opposite directions, declining in South Korea and rising in Brazil. The eight-year decline in the Korean rate of inflation is a relatively unusual phenomenon. Because Korean prices were increasing at a decreasing rate, one would expect the cost of holding money to fall and the velocity of money to decline. The tendency of inflation to accelerate, as in Brazil, is more common. Because of the acceleration in the Brazilian inflation, one would expect to find the opposite—a rise in velocity. The figures for South Korea and Brazil confirm these expectations.

A. SOUTH KOREA

Table 1 shows the sharp downward trend of income velocity in South Korea from 1953 to 1961 based on the official estimates of GNP. It also shows that during the same period the average monthly rates of change in two official price indexes, two free exchange rates, and the GNP deflator fell sharply. In 1953, when the rate of inflation was over 4 per cent per month, income velocity was approximately 18 per year. In 1960, when the rate of inflation had fallen to about .5 per cent per month, income velocity was 7.8 per year.

The statistical data on the money supply shown in table 1 include currency in circulation and all types of deposits in banks.[12] Estimates of gross national product in both current and constant prices have been made in Korea since 1953.[13]

The figures on the two uncontrolled exchange rates—the rate of exchange for greenbacks (United States currency) and for United States military payment certificates—were collected by the Bank

12. Currency in circulation excludes currency held by banking institutions. Deposits have been adjusted to exclude checks in process of collection, interbank deposits, and deposits of the national government and foreign official organizations. The research department of the Bank of Korea includes in the official series on the money supply all deposits payable on demand within 30 days. In this study, savings and time deposits are also included. This was done in order to avoid the impacts on the money supply series resulting from a change in the classification of notice deposits in 1955 from monetary deposits to savings and time deposits, and the introduction of a new type of savings deposit in 1959. Although these savings deposits are not included in the official series on the money supply, they are similar to passbook deposits which are included. See Appendix A, "The Money Stock in South Korea."

13. The estimates of GNP in table 1 were made prior to 1965. Upward revisions in the GNP series were made in both 1965 and 1966 (Bank of Korea, *Review of Korean Economy in 1964* [Seoul, 1965], pp. 134–35, and *Review of Korean Economy in 1965* [Seoul, 1966], pp. 124–25).

TABLE 1

South Korea: Income Velocity and the Rate of Inflation

YEAR	GROSS NATIONAL PRODUCT* (Billions of Hwan)	MONEY STOCK†	INCOME VELOCITY PER YEAR	AVERAGE MONTHLY RATE OF CHANGE‡				
	H/W	H/W		Exchange Rate for Greenbacks	Exchange Rate for MPC	Seoul Consumer Price Index§	Seoul Wholesale Price Index	GNP Deflator
1946	—	.2	—	—	—	—	15.3%	—
1947	—	.4	—	—	—	—	5.4	—
1948	—	.6	—	—	—	—	2.2	—
1949	—	1.0	—	8.0%	11.5%	3.5%	3.7	—
1950	—	1.7	—	3.9	3.7	9.7	8.8	—
1951	—	5.7	—	7.1	6.1	9.7	9.5	—
1952	—	11.0	—	6.8	7.1	6.1	5.9	—
1953	389.4	21.6	18.03	4.4	4.6	4.1	1.9	2.7%#
1954	566.7	47.0	12.06	4.8	5.5	3.3	3.4	3.4
1955	950.2	73.1	13.00	1.7	2.8	2.3	3.0	3.1
1956	1,219.8	113.7	10.73	1.6	.7	3.1	3.2	1.9
1957	1,629.9	136.3	11.96	.4	.6	-.2	-.6	.8
1958	1,720.8	175.0	9.83	.6	1.1	.3	.7	.0
1959	1,854.5	241.6	7.68	.6	.9	.6	.9	.6
1960	2,107.1	269.2	7.83	.0	-.2	.5	.7	.9
1961	2,414.1	320.1	7.54	-.2‖	.6‖	.3	1.4‖	1.0

* Bank of Korea, *Monthly Statistical Review*, vol. 27 (May 1963), table 1.

† From 1953 to 1961, average of monthly series, mid-month, from Bank of Korea, *Monthly Statistical Review*. Includes currency in circulation, monetary deposits, and savings and time deposits. From 1946 to 1952, average of end-of-quarter series.

‡ Average of monthly series for the exchange rates and price indexes. The monthly rate of change is measured by the natural logarithm of P_t/P_{t-1}, in which P_{t-1} and P_t are successive values of a monthly index and are expressed in terms of per cent per month. The annual rates of change in the GNP deflator were converted to monthly rates of change by linear interpolation using the GNP annual deflator as a midyear index.

§ Seoul retail price index prior to 1955.

‖ Average for first six months of the year.

Average for last six months of the year.

of Korea. Before June 1961, military payment certificates and green-backs were exchanged openly for Korean currency even though such transactions were illegal. Money changers on the streets of Seoul were readily available, and the black-market rates of exchange were matters of common knowledge and record. Military payment certificates were designed to be used solely within United States military establishments by American soldiers. Shortly after they were originally issued, they were also used by Korean wives of American servicemen to purchase goods from army post exchanges for resale in the Korean markets, even though United States army regulations forbid this type of trade.

Greenbacks had to be smuggled into Korea. They have probably been used as a store of value because of their advantage over holding depreciating hwan currency. Also, greenbacks have been used as foreign exchange, and the market for them may have been, for some people, a more convenient source of foreign exchange than the strictly controlled official channels. In June 1961, the new military government of Korea began to enforce vigorously the law against exchanges of both military payment certificates and greenbacks, and information on their rates of exchange was no longer available.

The use of free exchange rates as a measure of changes in prices is based on the purchasing power parity theory of exchange rates.[14] With prices in the United States remaining relatively stable from 1953 to 1961 while Korean prices were rising sharply, one would expect the free exchange rates to rise together with Korean prices. Table 2 compares the official indexes of prices with indexes of the uncontrolled exchange rates and shows that this is generally what happened— although the rise in the uncontrolled exchange rates over the entire period was more rapid than the rise in the official price indexes. Also, the rise in the uncontrolled exchange rates did not coincide exactly with the rise in the official price indexes. In some years the exchange rates rose more rapidly than the official price indexes, and in other years they rose less rapidly than prices.

The differences in the movements of the price indexes and the free exchange rates probably reflect the impact of price controls on the official price indexes. Although most of the data are gathered by employees of the Bank of Korea who visit the appropriate shops or places of business, some of them are official prices obtained from

14. See Leland B. Yeager, "A Rehabilitation of Purchasing-Power Parity," *Jour. Pol. Econ.*, 66 (1958):516–30. Yeager concluded that "people value currencies primarily for what they will buy and, in uncontrolled markets, tend to exchange them at rates that roughly express their relative purchasing powers."

TABLE 2

South Korea: Comparison of Official Price Indexes and
Indexes of Uncontrolled Exchange Rates, 1953–61
(Annual Indexes, 1953 = 100)

Year	Seoul Consumer Prices*	Seoul Wholesale Prices	GNP Deflator†	Exchange Rate for Greenbacks	Exchange Rate for Military Payment Certificates
1953.....	100.0	100.0	100.0	100.0	100.0
1954.....	137.1	128.2	138.4	194.0	201.9
1955.....	231.0	232.2	223.2	265.1	309.8
1956.....	283.9	312.9	285.7	331.9	389.6
1957.....	349.5	370.0	351.3	354.6	406.8
1958.....	337.3	346.0	346.6	405.5	495.2
1959.....	347.9	371.0	355.4	431.3	553.5
1960.....	376.3	429.3	395.5	467.7	577.8
1961.....	408.2	487.6‡	437.9	487.7‡	595.5‡

* Seoul retail price index prior to 1955.

† Based on the GNP in current prices divided by GNP in 1955 prices.

‡ Average for first six months of the year.

government departments (see Appendix B). An examination made in 1962 of the two hundred individual commodity prices in the new wholesale price index showed no change for approximately one-third of the items over the span of a full year.[15] Government controls may have caused the official price indexes to understate the rate of inflation when the rise in prices was relatively rapid. Then, when the inflationary pressures weakened and government prices were possibly raised, the official indexes may have overstated the rate of inflation. In addition, free exchange rates would not be expected to vary exactly as prices of goods and services because of the effects of such factors as capital movements and government transfers.

The interrelationships among the money supply, an index of the exchange rate for greenbacks, and an index of real output based on the official estimates of GNP in constant prices are shown in table 3. The exchange rate for greenbacks increased by more than four and a half times from 1953 to 1960. The total money supply rose by over twelve times. The much smaller increase in the exchange rate for greenbacks than in the money supply may be explained partly by the growth in real output. Since the index of real output increased by approximately 37 per cent, the money stock per unit of output rose by only nine times —still approximately double the increase in prices as measured by the exchange rate for greenbacks. This unusual increase in real cash balances

15. Gabriel F. Cazell, *The Korean Wholesale Price Index* (Seoul: Statistical Advisory Group, Surveys and Research Corporation, 1962), p. 51.

TABLE 3

Year	Average Money Stock	Exchange Rate for Greenbacks	Real Output*	Money Stock per Unit of Output	Real Value of Money Stock per Unit of Output†
1953.....	100.0	100.0	100.0	100.0	100.0
1954.....	217.6	194.0	105.2	206.8	106.5
1955.....	338.4	265.1	109.4	309.3	116.8
1956.....	526.4	331.9	109.7	479.9	144.8
1957.....	631.0	354.6	119.2	529.4	149.2
1958.....	810.2	405.5	127.5	635.5	156.9
1959.....	1,118.5	431.3	134.1	834.1	193.4
1960.....	1,246.3	467.7	136.9	910.4	194.8

* Based on the official estimates of GNP in 1955 prices.

† Calculated by (1) dividing the annual money stock in hwan by the index of the exchange rate for greenback, (2) obtaining an index with 1953 = 100 of this result, and (3) dividing this index by the index of real output.

per unit of output was probably caused by the decline in the rate of inflation. Because of the lower cost of holding money when inflation is less rapid, people apparently desired to hold more cash relative to their incomes.

The rise in the real value of the money stock per unit of output shown in table 3 is smaller, but probably more accurate, than the estimated rise in cash balances based on table 1. Table 3 shows a rise in these balances of 95 per cent. In table 1, real cash balances per unit of output based on estimates of the GNP rose 130 per cent. The smaller rise in real cash balances in table 3 than in table 1 is the result of the more rapid rise in the rate of exchange for greenbacks than in the GNP deflator.[16] Because many government-controlled prices are included in the official indexes of prices and in the GNP deflator, estimates of real cash balances based on free exchange rates are probably more reliable than those based on the official price indexes.

B. BRAZIL

Table 4 shows the upward trend of income velocity in Brazil from 1948 to 1965, together with the rise in the monthly rates of change in

16. From 1953 to 1960, the rate of exchange for military payment certificates rose more rapidly than the rate of exchange for greenbacks. Using the rate of exchange for military payment certificates as a measure of inflation, prices rose by 5.8 times during this period, and the real value of cash balances per unit of output rose approximately 60 per cent.

TABLE 4

BRAZIL: INCOME VELOCITY AND THE RATE OF INFLATION, 1948–65

YEAR	GROSS NATIONAL PRODUCT*	MONEY STOCK I†	MONEY STOCK II‡	INCOME VELOCITY PER YEAR I	INCOME VELOCITY PER YEAR II	AVERAGE MONTHLY RATE OF CHANGE§		
		(Billions of Cruzeiros)				Cost-of-Living Index	Wholesale Price Index	GNP Deflator
1948	CR 185	CR 47.7	CR 63.2	3.88	2.93	0.7%	0.7%	0.7%‖
1949	213	53.8	70.8	3.96	3.01	0.1	1.6	0.8
1950	251	66.8	85.3	3.76	2.94	0.3	1.4	1.1
1951	304	84.4	103.9	3.60	2.93	0.8	0.6	1.0
1952	350	95.1	115.6	3.68	3.03	1.8	1.2	1.0
1953	425	112.6	134.1	3.77	3.17	1.2	1.0	1.5
1954	551	136.7	160.2	4.03	3.44	1.8	2.3	1.4
1955	686	162.9	187.4	4.21	3.66	1.2	0.6	1.6
1956	878	196.5	221.0	4.47	3.97	2.1	1.9	1.4
1957	1,050	242.6	269.6	4.33	3.89	1.1	0.4	1.1
1958	1,300	323.9	354.9	4.01	3.66	1.7	2.0	1.6
1959	1,774	411.5	447.5	4.31	3.96	2.9	2.6	2.0
1960	2,397	570.5	618.5	4.20	3.88	2.3	2.5	2.3
1961	3,475	822.8	884.8	4.22	3.93	3.0	3.3	3.0
1962	5,436	1,268.4	1,337.4	4.29	4.06	4.0	3.5	4.0
1963	9,520	2,005.4	2,093.9	4.75	4.55	4.9	5.0	5.1
1964	18,726	3,737.0	3,876.0	5.01	4.83	5.2	5.6	4.6
1965	31,034	6,834.0	7,052.5	4.54	4.40	2.9	2.0	3.7#

* *International Financial Statistics*, Aug. 1967, p. 62, and *Supplement to 1966/67 Issues*, p. 28. Estimate of gross domestic product was used for 1965.

† *International Financial Statistics, Supplement on Money*, 1964, p. 17, and subsequent issues. Averages of monthly seasonally adjusted series. Money Stock I plus mid-year estimates of quasi-deposits, *International Financial Statistics, Supplement to 1966/67 Issues*, p. 27.

‡ Money Stock I plus mid-year estimates of quasi-deposits, *International Financial Statistics, Supplement to 1966/67 Issues*, p. 27.

§ The monthly rate of change in the price indexes is measured by the natural logarithm of P_t/P_{t-1} in which P_{t-1} and P_t are successive values of a monthly index, and is expressed in terms of per cent per month. Both price indexes are from *International Financial Statistics*. The annual rates of change in the GNP deflator were converted to monthly rates of change by linear interpolation using the GNP annual deflator as a midyear index.

‖ Average for last 6 months of the year.

Average for first 6 months of the year.

two official price indexes and the GNP deflator.[17] The two estimates of income velocity are based on different series of the money supply: Money Stock I which includes currency in circulation and monetary deposits, and Money Stock II which includes quasi-deposits in addition to the items included in Money Stock I. Quasi-deposits consist of long-term deposits in commercial banks and quasi-monetary liabilities of the monetary authorities.[18]

During the first ten years, from 1948 through 1957, there were several fluctuations in both income velocity and the rate of inflation, even though both income velocity and the rate of inflation tended to rise over the period. Table 4 shows that from 1948 to 1951, a short rise in both measures of velocity was followed by a two-year decline. There was then a rise in income velocity from 1951 to 1956. In 1951, when the rate of inflation was less than 1 per cent per month, Income Velocity I was 3.6 per year and Income Velocity II was 2.9 per year. By 1956, when the rate of inflation was about 2 per cent per month, they were respectively 4.5 and 4 per year. In 1957–58, both measures of income velocity again fell.

A sharper rise in the rate of inflation occurred from 1958 to 1964. Over this period, this rate rose from about 2 per cent per month to over 5 per cent per month. During the same period, Income Velocity I rose from 4 to 5 per year, and Income Velocity II rose from 3.7 to 4.8 per year. In 1965, both the rate of inflation and the velocity of money declined.

The interrelationships between the money stock, the cost of living index, and an index of real output are shown in table 5. The cost-of-

17. The cost-of-living index is from São Paulo. In earlier years, it was weighted according to budget expenditures of a municipal worker's family in 1936–37. In later years, it was weighted according to a wage earner's expenditures in 1951–52. It includes both "free and legal prices." A cost-of-living index for Rio de Janeiro is also available, but is not significantly different.

The wholesale price index refers mainly to Porto Alegre and São Paulo. Through 1948, it was based on 18 domestic and 7 imported items weighted by production and imports in 1946. In later years, it refers to all goods without regard to the distinction between exports, imports, and other commodities. In early years, cotton and coffee accounted for 35 per cent of the total weight, and in later years for 29 per cent of the total.

18. Quasi-deposits have been one of the casualties of the rapid inflation. In December 1948, the total amount of quasi-deposits was 16 billion cruzeiros, approximately 32 per cent of the total currency plus monetary deposits. In 1965, quasi-deposits amounted to 265 billion cruzeiros, 3 per cent of the total quantity of currency plus monetary deposits.

TABLE 5
BRAZIL: INDEX NUMBERS FOR SELECTED SERIES OF ANNUAL FIGURES, 1948–65
(1948 = 100)

Year	Index of Money Stock I	Index of Money Stock II	Cost-of Living Price Index	Index of Real Output*	Index of Money Stock per Unit of Output I	Index of Real Value of the Money Stock per Unit of Output I	Index of Money Stock per Unit of Output II	Index of Real Value of the Money Stock per Unit of Output II
1948	100.0	100.0	100.00	100.0	100.0	100.0	100.0	100.0
1949	112.8	112.0	99.08	116.2	97.1	98.0	96.4	97.3
1950	140.0	135.0	104.79	129.5	108.1	103.1	104.2	99.5
1951	176.9	164.4	112.75	145.7	121.4	107.8	112.8	100.1
1952	199.4	182.9	132.83	142.4	140.0	105.4	128.4	96.7
1953	236.1	212.2	161.83	141.9	166.4	102.8	149.5	92.5
1954	286.6	253.5	190.33	156.5	183.1	96.2	162.0	85.1
1955	341.5	296.5	225.25	164.6	207.5	92.1	180.1	80.0
1956	411.9	349.7	279.92	169.6	242.9	86.8	206.2	73.7
1957	508.6	426.6	334.00	169.9	299.4	89.6	251.1	75.2
1958	679.0	561.6	385.33	182.4	372.3	96.7	307.9	79.9
1959	862.7	708.1	527.83	181.7	474.8	90.0	389.7	73.9
1960	1,196.0	978.6	711.08	182.2	656.4	92.3	537.1	75.6
1961	1,724.9	1,400.0	982.75	191.1	902.6	91.8	732.6	74.5
1962	2,659.1	2,116.1	1,504.33	195.4	1,360.8	90.4	1,083.0	72.0
1963	4,204.2	3,313.1	2,644.00	194.6	2,160.4	81.7	1,702.5	64.4
1964	7,834.4	6,132.9	4,879.00	207.5	3,775.6	77.4	2,955.6	60.5
1965	14,327.0	11,159.0	7,893.00	212.5	6,742.1	85.4	5,251.3	66.6

* Based on the gross national product in current prices deflated by the cost-of-living price index.

living index rose by 79 times during this period. Money Stock I increased by over 143 times and Money Stock II increased by almost 112 times. The larger increase in the money stock than in prices is probably explained by the increase in real output. Assuming an income elasticity of one, an increase in the money supply matched by an equal percentage increase in real output would not result in an increase in prices. From 1948 to 1965, the index of real output, derived by using the cost-of-living index to deflate the GNP in current prices, more than doubled.[19]

The money stock per unit of output rose by 67 times for Money Stock I and by 53 times for Money Stock II. This is less than the rise in prices—the result one would expect. Because prices rose more rapidly than the increase in the money stock per unit of output, real cash balances per unit of output fell. When the rate of inflation increased, people in Brazil apparently desired to hold less cash relative to their incomes.

How does the change in real cash balances per unit of output in South Korea compare with that in Brazil? The average rates of inflation over the period studied were similar, but the rates moved in opposite directions. Table 3 shows that in South Korea the rise in real money balances per unit of output was substantial—approximately doubling when the rate of inflation fell from over 4 per cent per month to less than 1 per cent. Table 5 shows that when the inflation rose from less than 1 per cent to over 5 per cent per month in Brazil, the decline in these balances was quite small—declining less than 25 per cent for the narrower definition of money and 40 per cent for the broader definition. Why this difference?

Friedman and Schwartz have shown that over long periods of time increases in real income in the United States were related to increases in the quantity of real cash balances that people desired.[20] In both South Korea and Brazil, increases in real income were substantial and constitute probably the principal explanation of the different relationships between real cash balances and the rate of inflation. In Brazil, although the increase in real income caused real cash balances to tend to rise, the acceleration in the rate of inflation had the opposite effect. These two influences tended to offset each other although the net effect was a decline in real cash balances per unit of output. In South Korea,

19. By obtaining the index of real output in this way, the trends of real cash balances per unit of output shown in table 5 are the exact inverse of the trends of income velocity shown in table 4.

20. Milton Friedman and Anna J. Schwartz, *A Monetary History of the United States, 1867–1960* (Princeton: Princeton Univ. Press, 1963), pp. 678–86.

both the increase in real income and the deceleration in the rate of inflation worked in the same direction to increase real cash balances.

Rough estimates of the elasticity of M/PO (real cash balances per unit of output) with respect to the rate of inflation and real income may be made for South Korea and Brazil from the data in tables 1 to 5. Assume that changes in M/PO are a function of changes in the rate of change of prices and changes in real income. For both countries, data for the first two years of the periods studied may be compared with the same data for the last two years. From the two equations (one for each country) it is possible to estimate the elasticities that balance both equations. Using the rate of exchange for greenbacks as a measure of changes in the rate of inflation in South Korea and using the narrow definition of money and the cost-of-living index in Brazil, the rate-of-inflation elasticity is $-.19$, and the real income elasticity of M/PO is .39—which means an income elasticity of demand for real money balances of 1.39. Using the rate of exchange for military payment certificates in South Korea and the same data as above for Brazil, the rate-of-inflation elasticity is $-.14$ and the real income elasticity of M/PO is .19—an elasticity of 1.19 for real money balances. These measures of elasticity are reasonable, and the rate-of-inflation elasticity is similar to the estimates of the elasticity at the mean rate of inflation shown in table 7.[21]

3. Velocity and the Expected Rate of Inflation

To make a more detailed examination of these rapid inflations we must investigate the relationship between changes in velocity and changes in the *expected* rate of inflation as suggested in the studies by Cagan. In both South Korea and Brazil, people undoubtedly anticipated at least some of the rise in prices that later occurred.

In Korea, prices had been rising for over twenty years. For ten years before 1932 prices moved downward, but in the early 1930s a "reflation" policy initiated to stimulate recovery caused prices to turn upward. From the beginning of the war between Japan and China in 1937 until the end of World War II, war finance was the principal cause of inflation. After the war, the breakdown of price controls, and a large increase in the money supply that occurred when the Japanese government in Korea collapsed, caused the wholesale price index to

21. Estimates of these elasticities using the broader definition of money and the wholesale price index for Brazil give similar elasticities of M/PO with respect to the rate of inflation, but widely varying elasticities with respect to real income.

rise as rapidly as 16 per cent per month.[22] From 1947 to 1949, wholesale prices typically rose from 2 to 5 per cent per month, and then rose even more rapidly during the Korean War. Bloomfield and Jensen, who were advisors to the Korean Ministry of Finance in 1949–50, observed that Koreans had shifted to the use of hoarded goods or United States currency as stores of value—a typical reaction in countries with anticipated inflation.[23] They also reported that the unusually high rates of interest in the free market—from 5 to 20 per cent per month—probably were discounting an anticipated rise in prices. Very high interest rates were also noted by De Alessi, who was with the United States aid program in South Korea in 1956–57.[24] He reported a decline in these rates when the inflation slowed down in 1957.

Brazilians have experienced inflation during most of the period since 1840. From 1840 to 1940, wholesale prices increased thirteen-fold, and from 1940 to 1945, they more than doubled.[25] In more recent years, interest rates on business loans have been as high as 5 per cent per month, and business enterprises have developed a variety of techniques for operating successfully under inflationary conditions.[26] Even though nominal interest rates have been relatively high, Kafka reports that negative real interest rates have persisted, especially among banks—probably because the banks underestimated the acceleration in inflation that actually occurred.[27] Kafka also states that hoarding was common, and an interesting aspect of the Brazilian inflation has been the widespread hoarding of consumer durables, including passenger cars.

A. THE EXPECTED RATE OF INFLATION

The problem of measuring expected inflation was discussed in detail by Cagan in his study of hyperinflation. Techniques for estimating

22. A. I. Bloomfield and J. P. Jensen, *Banking Reform in South Korea* (New York: Federal Reserve Bank of New York, 1951), p. 27.

23. *Ibid.*, p. 32.

24. L. De Alessi, "An Analysis of Foreign Aid Administration in Korea," *Southern Economic Journal*, 25 (1958):69.

25. H. W. Spiegel, "A Century of Prices in Brazil," *Review of Economics and Statistics*, 30 (1948):57–62.

26. James W. McKee, Jr., "Operating in an Inflationary Economy," in William D. Falcon, ed., *Financing International Operations* (New York: American Management Association, 1965), pp. 45–52.

27. Alexandre Kafka, "The Brazilian Stabilization Program, 1964–66," *Jour. Pol. Econ.*, 75 (Supplement, August 1967):608.

expected variables generally have been described by Nerlove.[28] A relatively simple formula for estimating the expected rate in inflation is:

$$E_t = (1 - e^{-B})C_t + (e^{-B})E_{t-1}, \tag{2}$$

where E_t is the expected rate of inflation for any given month, C_t is the current rate of inflation that month, E_{t-1} is the expected rate of inflation of the previous month, B is the coefficient of expectation, and e is the base of the natural logs. Equation (2) may be derived from equation (3), which was used by Cagan:[29]

$$E_t = (1 - e^{-B}) \sum_{i=0}^{\infty} C_{t-i}e^{-Bi}. \tag{3}$$

Estimates of the expected rate of inflation made in this way become a weighted moving average of past rates of inflation where greater weight is given to more recent rates of inflation than to those in the more distant past. No doubt other factors, such as a change in the political party in power, may have important effects on expectations, too. And expectations may not be systematically formed as this theory of expectations formation asserts. But, over long periods of time, the assumption that current price expectations depend primarily on past experience seems reasonable, and has worked well in a wide range of economic phenomena. This technique is essentially the same as that for estimating permanent income.

In equation (2), the expected rate of inflation changes each month. It is assumed that the public revises its expected rate of inflation in proportion to the difference between the current rate of inflation and the expected rate of inflation last month. The coefficient of expectation, B, is the proportion of this difference by which the public revises its expectations. For example, assume that the value of B, the coefficient of expectation, is 5 per cent. This would mean that the value of $(1 - e^{-B})$ is approximately 5 per cent, and the value of e^{-B} is approximately 95 per cent. If, for example, the current rate of inflation were zero and the expected rate of inflation last month were 20 per cent, the expected rate of inflation this month would be reduced to 19 per cent. With a higher coefficient of expectation, the effect of the current rate of inflation on the expected rate would be larger. If, in the

28. M. Nerlove, *Distributed Lags and Demand Analysis for Agricultural and Other Commodities* (U.S. Department of Agriculture, Agricultural Marketing Service, Agricultural Handbook No. 141, June 1958).

29. Cagan, "Monetary Dynamics," p. 39.

example above, the coefficient of expectation were 10 per cent, the expected rate of inflation this month would be reduced to 18 per cent.

In order to use equation (2), it is necessary to have data on prices available for several years prior to the period under investigation. For example, to calculate the expected rate of inflation in South Korea for January 1953, the coefficient of expectation had to be applied to current rates of change of prices starting three to four years earlier.

For both countries, calculations were made to determine the co-efficients of expectation that resulted in expected rates of inflation most closely related to the actual levels of real cash balances. For South Korea, the best fits resulted from the use of coefficients of expectation of 4 and 5 per cent. However, the use of other coefficients of expectation ranging from 1 to 9 per cent also resulted in high coefficients of determination. For Brazil, in the period from 1958 to 1965, when the rate of inflation was relatively rapid, the best coefficients of expectation were 13 and 15 per cent. For the earlier period from 1948 to 1957, when the rate of inflation was relatively low, the best coefficient of expectation was 2 per cent. During the earlier period, the expected rate of inflation is not as closely related to real cash balances per unit of output as in the later period.

These coefficients of expectation are lower than some of those that fit Cagan's data best. This seems reasonable because of the lower rates of inflation in South Korea and Brazil than in the countries he examined. Cagan conjectured that the coefficient of expectation would be higher the more rapid the rate of inflation.[30] One would expect reactions to the rate of inflation to be quicker when the rate of inflation is more rapid because the chance of loss is greater. In the European hyper-inflations studied by Cagan, the coefficient of expectation varied between 5 per cent and 35 per cent. In Austria in 1921–22, Cagan used a co-efficient of expectation of 5 per cent, the same as used for South Korea in this study. It is interesting that the speed of inflation in Austria in the two years preceding the hyperinflation was 82 per cent per year— not far different from the 102 per cent annual rate of inflation in South Korea in 1952. In Hungary from 1922 to 1924, Cagan used a coefficient of expectation of 10 per cent and in Greece from 1943 to 1944 and in Hungary from 1945 to 1946, he used a coefficient of expectation of 15 per cent. These are similar to the coefficients of expectation used in this study for the period of relatively rapid inflation in Brazil from 1958 to 1965.

30. Cagan, "Monetary Dynamics," pp. 58–64.

The use of low coefficients seems reasonable because of the use of monthly indexes. Although monthly indexes usually fluctuate widely, a large change in the price index for only one month would probably not have a large impact on the rate of inflation that people expected. By using a low coefficient of expectation, sharp variations in the price index for only a month or two have only a small impact on the estimate of price expectations.

The low coefficients of expectation are consistent with a considerable lag between changes in the actual and expected rates of inflation. This suggests that adjustment to a higher cost of holding money balances is not immediate, but takes some time. With a coefficient of expectation of 5 per cent, there would be an 80 per cent adjustment within one year.

In this study, the coefficient of expectation was not adjusted with changes in the rate of inflation. If the actual coefficient of expectation varies with the rate of change of prices, this would be a shortcoming of the estimates made here.[31]

B. THE STATISTICAL RESULTS

The regression equation used for the correlation of the expected rate of inflation with real cash balances per unit of output is:

$$\log_e M/PO = -aE + b. \tag{4}$$

Equation (4) is derived from:

$$M/PO = e^{-aE+b}. \tag{5}$$

Equation (5) states that the level of real cash balances per unit of output is a function of the expected rate of change of prices per month. The equation is linear in form and a, which is the coefficient of the independent variable, and b, the constant term, are parameters. Although monthly data on the money stock, free exchange rates, and prices were available from published or official sources, monthly indexes of real output had to be estimated from annual series.

The regression equations for both South Korea and Brazil are shown in table 6. Free exchange rates were used as price indexes in two of the equations for South Korea. For the other two Korean equations, official price indexes for consumer and wholesale prices were used. Better fits and lower standard errors of estimate were obtained with the use of free exchange rates. The first two equations for Brazil refer

31. Maurice Allais has developed a model in which the coefficient of expectation changes with the rate of inflation, "A Restatement of the Quantity Theory of Money," *Amer. Econ. Rev.*, 56 (1966):1123–57.

solely to the period from 1958 to 1965, when the rate of inflation accelerated and was relatively rapid. The third equation for Brazil refers to the period from 1948 through 1957 and is based on the use of the cost-of-living index. During this earlier period, if the wholesale price index is used to estimate the expected rate of inflation and to calculate M/PO, there is not a significant relationship between the expected rate of inflation and real cash balances.

There is a high degree of serial correlation in the regressions in table 6. This is to be expected because of shifts over time in the true co-efficient of expectation or because of the effect of other variables than the expected rate of inflation on the demand for real cash balances.[32] Simple regressions for subperiods indicate that the coefficients of expectation resulting in the highest coefficients of determination have varied. The best coefficients of expectation for the two official price indexes in South Korea rose from 1953–54 to 1955–56, fell in 1957–58, and then rose again in 1959–61. Table 6 shows that the best coefficient of expectation for Brazil is considerably higher in 1958–65 than in 1948–57.

In table 6, the values of a, the coefficient of the independent variable, were larger in South Korea and Brazil than in most of the countries studied by Cagan. This is as one would expect since a tends to be larger the smaller the value of the coefficient of expectation. This is because a lower coefficient of expectation will reduce the value of E (see equation [4]). For the seven hyperinflations in Europe studied by Cagan, the average coefficient of the independent variable was 4.68. In two countries that Cagan examined, Austria and Hungary after World War I, the value of the coefficients of expectation were .05 and .1, respectively, and the value of a was 8.55 and 8.70. This is not far different from the value of a for South Korea, when the exchange rate for military payment certificates was used, and is slightly larger than the value of a for Brazil during the period of accelerated inflation from 1958 to 1965. In Deaver's equation relating annual data on real cash balances to the expected inflation, the value of a (converted to a monthly basis) was 12.6, not far different from the values of a in several of the equations in table 6.

In these regression equations, the elasticity of demand for real cash balances per unit of output is measured by $-aE$. Since the value of E varies, the measure of elasticity also varies. For both South Korea and Brazil, the demand for real cash balances per unit of output with respect to the expected rate of inflation has been inelastic. In South

32. Cagan, "Monetary Dynamics," p. 58.

TABLE 6

Results of Simple Regressions of the Logarithm
of the Real Value of the Money Stock Per Unit of Output
(M/PO) on the Expected Rate of Inflation (E)

Price Index*	Regression Equation†	Standard Error of the Estimate	Coefficient of Determination
South Korea, Jan. 1953–June 1961 (102 months)			
Greenbacks....... ($B = .05$)	$M/PO = 5.35105 - 13.5651E$ (.41213)	.07746	.915
Military payment certificates .... ($B = .05$)	$M/PO = 5.11372 - 9.6051E$ (.40644)	.07823	.848
Seoul wholesale price index.... ($B = .05$)	$M/PO = 5.48703 - 15.2062E$ (.78325)	.12645	.790
Seoul consumer price index.... ($B = .05$)	$M/PO = 5.54592 - 15.2523E$ (.57786)	.10735	.874
Brazil, Jan. 1958–Dec. 1965 (96 months)			
Cost-of-living index......... ($B = .15$)	$M/PO = 4.66605 - 6.0071E$ (.26521)	.03152	.845
Wholesale price index......... ($B = .13$)	$M/PO = 4.66129 - 6.1291E$ (.25114)	.03170	.864
Brazil, Jan. 1948–Dec. 1957 (120 months)			
Cost-of-living index......... ($B = .02$)	$M/PO = 4.89755 - 30.6463E$ (1.96227)	.04371	.674

* The coefficient of expectation, B, is the rate at which the expected rate of inflation is affected by the current monthly rate of inflation.

† The standard error of the regression coefficient is shown in parentheses below the regression coefficient.

Korea, at a mean expected rate of inflation of between 2.7 per cent and 3.0 per cent per month, the elasticity of demand for real cash balances per unit of output was approximately −.40 for three of the price indexes used and −.30 for the fourth (see table 7). Assuming an elasticity of −.40, if the expected rate of inflation increased from its mean, 2.7 per cent per month, to 5.4 per cent per month, the level of real cash balances per unit of output would decrease about 40 per cent. In Brazil from 1958 to 1965, at a mean expected rate of inflation of approximately 3.1 per cent per month, the elasticity of demand for real cash balances per unit of output was −.19. For the period from 1948 to 1957, at a mean expected rate of inflation of 1 per cent per month, the elasticity of demand for real cash balances per unit of output was −.32.

It is interesting that the elasticities of M/PO with respect to the mean expected rates of inflation shown in table 7 are similar to some of the estimates of the interest elasticity of velocity in the United States from 1910 to 1958 made by Brunner and Meltzer. In demand functions for money, the rate of change of prices is a variable similar to the nominal rate of interest. Both reflect the cost of holding money or the rate of return received for holding other assets than money. For velocity defined as the ratio of income to the money stock, Brunner and Meltzer estimated mean interest elasticities ranging from .34 to .44.[33] The rates of interest used in their studies were yields on twenty-year corporate bonds.

TABLE 7

The Elasticity of the Index of the Real Value of the Money Stock per Unit of Output (M/PO) with Respect to the Mean Expected Rate of Inflation $(\bar{E})$

	South Korea, Jan. 1953–June 1961 (102 months) (1953 = 100)				
Price Index	Mean M/PO	Minimum M/PO	Month of Minimum M/PO	Maximum M/PO	Month of Maximum M/PO
Greenbacks.........	143.2	68.5	Jan. 1953	226.3	June 1961
Military payment certificates.......	123.7	68.5	Jan. 1953	173.7	Sept. 1960
Seoul wholesale price index.......	160.1	64.3	Feb. 1953	234.9	July 1959
Seoul consumer price index.......	168.0	73.2	Feb. 1953	255.2	March 1960

Price Index	Mean E	Maximum E	Month of Maximum E	Minimum E	Month of Minimum E	Elasticity of M/PO with Respect to $\bar{E}$
Greenbacks......	2.85%	7.01%	Jan. 1953	0.10%	June 1961	.386
Military payment certificates.....	3.08	7.15	Jan. 1953	0.17	Sept. 1960	.295
Seoul wholesale price index.....	2.70	6.63	Feb. 1953	0.73	July 1959	.410
Seoul consumer price index.....	2.77	6.88	Feb. 1953	0.47	June 1961	.421

33. Karl Brunner and Allan H. Meltzer, "Predicting Velocity: Implications for Theory and Policy," *Journal of Finance*, 18 (1963):351.

TABLE 7—*Continued*

Brazil, Jan. 1958–Dec. 1965 (96 months)
(1948 = 100)

Price Index	Mean M/PO	Minimum M/PO	Month of Minimum M/PO	Maximum M/PO	Month of Maximum M/PO
Cost-of-living index..	87.4	74.7	Jan. 1965	99.8	June 1958
Wholesale price index............	87.3	72.3	April 1964	101.7	March 1958

Price Index	Mean E	Maximum E	Month of Maximum E	Minimum E	Month of Minimum E	Elasticity of M/PO with Respect to $\bar{E}$
Cost-of-living index.........	3.25%	5.39%	July 1964	0.95%	Feb. 1958	.195
Wholesale price index.........	3.13	5.58	March 1964	0.35	Feb. 1958	.192

Brazil, Jan. 1948–Dec. 1957 (120 Months)
(1948 = 100)

Price Index	Mean M/PO	Minimum M/PO	Month of Minimum M/PO	Maximum M/PO	Month of Maximum M/PO
Cost-of-living index..	97.3	81.9	Oct. 1956	112.0	Jan. 1951

Price Index	Mean E	Maximum E	Month of Maximum E	Minimum E	Month of Minimum E	Elasticity of M/PO with Respect to $\bar{E}$
Cost-of-living index..........	1.04%	1.40%	Oct. 1957	0.74%	Dec. 1951	.319

In hyperinflations in which the rate of inflation is increasing, a flight from cash may develop and the inflation becomes self-generating. Cagan concluded that the conditions necessary for a self-generating inflation depend on the product of the two parameters—the coefficient of expectation, B, and the coefficient of the independent variable, a, and that a flight from cash would occur if aB were greater than one, but not if it were less than one.[34] Because the rate of inflation in South Korea was decreasing, the possibility that the inflation might become explosive was not a problem. The inflation in Brazil was not rapid

34. The following equation shows that if aB is less than unity, prices may be in stable equilibrium, but not if aB is greater than unity (Cagan, "Monetary Dynamics," p. 65):

$$\frac{\partial\left(\dfrac{d \log P}{dt}\right)}{\partial P} = \frac{-B}{1 - aB}\left(\frac{1}{P}\right)$$

enough to be explosive even though the rate of inflation rose. The product of aB was .61 for the period from 1948 to 1957 and approximately .90 for the period from 1958 to 1965.

Scatter diagrams illustrating the relationship between the expected rate of inflation and the index of real cash balances per unit of output in South Korea are shown in charts 1 and 2. Charts 3 and 4 show the series of the actual and predicted real values of the money stock per unit of output. The predicted series were calculated from the equations in table 6 and depend on the values of the expected rate of inflation. Charts 1–4 are based on the use of the free exchange rates as price indexes. Figures using the official price indexes show a similar relationship, but the relationship is not as close.

A scatter diagram for Brazil for the period from 1958 to 1965 is

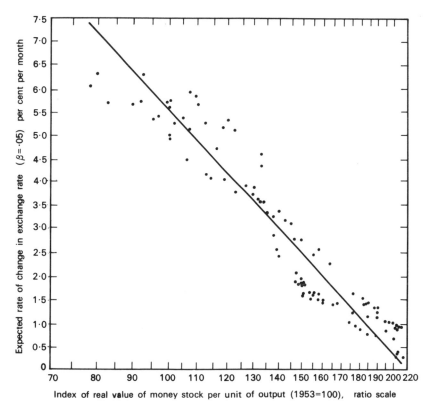

CHART 1. South Korea: Scatter diagram of expected rates of change in the rate of exchange for greenbacks and indexes of real value of money stock per unit of output, January 1953–June 1961.

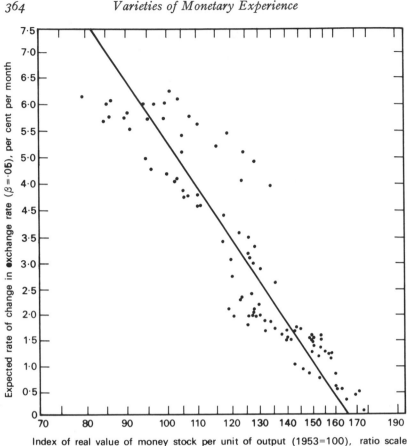

CHART 2. South Korea: Scatter diagram of expected rates of change in the rate of exchange for military payment certificates and indexes of real value of money stock per unit of output, January 1953–June 1961.

shown in chart 5, and the series for the actual and predicted real value of the money stock per unit of output are shown in chart 6. These figures are based on the use of the cost-of-living index. Figures based on the wholesale price index show approximately the same relationship. The estimates of actual real cash balances per unit of output are based on the narrow definition of money because of the lack of sufficient monthly data on quasi-deposits.

For both South Korea and Brazil, these figures show a close relationship between the trend in the actual and predicted indexes and in the turning points and shorter movements. When the expected rate of inflation rose, prices increased more rapidly than the money supply per

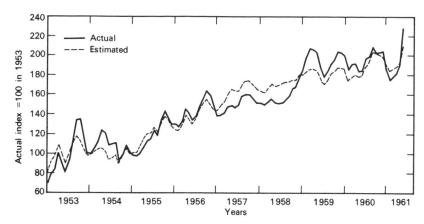

CHART 3. South Korea: Index of real value of money stock per unit of output, January 1953–June 1961, using rate of exchange for greenbacks as price index.

unit of output. When the expected rate of inflation fell, the rise in prices was less than the increase in the money supply per unit of output.

The scatter diagrams for South Korea and Brazil show that the relationship between the expected rate of inflation and real cash balances per unit of output is not linear, but fluctuates first above and then below the linear regression line as the rate of inflation rises. This is the kind of relationship one would expect if changes in the rate of

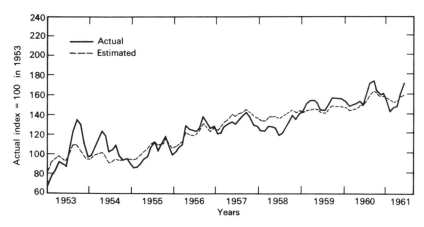

CHART 4. South Korea: Index of real value of money stock per unit of output, January 1953–June 1961, using rate of exchange for military payment certificates as price index.

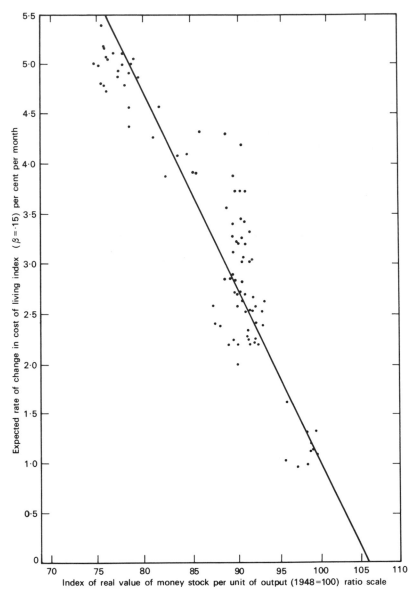

CHART 5. Brazil: Scatter diagram of expected rates of change in index of cost of living and indexes of real value of money stock per unit of output, January 1958–December 1965.

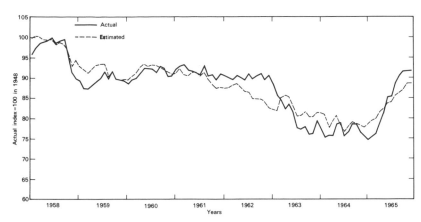

CHART 6. Brazil: Index of real value of money per unit of output, 1958–65, using cost-of-living index.

inflation lag behind changes in the rate of expansion in the money supply.

The nonlinear relationship can also be seen in the relationship between the actual and predicted series of the real value of the money stock per unit of output. In South Korea, when the rate of increase in the money stock was reduced, the immediate impact was for the actual M/PO in charts 3 and 4 to be below the estimated M/PO. Table 8 shows that the rate of increase in the money stock in South Korea was reduced sharply from mid-1954 to mid-1955, from 1957 to mid-1958, and in 1960. There was also the monetary reform in February 1953 in which a large amount of deposits was frozen. Charts 3 and 4 show that corresponding to each of these periods of contraction in the rate of increase in the money stock, actual real cash balances per unit of output fell below the predicted amount. But eventually, as the rate of expansion in the money stock remained at the new lower level, the actual series for M/PO rose above the estimated series. This is probably because the rate of inflation finally fell to the new lower rate of expansion in the money supply. Because of the slower rate of expansion in the money supply, people would reduce their rate of spending causing the inflation to become less rapid. And the slower rate of inflation would cause actual real cash balances to rise.

In Brazil, if it is assumed that prices lag behind changes in the money supply, when the rate of expansion in the money stock increased, the immediate effect would be to cause actual M/PO to be above estimated M/PO. Chart 6 shows several examples of this. In 1959, the rate of

TABLE 8

MONTHLY RATES OF INCREASE IN THE MONEY STOCK
IN SOUTH KOREA AND BRAZIL

SOUTH KOREA			BRAZIL	
Year	Half of Year	Monthly Rate of Increase in the Money Stock*	Year	Monthly Rate of Increase in the Money Stock†
1953....	1st	6.84%	1948....	0.49
	2d	7.29	1949....	1.27
1954....	1st	7.58	1950....	2.47
	2d	2.91	1951....	1.21
1955....	1st	3.20	1952....	1.17
	2d	4.45	1953....	1.45
1956....	1st	3.71	1954....	1.64
	2d	2.51	1955....	1.32
1957....	1st	−0.17	1956....	1.65
	2d	2.47	1957....	2.41
1958....	1st	1.63	1958....	1.58
	2d	3.16	1959....	2.87
1959....	1st	2.94	1960....	2.65
	2d	1.17	1961....	3.36
1960....	1st	0.79	1962....	4.05
	2d	−0.14	1963....	4.09
1961....	1st	1.85	1964....	5.15
			1965....	4.64

* Six-month average of monthly rates of change. For definition of money stock, see table 1.

† Twelve-month average of monthly rates of change. For definition of money stock, see Money Stock I, table 4.

increase in the money stock rose sharply and caused the actual series to rise and coincide with the estimated series during a portion of the year. In 1960, as the new more rapid rate of expansion in the money stock held steady, the actual series fell below the estimated series. This was probably the result of the rate of inflation catching up with the previous acceleration in the rate of increase in the money supply. During 1961 and 1962, there was a continuous rise in the rate of increase in the money stock, and actual M/PO was above estimated M/PO. But in 1963, when the rate of expansion in the money stock leveled off, actual M/PO again fell below estimated M/PO.

4. CONCLUSION

The period from 1953 to 1961 is not the first time since World War II that the velocity of money in South Korea has declined while prices were rising rapidly.[35] A decline in velocity in 1947–49, which was noted

35. Bloomfield and Jensen, *Banking Reform*, p. 32.

by Bloomfield and Jensen, can also be explained by a decline in the rate of inflation. For the 1945–52 period, the statistical data on the money supply are not as good as for the later period, and income statistics are not available. However, estimates of real cash balances per capita and of the expected rate of inflation based on the Seoul wholesale price index may be made for this earlier period. The monthly index of real cash balances per capita with the base year 1947 rose from an average of 99.7 in 1947 to 120.1 in 1949. The expected rate of inflation per month using a coefficient of expectation of .10 fell from an average of 7.3 per cent in 1947 to 3.5 per cent in 1949. A simple regression of the real value of the money stock per capita versus the expected rate of inflation for the forty-month period from January 1947 to April 1950, just prior to the outbreak of the Korean War, yields a coefficient of determination of .75.[36]

The experience in South Korea and Brazil shows the basic role of the rate of expansion of the money supply as a factor affecting the rate of inflation. In these countries, income velocity fell when the rate of inflation slowed down and rose when the rate of inflation increased. But the rate of inflation was itself related to the rate of expansion of the money supply. Rises in the price level and in total money income appear to be significantly determined by both the direct impact of changes in the rate of expansion of the money stock and the indirect impact of changes in velocity caused by changes in the rate of expansion in the money supply.[37]

In Brazil, the accelerated rate of increase in the money supply was primarily the result of efforts to promote economic growth.[38] Particularly ambitious development programs were introduced in 1958 and were financed by budget deficits and bank credit. More rapid increases in the money stock than people had been accustomed to probably had a stimulating effect on real output as long as they kept getting larger. Holders of the additional money would try to reduce their cash balances to the desired level, but as a whole they would not be able to do so. In the attempt, they would bid up the prices of financial assets and lower interest rates. This would both stimulate the demand for and encourage the production of physical assets.

36. The linear regression equation for the logarithm of real cash balances per capita is $4.90480 - 4.34084E$, where E is the expected rate of inflation. A coefficient of expectation of .10 gives a better fit than .05.

37. See Milton Friedman, "Interest Rates and the Demand for Money," *Journal of Law and Economics*, 9 (1966): 78.

38. Kafka, "Brazilian Stabilization Program," pp. 596–97.

In South Korea, the decline in the rate of increase in the money supply was the result of efforts by the government to curtail the monetary expansion. United States advisors in Korea were continuously exerting pressure on the government to slow down the inflation. An additional factor that contributed to the slower rate of increase in the money supply in South Korea was the increase in economic aid from the United States. Measured in hwan, the value of American aid rose from 14.5 per cent of GNP in 1953 to 25.9 per cent in 1956 (see table 9).

TABLE 9

SOUTH KOREA: FOREIGN AID AS A PER CENT OF GNP
AND THE MONTHLY RATE OF CHANGE IN THE MONEY STOCK

Year	Monthly Rate of Increase in the Money Stock per Unit of Output*	Amount of Foreign Aid in Dollars† (In Millions)	Amount of Foreign Aid in Hwan‡ (In Billions)	Foreign Aid in Hwan as a Percentage of GNP
1953...	6.6%	$194.2	H/W 56.5	14.5%
1954...	4.9	153.9	86.9	15.3
1955...	3.7	236.7	182.7	19.2
1956...	2.7	326.7	315.7	25.9
1957...	0.5	382.9	395.3	24.3
1958...	1.9	321.3	379.3	22.0
1959...	1.8	222.2	279.0	15.0
1960...	0.1	245.4	334.2	15.9
1961...	2.9	199.2	282.7	11.4

* Twelve-month average of monthly rates of change.

† Bank of Korea, *Monthly Statistical Review*, 14 (1960):74, and ibid., 16 (1962):70.

‡ The value of foreign aid in dollars multiplied by the uncontrolled rate of exchange for greenbacks. In 1961, data on the exchange rate were available only up to June.

Proceeds from the sale of aid goods were an important source of revenue for the Republic of Korea, and the larger the amount of aid received, the less need to provide revenue through the creation of money.[39] Also, although many governmental agencies and other organizations received aid goods at prices below the free market level, such aid made it possible for them to borrow smaller amounts from banks. As a result, larger amounts of foreign aid tended to reduce the extent to which Korean banks expanded credit by creating additional supplies of money.

39. See C. D. Campbell and G. Tullock, "Aspects of Korea's Systems," pp. 342–46. In countries in which the increase in the money supply is closely related to the volume of dollar reserves, the relationship between dollar aid and the money supply is different than in Korea. In such countries an increase in dollar aid tends to increase their dollar reserves and thus the money supply.

The experience in South Korea illustrates some of the problems involved in a transition from inflation to price stability.[40] The Republic of Korea reduced the rate of increase in the money stock from approximately 7 per cent per month in 1953 to nearly 1 per cent in 1957. If the expansion in the money supply had been stopped completely, deflation rather than price stability would have resulted. With no increase in the money supply and a decline in velocity because of changing price expectations, prices would have fallen. However, in 1958–59 the 2 per cent average monthly increase in the money supply more than offset the decline in velocity and caused a small rise in prices. In 1960 there was practically no increase in the money supply, and further progress was made toward price stability. In 1961, the rate of increase in the money supply rose more sharply than was consistent with price stability, and the attempt to go from rapid inflation to price stability appears to have ended. The rate of increase in the consumer price index was 1.3 per cent per month in 1962 and 2.1 per cent in 1963.

Although this study has concluded that the unusual decline in the velocity of money in South Korea was the result of a decline in the rate of inflation, other explanations have been suggested. One of these is that the decline in velocity at a time when prices were still rising rapidly was the result of a failure on the part of the bulk of the population fully to grasp what was happening to the purchasing power of their money. If the rate of inflation is accelerating and people do not recognize what is happening to the value of their money, velocity may be relatively low. This is because prices do not rise as fast as the money supply. But the low level of velocity will probably be temporary. As soon as persons recognize what is happening, the price rise will speed up, and velocity will rise. In South Korea, this possibility did not occur because the rate of inflation was decelerating rather than accelerating. It is changes in the actual rate of inflation relative to the rate people are accustomed to that is significant. If the rate of inflation slows up, as it did in South Korea, holding money becomes less expensive than it had been and people tend to hold more relative to their incomes.

Another quite different reason given for the unusual decline in velocity in Korea is that Koreans expected the inflation would soon come to an end. They might have anticipated an exceptionally good rice harvest or larger volume of economic aid. Actually, during most of

40. For interesting discussions of the problem of stopping inflation, see Robert A. Mundell, "Growth, Stability, and Inflationary Finance," *Jour. Pol. Econ.*, 73 (1965):107–9, and Gordon Tullock, "Effects of Stabilization," *ibid.*, 71 (1963): 413–15.

the period in South Korea from World War II to 1957, there was almost no basis for believing that the inflation would soon come to an end. In this study it has been assumed that Koreans did not expect a slower rate of inflation until after they had experienced it, and then they revised their expectations gradually.

In Brazil, the rise in velocity was related to a rise in the expected rate of inflation. One of the most common fears concerning the rapid inflation in Brazil is that it is on the verge of reaching the runaway stage. The experience in Brazil does not support these fears and indicates that increases in the velocity of money may be very moderate in an expanding economy in which there is an accelerated inflation. Whenever the rate of inflation slowed down in Brazil, real cash balances tended to rise. Increases in real income were probably tending to raise the amount of real cash balances that people desired.

A common explanation of the rapid inflation in Brazil is the structuralist thesis that inflation is the result of economic growth. This point of view gives principal emphasis to such factors as the inelastic supplies of agricultural products, growing population, upward pressure on import prices, downward rigidity of industrial prices and wages, and political instability. The money supply in this approach is not considered a cause of the inflation, but it usually plays an important role in solving the dilemma created by the basic causes. This study supports the point of view that the increase in the money supply was an essential element in the Brazilian inflation. It also concludes that changes in the rate of inflation, which are not well explained by the structuralist thesis, are significantly related to the rate of increase in the money supply. There is not only a direct effect on prices of the increase in the money stock, but also an indirect effect through the impact of changes in the rate of inflation on the velocity of money.

APPENDIX A
THE MONEY STOCK IN SOUTH KOREA

Monthly figures on the total money stock in South Korea from 1953 to 1961 are shown in table 12. The total money stock includes currency in circulation, monetary deposits, and savings and time deposits.

The Bank of Korea has been the sole issuer of Korean bank notes since 1910. Following World War II, currency in circulation was defined, as it is in the United States, to include all bank notes issued less the amount held by banking institutions.[41] During most of the period from 1953 to 1961, currency in South Korea included almost no coins. Smaller-sized notes were used in place of coins for the small denominations. Coins were issued in October 1959 and are now used as part of the medium of exchange. United States currency and United States military payment certificates, the latter designed to be used solely on American military installations, have also circulated in the Korean economy. Statistical data on these forms of currency are not available, and they are not included in the total amount of currency in circulation. The ratio of currency in circulation to the total money stock—including all kinds of deposits—declined from over 60 per cent in 1953–54 to 41 per cent in July 1959. It then rose to 46 per cent in July 1960 and remained at that level up to June 1961.

The relative importance of the six principal types of bank deposits in 1961 is shown in table 10. Monetary deposits include all deposits that are legally payable on demand thirty days after deposit. They include, in addition to checking deposits, interest-bearing passbook deposits which in the United States would be classified as time deposits. "Other

41. During the Japanese occupation, Bank of Chosen notes circulated in Japanese-controlled areas outside of Korea, and currency in circulation in Korea included Bank of Japan, Bank of Taiwan, and Japanese military and occupation notes. These notes were exchangeable one for one. Prior to the end of World War II, currency in circulation in Korea was defined as the total amount of Bank of Chosen notes issued less the amount in circulation outside Korea, plus the amount of Japanese notes and coins in circulation in Korea. In 1945–46, the United States military government in Korea had the Japanese currencies removed from circulation. See Bloomfield and Jensen, *Banking Reform*, pp. 106–7.

TABLE 10

SOUTH KOREA: TYPE OF DEPOSIT AS A
PERCENTAGE OF TOTAL DEPOSITS,
JANUARY 1961

Type of Deposit	Percentage of Total Deposits*
Monetary deposits	
Passbook deposits..............	27.6%
Checking deposits..............	21.2
Other deposits.................	20.5
Savings and time deposits	
Savings deposits...............	14.8
Time deposits.................	11.4
Notice deposits...............	4.6
Total deposits...............	100.0

* Total deposits in the commercial banks, Agricultural Bank, Korean Reconstruction Bank, and Bank of Korea, not including an adjustment for checks in process of collection and interbank deposits.

deposits" consist primarily of cashier's checks not yet cleared. The way in which total monetary deposits are estimated is similar to that in the United States. It is a net figure after making allowance for checks and bills in process of collection. It also excludes interbank deposits and deposits of the national government and foreign official organizations.[42]

Savings and time deposits are included as part of the money stock in this study, although they are not included in the official Korean statistics on the money supply. The kinds of deposits included in savings and time deposits are similar to passbook deposits that are included in monetary deposits. Notice deposits were classified as monetary deposits prior to June 1955 and are included in this study. They pay interest, and after a depository period of one month, a three-day notice is required prior to withdrawal. Time deposits also pay rates of interest that vary with the duration of the deposit, and as in the United States, interest is paid only after the period of time specified in the contract. Savings deposits were initiated in 1959. They pay a rate of interest, may be held only by individuals and nonprofit organizations, and had a ceiling of three million hwan for any one account prior to the monetary reform in 1962.

In February 1953, a monetary reform changed the unit of account from won to hwan, and the conversion ratio was 100 to 1. The exact

42. For a description of the revisions in the money supply series made in 1955–56, see Bank of Korea, *Monthly Statistical Review*, 71 (Aug. 1955–Jan. 1956):3.

timing of the reform was kept secret, although the advisability of a reform had been under consideration for several years. Because of the lack of any forewarning, an acceleration of the rise in prices preceding the reform was avoided. The principal objectives of the reform, in addition to controlling inflation, were to collect unpaid taxes and overdue loans, and to simplify calculations. People were required to surrender won notes and checks and to declare won bank deposits and other monetary obligations within nine days after the announcement. The initial exchange that was permitted was limited to 500 hwan per person. Holdings in excess of this amount were placed in "frozen" time deposits for a period of one to three years depending on the asset converted.

In this study the data on the money stock were converted to midmonth, seasonally adjusted figures. The seasonal variations in the total money stock are shown in table 11. Following the harvest season, from August to January, the total money stock usually rises sharply because of large increases in bank loans made to purchase rice for government distribution to the urban population and the Korean army. The seasonal variations in the total money stock are similar to those for currency in circulation and the opposite of those for total deposits.

TABLE 11

SOUTH KOREA: SEASONAL VARIATIONS IN THE
TOTAL MONEY STOCK, CURRENCY IN
CIRCULATION, AND TOTAL DEPOSITS

MONTH	RATIO TO 12-MONTH MOVING AVERAGE, 1953–60		
	Total Money Stock	Currency in Circulation	Total Deposits
Jan...........	104.1	109.5	97.8
Feb..........	103.4	106.7	101.9
Mar.........	100.2	95.9	104.0
Apr..........	100.3	94.4	107.3
May.........	99.5	92.8	106.6
June........	98.8	94.7	102.6
July........	96.7	93.7	99.6
Aug.........	96.5	94.1	99.2
Sept.........	99.1	100.1	97.9
Oct..........	97.4	98.4	96.0
Nov..........	100.3	105.6	94.4
Dec..........	103.7	114.0	92.9

TABLE 12

SOUTH KOREA: MONEY STOCK, 1953–61
(In Millions of Hwan)

End of Month	Currency in Circulation	Monetary Deposits	Savings and Time Deposits	Total Money Stock
1953				
Jan......	10,024*	4,838*	275*	15,137*
Feb......	6,890	4,866	2,881†	14,637
Mar......	9,976	3,794	2,091	15,861
Apr......	10,001	5,148	2,026	17,175
May.....	10,870	5,626	2,041	18,537
June.....	12,284	5,940	2,074	20,298
July.....	12,870	6,293	2,130	21,293
Aug......	14,310	7,285	2,138	23,733
Sept.....	17,306	8,103	2,231	27,640
Oct......	18,714	8,401	2,277	29,392
Nov......	20,493	8,382	2,304	31,179
Dec......	22,334	7,982	2,385	32,701
1954				
Jan......	22,647	8,995	2,462	34,104
Feb......	24,245	9,735	2,673	36,653
Mar......	24,207	12,089	2,629	38,925
Apr......	25,273	15,455	2,636	43,364
May.....	27,452	15,618	2,724	45,794
June.....	30,406	15,377	2,997	48,780
July.....	31,251	15,867	3,040	50,158
Aug......	31,620	16,601	3,296	51,517
Sept.....	33,517	16,721	3,478	53,716
Oct......	34,864	15,580	3,478	53,922
Nov......	37,059	16,678	3,601	57,338
Dec......	39,979	18,100	3,860	61,939
1955				
Jan......	40,181	20,090	3,998	64,269
Feb......	39,510	21,153	4,196	64,859
Mar......	35,767	22,375	4,851	62,993
Apr......	35,576	24,273	4,864	64,713
May.....	36,153	25,901	4,970	67,024
June.....	40,595	24,467	5,167	70,229
July.....	42,516	23,927	5,261	71,704
Aug......	42,260	28,053	6,603	76,919
Sept.....	49,210	26,376	7,770	83,356
Oct......	45,125	29,807	6,890	81,822
Nov......	48,990	30,553	6,747	86,290
Dec......	58,777	34,746	6,990	100,513

SOURCE: Bank of Korea, *Monthly Statistical Review.*

* Prior to the monetary reform in February 1953, in hundred million won.

† Excludes deposits amounting to 712 million hwan that were frozen and used for the payment of overdue taxes and loans.

TABLE 12—*Continued*

End of Month	Currency in Circulation	Monetary Deposits	Savings and Time Deposits	Total Money Stock
		1956		
Jan......	54,792	40,735	7,296	102,823
Feb......	55,549	41,612	8,452	105,613
Mar......	49,796	40,348	13,068	103,212
Apr......	50,071	48,367	10,241	108,679
May.....	53,426	50,290	9,549	113,265
June.....	54,361	44,650	13,608	112,619
July.....	53,120	47,872	10,377	111,369
Aug......	54,960	46,707	9,676	111,343
Sept......	60,909	43,062	15,546	119,517
Oct......	59,837	49,601	12,853	122,291
Nov......	69,822	52,484	11,677	133,983
Dec......	73,338	47,587	14,222	135,147
		1957		
Jan......	71,872	51,166	10,609	133,647
Feb......	68,708	51,144	11,570	131,422
Mar......	63,621	56,618	12,196	132,435
Apr......	59,947	57,045	11,852	128,844
May.....	58,210	58,791	11,457	128,458
June.....	61,191	58,097	12,691	131,979
July.....	62,024	60,312	12,426	134,762
Aug......	64,936	59,200	12,495	136,631
Sept......	65,716	59,333	14,946	139,995
Oct......	68,963	57,316	14,173	140,452
Nov......	76,926	57,670	13,919	148,515
Dec......	86,048	59,136	15,124	160,308
		1958		
Jan......	81,467	68,444	14,574	164,485
Feb......	82,991	74,444	14,749	172,184
Mar......	74,292	72,764	16,141	163,197
Apr......	78,202	76,208	15,776	170,186
May.....	74,445	75,988	16,472	166,905
June.....	72,931	76,210	17,414	166,555
July.....	74,148	74,876	17,385	166,409
Aug......	79,110	74,329	17,309	170,748
Sept......	88,368	77,413	19,495	185,276
Oct......	88,648	78,772	20,352	187,772
Nov......	98,805	79,477	20,368	198,650
Dec......	111,057	81,496	19,161	211,714

TABLE 12—*Continued*

End of Month	Currency in Circulation	Monetary Deposits	Savings and Time Deposits	Total Money Stock
		1959		
Jan......	108,015	100,012	18,920	226,947
Feb......	111,384	111,810	19,953	243,147
Mar......	98,669	112,041	27,337	238,047
Apr......	98,488	111,505	30,117	240,110
May....	96,585	112,957	33,450	242,992
June.....	93,973	112,730	33,393	240,096
July.....	95,501	111,409	33,254	240,164
Aug......	98,900	98,960	39,390	237,250
Sept......	101,954	101,760	42,482	246,196
Oct......	106,194	100,971	41,627	248,792
Nov......	111,744	98,895	44,612	255,251
Dec......	123,595	86,305	54,853	264,753
		1960		
Jan......	128,915	88,824	59,031	276,770
Feb......	121,724	95,506	65,796	283,026
Mar......	111,659	99,413	69,650	280,722
Apr......	118,588	93,058	63,646	275,292
May....	113,401	94,051	64,207	271,659
June.....	117,873	89,025	62,890	269,788
July.....	118,952	84,941	60,412	264,305
Aug......	117,384	86,205	58,646	262,235
Sept......	123,590	75,688	54,373	253,651
Oct......	117,568	81,998	54,064	253,630
Nov......	129,155	84,401	54,379	267,935
Dec......	139,319	79,758	56,951	276,028
		1961		
Jan......	128,300	89,300	56,400	274,000
Feb......	132,000	90,500	57,000	279,500
Mar......	115,400	99,700	59,800	274,900
Apr......	118,900	100,700	61,400	281,000
May....	129,400	103,300	58,100	290,900
June.....	132,000	113,600	62,400	308,000
July.....	137,000	124,700	66,500	328,200
Aug......	151,500	122,400	71,900	345,800
Sept......	154,200	128,800	76,900	359,900
Oct......	153,800	129,200	80,200	363,200
Nov......	166,500	130,600	84,200	381,300
Dec......	166,600	145,600	90,800	403,000

APPENDIX B
KOREAN PRICE INDEXES AND
UNCONTROLLED EXCHANGE RATES

Table 17 includes the available monthly figures from 1945 to 1961 for the Seoul wholesale price index, the Seoul consumer price index (the Seoul retail price index prior to 1955), and the rate of exchange for greenbacks (United States currency) and United States military payment certificates. During the early part of the Korean War, the price indexes are not available for some months. Also, during the period in which the government was located in Pusan, the wholesale price index was collected there rather than in Seoul. Data on the unofficial exchange rates are not available until January 1948.

THE SEOUL WHOLESALE PRICE INDEX

The Seoul wholesale price index[43] has been published monthly from 1910 to 1961, when it was replaced by the new wholesale price index (initiated in 1955). From 1949 to 1961 it included the prices of 45 commodities. The groups of commodities and their weights are shown in Table 13. Some of the prices in the index are free market prices collected by the research department of the Bank of Korea from wholesale stores and dealers in Seoul, and some are official prices

TABLE 13

SOUTH KOREA: NUMBER AND KIND OF
COMMODITIES IN THE SEOUL WHOLESALE PRICE
INDEX AND THEIR WEIGHTS

Group	Number of Commodities	Weight
Grains....................	7	39
Meat, eggs, fish............	3	6
Textile raw materials.......	3	10
Textiles...................	6	8
Building materials..........	8	3
Fertilizer.................	3	2
Fuel......................	4	7
Miscellaneous..............	11	25
Total...................	45	100

43. See "General Explanation of the New Wholesale Price Index," Bank of Korea, *Monthly Statistical Review*, 12 (1958), 39–53.

obtained from government departments. The official prices are not changed often. Table 14 shows that the Seoul wholesale price index has typically risen from April to September and fallen during the harvest season from September to November. The seasonal variations in this index are similar to the seasonal variations in the price of grain.

TABLE 14

SOUTH KOREA: SEASONAL VARIATIONS IN PRICE INDEXES

MONTH	RATIO OF MONTHLY PRICE INDEX TO 12-MONTH MOVING AVERAGE		
	Seoul Wholesale Price Index (1953–60)	Price of Grains* (1953–60)	Seoul Consumer Price Index (1956–60)
Jan.........	97.80	89.66	97.44
Feb.........	99.32	91.15	99.05
Mar.........	97.33	91.54	99.52
Apr.........	95.89	94.38	102.85
May........	98.88	103.51	104.23
June.......	102.17	112.91	102.08
July........	102.66	115.32	101.00
Aug........	104.85	115.54	101.38
Sept........	105.82	111.57	101.61
Oct.........	100.70	97.37	98.74
Nov........	96.33	87.89	95.51
Dec.........	98.02	89.12	96.59

* Grain component of the Seoul wholesale price index.

THE SEOUL CONSUMER PRICE INDEX AND THE SEOUL RETAIL PRICE INDEX

The Seoul retail price index was published from 1936 to 1955, when it was replaced by the Seoul consumer price index.[44] From 1949 to 1955 the Seoul retail price index included the prices of forty-three commodities. The groups of commodities and their weights are shown in table 15. The Seoul consumer price index initiated in 1955 includes the prices of 154 items as listed in table 16. Fifteen of the items in the consumer price index are services. The weights of all items were based on a cost-of-living study of families of salaried employees and wage earners in Seoul in 1955. Data are gathered directly by employees of the Bank of Korea who visit the appropriate shops or places of business. The seasonal variations in the Seoul consumer price index shown in table 12 are slightly different from the seasonal variations in the Seoul wholesale price index. The Seoul consumer price index has typically risen from November to May and fallen from May to November.

44. See "The New Seoul Consumer Price Index," Bank of Korea, *Monthly Statistical Review*, 11 (1957):55–96.

TABLE 15

NUMBER AND KIND OF COMMODITIES IN
THE SEOUL RETAIL PRICE INDEX
AND THEIR WEIGHTS

Group	Number of Commodities	Weight
Food............	21	62.7
Fuel and light.....	5	18.1
Clothing..........	14	12.9
Miscellaneous......	3	6.3
Total...........	43	100.0

TABLE 16

NUMBER AND KIND OF COMMODITIES IN
THE SEOUL CONSUMER PRICE INDEX
AND THEIR WEIGHTS

Group	Number of Commodities	Weight
Food............	62	48.39
Housing..........	16	13.05
Fuel and light.....	8	8.02
Clothing..........	36	13.12
Miscellaneous......	32	17.42
Total...........	154	100.00

TABLE 17

SOUTH KOREA: INDEXES OF PRICES AND UNCONTROLLED
EXCHANGE RATES, 1945–61

Month	Seoul Wholesale Price Index (1947 = 100)	Seoul Retail Price Index (1947 = 100)	Exchange Rate for Greenbacks (In Won)	Exchange Rate for Military Payment Certificates (In Won)
1945				
Aug..........	17.0	15.9		
Sept..........	11.2	12.4		
Oct..........	9.3	11.7		
Nov..........	9.4	14.3		
Dec..........	11.8	15.9		

TABLE 17—*Continued*

Month	Seoul Wholesale Price Index (1947 = 100)	Seoul Retail Price Index (1947 = 100)	Exchange Rate for Greenbacks (In Won)	Exchange Rate for Military Payment Certificates (In Won)
		1946		
Jan..........	19.8	21.4		
Feb..........	28.2	30.4		
Mar..........	48.8	49.5		
Apr..........	49.9	48.5		
May.........	46.0	42.1		
June.........	51.6	51.7		
July.........	56.0	64.8		
Aug..........	77.5	69.6		
Sept.........	90.4	81.7		
Oct..........	57.6	70.3		
Nov..........	59.8	57.0		
Dec..........	74.4	68.7		
		1947		
Jan..........	89.9	87.1		
Feb..........	91.9	94.5		
Mar..........	89.6	95.0		
Apr..........	84.0	86.4		
May.........	85.7	83.8		
June.........	89.8	89.8		
July.........	96.8	97.1		
Aug..........	97.1	98.9		
Sept.........	102.3	100.8		
Oct..........	110.8	107.0		
Nov..........	119.7	119.2		
Dec..........	142.4	140.3		
		1948		
Jan..........	149.6	145.7	450	400
Feb..........	149.1	149.7	450	400
Mar..........	149.2	149.3	450	400
Apr..........	147.4	135.7	450	400
May.........	149.3	138.9	500	500
June.........	162.7	145.9	500	500
July.........	168.3	154.8	500	500
Aug..........	177.9	165.9	500	500
Sept.........	180.1	174.2	1,000	600
Oct..........	168.2	163.1	1,000	600
Nov..........	168.2	153.9	1,088	588
Dec..........	185.0	166.4	1,088	588

TABLE 17—*Continued*

1949

Jan.	180.2	164.6	1,088	588
Feb.	174.7	162.4	1,063	590
Mar.	177.7	167.1	1,207	843
Apr.	187.2	172.5	1,292	925
May	196.9	172.9	1,300	960
June	201.6	178.1	1,550	1,230
July	226.0	200.1	1,670	1,290
Aug.	244.0	206.3	1,750	1,438
Sept.	254.7	206.3	1,825	1,475
Oct.	271.9	214.3	2,390	1,798
Nov.	269.3	225.3	2,550	1,930
Dec.	289.9	257.2	2,834	2,314

1950

Jan.	322.0	286.7	3,588	2,703
Feb.	334.6	298.4	3,675	2,313
Mar.	332.3	315.0	3,170	2,506
Apr.	339.8	313.7	2,975	2,350
May	334.5	294.9	2,275	2,033
June	348.0	315.8	2,176	1,991
July	—	669.0	2,162	1,409
Aug.	—	741.8	2,654	1,902
Sept.	—	956.0	2,679	1,854
Oct.	—	899.7	2,577	2,274
Nov.	—	860.3	3,420	3,320
Dec.	831.1	825.5	4,490	3,573

1951

Jan.	—	—	6,561	4,002
Feb.	—	—	6,081	4,180
Mar.	—	—	7,310	5,540
Apr.	1,564.5*	—	8,490	5,460
May	1,545.5*	—	8,700	5,861
June	1,670.8*	—	8,300	5,950
July	2,033.4*	—	8,770	6,200
Aug.	2,217.8*	2,787.5	10,920	6,690
Sept.	2,550.2*	2,764.0	12,830	7,150
Oct.	2,851.8*	2,393.0	10,790	7,370
Nov.	2,565.2*	2,427.5	10,180	6,990
Dec.	2,599.2*	2,653.3	10,526	7,405

1952

Jan.	2,629.9*	2,932.2	11,446	7,602
Feb.	3,008.2*	3,515.8	12,388	8,312
Mar.	3,676.5*	4,312.5	13,537	9,431
Apr.	3,789.3*	4,518.8	14,530	9,738
May	4,769.7*	4,894.0	14,055	9,195
June	5,136.6*	4,968.2	16,337	10,408
July	5,594.5*	5,225.3	16,700	11,900
Aug.	5,980.4*	5,680.7	16,800	12,200
Sept.	6,197.7*	6,090.1	17,100	11,400
Oct.	5,872.1*	5,304.8	17,400	12,300
Nov.	5,097.5*	5,110.8	19,800	15,000
Dec.	5,256.8*	5,540.5	23,800	17,300

* Index compiled in Pusan.

TABLE 17—*Continued*

Month	Seoul Wholesale Price Index (1947 = 100)	Seoul Retail Price Index (1947 = 100)	Exchange Rate for Greenbacks (In Won)	Exchange Rate for Military Payment Certificates (In Won)
		1953		
Jan..........	5,528.8*	5,969.5	28,600	20,400
			(In Hwan)	(In Hwan)
Feb..........	6,215.9*	6,825.3	250	179
Mar..........	5,974.2*	6,871.3	249	175
Apr..........	5,717.3*	7,219.2	227	178
May.........	5,711.2*	6,731.6	273	197
June........	6,147.0*	6,823.8	332	222
July........	6,249.6*	7,396.6	313	195
Aug..........	6,089.4	7,861.7	270	182
Sept..........	5,869.8	8,088.7	263	187
Oct..........	5,610.4	7,676.9	289	215
Nov..........	5,663.8	8,049.5	341	261
Dec..........	6,635.0	9,092.4	401	299
		1954		
Jan..........	5,989.1	8,640.2	413	300
Feb..........	6,051.7	8,452.7	417	299
Mar..........	6,135.0	9,009.9	429	300
Apr..........	6,055.2	8,960.8	439	311
May.........	6,369.2	8,269.7	483	352
June........	6,730.3	8,287.8	576	439
July........	7,269.7	9,129.2	599	452
Aug..........	8,093.6	9,840.1	614	448
Sept..........	9,107.6	11,299.7	741	500
Oct..........	9,940.7	12,528.1	700	528
Nov..........	9,752.8	13,592.1	656	530
Dec..........	10,030.7	13,446.4	711	576
		1955		
Jan..........	11,299.9	87.0†	772	629
Feb..........	11,760.9	90.7	803	640
Mar..........	11,507.6	91.6	778	622
Apr..........	11,266.1	92.9	748	605
May.........	12,431.4	96.3	729	610
June........	14,011.7	102.7	753	577
July........	14,591.7	106.5	735	579
Aug..........	16,494.6	110.6	803	662
Sept..........	17,729.1	116.1	765	657
Oct..........	16,046.8	107.9	730	634
Nov..........	14,318.2	98.0	775	706
Dec..........	14,330.2	99.8	872	805

* Index compiled in Pusan.
† Figures in this column give Seoul Consumer Price Index (1955 = 100).

TABLE 17—*Continued*

Month	Seoul Wholesale Price Index (1947 = 100)	Seoul Consumer Price Index (1955 = 100)	Exchange Rate for Greenbacks (In Hwan)	Exchange Rate for Military Payment Certificates (In Hwan)
	1956			
Jan.........	14,553.0	102.5	931	831
Feb.........	15,376.0	106.5	975	831
Mar.........	15,471.1	108.5	957	819
Apr.........	16,287.5	114.3	892	725
May........	18,417.9	125.1	972	779
June........	20,013.3	126.1	1,048	817
July........	20,508.2	126.9	1,018	818
Aug.........	21,212.0	131.2	953	793
Sept.........	21,523.7	134.5	918	744
Oct.........	19,618.7	128.8	903	805
Nov.........	19,544.0	129.7	979	880
Dec.........	20,950.0	139.9	1,051	874
	1957			
Jan.........	21,921.1	149.6	1,104	912
Feb.........	21,928.1	152.3	1,068	881
Mar.........	22,499.7	156.9	1,060	843
Apr.........	23,187.0	165.8	1,012	826
May........	22,919.9	161.9	984	791
June........	23,426.7	155.5	1,014	822
July........	22,959.1	152.9	1,027	818
Aug.........	23,340.7	155.3	995	806
Sept.........	22,554.0	148.4	988	792
Oct.........	20,829.1	141.6	993	824
Nov.........	19,774.7	137.8	1,043	895
Dec.........	19,502.7	137.4	1,102	935
	1958			
Jan.........	19,551.5	139.6	1,134	997
Feb.........	19,686.2	143.5	1,176	1,023
Mar.........	19,873.0	141.8	1,165	989
Apr.........	19,739.4	146.0	1,142	996
May........	20,583.4	149.3	1,171	1,012
June........	20,706.7	148.7	1,184	1,067
July........	20,756.7	148.0	1,189	1,054
Aug.........	20,589.4	147.3	1,190	1,035
Sept.........	21,267.5	150.6	1,208	1,026
Oct.........	22,296.5	150.9	1,201	1,015
Nov.........	21,239.3	144.5	1,219	1,071
Dec.........	21,142.3	142.1	1,188	1,065

TABLE 17—*Continued*

Month	Seoul Wholesale Price Index (1947 = 100)	Seoul Consumer Price Index (1955 = 100)	Exchange Rate for Greenbacks (In Hwan)	Exchange Rate for Military Payment Certificates (In Hwan)
		1959		
Jan.........	21,115.0	144.6	1,186	1,098
Feb.........	21,110.7	146.3	1,178	1,100
Mar.........	20,422.5	147.3	1,162	1,115
Apr.........	20,238.4	150.3	1,173	1,116
May........	21,592.7	152.1	1,191	1,138
June........	21,949.5	149.3	1,296	1,199
July........	21,974.3	148.6	1,396	1,226
Aug.........	22,674.8	149.6	1,355	1,178
Sept.........	23,617.1	157.7	1,297	1,125
Oct.........	23,184.5	157.2	1,292	1,152
Nov.........	23,433.1	151.1	1,263	1,170
Dec.........	23,604.9	153.4	1,280	1,188
		1960		
Jan.........	23,744	152.9	1,320	1,223
Feb.........	24,386	156.6	1,449	1,292
Mar.........	24,727	158.6	1,440	1,305
Apr.........	25,069	165.2	1,432	1,289
May........	25,431	166.2	1,473	1,249
June........	25,804	164.7	1,464	1,282
July........	26,675	166.1	1,371	1,196
Aug.........	27,228	167.9	1,342	1,110
Sept.........	26,941	167.7	1,245	1,061
Oct.........	25,601	165.3	1,250	1,096
Nov.........	25,262	160.8	1,272	1,152
Dec.........	25,689	163.2	1,284	1,156
		1961		
Jan.........	27,876	173.0	1,398	1,206
Feb.........	29,079	177.3	1,483	1,289
Mar.........	28,947	178.0	1,473	1,271
Apr..	29,170	178.7	1,465	1,268
May........	29,970	182.9	1,433	1,197
June........	29,082	172.1	1,269	1,195
July........		176.5		
Aug.........		179.6		
Sept.........		182.2		
Oct.........		181.4		
Nov.........		170.2		
Dec.........		168.3		

Index